Language, Literacy and Education:
A Reader

Edited by
Sharon Goodman, Theresa Lillis, Janet Maybin, Neil Mercer

Trentham Books
Stoke on Trent, UK and Sterling, USA

in association with

Trentham Books Limited
Westview House, 734 London Road
Oakhill, Stoke on Trent
Staffordshire, England ST4 5NP

22883 Quicksilver Drive, Sterling
VA 20166-2012, USA

First published 2003

**British Library Cataloguing-in-
Publication Data**
A catalogue record for this book is
available from the British Library

ISBN: 1 85856 288 0

Designed and typeset by Trentham Print
Design Ltd., Chester and printed in Great
Britain by Cromwell Press Ltd., Wiltshire.

Grateful acknowledgement is made to the following sources for permission to
reproduce material within this product.

Text
Reprinted from Rojas-Drummond, S. (2000) 'Guided participation, discourse and
the construction of knowledge in Mexican classrooms', *Social Interaction in
Learning and Instruction*. Copyright © 2000 Elsevier Science Ltd. All rights
reserved. With permission from Elsevier Science

Machado, de Almeida and Mattos, A. (2000) 'A Vygotskian approach to evaluation
in foreign language learning contexts', *ELT Journal*, Vol. 54/4, October 2000.
Copyright © Oxford University Press. Reprinted by permission of Oxford
University Press

Olson, D. (1996) 'Literate Mentalities: Literacy, consciousness of language, and
modes of thought', *Modes of Thought: Explorations in Culture and Cognition*,
Cambridge University Press. Copyright © Cambridge University Press 1996

Street, B. (1997) 'The implication of the 'New Literacy Studies' for Literacy
Education', in *English in Education – Literacy*, Vol. 31, No. 1, Autumn 1997, The
National Association for the Teaching of English

Hicks, D. (1995) 'Discourse, Learning and Teaching', in Apple, M. (ed) *Review of
Research in Education* No. 21, American Educational Research Association

Torrance, H. and Pryor, J. (1998) 'Classroom assessment and the language of
teaching', *Investigating Formative Assessment: Teaching, learning and assessment
in the classroom*, pp.44-52, Open University Press

Bucholtz, M. (1999) 'Why be normal?: Language and identity practices in a
community of nerd girls', *Language in Society*, Vol. 28, No. 2, June 1999,
Cambridge University Press. Copyright © 1999 Cambridge University Press

Gutiérrez, K. D., Baquedano-López, P. and Tejeda, C. (1999) 'Rethinking diversity:
hybridity and hybrid language practices in the third space', in *Mind, Culture and
Activity*, 6(4) 286-303, Lawrence Erlbaum Associates, Publishers. Copyright ©
1999, Regents of California on behalf of the Laboratory of Comparative Human
Cognition

Ramanathan, V. (1999) 'English is here to stay: A critical look at institutional and
educational practices in India', *TESOL Quarterly*, Vol. 33, NO. 2, Summer 1999.
Copyright © 1999 Teachers of English to Speakers of Other Languages, Inc.

Janks, H. (1993) *Language and Position*, Hodder and Stoughton in association with
Witwatersrand University Press. Copyright © Hilary Janks

Wallace, C. (2002) 'Local literacies and global literacy', in Block, D. and Cameron,
D. (eds) *Globalisation and Language Teaching*, Routledge

Snyder, I. (2001) 'A New Communication Order: researching literacy practices in
the Network Society, *Language and Education*, Vol. 15, No. 2 and 3, pp.117-131,
Multilingual Matters Ltd

Swanwick, R (2002) 'Sign bilingual deaf children's approaches to writing',
Deafness and Education International, 4 (2) pp.65-83, Whurr Publishers Limited

Adapted from Gregory, E. and Williams, A. (1998) 'Family literacy history and
children's learning strategies at home and at school: perspectives from ethnography
and ethnomethodology', in *Studies in Educational Ethnography*, volume 1,
pp.19.46. Copyright © 1998 by JAI Press Inc. Reprinted by permission of Elsevier
Science

Every effort has been made to contact copyright holders. If any have been
inadvertantly overlooked the publishers will be pleased to make the necessary
arrangements at the first opportunity.

List of Contents

PART FOUR: MULTIMODAL COMMUNICATION

About the editors and authors of this Reader

Svenja Adolphs is Research Associate at the Centre for Research in Applied Linguistics, School of English Studies, University of Nottingham, UK. Her research interests include spoken language corpora; suggestions in casual conversation; lexical patterning and language corpora.

Patricia Baquedano-López is Assistant Professor in Language, Literacy and Culture at the Graduate School of Education, University of California, Berkeley. Her research interests include the study of language socialisation, language development and use, as well as the study of literacy practices in and out-of-school.

Mary Bucholtz is Assistant Professor in the Department of Linguistics at the University of California, Santa Barbara. Her research focuses on the relationship between language and identity, especially gender, race and youth.

Ronald Carter is Professor of Modern English Language in the School of English Studies at the University of Nottingham. He is the author and editor of over forty books and nearly ninety articles on literary, educational and applied linguistics.

Lynn Mario T. Menezes de Souza is Assistant Professor of Language and Linguistics in the Department of Modern languages in the University of São Paulo, Brazil. With a background in Linguistics, Applied Linguistics and a doctorate in Semiotics and Communications Studies, his present research interests cover the interfaces between language, culture, ideology, pedagogy and ethnography, all of which converge in issues related to literacy.

Sharon Goodman is Lecturer in the Centre for Language and Communications at The Open University, UK. Her research interests include linguistics, visual and verbal communication and academic literacies.

Eve Gregory is Professor of Language and Culture at Goldsmiths College, University of London. She has conducted research projects on children's out of school literacy and particularly, the role of siblings in the teaching and learning of literacy.

Kris Gutiérrez is Professor in the Graduate School of Education and Information Studies and director of the Centre for the Study of Urban Literacies at University of California, Los Angeles. Her research focuses on studying the literacy practices of urban schools. In particular, her research concerns itself with the social and cognitive consequences of literacy practices in formal and non-formal learning contexts.

Deborah Hicks is Associate Professor of Education at the University of Cincinnati. She completed a doctorate at the Harvard Graduate School of Education, with a focus on language and literacy practices. She is known for her interdisciplinary studies of classroom discourse and learning. Her current work is focused on researching and writing histories of girlhood in an urban Appalachian community, in which both urban spaces and rural histories inform students' identities.

Carey Jewitt is a researcher based in the Department of Culture, Communications and Societies at the Institute for Education, University of London. She has a particular interest in the analysis of visual representations.

Gunther Kress is Professor of Education/English at the Institute of Education, University of London. He has a specific interest in the interrelations in contemporary texts of different modes of communication – writing, image, speech, music – and their effects on forms of learning and knowing. He is interested in the changes brought about by the shift in the major media of communication 'from the page to the screen' and their effects and consequences.

Theresa Lillis is lecturer at the Centre for Language and Communications at The Open University, UK. She has worked as a teacher in a range of educational contexts, including secondary, adult and higher education. Her research interests include widening access to higher education, academic writing, gender and collaborative research methodologies.

Andréa Machado de Almeida Mattos is an experienced teacher and researcher in the field of English as a foreign language. She has published both in Brazil and internationally.

Janet Maybin is senior lecturer in the Centre for Language and Communications at The Open University. She researches and writes on children's and adults' informal language and literacy practices.

Neil Mercer is Professor and Director of the Centre for Language and Communications at The Open University, UK. He has carried out extensive research into the use of language, teaching and learning in schools. His books and other publications have been translated into four languages.

Caroline McKinney is a teacher and researcher in South Africa. She has worked as a curriculum developer and materials writer in a range of educational contexts, including adult, basic, further and higher education. Her research interests include transformation in the higher education sector in South Africa and critical approaches to language and literacy.

Gemma Moss is based in the Education Policy Research Unit, Institute of Education, University of London, where she is directing a sequence of funded research projects. Her research interests include: literacy policy; gender and literacy; the formation of the English curriculum; and the relationship between home and school literacy practices.

David R. Olson is Professor of Applied Cognitive Science at the Ontario Institute for Studies in Education. His research on cognition, cognitive development and literacy has resulted in ten authored and edited books and some 200 articles.

John Pryor works with micro-sociological, ethnographic and collaborative approaches in researching a wide range of issues in education. He has published on assessment, gender, groupwork, teacher research and African education. He is a Lecturer in Education at the University of Sussex where he convenes the MA in Education studies.

Vai Ramanathan is Associate Professor in the Linguistics Department at the University of California at Davis. Her research interests include global English, as well as L1 and L2 literacy and teacher-education.

Sylvia Rojas-Drummond is Professor at the Faculty of Psychology, Graduate Division, National Autonomous University of Mexico. There she directs the Laboratory of Cognition and Communication.

Ilana Snyder is Associate Professor, Faculty of Education, Monash University. Her work focuses on new technologies in teaching and learning.

Brian V. Street is Professor in Language and Education at King's College London. His interests include language in education, languages and literacies in cross-cultural perspective, academic literacies and literacy in development. He is particularly interested to link theories of language and literacy to current educational issues, including academic literacies in Higher Education, and to the communicative demands of the 'new work order'.

Ruth Swanwick is lecturer in deaf education in the School of Education, University of Leeds. She is course tutor for the Advanced Diploma in the Education of Deaf Children. Her research interests include the bilingual language development of deaf children and the role of British Sign Language in deaf children's literacy development.

Carlos Tejeda is Assistant Professor in the Charter College of Education at California State University, Los Angeles. His research focus is grounded in spatial and sociocultural theories of learning in decolonizing pedagogical contexts. Professor Tejeda is affiliated with the Centre for the Study of Urban Literacies at the University of California, Los Angeles.

Harry Torrance is Professor of Education at the University of Sussex. He has directed numerous research projects investigating classroom assessment and school-based examining, and has published widely in the fields of assessment and evaluation. He is currently working with an European funded network studying internet-based assessment.

Catherine Wallace is senior lecturer in Education, School of Culture Language and Communication, Institute of Education, University of London. Her main areas of research and teaching are critical language study, the teaching of reading, language and literacy for bilingual learners, globalisation and language teaching, materials development.

Ann Williams is Research Fellow at the University of London. She has worked on several funded projects in the fields of language change, variation in urban dialects and literacy in inner city communities.

Anita Wilson is a prison ethnographer. At present she holds a Spencer Post-Doctoral Fellowship (New York) based at Lancaster University, England and is currently looking at the literacy-related practices of prisoners in Europe and America.

Introduction: mapping the traditions of a social perspective on language and literacy

Theresa Lillis

About this Reader

Language and literacy figure prominently in educational debates at national and international levels. Some of the many questions raised are; which languages, or types of languages, should be the medium of education? What is the relationship between language and learning? What kinds of literacy should be taught in schools and why? How can teachers use language effectively to ensure that learning takes place? Why do some people learn the discourses of education, whereas others do not? What is the relationship between language, identity and learning? Within the context of a changing communicative landscape which involves an ever increasing use of new technologies, the global influence of particular languages, notably English, and fundamental debates about the purpose of education, such questions become more and more complex and the importance of answering them more urgent.

Questions about language, literacy and education have generated considerable research over the past 50 years which has drawn on a number of academic traditions including sociolinguistics, psychology, anthropology and sociology. This research, whilst potentially of great interest to many working in education, is often dispersed across specialist academic publications and is not easily available to students or teachers.

This Reader provides an easily accessible, single volume collection of readings which illustrate both the variation in research on language and literacy and the common, underlying themes. The Reader consists of twenty chapters, seven of which have been specially commissioned. Together they offer readers the opportunity to become familiar with some of the ways in which researchers are grappling with key questions about language, literacy and education. The Reader is organised around four key themes: *Talk and the Processes of Teaching and Learning; Literacy and Education; Discourse and Identity; Multimodal Communication.* As a collection, the Reader explores both theory and empirical research; it illustrates a range of educational contexts, including mainstream schooling, English as a foreign language, sign bilingual deaf education, indigenous community learning; it focuses on informal contexts such as the home, the playground, local communities; it considers diverse participants, including children and adults, bilingual and monolingual learners. The Reader will be of relevance to anyone interested in language and education including students of language and literacy, teachers in mainstream primary and secondary classrooms, teachers of English as a foreign or an additional language, teacher trainers and lecturers in English. This Reader is required reading for the Open University course: *Language and Literacy in a Changing World* (E844) which forms part of an MA in Education and MA in Education/Applied Linguistics.

A social perspective on the study of language and literacy

The theoretical perspective on language and literacy adopted by most of the writers in this Reader can be described as a *social perspective*. Broadly speaking, a social perspective on language involves the following three positions:

- Language is conceptualised as language-in-use rather than language as an abstract system

- Language-in-use inevitably involves a focus on the social context in which language occurs

- Language-in-use acknowledges variation as a fundamental aspect of language

A social perspective on language stands in contrast to a powerful tradition of viewing language as an abstract, grammatical system independent of language users and contexts (for further discussion, see Mesthrie *et al* 2000 chapter 1).

However, it is important to note that there is no one unified 'social perspective' or approach to the study of language. Rather, there is a plethora of theoretical frameworks, concepts and analytical tools that have emerged from distinct intellectual traditions. In reading the chapters in this book and thinking about the ways in which researchers are exploring key questions about language and literacy, it may be useful to consider the following brief maps of some of the different traditions researchers are working within.

Mapping traditions

A 'tradition' is a cluster of culturally and historically specific beliefs and practices which are forged by people in different contexts over time. Traditions, or aspects of them, may remain quite distinct or merge with others depending on a number of complex issues. In approaching the range of intellectual traditions that are influencing and informing current research on language and literacy, it is useful to map traditions along the following dimensions.

Academic disciplines
Paradigmatic shifts
Geo-historical contexts
Ideological positions

Mapping the traditions influencing language and literacy research in this way obviously involves some over-simplification. The dimensions themselves are problematic, for example what exactly constitutes a discipline is far from straightforward, and each of the dimensions overlap. However, they provide a useful starting point from which to begin thinking about the range of concepts and frameworks that are influencing the study of language and literacy, as illustrated in this Reader.

Map 1 Academic disciplines

Perhaps the most obvious way of mapping the intellectual traditions influencing the study of language and literacy is to focus on academic disciplines or sub-disciplines. The following are some of the key academic disciplines that are being drawn on by researchers in the study of language and literacy.

- **Sociolinguistics** There are three core positions in sociolinguistics which underpin most, if not all, social perspectives on language and literacy, as illustrated in the chapters in this Reader. The first is that there is a fundamental link between language and society. The second is that linguistic variation – according to, for example, participants, settings, topics and functions – is a basic feature of language. The third is that all languages and linguistic varieties are of equal value and importance, with no one language or variety being intrinsically superior to any other. This position requires a descriptive approach to the study of language, where the aim is to describe without evaluation, rather than a prescriptive approach, where the aim is to set out what kinds of language or literacy should be used (see Holmes 2001, Mesthrie *et al* 2000).

• **Applied linguistics** Research in the learning and acquisition of language in monolingual, bilingual and multilingual contexts is a key focus in applied linguistics and provides a rich resource for all interested in the relationship between language and learning (see for example, Ellis 2001, Beaumont and O'Brien eds. 2000). In addition, specific linguistic tools of analysis have been developed which are used for both research and teaching. For example, analytic tools from systemic functional linguistics (Halliday 1994) are widely used for research and teaching purposes. The influence of work in applied linguistics is evident in many chapters in the Reader, for example in the discussion on the discourses and genres of teaching in the chapter by Hicks, and the debate surrounding communicative language teaching in the chapter by Wallace.

• **Anthropology** Anthropology focuses on understanding everyday events, and the meanings attached to these events by the participants in them, in diverse social and cultural contexts. A particularly important contribution from anthropology to the study of language and literacy has been the development of ethnography as a research methodology. Ethnography emphasises the need to pay attention to the detail of local social cultural contexts of language use and attaches great importance to the perspectives of research participants. It has become a key methodology in literacy research, particularly in what is known as New Literacy Studies (for examples see Brice Heath 1983; Street 1995; Barton and Hamilton 1998). The influence of such work is evident in several chapters in this Reader, notably those by Street, Wallace, Gregory and Williams and Wilson.

• **Sociocultural theory** Sociocultural theory is a distinctive field within the broader area of social psychology and focuses on the link between language and learning, both of which are viewed as fundamentally social phenomena. Sociocultural theory has been particularly important in studies of teaching and learning in formal contexts, with a particular emphasis to date on spoken interaction in classroom contexts (see, for example, Mercer 2000); in theorising and researching the ways in which individuals become active members of communities (Lave and Wenger 1991); and in theorising and exploring the relationship between language and meaning making (Bakhtin 1981, 1984, 1986). Sociocultural theory is used in several chapters in this Reader, notably in those by Rojas-Drummond, Andréa Machado de Almeida Mattos, Gutierrez *et al* and Maybin.

• **Sociology** Given the importance attached to social context, many researchers adopting a social perspective on language draw on a range of concepts and theories from the discipline of sociology. These have included the use of specific social categories such as social class, gender, ethnicity as well as macro social theories, such as Marxism (see Trudgill 1975 for classic example of the use of specific social categories in language study; see Fairclough 1992 for example of the use of macro theory). Chapters in this Reader which focus more explicitly on sociological concepts and theory are those by Street, McKinney, Ramanathan and Wallace.

- **Philosophy** In exploring relationships between language, social context and meaning making, some researchers draw explicitly on philosophy, in particular the philosophy of language. Key concepts under scrutiny in current research on language and literacy are the 'self' – in terms of agency, identity and subjectivity – and the self's relation to social practices (see discussion for example in Butler 1997; Gee 1996). Chapters in this Reader which explicitly focus on identity are those by Bucholtz, McKinney and Maybin. An area which draws on philosophy, as well as sociology, and which is being used in studies of language and literacy, is post-colonial theory (Bhabha 1994) . Specific concepts from post-colonial work are drawn on in the chapters by Gutierrez *et al* and Wilson.

Some researchers work firmly within one disciplinary or sub-disciplinary tradition whilst others draw on concepts from several. For example, in this Reader, Rojas-Drummond works with concepts mainly from one tradition – the field of sociocultural theory – whilst Wallace draws on several, including New Literacy Studies, language teaching theory from applied linguistics and World Englishes which draws on postcolonial theory.

Map 2 Paradigmatic shifts

In mapping a social perspective on language there is evidence of several important paradigmatic shifts, that is significant changes in understandings about the nature of language and literacy. The following shifts can be identified:

- from the study of 'language' as an abstract system to an emphasis on language as socially situated 'discourse'

- from the study of literacy as individual cognitive activity to literacy as a profoundly social practice (see Street 1995; Barton, Hamilton and Ivanič 2000)

- from a conceptualisation of social categories such as social class and sex/gender as fixed and stable, to an emphasis on aspects of identity as diverse and always in process (see for example Gee 1996; for example discussions on gender, see Cameron 1997, Johnson and Meinhof eds. 1997)

- from an overriding concern with 'theories of language' to a central concern with 'social theory' (see for example Chouliaraki and Fairclough 1999)

- from a concern with the verbal aspects of language to a focus on a range of semiotic resources, including the visual (see Kress and van Leeuwen 1996, 2001)

Whilst it is certainly possible to identify these positions on the nature of language as 'shifts' and thus to construct understandings about language as changing diachronically (over time), it is important also to view these positions synchronically (as current), continuing to be debated and explored. As is clear from the range of chapters in this Reader, there are many points of unresolved tension. For example, whilst most of the chapters in this book focus on language in social context, exactly what constitutes 'social context' is hotly disputed. Does 'social context', refer to the immediate context in which specific instance of language occurs, for example in a particular classroom, or does it refer to the wider society? And how is the wider society to be conceptualised? Does language take place *in* a context, or are contexts created through specific uses of language? The chapters in this Reader deal with context in a number of ways. Notions of context as a physical space in which language occurs include immediate local contexts, such as the classroom as in the chapter by Torrance and Pryor, and more global notions of context, as in the chapter by Ramanathan who focuses on the differential educational experiences of college students within the context of the geo-politics of English. At the same time, both these chapters focus on how local interactions and uses of language serve to constitute these contexts. Chapters by Maybin and Bucholtz in particular emphasise the *performative* aspect of language, and context: through particular kinds of interaction, individuals act out particular kinds of identities and actively work at constructing particular kinds of contexts.

Map 3 Geo-historical contexts

It is also possible to map different intellectual traditions in approaches to the study of language geo-historically, that is as emerging out of specific geographical/cultural sites. Traditions emerge in response to specific local concerns and interests. For example, one strand of sociolinguistics emerged from the US at a time when there was a concern to record fast disappearing indigenous languages; in the UK sociolinguistics emerged following a key interest in everyday spoken, rather than written language, and a commitment to mapping types of language use against socially diverse groups of users. In contrast, sociocultural approaches to language emerged from the Soviet Union in the 1930s at a time when intellectual interests focused for the main part on the relation between traditional methodologies and Communist doctrines: what, for example, would psychology, linguistics, and literary theory look like when illuminated by Marxist theory? (see discussion in Holquist 2002). In more recent times 'postcolonial theories' as the name indicates have emerged from places such as India and Africa as a way of exploring key aspects of experience and theory from a specifically postcolonial perspective. Within the context of significant changes in global power relations, postcolonial theory raises complex questions about, not least, any presumed negative or positive views about the teaching of English world-wide, the inherent values of either monolingual or multilingual education programmes, and the relationship between the spread of English and global economies (see for example Kachru 1985, 1992; Pennycook 1994, 1998).

To acknowledge the geo-historical location of different traditions is to emphasise that theoretical and analytical frameworks are developed in response to local interests and traditions. However, this is not to suggest that theories and research which emerge in one specific geo-historical context remain bound to these contexts. An obvious example is the way in which work from the Soviet sociohistorical tradition of the 1930s is being drawn on in much Western academic research on teaching and learning. This is exemplified in this Reader in the Chapters by Rojas-Drummond and Machado de Almeida Mattos, who draw on the work of Vygotsky (1978, 1986) as well as in the chapter by Maybin where she uses the work of Bakhtin (1984) to explore chil-dren's talk in the context of UK primary schools. Likewise, the key concept of 'third space' which has emerged from postcolonial theory (Bhabha,1994) is used by Gutiérrez *et al* in their chapter on teaching and learning in bilingual contexts, and Wilson in her chapter on prison literacies.

Acknowledging the historical and geo-cultural locations of different intellectual tradition should ward against acceptance of easy claims to innovation in academic research, from any one parti-cular site in the academy. For what may seem 'new' in one context or intellectual tradition may be old or, at least familiar in others. A good example of the link between 'new' and 'old' in this volume is the work on multimodality which, whilst a relatively recent concern in some areas of Western linguistics as exemplified in the chapter by Jewitt and Kress, has a long-standing tradition in other fields, such as indigenous community literacy discussed by de Souza and deaf/sign language by Swanwick. Bringing these chapters together in one volume offers readers the opportunity to explore in more detail what each specific tradition, and researchers, have to offer.

Map 4 Ideological positions

All intellectual traditions embody worldviews and this is necessarily also the case with traditions of language and literacy study.

> Language is so intimately connected with social life and human behaviour that any model of language tends to embody assumptions and value judgements which cannot be challenged by empirical data because they already circumscribe what kind of data is regarded as relevant to the theory. In this respect, a model of language can also be said to represent an ideology of language (Graddol 1994: page 80)

All theories and approaches to the study of language are ideological to the extent that they implicitly reflect and constitute particular worldviews, such as values and beliefs about society, about language and about the individual. The ways in which views of society explicitly connect with approaches to the study of language can be illustrated in the ways in which the notion of linguistic 'variation', core to all social perspectives on language and literacy, is theorised from three broadly defined ideological positions.

- *Liberal/Humanist* Linguistic variation is viewed as a fundamental aspect of language and is to be celebrated rather than treated as a problem. Where there are discussions about which language or type of language should be used, the notion of 'appropriateness' is brought to bear: participants are free to choose which language or type of language they use but such choices are (or should be) influenced by what is 'appropriate' to any specific context. For example, it may be appropriate to use standard English in a formal interview situation, but equally appropriate to use a different ('non-standard') dialect when talking with friends.

- *Critical/Neo-Marxist* In 'critical' social theories of society, such as (neo) Marxist or feminist, variation is also seen as a fundamental aspect of human language but such variation is understood as being always embedded in social relations of power. Critical theories emphasise the conflicting interests of social groups within society and hence the unequal power relations in any instance of language use. Within this framework, the notion of appropriateness used in liberal/humanist approaches is criticised for its inattention to power and the assumption that individuals can freely choose the kind of language they use. For example, in formal education contexts such as schools and universities, specific languages or dialects are designated as the medium of education and students and teachers are required to use them.

- *Post-structuralist* Structuralist accounts of society emphasise the patterns or structures that make up society and the relations between them. In contrast, within post-structuralism, the ordered nature of society offered by this emphasis on identifiable structures gives way to a view of society which is hugely complex, and probably unknowable. Variation, within this frame, is a fundamental feature of language, but in a more complex and precarious sense than in either the liberal/humanist or critical approaches. Society is viewed as infinitely complex, varying according to the perspectives from which it is viewed. Likewise, the individual is a fluid phenomenon always in a process of 'becoming'; a process in which language plays a central role. Consider the example of analysing spoken interaction of men and women. Stated briefly, structuralists would tend to view participants as male and female who interact in particular ways *because of* their sex/gender, whereas post-structuralists would focus on the ways in which participants work at constructing themselves as male or female through their interactions.

In the chapters in this Reader, as in much academic writing, the ideology or worldviews of writers are often implicit, and left to the reader to discern. Examples of more explicitly stated ideological positions are evident in the chapters by Street, Wallace and McKinney, all of whom, albeit in different ways, adopt critical perspectives. Post-structuralist influence is particularly evident in the chapters by Maybin and Bucholtz.

Ideology also influences the process of knowledge construction, albeit in complex ways. Most obviously, much research in the tradition of liberal humanism or critical approaches continues to work from within a positivist approach to knowledge making where the emphasis is on developing methods which seek to describe reality 'as it really is'. The researcher within this frame claims a special kind of authority over the people or phenomenon being observed, acting as 'interpreter of the world' (Reynolds in Lather 1991, p59). In contrast, researchers working a post-structuralist tradition question the possibility of offering any neutral or objective account of reality, as the phenomena being observed will always only ever be partial (observed at a particular moment in time and context) and always shaped by the particular researchers' perspectives. In this Reader, several chapters, notably those by Gregory and Williams, Carter and Adolphs, and Moss, focus explicitly on research methodology and the difficult questions surrounding the description and documentation of reality. The chapter by Wilson also explicitly discusses the part played by the researcher in the research process.

One way of conceptualising the different intellectual traditions that are being drawn on in the study of language and literacy is to think of them as conversations in which different people participate at different times. The chapters in this Reader illustrate some of the ways in which researchers are engaging in these conversations, according to their specific interests. They illustrate the different ways in which it is possible to use the rich array of conceptual tools and frameworks available to all who are interested in exploring the place and role of language and literacy in education.

The four parts of the Reader

The chapters in the Reader are organised around four key themes: *Talk and the processes of Teaching and Learning; Literacy and Learning; Discourse and Identity; Multimodal Communication.* The themes in the first two parts have long been of concern to educationalists and language and literacy researchers; the chapters in parts three and four focus on themes that are becoming increasingly prominent. Each of the chapters in the four parts draws on different elements of the intellectual traditions outlined above.

Part one: Talk and the processes of teaching and learning The four chapters in this part illustrate a sociocultural approach to the study of language and learning. All four chapters draw on this tradition, in particular, on work by Vygotsky (1978, 1986) and key writers in this field such Bruner (1986, 1990) and Rogoff (1990). Foundational concepts used in sociocultural research, such as the *zone of proximal development* (ZPD) and *scaffolding,* are further elucidated based on classroom based research in both monolingual and bilingual contexts. The opening chapter by

Deborah Hicks brings together work from different strands of sociocultural theory to outline a sociocultural perspective on discourse and learning. In chapter 2, Harry Torrance and John Pryor focus on the importance of teacher talk in the processes of learning but emphasise the difficulties surrounding the use of language as a tool for assessing classroom learning. In Chapter 3, Sylvia Rojas-Drummond explores the usefulness of the notion of scaffolding and the different interactional forms this takes in her focus on episodes of teaching and learning. Chapter 4 by Andréa Machado de Almeida Mattos illustrates that, whilst much sociocultural research has focused on spoken interaction in mainstream primary classrooms, key sociocultural analytic tools are just as relevant to the foreign language learning classroom.

Part two: Literacy and learning This part includes five chapters which illustrate some of the central debates surrounding literacy and learning and the different intellectual traditions being drawn on in literacy research. The first two chapters by David Olson and Brian Street reflect two potentially opposing views on the nature of literacy: Street offers a 'social practice' view of literacy drawn from an anthropological perspective; in contrast Olson adopts what can be described as a cognitive perspective on literacy. Olson's chapter is unusual in this Reader in not adopting a social perspective; it is included because of the importance of Olson's work in its own right but also, perhaps surprisingly, because key concepts within this perspective are drawn on in some strands of social perspectives on language and literacy. There are, for example, striking parallels between Olson's notion of 'scientific thinking' in Chapter 5 and Wallace's discussion of 'literate English' in chapter 7 in her focus on the teaching of English as a foreign language. The chapters by Gregory and Williams and by Moss focus on ways of researching the literacy practices of primary aged children both at home and at school. The chapters in this part of the Reader draw on key notions from New Literacy Studies such as *autonomous* versus *ideological* models of literacy, *literacy practices* and *literacy events.*

Part three: Discourse and identity This part consists of five chapters which focus on a theme which has recently become more significant in education research: the relationship between language and identity. This relationship is discussed in the contexts of formal and informal discourse practices, involving younger children and adolescents, monolingual and bilingual contexts, school through to higher education. The chapters draw on core concepts from sociolinguistics and sociocultural theory and illustrate both ethnographic and text based methodologies. Post-structuralist approaches to identity and language are explored across the chapters in different ways.

Three of the five chapters focus on school aged children. Chapter 10 by Mary Bucholtz and Chapter 11 by Janet Maybin explore the relationship between spoken interaction and identity. Bucholtz focuses on teenage girls, Maybin focuses on children aged between 10 and 12. Kris Gutiérrez, Patricia Baquedano-López and Carlos Tejeda also focus on identity and difference, drawing on Bhabha's notion of the third space to explore new possibilities for learning in bilingual contexts.

Chapters 13 and 14 focus on older students. Chapter 13 by Carolyn McKinney focuses identity in relation to critical literacy pedagogy at university level in South Africa and in Chapter 14 Vai Ramanathan focuses on the experiences of college students in India. She explores the local institutional practices of streaming according to language background and the impact this has on the educational opportunities for learners from different social backgrounds.

Part four. Multimodal communication This final part of the Reader consists of six chapters which illustrate the growing focus on a broader range of semiotic resources than just verbal language. Chapters draw on work in sociolinguistics and applied linguistics, as well as New Literacy Studies. In Chapter 15, de Souza explores the multimodal text making practices of the Kashinawá people in Brazil. De Souza argues that, in contrast to Western textual practices, images are central to the concept of text in indigenous Kashinawá culture. Likewise, multimodal practices are fundamental to the focus of the following chapter where Ruth Swanwick focuses on Deaf education. Swanwick illustrates the three principal modes used in Deaf sign bilingual education: visual sign, spoken English and written English. In Chapter 17 Carter and Adolphs challenge assumptions about differences between the two modes of verbal language – spoken and written – and emphasise the creativity of everyday spoken language. The final three chapters in the Reader illustrate the ways in which the notion of multimodality is explicitly being researched and theorised as a significantly 'new' dimension of language and literacy. Chapter 18 focuses on multimodality as a key aspect of communication using new technologies. Drawing on new literacy studies and multimodal approaches to communication Snyder emphasises the ways in which new technology facilitates, even demands, the use of visual and aural modes as well as verbal language. In Chapter 19 Jewitt and Kress focus on the multimodal nature of the science classroom, thus challenging much classroom based research which focuses principally, or solely, on verbal aspects of meaning making. The final chapter by Wilson brings together a key notion from postcolonial theory, 'third space', with current multimodal research to explore the literacy practices of prisoners. Through careful ethnographic research she shows how, contrary to many claims about 'illiteracy' or 'poor literacy', a wide range of literacy practices form an important part of prisoners' daily lives.

Acknowledgements

The editors would like to thank all those who have been involved in the production of this Reader. In particular, we are grateful to all the contributors to this book, the course manager Fulden Underwood, the course secretary Virginia Alitta and the copublishing advisor, Gill Gowans. Thanks also to the external assessor, Roz Ivanič, for her supportive advice on this text and the Open University course of which this Reader is a part.

References

Bakhtin, M. (1981) Discourse in the novel. In M. Holquist (ed) *The Dialogic Imagination. Four essays by M. Bakhtin.* Trans. C. Emerson and M. Holquist. Austin: University of Texas Press

Bakhtin, M. (1984) *Problems of Dostoevsky's Poetics.* Trans. C. Emerson. Minnesota: Manchester University Press

Bakhtin, M. (1986) The problem of speech genres. In C. Emerson and M. Holquist (eds) *Speech Genres and other late essays,* trans. V.W. McGee. Austin, Texas: University of Texas Press

Barton, D. and Hamilton, M (1998) *Local literacies.* London: Routledge

Barton, D., Hamilton, M. and Ivanič, R. (2000) *Situated literacies. Reading and writing in context.* London: Routledge

Beaumont, M. and O'Brien, T. (2000) *Collaborative research in second language education.* Stoke-on-Trent: Trentham

Bhabha, H.K. (1994) *The Location of Culture.* London: Routledge

Bruner, J.S. (1986) *Actual minds, possible worlds,* Cambridge, MA: Harvard University Press

Bruner, J. (1990) *Acts of meaning.* London: Harvard University Press

Butler, J. (1997) *Excitable speech. A politics of the performative.* New York: Routledge

Cameron, D. (1997) Theoretical debates in feminist linguistics: questions of sex and gender, in R. Wodak (ed) *Gender and discourse.* London: Sage

Chouliaraki, L. and Fairclough, N. (1999) *Discourse in late modernity. Rethinking critical discourse analysis.* Edinburgh: EUP

Ellis, R. (2001) Second language acquisition: research and language pedagogy. In C. Candlin and N. Mercer (eds) *English language teaching in its social context.* London: Routledge

Fairclough, N. (1992) *Discourse and social change.* Cambridge, Polity

Gee, J.P. (1996) (2nd ed) *Social linguistics and literacies: Ideologies in discourses.* Basingstoke: Falmer Press

Graddol, D. (1993) Three models of language description. In D. Graddol and O. Boyd-Barrett, *Media texts: authors and readers.* Clevedon: Multilingual Matters/The Open University Press

Halliday, M.A.K.(1994) *An introduction to functional grammar.* London: Edward Arnold

Heath, S. B. (1983) *Ways with words.* Cambridge: CUP

Holmes, J. (2001) (2nd ed) *An introduction to sociolinguistics.* London: Longman

Holquist, M. (2002) (2nd ed) *Dialogism. Bakhtin and his world.* London: Routledge

Johnson, S. and Meinhof, U. (1997) (eds) *Language and masculinity.* Oxford: Blackwell

Kachru, B. (1985) *Standards, codifications, and sociolinguistic realism: the English language in the outer circle.* Cambridge: CUP

Kachru, B. (1992) (ed) *The other tongue: English across cultures.* Urbana: University of Illinois Press

Kress, G. and van Leeuwen, T. (1996) *Reading images: the grammar of visual design.* London: Routledge

Kress, G. and van Leeuwen, T. (2001) *Multimodal discourse. The modes and media of contemporary communication.* London: Arnold

Lather, P. (1991) *Getting smart: Feminist research and pedagogy with/in the postmodern.* London: Routledge

Lave, J. and Wenger, E. (1991) *Situated learning: legitimate peripheral participation.* Cambridge and New York: CUP

Mercer, N.M. (2000) *Words and minds.* London: Routledge

Mesthrie, R., Swann, J., Deumert, A. and Leap, W. (2000) *Introducing sociolinguistics.* Edinburgh: EUP

Pennycook, A.(1994) *The cultural politics of English as an international language.* London: Longman

Pennycook, A. (1998) *English and the discourses of colonialism.* London: Routledge

Rogoff, B. (1990) *Apprenticeship in thinking. Cognitive development in social context.* New York: OUP

Street, B. (1995) *Social Literacies: critical approaches to literacy in development, ethnography and education.* London: Longman

Trudgill, P. (1975) *Accent, dialect and the school.* London: Edward Arnold

Vygotsky, L.S. (1978) *Mind in society, the development of higher mental processes.* Cambridge MA: Harvard University Press

Vygotsky, L.S. (1986) *Thought and language,* ed and trans A Kozulin. Cambridge MA: MIT press

PART ONE
Talk and the processes of teaching and learning

Introduction

The chapters in Part 1 are all concerned with talk and the processes of teaching and learning. Based on recent research, they offer a range of insights into the way spoken language is used in the everyday life of classrooms. They also exemplify an increasingly influential approach to the analysis of language and education, usually known as *sociocultural research.*

Derived initially from the work of Lev Vygotsky, sociocultural researchers adopt a particular view of how language and social interaction are involved in the processes of human development and learning. From a sociocultural perspective, education and cognitive development are seen as cultural processes, whereby knowledge is not only possessed individually but distributed amongst members of communities. The way that children come to understand the world is explained through their involvement in social events, which are themselves shaped by cultural and historical factors. Sociocultural researchers therefore share the view that we cannot understand the nature of thinking, learning and development without taking account of the intrinsically social, historical and communicative nature of human life. Education is thus a process of dialogue, with the interactions amongst students and teachers reflecting the historical development, cultural values and social practices of the societies and communities in which educational institutions exist. This implies that education might be better described as a situated, contextualized process of teaching-and-learning, rather than there being separate processes of 'teaching' and 'learning'. Educational success, and failure, may then be explained as much by the quality of educational dialogue as by the intrinsic capability of individual students or the didactic presentational skills of individual teachers.

The author of Chapter 1, Deborah Hicks, is a leading American researcher in the study of classroom talk, whose work has developed the application of sociocultural theory to education in schools. She provides an introduction to a sociocultural perspective on discourse, learning and teaching (though she uses the term 'socio-cognitive' to describe the approach we have called 'sociocultural') and illustrates it with a review of relevant research. The research she reviews is mainly North American, but the perspective she endorses is essentially similar to that now adopted by many researchers elsewhere in the world. Hicks provides a definition of 'discourse', a term which is commonly used in the social sciences but open to a variety of interpretations. Her interpretation of this concept, with references to both linguistic form and socially situated practices, is one which is particularly well suited to the analysis of communication in classrooms.

In Chapter 2, the British researchers Harry Torrance and John Pryor discuss language as a tool for assessing learning and understanding in the classroom. Using examples from their own research, they show how assessment is an intrinsic part of the normal interactions between

.hers and learners. In doing so, they provide some powerful and salutary illustrations of how .ifficult it can be for teachers and learners to communicate effectively. Torrance and Pryor also show how the kinds of questions used by teachers can have a strong influence on the process of classroom education and on the ways children demonstrate their understanding. One implication of their analysis would seem to be that if teachers were able to gain more insightful under-standing of the pragmatics of classroom dialogue, this would be likely to change the ways they manage classroom interaction.

Two concepts emerging from sociocultural theory have become quite widely adopted by educational researchers – 'scaffolding' and the Zone of Proximal Development (ZPD). One useful way to explore the meaning and value of these concepts is to apply them in an analysis of actual episodes of teaching and learning. In Chapter 3, Sylvia Rojas-Drummond does exactly this as she describes a programme of applied research in schools in Mexico City. The research generated a methodology for differentiating the kinds of interactional strategies teachers employed and relating them to the kinds of learning which took place. In this way, like Torrance and Pryor, she is able to use a sociocultural analysis of classroom events to draw some general, practical conclusions about the process of teaching-and-learning.

Language is both the medium and the message of education. It enables the process of teaching and learning to take place; and one of the principal goals of education is the development of students' ability to use language. Nowhere is this more apparent than when students are learning a second or additional language. It is only relatively recently that the sociocultural perspective has been applied to research on language teaching, but it has now begun to be a significant influence. An example of this kind of research as carried out by a teacher-researcher is provided by the final chapter in Part 1, in which Andréa Machado de Almeida Mattos uses sociocultural concepts to make an evaluative analysis of how talk is used by a group of Brazilian students of English.

CHAPTER I
Discourse, teaching and learning
Deborah Hicks

What Is Discourse?

The term *discourse* implies a dialectic of both linguistic form and social communicative practices. One can talk of discourse in terms of oral and written texts that can be examined after the fact and socially situated practices that are constructed in moment-to-moment interaction (Fairclough, 1992; Gee, Michaels, and O'Connor, 1992). Thus, use of the term *discourse* implies a decision about how classroom communication is to be theoretically positioned in research on teaching and learning.

A literary theorist and philosopher of language and interpretative sciences from the former Soviet lands, Mikhail Bakhtin, wrote at length about such issues as these. Contrasting his own work with the work of linguists and philologists interested more in the formal structure of language, Bakhtin (1981, 1986) developed a theory of language centered around dialogic *utterances* as opposed to grammatical sentences (see also Morson and Emerson, 1990). Whereas sentences were defined by their formal structure (as has been described by any number of linguists), utterances were defined by changes of speaking subjects. Hence, the unit of analysis for studies of language became a unit of social communication:

> The terminological imprecision and confusion in ... linguistic thinking result from ignoring the *real unit* of speech communication: the utterance. For speech can exist in reality only in the form of concrete utterances of individual speaking people, speech subjects. Speech is always cast in the form of an utterance belonging to a particular speaking subject, and outside this form it cannot exist. (Bakhtin, 1986, p.71)

Bakhtin, and other scholars of language and linguistics who share his theoretical perspective on language, would acknowledge that words can have semantic content, what one might refer to as their 'dictionary meaning,' and that sentences can have stable grammatical form. However, once a word, phrase, or sentence is uttered or written, it assumes meaning that is inherently social in nature. As Bakhtin wrote, an utterance has 'expressive intonation' and receives its meaning by virtue of its position in a chain of speech communication (1986, pp. 90-91). Vygotsky (1986, 1987) made a similar point when he wrote that words have meaning (i.e., dictionary meaning), but only speech has *sense*. In other words, spoken and written language acquires meaning only through social usage. Meaning is socially constituted.

Many educators who explore relations between classroom communication and children's learning draw upon a model of language as a cognitive resource. Language unquestionably serves as

*   First published in M. Apple (ed.) *1995 Review of Research in Education*, pp49-72. Washington: American Educational Research Association.

a symbolic mediator of children's thinking and learning; indeed, this is the central theme of the sociocognitive (or social constructivist) research that has emerged largely in response to Vygotsky's writings on 'mind in society' (1978) and 'thinking and speech' (1986,1987). The topic of how language mediates children's learning will also emerge as a centerpiece of the present review. At the same time, it is crucial that language not be depicted solely as an intra-individual symbolic resource, a cognitive abstraction that is similar in kind to the mathematical formalisations developed to describe numerical relationships. Drawing upon the work of Bakhtin and the subsequent work of numerous theorists of language and meaning (e.g., Fairclough, 1989, 1992; Gee, 1990, 1992; Gumperz, 1982; Halliday, 1978; Halliday and Hasan, 1989; Hymes, 1974; Lemke, 1990), I will assume that language is an inherently social construct and that its meaning is constituted *relationally* between speaker and hearer or between author and reader. This theoretical depiction of language and meaning is a fulcrum for the review of research on classroom communication that follows.

Two important aspects of this theoretical perspective on discourse deserve elaboration before I move forward with the review. The first concerns the duality of discourse as textual products (both oral and written) and constitutive discursive practices (see Fairclough, 1992). Classroom interactions like whole class discussions, sharing time, journal writing, and science problem solving result in oral and written texts that can be examined after the fact. Moreover, oral and written texts in the classroom have stable generic forms associated with particular activity structures. Children need not learn anew every day the forms of discourse associated with Morning Circle; this knowledge becomes part of a shared history within the classroom. The existence of such stable discourse genres is a symbolic resource that enables teachers and children to construct what Edwards and Mercer (1987) refer to as 'common knowledge'. At the same time, classroom discourses are not 'givens' but, rather, social constructions. Classroom contexts like Morning Circle can be examined in terms of how they are constituted by discourse and joint action. Comments by Erickson and Shultz (1981) about the meaning of *context* could be considered equally true of discourse:

> Contexts can be thought of as not simply *given* in the physical setting – kitchen, living room, sidewalk in front of drug store – nor in combinations of persons (two brothers, husband and wife, firemen). Rather, contexts are constituted by what people are doing and where and when they are doing it. As McDermott (1976) puts it succinctly, people in interaction become environments for each other. Ultimately, social contexts consist of mutually shared and ratified definitions of situations and in the social actions persons take on the basis of these definitions (Mehan *et al.*, 1976). (p. 148)

This duality of discourse has been manifested in research on both the social interactional processes constituted by discourse (Dorr-Bremme, 1992; Erickson, 1988, 1996; Hicks, 1994; Yackel, Cobb, Wood, Wheatley and Merkel, 1990) and the discourse organisation or thematic content of the texts produced from those interactions (Gee, 1986; Lemke, 1990, 1992; Mehan, 1979; Michaels, 1981). The latter research lens on discourse has drawn upon theory and method from the fields of sociolinguistics (see Cazden, John and Hymes, 1972; Gumpez and Hymes, 1986; Hymes, 1974) and social semiotics (Halliday, 1978; Halliday and Hasan, 1989) in which the emphasis is on relations between community membership and linguistic form and function. The former has emerged out of a tradition of interactional sociolinguistics (Erickson, 1988; Gumperz, 1982, 1986) in which the emphasis is on how discourse and joint activity are constitutive of everyday life. Taken together, these two perspectives offer complementary means of exploring how classroom knowledge is 'talked into being' (Green and Dixon, 1993).

A second point of elaboration concerns the embodiment of ideologies in discourse. Discourses can never be neutral or value free; discourses always reflect ideologies, systems of values, beliefs, and social practices (Fairclough, 1989; Foucault, 1972; Gee, 1990). As James Paul Gee writes, discourses are identity tool kits replete with socially shared ways of acting, talking and believing. An example that Gee has used is a simple but powerful one: If I (a female, middle-class academic) walk into a motorcycle bar, I may speak the language of that setting, but I don't speak the discourse. I would be immediately recognised by my appearance, actions and language use as a non-member of the social group that is identified with that setting. Gee (1989, 1990) uses the term *Discourse* (as opposed to its lowercase variant) to describe the 'tool kit' that participants in a community share. Gee and other social theorists (Rosaldo, 1989, for instance) also make the point that social actors can participate in multiple Discourses, some of which may be conflicting identities for them. For instance, my own working-class roots can be in conflict with the Discourses that I must assume for the purpose of being an academic; similarly, academic Discourses may be in conflict with the Discourses that are associated with my being a woman (Ellsworth, 1989; Hollingsworth, 1994).

It is important to add that academic discourses also embody such ideologies; they are also Discourses. Thus, learning to 'talk science' or 'talk math' involves more than just learning a set of linguistic forms; it also involves learning beliefs and values (Lampert, 1990; Lemke, 1990; Yackel *et al.*, 1990). Gee (1989, 1990) and Lemke (1990) both point out that the ideologies embodied in such academic discourses may be in conflict with some children's home and community discourses. Minimally, these academic discourses may be unfamiliar to children who have not experienced at home what Scollon and Scollon (1981) term *essayist literacy*.

In discussing how discourses embody ideologies, I have come full circle to the discussion that began this section: that of Bakhtin's writings on dialogic utterances as the 'real' units of language and meaning. Central to Bakhtin's theory was the premise that utterances retained ideological remnants of their past usage within sociohistorical contexts. Although the forms of inquiry Bakhtin used were grounded primarily in literary analysis, his theories are nonetheless extremely relevant to current research on classroom communication. As the review of research that follows will make clear, viewing discourses as value-laden ideological systems has become a major theme within the field of research on discourse and classroom learning. It is a particularly important dimension of current research on *intertextuality,* the ways in which texts derive their meaning 'against the background of other texts, and the discourses of other occasions' (Lemke, 1992, p.257).

Discourse as a mediator of children's learning

In his book *The Forbidden Experiment*, Roger Shattuck (1980) describes how a young French doctor named Jean-Marc Gaspard struggled to bring the 'wild boy of Aveyron,' captured in the woods in the year 1800, to a more socialised state of existence. Central to the motives of the young physician were his efforts to teach the boy, named Victor, language. Although the physician's efforts were only partially successful, his ambitious goal of educating a completely unsocialised and therefore speechless child attests to the importance placed upon language as a symbolic tool of society. Throughout the history of psychology, language has been viewed as a crucial link in explaining how children become fully functional members of a social world.

In the field of psychology, language has been most consistently depicted as a symbolic system used by children to construct abstract representations of events, semantic categories, and hierarchical and sequential relationships. For instance, Katherine Nelson and her research colleagues (see Nelson, 1986, 1989) have done extensive work on how children construct abstract event representations through their recurrent participation in social events partly constituted by language practices. This type of theorising about language and cognition has achieved prominence in the cognitive constructivist theories and pedagogies now prevalent in the field of education (Fosnot, 1989; Magoon, 1977; von Glaserfield, 1989).

The publication of English translations of the collected writings of L.S. Vygotsky (see Vygotsky, 1962, 1978, 1986, 1987; see also Kozulin, 1990; Wertsch, 1985b; Yaroshevsky, 1989) has profoundly influenced recent cognitivist research on language. Vygotsky referred to his theory of development as a sociocultural or sociohistorical one, and he positioned *social speech* as the primary unit of psychological analysis. His sociocultural and sociohistorical theories of learning were grounded in his intense interest in how language and other culturally significant symbolic systems mediated human thinking. Unlike animals, who were limited to lower and biologically determined forms of thinking, human thinking was transformed, or interrupted (Emerson, 1993), by the introduction of language. Since the appearance in the 1970s and 1980s of Vygotsky's collected writings, there has been a deluge of research and writing conducted from a sociocognitive perspective. In such research, language and literacy have been explored as 'cultural amplifiers' (Cole and Griffin, 1980), and learning has been depicted as a process of apprenticeship into social practices (for examples of sociocognitive/sociocultural research and theorising, see del Rio, Alvarez, and Wertsch, 1994; Forman, Minick, and Stone, 1993; Minick, 1989; Moll, 1990; Rogoff, 1990; Tharpe and Gallimore, 1988; Wertsch, 1985b, 1991). Social constructivist research on teaching and learning is also rooted in such sociocognitive/sociocultural theories (see O'Loughlin, 1992).

Sociocognitive research has been extremely informative about how discourse is a mediator of children's learning in classrooms and other educational settings. Studies of caretaker and child interactions in home settings and teacher and student interactions in classroom settings have drawn upon sociocognitive theory to explain how children learn in what Vygotsky termed the 'zone of proximal development' (Vygotsky, 1978; see also Rogoff and Wertsch, 1984). A central metaphor that has emerged from this work is that of *scaffolding* (Wood, Bruner, and Ross, 1976). As caretaker and child engage in joint activity, the more capable adult or peer initially physically structures the activity for the child or provides explicit verbal directions that direct the child's activity. At this early point in the history of the child's participation in a social activity, the child's situational understanding may be quite different from that of the adult's (Wertsch, 1984). However, through repeated joint participation in an activity structure during which the adult gradually does what Cazden (1983) terms 'upping the ante,' the understanding of child and adult become more similar (Wertsch, 1984). Through her or his repeated engagement in activity that is often mediated by discourse, the child's situational understandings are shaped so that she or he can be a full participant in a social world.

To illustrate the mediational role of discourse and joint social activity, I will draw upon some interactional data on children's discourse and learning in an urban first-grade classroom. In this example, taken from a regular morning journal writing activity, the classroom teacher has approached a child who has drawn a horse figure in her journal. This particular example occurred midyear (January) when children in the classroom were expected not only to draw something in their journals but also to write something using invented (phonetically derived) spellings. Moreover, children had been encouraged, and generally themselves preferred, to compose fictional stories or narratives of personal experience. Suggested 'story starters' (e.g., *One day a ...*) had been written in large letters on poster board, and children working together in desk groupings often jointly composed stories around topics of shared interest. Thus, as Teacher Rhoda (as the children referred to their classroom teacher) approached the grouping of desks where Janeen (the child in question) was working, she restructured the task for Janeen so that the activity became one of story writing as opposed to drawing. In Example 1, Janeen acquires a different situational understanding of the task at hand, and discourse plays an important role in the *joint accomplishment* of this understanding.

Example I: The Mediational Role of Discourse[1]
Janeen (J) is drawing a figure in her journal. Emma (E), to Janeen's left, is observing and writing about two silkworms on her desk. Christine (C) and Chen Ju (CJ) are seated across from Janeen.

J:	*draws in journal, with pencil*
	I made a mistake and put this (unclear) [*she erases*]
	wanna be in my play? [*J looks to E*]
	huh?
	wanna be in my play? [*J turns her torso to E*]
	draws a single line across bottom of page
	this gonna be the grass
	colours the lower part of the drawing, often placing her head very
	close to the journal page

Teacher Rhoda (TR) approaches Janeen's desk area.

TR:	oka:y Aleisha # how you doin? [*J reaches into crayon basket*]
J:	*begins to color*
TR:	what are you writing about (.) Aleisha?
	I mean Janeen [*TR moves directly behind J*]
	what are you writing about? [*TR scratches J's back*]
J:	a horse [*softly*] [*TR leans over J*] TR: huh? what?
J:	a horse =
TR:	= a horse (.) okay
	I want you to put your crayon down now [*TR places J's pencil on journal*]
	I want you to take your pencil and put the title up there [*TR points to journal*] # a horse
J:	*writes* The

Teacher Rhoda leaves Janeen's desk area. Janeen continues to write.

J:	ho:::rse [*turns torso toward E*]
h::	[*articulates as she writes haerto*]
	sits back in chair then resumes writing

Later during Journal Writing, Teacher Rhoda approaches the desk area once again. She moves to Janeen's desk.

TR:	alright now # okay
	what's it [the journal entry] called now?
J:	the horse
TR:	the horse J: h:: [*TR slides journal closer to J*]
TR:	okay
	Teacher Rhoda interrupts her work with Janeen to establish order in the classroom
	now (.) the horse

	what's the story gonna be # tell me
J:	*holds pencil poised over journal*
TR:	how does it start? J: the horse =
	= was TR: the–
TR:	go ahead
	the horse was ...
	J begins to write in her journal, as TR leaves the desk area
J:	*leans back in chair*
	the horse was [softly]

By the end of Journal Writing, Janeen has composed the following written entry:

Written:
The haerto
The haerto WasWakingonThe
graysen AnD aBaBYAnD The BaBy
Jump up AnD htae har hD
Gloss:
The Horse
The horse was walking on the grass. And a baby. And the baby jump up
and hit her head.

The kind of social interchange that occurs in Example 1 is illustrative of the way in which such forms of understanding initially occur relationally between persons before they are *internalised* (Emerson, 1983; Toulmin, 1979, 1984; Vygotsky, 1986; Wertsch and Stone, 1985) by the child. The discourses and activity structures constitutive of meaning construction are inherently social, such as the story form that Janeen appropriated for journal writing. For sociocognitive theorists, a central research question is therefore that of how children appropriate the discourses characteristic of informal (e.g., home, playground) and formal institutional (e.g., school, church) settings (Gee, 1990; Wertsch, 1991).

Academic Discourses in the Classroom
The following written text was also produced by Janeen, the first grader introduced in Example 1. The text was written during a 6-week unit on silkworms that involved observing and documenting the growth and metamorphosis of these caterpillarlike creatures.

Example 2: Academic Writing[2]
Written:
Facts About Silkworms
1. They turn into moths.
2. Wen They are Little They
    eies are gery and Wen They Are big
    They eies are Black.
3. The silkworms make cocon.
4. The silkworms have spaet on them.
5. The silkworm have 8 Leg.

Gloss:
Facts About Silkworms
1. They turn into moths.
2. When they are little their eyes are grey and when they are big their eyes are black.
3. The silkworms make cocoon.
4. The silkworms have spot on them.
5. The silkworms have 8 leg.

L+LIn SS

Probably no educator would take exception with my identifying this piece of writing as a science text. It is essayist in style, it is grounded in observation and description (two very 'scientific' activities), and the topic is one typical of the biological sciences. Disciplines such as science and mathematics are partly constituted by textual genres and discursive practices, and learning science or learning math cannot be separated from these practices. In fact, many educators (teachers and researchers) would view Janeen's science diary entry as one form of evidence that she has learned science. Similarly, some theorists would suggest that 'learning science' is a process that is framed by discourse genres, forms of activity, and ways of establishing semantic links among events, objects and persons (see Lemke, 1988, 1990; Rosebery, Warren and Conant, 1992). Other researchers have explored similar issues with respect to mathematics instruction (Ball, 1991, 1993; Bill, Leer, Reams, 1992; Hiebert and Wearne, 1993; Lampert, 1990; Spanos, Rhodes, Corasaniti Dale, and Crandall, 1988).

Literacy is generally thought of as the ability to read and write. However, some theorists have extended the meaning of literacy to encompass more than just the ability to read and write. Full literacy, according to some, entails mastery of secondary or formal institutional, often academic discourses (Gee, 1989). These secondary discourses typically involve ways of describing, explaining and questioning that are dissimilar to 'ordinary' conversation. They entail what Vygotsky (1986, 1987) termed *nonspontaneous* forms of thinking and talk, such as explicit focusing on particular kinds of relationships that are verbalised or written and often subjected to public confirmation. The discourses typical of academic disciplines may be thought of as *literacies*, in this broader sense (Michaels and O'Connor, 1990). A similar theoretical perspective has been voiced in documents like the National Council of Teachers of Methematics (NCTM) teaching and evaluation standards, which call for the need for children to become 'mathematically literate' (NCTM, 1989, p.18). Mathematical literacy in this sense would involve far more than children being able to record their reasoning processes in math journals. It would also involve ways of talking and forms of reasoning that characterise the discipline, such as hazarding a solution to a problem, explaining to one's peers how one arrived at the solution, and engaging in a dialogue about possible alternative solutions (Lampert, 1990; NCTM, 1989, 1991). A written record of one's solution processes would then be an additional link in the construction of mathematical discourse.

How do teachers teach and children learn these more formal academic discourses? There have been some efforts to incorporate the explicit teaching of academic genres into literacy instruction (see Reid, 1987, for a discussion of the controversy surrounding 'genre instruction'). However, a sociocognitive perspective on discourse would suggest that children learn academic discourses through their repeated participation in meaningful social activity (Rogoff, 1990). Classroom teachers set the stage for this learning process by providing the discursive 'slots' that enable novice learners to participate in disciplinary practices. This can occur within group discussions in which the teacher orchestrates classroom discourse (NCTM, 1991, p. 35), or it can occur in small group or one-on-one conferences.

It is thus important to note that academic discourses are negotiated situationally within the classroom. Although there are commonalities within disciplines (and these commonalities are reinforced by the publication of teaching and evaluation standards), what it means to 'talk science', 'talk history,' or 'talk mathematics' is constructed through locally situated, everyday social interaction. This is graphically illustrated by cross-cultural differences in how teachers orchestrate children's learning within disciplines (see, for instance, Stigler, Fernandez, and Yoshida, 1992, on the discourse of mathematics instruction in Japan and in the United States). However, each classroom is also a distinct local site for the construction of meaning. In the words of Heidi Brilliant-Mills (1993), a researcher in the Santa Barbara Discourse Group who has studied the construction of mathematics discourse in a sixth-grade classroom,

> the words selected, the patterns of interaction experienced, and the range of events constructed by members define what counts as mathematics, mathematical actions, and being mathematicians. Viewing language as social action and meaning making, members of a classroom group construct particular patterns of social performance that make visible how teachers and students understand mathematics. It is important, therefore, to understand the ways in which a register and patterns of interaction are constructed because there is no one register or pattern of interaction for mathematics for students. Registers are *situationally constituted* through the patterns of interaction that serve to define what counts as mathematics and what being a mathematician means in particular settings. (p.302, italics added)

An example of the situational construction of academic discourse comes once again from my case study of one first grader, Janeen. In Example 2, we saw an example of Janeen's science diary entry, one reflective of the formal discourses of science as an academic discipline (or literacies). Approximately one year before the writing of the science text shown in that earlier example, I documented an episode of science diary writing that was also centered on children's observations of silkworms. Like all the children in the classroom, Janeen had been given several silkworms to observe over an entire cycle of growth and metamorphosis. In Example 3, Teacher Rhoda structures the modes of activity and forms of discourse that constitute scientific work. Through physical movement (handing Janeen a magnifying glass) and leading questions ('what d'ya see?'), she molds Janeen's observations of and comments about the silkworms. Thus, in Example 3, we see the joint construction of a scientific discourse, one that will later become a means for Janeen's independent science work.

Example 3: Situationally Constructed Academic Discourses
Janeen (J) is working on a science diary entry. Thus far, she has written the words 'The silkworm' in her science diary. Emma (E) is seated to her left. Teacher Rhoda (TR) approaches the desk area.

TR:	now what d'ya got here?
J:	the silkworm # is [*reading*]
TR:	*empties silkworms (in a plastic tray) onto J's science diary*
	which one is it?
	which one are you looking at?
J:	*points to a silkworm*
TR:	take one to look at
	okay we really have to look at 'im
J:	*looks intently at silkworms on her science diary page*
TR:	now (.) where is this guy?
	here he is [*indicates one of the silkworms*]
	is this the one you wanna look at?
J:	*nods yes*
TR:	let's take 'im over here
	separates silkworm from other ones on diary page
	let 'im crawl right there =
E:	= *see* # it's not (.) don't be afraid of touching it

TR:	now # you can take a good look at 'im like this too [*hands J a magnifying glass*]
J:	*looks at silkworm through magnifying glass*
TR:	can you see 'im (.) alright?
J:	*nods yes*
TR:	yeah (.) what d'ya see? [*takes J's hand and guides her to move the magnifying glass closer to silkworm*]
J:	he goin like this [*moves her head up and back*]
TR:	he's going like that?
	what d'ya think that was?
	what is that?
	he's going like –
J:	he was liftin his head
TR:	<u>okay</u>!
	the silkworm # was [*writing in J's science diary*]
	lifting?
J:	his
TR:	his head [*writing*]
	al<u>right</u>

This discussion of situationally constituted academic discourses recalls my earlier discussion of the duality of discourses as texts and socially situated interactional processes. It is meaningful to examine both dimensions of discourse, and, with the advent of video technology and *micro-ethnographic* methods of analysis (see Erickson, 1992), both can be examined after the actual occurrence of episodes of social activity. Indeed, much current work on classroom discourse combines studies of textual products (again, both oral and written texts) and studies of social-interactional processes.

A related theoretical perspective on discourse and learning has emerged in the field of psychology under the rubric of *discursive psychology* (Edwards and Potter, 1992; Harre and Gillett, 1994) or *social constructionism* (Gergen, 1985; Shotter, 1993). Although grounded more in post-modernist views of discourse and the self than in the analysis of face-to-face social interaction, such theories share an interest in how discourse is constitutive of social life. In the case of discourse-oriented theories of psychology and education (see, in particular, Edwards, 1993; Edwards and Mercer, 1987; Walkerdine, 1990), the emphasis is on how discursive practices constitute what is more typically referred to as *cognition* and how speaking subjects are given social identities through their positionings in discourse. Although having different intellectual histories, interactional sociolinguistic and social constructionist educational research sometimes touch upon similar topics of inquiry (compare, for example, Dorr-Bremme's 1992 study of how children's classroom identities are socially constituted with Edwards's 1993 study of how children's conceptual understandings are constructed through talk).

This concludes my discussion of theoretical perspectives on discourse and learning. I might summarise this section by stressing that discourse is an inherently social construct that mediates, indeed partly constitutes, the teaching and learning that take place in classrooms. Through meaningful classroom activity, children appropriate the discourses that situationally define 'what counts' as knowing within disciplines. In the following section, I turn to current research on classroom discourse. I explore prominent classroom genres, such as the Initiation-Response-Evaluation(IRE)/Initiation-Response-Follow-up(IRF) instructional sequence; efforts at educational reform tied to discourse; the 'embeddedness' of classroom discourses in community-based discourses; and the heterogeneous discourses that are woven into one text or turn of talk. Each of these topics is elaborated through reference to work of current researchers in the field. Because of the breadth of this field, I cannot hope to cover all of the research that would fall under a given topic. Rather, I provide exemplars that will, I hope, enrich readers' understanding of the research topics currently being addressed within the field of classroom discourse.

RESEARCH ON DISCOURSE AND LEARNING IN THE CLASSROOM

This section begins with a limited discussion of children's appropriation of discourse in the pre-school years. A discussion of preschool language development will orient the reader to the importance of understanding how community-based discourse practices that children experience at home later become a means for their participation in classroom activities. Many sociolinguistic researchers believe that community-based discourse practices are a primary conduit through which children structure their school experiences. If these practices are consonant with those found in formal classroom settings, children typically learn academic discourses with ease. If not, then children may encounter difficulties. The tenet of most educational standards that all children have access to academic learning is invoked here as I discuss differences in the discourse-related experiences that young children bring to their classrooms.

Discourse and social activity in the preschool years

In the first section of this review, I discussed current thinking on how discourse mediates children's learning. I noted that as children participate in repeated social events, they gradually assume more control over their activity. Activity that was once performed with extensive input from a caretaker can later be performed independently by the child. The term *repeated* is an important one to emphasise. Social events such as listening to bedtime stories, taking a bath, having dinner, and going to day care become routine aspects of children's lives. As they participate in the day-to-day routines that make up their preschool lives, children also learn the forms of discourse associated with those routines.

An example from the literature on young children's language and literacy development is illustrative of how children internalise forms of discourse that initially occur as part of their daily routines. This example is drawn from language data recorded by a prominent child language researcher, Catherine Snow, as she interacted with her then 3-year-old son, Nathaniel. In the example, mother and child are jointly reading a Dr. Seuss book, *Hop on Pop*, that is a familiar one to Nathaniel. The mother structures the book reading so that Nathaniel can successfully fill in the conversational 'slots' left open by her pauses at the ends of familiar phrases from the text.

Example 4: Discourse Development in the Preschool Years

Printed text:	*Conversation at 37 months, 26 days:*	
Hop on Pop	M:	hop on pop
	by ...	
Dr. Seuss	N:	Dr. Seuss
PAT PAT	M:	Pat pat
They call him Pat.		they call him pat
PAT SAT		Pat sat
Pat sat on hat.		Pat sat on
	N:	the hat
PAT CAT	M:	Pat cat
Pat sat on cat.		Pat sat on
	N:	a cat

PAT BAT	M:	Pat bat
Pat sat on bat.		Pat sat on
	N:	a bat (Snow, 1983, p.181)

In the same way that young children gradually assume more and more control over their activity, they become more adept at the use of discourse forms that they encounter in such repeated episodes of social activity. Discourse genres like the book-reading dialogue above, along with social roles and activities, become part of the child's increasingly complex repertoire of language knowledge and practices. Social discursive routines that are initially quite simple later become part of a more complex system. For instance, the very young child's participation in social routines such as 'peekaboo' and 'hide and seek' later emerge as the differentiated social roles and speech forms that the child assigns to various characters in her or his symbolic play (Rubin and Wolf, 1979; Wolf and Hicks, 1989). Young children in the preschool years develop a repertoire of discourse types linked to specific recurring social activities (see, in particular, Julie Gerhardt's analysis in Nelson, 1989, of one child's development of a repertoire of discourse types).

Ways with words

The segment of mother-child dialogue in Example 4 looks much like a discourse genre familiar to scholars of classroom discourse. The pattern in which the mother initiates a phrase from the book and the child fills in the slot left open by her pause resembles what scholars of classroom discourse have termed the Initiation-Response-Evaluation (IRE) (Cazden, 1986, 1988; Mehan, 1979) or Initiation-Response-Follow-up (IRF) (Sinclair and Coulthard, 1975; Wells, 1993) sequence. In the case of the mother-child interchange in Example 4, there is no overt evaluation; the mother does not explicitly label the child's responses as right or wrong, good or bad. However, the social activity in which the two participate is instructional in nature, the discourse form that ensues is one that entails an obligatory response from the child (although one scaffolded by the mother), and the focus of attention is a written text. All of these factors make this activity one that is highly compatible with the communicative activities that children typically encounter in the classroom. Moreover, like many academic discourses, the talk during this episode is grounded in what Scollon and Scollon (1981) term *essayist literacy*. Essayist literacy, manifested in written genres such as fiction and scientific texts, entails a more distant relationship between speaker and hearer. A trademark of Western literacy is the way in which authors distance themselves from events by creating an authorial voice removed from moment-to-moment exchange with the reader. Such literate practices have, according to the Scollons, become part of the 'presentation of self,' the ways in which many Western middle-class speakers position themselves vis-à-vis other persons and other texts.

The work of the Scollons, and that of other anthropologists and sociolinguists, has revealed important differences across communities and cultures in children's language socialisation. Returning to James Paul Gee's terminology, one might say that children in different communities are enculturated into different Discourses reflecting the language practices, values, and ways of acting and believing characteristic of their communities. Moreover, not all of these Discourses are ones that closely match the essayist forms of discourse described by Scollon and Scollon.

Research that illustrates this point comes from Shirley Brice Heath's ethnographic study of the language socialisation of children in three communities in the Piedmont. Heath (1982, 1983) found that as children participated in differing kinds of social events, they were socialised into different 'ways with words.' Heath focused, in particular, on the *narrative* practices, or talk about events, that she uncovered through research in three communities: two working-class communities, one Black and one White, of present and former millworkers and one community of 'townspeople,' White and Black middle-class members of a nearby town. This work, spanning nearly a decade, revealed narrative practices that were important links to children's later participation in classrooms. For instance, children from Trackton, a Black working-class community, were participants in rich oral language traditions. Heath noted the amazing abilities of some of the young members of this community to engage in verbal repartee and story telling. However, events were not subjected to 'stop-action' framing and verbal elaboration; adult caretakers did not break up events and place them in a narrative frame in a way that would resemble an instructional conversation ('now let's see what happens when we mix in the flour'). As one elder member of the Trackton community elaborated in reference to her grandchild Teegie's learning:

> He gotta learn to *know* 'bout dis world, can't nobody tell 'im. Now just how crazy is dat? White folks uh hear dey kids say sump'n, dey say it back to 'em, dey aks 'em 'gain 'n 'gain 'bout things, like they 'posed to be born knowin'. You think I tell Teegie all he gotta know to get along? He just gotta be keen, keep his eyes open, don't he be sorry. Gotta watch hisself by watchin' other folks. Ain't no use me tellin' 'im: 'Learn dið, learn dat. What's dis? What's dat?' He just gotta learn, gotta know: he see one thing one place one time, he know how it go, see sump'n like it again, maybe it be de same, maybe it won't. He hafta try it out. (Heath, 1983, p.84)

Heath found that in classroom settings, children from Trackton found 'known information' questions unfamiliar and difficult. Worksheets that required them to siphon off subparts of words and sentences or to single out one particular aspect of an event were dissimilar to the ways with words of their community. Children from Roadville, a working-class mill community, also experienced difficulties with school language practices. The need in the later elementary years to expand upon facts, providing explanation and elaboration or engaging in fictional story writing, was difficult for children whose primary language socialisation had involved 'sticking to the facts'.

Such ethnographic forms of research on preschool language socialisation within communities provide important detail on issues that are often associated with educational achievement, such as time spent interacting with books (Wells, 1986). For instance, Heath (1982, 1983) and Miller (1982; see also Miller, Nemoianu, and DeJong, 1986) found that working-class mothers engaged in book reading with their children. However, the emphasis in these book-reading sessions was often on the labeling of items ('what's that?') or on the recall of information directly from the text. Such book-reading sessions did not resemble the instructional conversations (Tharpe and Gallimore, 1988) that characterise middle-class language socialisation practices and that characterise the discourses within many academic disciplines, extending from the given or known to the realm of the hypothetical or fictional.

I will return to this topic of the 'ways with words' children bring to their primary grade classrooms in a later subsection, where I discuss the intersection of community discourses and learning that occurs in classrooms. In that later section and in my concluding statements, I will point out that classrooms cannot be viewed as divorced from the community-based language practices of children. If the goal of allowing all children full access to academic knowledge is to be met, researchers across disciplines must look seriously at how children's primary discourses do or do not mesh with the expectations of formal schooling. First, however, I need to provide an overview of the forms of classroom discourse, or genres, that are linked to both 'traditional' instruction and instruction grounded in recent reform efforts.

Discourse genres in the classroom

As any primary grade teacher knows, one of the biggest tasks facing young children entering school is that of mastering the forms of discourse and social activity appropriate within different settings. Participating in a whole class discussion involves a different set of social roles, forms of discourse, and modes of activity than, for instance, engaging in symbolic play with peers. Each form of classroom activity has an associated set of *participant structures*, ways in which participants in the activity socially and linguistically orient themselves to one another and to the activity at hand (Au, 1980; Erickson and Shultz, 1981; Harness-Goodwin, 1990; O'Connor and Michaels, in press). Erickson (1996) provides a fascinating study of just how difficult the process of 'learning the ropes' is. Children must learn not only what to say and how to say it but also when to say it. Appropriate timing can be as critical as getting the 'right' answer; children have to be attuned to any number of contextualisation cues (Gumperz, 1982) in order to participate successfully in classroom discussions. In class discussions, what counts as 'right' may depend as much on the social appropriateness of a response – its adherence to the exigences of a certain discourse genre or participant framework – as on children's academic 'content knowledge' (Edwards, 1993).

Intimately linked to participant frameworks are the forms of discourse that are partly constitutive of them. Classrooms, like any other social setting, are characterised by stable discourse genres: forms of talk and writing that can be attributed to particular groups of speakers or writers doing certain things at a given location, often at certain times of the day (see Bakhtin, 1986, for a theoretical discussion of *speech genres*). Speakers, typically unconsciously, recognise bounded events as *speech activities* (Gumperz, 1982) that are defined by modes of discourse and forms of activity. As I noted earlier, children entering the classroom in the early morning hours do not need to be told how to participate in Morning Circle; they know through repeated participation the forms of talk and participant structures that define that speech activity. Without the existence of these 'relatively stable types of ... utterances' (Bakhtin, 1986, p.60), classroom communication and learning would be impossible.

IRE/IRF: the unmarked case?

Across the literature on classroom discourse, certainly the most robust form of talk documented has been that of the Initiation-Response-Evaluation (Cazden, 1988; Mehan, 1979) or Initiation-Response-Follow-up (Sinclair and Coulthard, 1975; Wells, 1993) sequence. This genre has come to be viewed as what linguists call the *unmarked case*; it constitutes somewhat of a norm. Perhaps the robustness of the IRE/IRF sequence across classroom settings can be related back to the example of mother-child interaction shown in Example 4. There, as the more capable adult in that example assumed an instructional role, she provided conversational slots so that the child could successfully participate in joint book reading. The provision of such slots or openings for learners may be a means through which caretakers, and teachers, provide access to discourses and forms of knowledge beyond the child's independent means.

The IRE/IRF organisation of classroom lessons has been documented largely for group dis-cussion activities in which the teacher asks a question, a child (or a group of children) responds, and the teacher follows through with a comment, often evaluative in nature. The following example from Courtney Cazden's own teaching illustrates the typical triadic structure of classroom lessons. In this example, the teacher has been eliciting children's birthplaces as a means of helping them learn about geography, distance, and family origins. One student, Prenda, has been called on to identify her birthplace and then to find it on a map.

Example 5: The IRE/IRF Sequence in Classroom Lessons

Teacher: Uh, Prenda, ah, let's see if we can find, here's your name. Where were you born, Prenda? [*initiation*]

Prenda: San Diego. [*response*]

Teacher: You were born in San Diego, all right. [*evaluation*]

Teacher: Uhm, can you come up and find San Diego on the map? [*initiation*]

Prenda: (goes to board and points) [*response*]

Teacher: Right there okay. [*evaluation*] (Cazden, 1988, p. 32)

In some cases, the IRE/IRF sequence has come to be associated with broader teaching practices or philosophies, such as the direct instruction of skills or the elicitation of so-called *known-information* questions, questions where the teacher is seeking the 'right answer.' The IRE sequence has, for some educational researchers, come to be associated with a 'skill and drill' mode of instruction, and reform efforts have therefore made such modes of communication one of their primary targets of change. However, Longo (1994) and Wells (1993) point out that more directive or evaluative instruction can coexist with the forms of talk associated with inquiry learning or 'teaching for understanding' (for discussions of discourse grounded in inquiry, see Ball, 1991; Hiebert and Wearne, 1993; Lampert, 1990; Tharpe and Gallimore, 1988). This is particularly the case when one extends the IRE sequence to include all forms of discourse that are triadic in structure, which ultimately is the case for most classroom discourses.

In his article 'Reevaluating the IRF Sequence,' Gordon Wells (1993) describes how one classroom teacher moved between direct modes of instruction involving a triadic form of discourse with explicit evaluation and discourse that resembled more what Tharpe and Gallimore (1988) refer to as an *instructional conversation*. This can be illustrated by the following two examples from his article. In the first, three students in a third-grade classroom have been developing methods for measuring time. They have access to a science textbook, as well as various artifacts (bottles, measuring jugs). The teacher holds a conference with the students to make sure that they understand the goals of the cooperative task.

Example 6a: Reevaluating the IRF Sequence

The teacher (T) and students (Emily [EJ], Lily [L], Veronica [V]) have been looking at the textbook they are using, in which instructions are given for performing the activity.

T: Here the picture (a cartoon of children doing the activity) suggests that you can clap, but are there other ways that you can use to figure out how long it takes for the bottle to empty?

E: Stamp your feet

T: Stamp your feet, good (.) another way?

E: Er snap

T: Snap....

OK, besides using your hands and feet, what other methods could you think of?

L: Stop watch

T: No, you're not supposed to use a clock and a watch

V: (unintelligible)

T: OK, so I put the problem to you: Think of as many ways as you can (.) to figure out the time it takes (.) for you [Emily] to empty the bottle compared to her [Lily], compared to er Veronica
        Now the next problem I would like you to think about is ... what are – what the three of you are doing (.) is it a fair test?
        The meaning of 'fair test' is if you empty a bottle-say if you [Emily] fill the bottle half (.) and Veronica fills her bottle full (.) would it be a fair test?
V: No
E: No (.) you have to – if I filled my bottle half and to make that a fair test she would fill her bottle half
T: That's right. . . . (Wells, 1993, pp.18-19)

This example illustrates a fairly direct mode of instruction in which the teacher overtly evaluates students' responses to her questions. In a later conference, however, the discussion resembles more an instructional conversation. This conference occurred after Emily, Lily, and Veronica had worked cooperatively to devise 'fair' methods of measuring time. In Example 6b, the teacher's role has shifted to one of a conversational partner inquiring about the work of the three students. Her follow-ups to students' responses often take the form of further questions, clarifying the students' ideas or *revoicing* them (for slightly different depictions of revoicing, see Bill *et al.*, 1992; O'Connor and Michaels, 1996). In Example 6b, the teacher's follow-up questions or re-voicings allow the students to have the last word.

Example 6b: Re-evaluating the IRF Sequence
T: So how are you all doing?
E: Fine
T: What did you all do?
E: Well, what we did was we used cups and then we started um – I start clapping when we (got back) and we counted the exact with the cups –
V: Like whenever <u>anyone</u> –
E: <u>and then</u> we started pouring the bottles

        We [Emily and Veronica] were about the same (.) three and she [Lily] had four
        And right now we're wondering why she had four because probably she um (.) poured out slowly (.) or – and probably we poured it out real fast
T: You used these containers? (*pointing to plastic cups*)
E: No, we used the Five Alive-
T: The Five Alive bottles?
E: Yeah, these [cups] are to keep the beat
T: OK, so you – so that is a good observation – you observed (.) that Lily's count (.) was much (.) less-more or less'?
E: More
T: – more (.) than both of you (.) and you figured that it's because of the way she poured it. ... (Wells, 1993, p.23)

Wells (1993) concludes that the IRF discourse genre can encompass a number of different instructional functions depending on the tasks and goals in question. It may be that the IRF genre is an overarching form of discourse organisation (the unmarked case) reflecting the teacher's greater authority and more mature understanding of disciplinary practices and concepts. However, if one extends the IRE to include all forms of triadic discourse (or IRF), as Wells has done, this genre can be viewed as encompassing a constellation of quite heterogeneous speech activities. In other words, although the discourse *structure* of the IRF may be constant across instructional settings, its *functions* may vary widely.

Other classroom genres

Triadic forms of discourse may characterise much of classroom instruction, even instruction that is more conversational in nature. However, teachers or students sometimes engage in a more monologic form of talk. A child in a mathematics classroom may be asked to elaborate on how she arrived at her answer to a problem. As the child speaks, she constructs a short history of her solution to the problem, what Paul Longo (1994) refers to as a 'mathematical narrative.' A child in First Circle or Morning Circle might be invited to tell a narrative of personal experience. Other children seated in a circle on the rug area listen as the child relates a personally experienced event, sometimes centered around an object that she has brought to school. In these kinds of communicative interactions, the speaker is given the floor for a much longer period of time. The rules of the game – the participant frameworks that define social roles and obligations – have shifted somewhat so that the speaker no longer expects an immediate response. Moreover, the responses from both the classroom teacher and fellow students often serve to clarify or extend points from the speaker's narrative rather than evaluate the correctness of the speaker's answer.

Narrative discourses, oral and written texts representative of a series of connected events, may be another overarching discourse genre in the classroom, one with many variations in both form and function. A narrative of personal experience or explanation can crop up in nearly any classroom discussion. Indeed, some classroom communicative activities are constituted largely by narrative discourses. Two examples that come to mind are (a) Morning Circle or First Circle and Sharing Time, where children construct narratives of personal experience (Dorr-Bremme, 1992; Kantor, Green, Bradley, and Lin, 1992; Michaels, 1981), and (b) Journal Writing, where children typically write journal entries grounded in fictional or personally experienced events (Dyson, 1989, 1993; Hicks and Kanevsky, 1992).

Some educators and educational psychologists have argued that narrative discourse is developmentally more accessible to young children. Kieran Egan (1988, 1993), for instance, has argued that young children acquire new knowledge most easily when potentially difficult concepts are embedded in story form. An abstract concept such as 'good versus evil' is easily understood by young children when it is embodied in the characters of the Teenage Mutant Ninja Turtles (the good guys) engaged in battle against Splinter and his foot soldiers (the bad guys). Others have suggested that narrative discourse be viewed as a constellation of discourse genres, some having story form ('Once upon a time ...') and others representative of more essayist forms ('This is how I got my answer...') In my own work on narrative discourse and classroom learning (see Hicks, 1993), I have argued that narrative discourses should be examined in light of the speech activities in which participants are engaged. In this sense, narrative can be explored as a family of discourse genres in which children and teachers construct extended oral or written texts that order, describe, explain, or employ events, both real and fictional.

Studies of children's language use and classroom learning have suggested a relationship between such extended talk about events and children's successful participation in school tasks (Snow and Kurland, 1996). In large part, such studies have connected children's narrative performances with their literacy learning. Since oral narrative genres represent extended discourse in which the speaker constructs a *text* as opposed to a single utterance, studies of children's oral narratives have been viewed as a possible window onto their classroom literacy learning. Such work has often been focused on sociolinguistic differences in the narratives constructed by children from differing communities. Recall that Heath's ethnographic study of communities' ways with words revealed important differences in narrative socialisation. In subsequent studies of children's classroom narratives, Michaels (1981) found cultural differences that supported Heath's work. The Sharing Time narratives of Black children were rooted more in an oral discourse style, where events were connected through linguistic devices like repetition, such as one might find in poetry. The Sharing Time narratives of White children tended to be more essayist or 'literate' in nature, in that a single topic was chosen and events connected to the topic were related in a sequential manner. Researchers like Sarah Michaels have concluded that differing forms of narrative discourse may provide children with differential access to literacy. As Scollon and Scollon (1981) note in a chapter titled 'The Literate Two Year Old,' preschool children in many middle-class families may be literate long before they are able to read and write.

Research on narrative discourse genres in the classroom, however, is not only important for understanding children's abilities to read and write, as literacy has been traditionally viewed. Extending from the theoretical perspectives that I described in the first section, narrative discourses could be viewed as a window onto children's appropriation of literacies, in the broader sense. Talking and writing science does not simply require the construction of texts with sequenced events; it requires the production of certain *kinds* of narrative texts. The latter is not always an easy task for young children.

In this discussion of 'other' classroom discourse genres ('other' in contrast to IRE/IRF triadic discourses), I have concentrated largely on narrative genres: stories, reports, and descriptions or explanations that result in an extended turn of talk. There are many other genres of classroom discourse that one could identify. Some of these might be positioned as subgenres of the two larger ones that I have focused on here. Lemke (1990), in his study of classroom science talk, identifies any number of what Gumperz (1982) would term speech activities, in which participants share assumptions about who does the talking and what forms of talk are appropriate. Speech activities such as Going Over Homework, Calling the Roll, and Class Announcements are all repeatedly experienced forms of social activity that are partly constituted by discourse practices. Each of these speech activities can be identified by characteristic forms of discourse that are fairly predictable from the setting. For instance, Calling the Roll or Attendance might be identified by a sequence of exchanges in which the teacher nominates a child to take attendance, the child calls the roll, and other children respond 'here' or 'present.'

It is in this sense that written and oral discourse genres are intimately connected to classroom activity structures (Lemke, 1990; Wells, 1993). A journal entry that has story form, as did Janeen's 'horse' entry in Example 1, for instance, emerges in response to a particular activity structure: Journal Writing. One could examine any number of classroom genres and their concomitant frames of social activity. Instead, I have chosen to focus on two overarching genres that have played an important role in researchers' efforts to understand links between classroom discourse and classroom learning.

Notes

1. The following transcription symbols are used in Example 1 and other examples throughout this review: (.) indicates very short pause or breath intake, # indicates longer pause, vowel: indicates lengthened vowel, underlining indicates stress on word, caps indicates increased volume, = indicates absence of pause between utterances. Overlapping utterances by more than one speaker are thus marked by their horizontal placement on one line or vertical placement underneath one another.

2. Janeen is a member of an urban African American community that makes use of grammatical forms typical of what sociolinguists refer to as vernacular Black English or simply Black English (see Wolfram and Fasold, 1974, for

discussion). In my gloss of Janeen's science diary writing, I have maintained these grammatical forms rather than attempting to 'correct' them to mainstream standard English.

References

Au, K. (1980) Participation structures in a reading lesson with Hawaiian children: Analysis of a culturally appropriate instructional event. *Anthropology and Education Quarterly,* 11, 91-115.

Bakhtin, M. M. (1981) *The dialogic imagination: Four essays by M. M. Bakhtin* (M. Holquist, Ed., C. Emerson and M. Holquist, Trans.). Austin: University of Texas Press.

Bakhtin, M. M. (1986) *Speech genres and other late essays* (C. Emerson and M. Holquist, Eds., V. McGee, Trans.). Austin: University of Texas Press.

Ball, D. (1991, November). What's all this talk about 'discourse'? *Arithmetic Teacher*, 44-48.

Ball, D. (1993). With an eye on the mathematical horizon: Dilemmas of teaching elementary school mathematics. *Elementary School Journal*, 93, 373-397.

Bill, V., Leer, M., Reams, L., and Resnick, L. (1992). From cupcakes to equations: The structure of discourse in a primary mathematics classroom. *Verbum,* 1-2, 63-85.

Brilliant-Mills, H. (1993) Becoming a mathematician: Building a situated definition of mathematics. *Linguistics and Education*, 5, 301-334.

Cazden, C. (1983) Adult assistance to language development: Scaffolds, models, and direct instruction. In R. Parker and F. Davis (Eds.), *Developing literacy: Young children's use of language*. Newark, DE: International Reading Association.

Cazden, C. (1986) Classroom discourse. In M. E. Wittrock (Ed.), *Handbook of research on teaching* (3rd ed., 432-463). New York: Macmillan.

Cazden, C. (1988) *Classroom discourse: The language of teaching and learning*. Portsmouth, NH: Heinemann.

Cazden, C., John, V. P., and Hymes, D. (Eds.). (1972) *Functions of language in the classroom*. New York: Teachers College Press.

Cole, M., and Griffin, R (1980) Cultural amplifiers reconsidered. In D. Olson (Ed.), *The social foundations of language and thought: Essays in honor of Jerome S. Bruner* (343-364). New York: Norton.

Dorr-Bremme, D. (1992, April) Discourse and social identity in a kindergarten/first grade classroom. Paper presented at the annual meeting of the American Educational Research Association, San Francisco.

Dyson, A. H. (1989) *Multiple worlds of child writers: Friends learning to write*. New York: Teachers College Press.

Dyson, A. H. (1991) Towards a reconceptualisation of written language development. *Linguistics and Education*, 3, 139-161.

Dyson, A. H. (1993) *Social worlds of children learning to write in an urban school*. New York: Teachers College Press.

Edwards, D. (1993) Concepts, memory, and the organisation of pedagogic discourse: A case study. *Educational Research,* 19, 205-225.

Edwards, D., and Mercer, N. (1987) *Common knowledge*. London: Methuen.

Edwards, D., and Potter, J. (1992) *Discursive psychology.* Newbury Park, CA: Sage.

Egan, K. (1988) *Primary understanding: Education in early childhood.* New York: Routledge.

Egan, K. (1993) Narrative and learning: A voyage of implications. *Linguistics and Education,* 5, 119-126.

Ellsworth, E. (1989) Why doesn't this feel empowering? Working through the repressive myths of critical pedagogy. *Harvard Educational Review*, 59, 297-324.

Emerson, C. (1983) The outer word and inner speech: Bakhtin, Vygotsky, and the internalisation of language. *Critical Inquiry,* 10, 245-264.

Emerson, C. (1993, October) Bakhtin and Vygotsky in the context of post-communist education. Paper presented at the College of Education Colloquium Series, University of Delaware, Newark.

Erickson, F. (1988) Ethnographic description. In H. von Ulrich Ammon, N. Dittmar, and K. Mattheier (Eds.), *Sociolinguistics*. Berlin: Walter de Gruyter.

Erickson, F. (1992) Ethnographic microanalysis of interaction. In M. LeCompte, W. Millroy, and J. Preissle (Eds.), *The handbook of qualitative research in education* (201-225). New York: Academic Press.

Erickson, F. (1996) Going for the zone: The social and cognitive ecology of interaction in classroom conversations. In D. Hicks (Ed.), *Discourse, learning, and schooling: Sociocultural and sociocognitive perspectives.* New York: Cambridge University Press.

Erickson, F., and Shultz, J. (1981) When is a context?: Some issues and methods in the analysis of social competence. In J. Green and C. Wallat (Eds.), *Ethnography and language in educational settings* (147-160). Norwood, NJ: Ablex.

Fairclough, N. (1989) *Language and power.* London: Longman.

Fairclough, N. (1992) Intertextuality in critical discourse analysis. *Linguistics and Education*, 4, 269-293.

Forman, E., Minick, N., and Stone, A. (Eds.). (1993) *Contexts for learning: Sociocultural dynamics in children's development.* New York: Oxford University Press.

Fosnot, C. T. (1989) *Enquiring teachers, enquiring learners: A constructivist approach for teaching.* New York: Teachers College Press.

Foucault, M. (1972) *The archaeology of knowledge and the discourse on language* (A. M. Sheridan Smith, Trans.). New York: Pantheon Books.

Gee, J. P. (1986) Units in the production of narrative discourse. *Discourse Processes*, 9, 391-422.

Gee, J. P. (1989) What is literacy? *Journal of Education*, 171,18-25.

Gee, J. P. (1990) *Social linguistics and literacies: Ideology in discourses.* New York: Falmer.

Gee, J. P. (1992) *The social mind: Language, ideology, and social practice.* New York: Bergin and Garvey.

Gee, J. P., Michaels, S. and O'Connor, M. C. (1992) Discourse analysis. In M. LeCompte, W. Millroy, and J. Preissle (Eds.), *The handbook of qualitative research in education* (227-291). New York: Academic Press.

Gergen, K. (1985) Social constructionist inquiry: Context and implications. In K. Gergen and K. Davis (Eds.), *The social construction of the person* (3-18). New York: Springer-Verlag.

Green, J., and Dixon, C. (1993) Talking knowledge into being: Discursive and social practices in classrooms. *Linguistics and Education*, 5, 231-239.

Gumperz, J. (1982) *Discourse strategies.* New York: Cambridge University Press.

Gumperz, J. (1986) Interactional sociolinguistics in the study of schooling. In J. Cook-Gumperz (Ed.), *The social construction of literacy* (45-68). New York: Cambridge University Press.

Gumperz, J., and Hymes, D. (Eds.). (1986) *Directions in sociolinguistics: The ethnography of communication.* New York: Basil Blackwell.

Halliday, M. A. K. (1978) *Language as social semiotic.* London: Edward Arnold.

Halliday, M. A. K., and Hasan, R. (1989) *Language, context, and text.* London: Oxford University Press.

Harness-Goodwin, M. (1990) *He-said-she-said: Talk as social organisation among Black children.* Bloomington: Indiana University Press.

Harre, R., and Gillett, G. (1994). *The discursive mind.* Thousand Oaks, CA: Sage.

Hartman, D. (1992) Intertextuality and reading: The text, the author, and the context. *Linguistics and Education*, 4, 295-311.

Heath, S. B. (1982) What no bedtime story means: Narrative skills at home and at school. *Language in Society,* 11, 49-76.

Heath, S. B. (1983) *Ways with words: Language, life, and work in communities and classrooms.* New York: Cambridge University Press.

Hicks, D. (1993) Narrative discourse and learning: An essay response to Kieran Egan's 'Narrative and learning: A voyage of implications.' *Linguistics and Education*, 5, 127-148.

Hicks, D. (1994) Individual and social meanings in the classroom: Narrative discourse as a boundary phenomenon. *Journal of Narrative and Life History*, 4, 215-240.

Hicks, D., and Kanevsky, R. (1992) Ninja Turtles and other superheros: A case study of one literacy learner. *Linguistics and Education*, 4, 59-105.

Hiebert, J., and Wearne, D. (1993) Instructional tasks, classroom discourse, and students' learning in second-grade arithmetic. *American Educational Research Journal,* 30, 393-425.

Hollingsworth, S. (1994) *Teacher research and urban literacy education: Lessons and conversations in a feminist key.* New York: Teachers College Press.

Hymes, D. (1974) *Foundations in sociolinguistics: An ethnographic introduction.* Philadelphia: University of Pennsylvania Press.

Kantor, R., Green, J., Bradley, M., and Lin, L. (1992) The construction of schooled discourse repertoires: An interactional sociolinguistic perspective on learning to talk in preschool. *Linguistics and Education,* 4,131-172.

Kozulin, A. (1990) *Vygotsky's psychology: A biography of ideas.* Cambridge, MA: Harvard University Press.

Lampert, M. (1990) When the problem is not the question and the solution is not the answer: Mathematical knowing and teaching. *American Educational Research Journal*, 27, 2963.

Lemke, J. L. (1988) Genres, semantics, and classroom education. *Linguistics and Education,* 1, 81-99.

Lemke, J. L. (1990) *Talking science: Language, learning, and values.* Norwood, NJ: Ablex.

Lemke, J. L. (1992) Intertextuality and educational research. *Linguistics and Education,* 4, 257-267.

Longo, P. (1994, February) *The dialogical process of becoming a problem solver: A sociolinguistic analysis of implementing the NCTM standards.* Paper presented at the Ethnography in Education Research Forum, University of Pennsylvania, Philadelphia.

Magoon, A. J. (1977) Constructivist approaches in educational research. *Review of Educational Research,* 47, 651-693.

McDermott, R. (1976) *Kids make sense: An ethnographic account of the interactional management of success and failure in one first grade classroom.* Unpublished doctoral dissertation, Stanford University, Stanford, CA.

Mehan, H. (1979) *Learning lessons: Social organisation in the classroom.* Cambridge, MA: Harvard University Press.

Michaels, S. (1981) 'Sharing time': Children's narrative styles and differential access to literacy. *Language in Society,* 10, 423-442.

Michaels, S., and O'Connor, M. C. (1990) *Literacy as reasoning within multiple discourses: Implica tions for policy and educational reform.* Paper presented at the Council of Chief State School Officers 1990 Summer Institute, Newton, MA.

Miller, P. (1982) *Amy, Wendy, and Beth: Language learning in South Baltimore.* Austin: University of Texas Press.

Miller, P., Nemoianu, A., and DeJong, J. (1986). Early reading at home: Its practice and meaning in a working class community. In B. Schieffelin and P. Gillmore (Eds.), *The acquisition of literacy: Ethnographic perspectives* (3-15). Norwood, NJ: Ablex.

Minick, N. (1989) *L. S. Vygotsky and Soviet activity theory: Perspectives on the relationship between mind and society* (Technical Reports Special Monograph No. 1). Newton, MA: The Literacies Institute.

Moll, L. (Ed.). (1990) *Vygotsky and education: instructional implications and applications of sociohistorical psychology.* New York: Cambridge University Press.

Morson, G. S., and Emerson, C. (1990) *Mikhail Bakhtin: Creation of a prosaics.* Stanford, CA: Stanford University Press.

National Council of Teachers of Mathematics. (1989) *Curriculum and evaluation standards for school mathematics.* Reston, VA: Author.

National Council of Teachers of Mathematics. (1991) *Professional standards for teaching mathematics.* Reston, VA: Author.

Nelson, K. (1986) *Event knowledge: Structure and function in developmen.t* Hillsdale, NJ: Erlbaum.

Nelson, K. (1989) *Narratives from the crib.* Cambridge, MA: Harvard University Press.

O'Connor, M. C., and Michaels, S. (1996) Shifting participant frameworks: Orchestrating thinking practices in group discussion. In D. Hicks (Ed.), *Discourse, learning, and schooling: Sociocultural and sociocognitive perspectives.* New York: Cambridge University Press.

O'Loughlin, M. (1992) Rethinking science education: Beyond Piagetian constructivism toward a sociocultural model of teaching and learning. *Journal of Research in Science Teaching,* 29, 791-820.

Reid, I. (Ed.). (1987) *The place of genre in learning. Current debates.* Geelong, Australia: Deakin University Press.

del Rio, P., Alvarez, A., and Wertsch, J. (1994) *Explorations in socio-cultural studies* (Proceedings of the first annual Conference on Socio-Cultural Research, Vols.1-4). Madrid: Infancia y Aprendizaje Foundation.

Rogoff, B. (1990) *Apprenticeship in thinking: Cognitive development in social con-text.* New York: Oxford University Press.

Rogoff, B., and Wertsch, J. (Eds.). (1984) *Children's learning in the 'zone of proximal development'* (New Directions for Child Development 23). San Francisco: Jossey-Bass.

Rosaldo, R. (1989) *Culture and truth: The remaking of social analysis.* Boston: Beacon Press.

Rosebery, A., Warren, B., and Conant, F. (1992) Appropriating scientific discourse: Findings from minority classrooms. *Journal of the Learning Sciences,* 2, 61-94.

Rubin, S., and Wolf, D. (1979) The development of maybe: The evolution of social roles into narrative roles. In E. Winner and H. Gardner (Eds.), *Fact, fiction, and fantasy in childhood* (New Directions for Child Development, Vol.6, 15-28). New York: Jossey-Bass.

Scollon, R., and Scollon, S. B. (1981) *Narrative, literacy, and face in interethnic communication.* Norwood, NJ: Ablex.

Shattuck, R. (1980) *The forbidden experiment: The story of the wild boy of Aveyron.* New York: Farrar Strauss Giroux.

Shotter, J. (1993) *Cultural politics of everyday life: Social constructionism, rhetoric and knowing of the third kind.* Toronto: University of Toronto Press.

Sinclair, J. M., and Coulthard, R. M. (1975) *Towards an analysis of discourse: The English used by teachers and pupils.* London: Oxford University Press.

Snow, C. (1983) Literacy and language: Relationships during the preschool years. *Harvard Educational Review*, 53, 165-189.

Snow, C. and Kurland, B.F. (1996) Sticking to the point: Talk about magnets as a context for engaging in scientific discourse. In D. Hicks (Ed.), *Discourse, learning, and schooling*. New York: Cambridge University Press.

Spanos, G., Rhodes, N., Corasaniti Dale, T., and Crandall, J. (1988) Linguistic features of mathematical problem solving: Insights and applications. In R. Cocking and J. Mestre (Eds.), *Linguistic and cultural influences on learning mathematics*. Hills-dale, NJ: Erlbaum.

Stigler, J., Fernandez, C., and Yoshida, M. (1992, August). Traditions of school mathematics in Japanese and American elementary classrooms. Paper presented at the International Conference for Mathematics Education, Quebec City, Canada.

Tharpe, R. G., and Gallimore, R. (1988) *Rousing minds to life: Teaching, learning, and schooling in social context*. New York: Cambridge University Press.

Toulmin, S. (1979) The inwardness of mental life. *Critical Inquiry,* 6, 1-16.

Toulmin, S. (1984) *The inner life: The outer mind* (Heinz Werner Lecture Series, Vol. 15). Worcester, MA: Clark University Press.

von Glaserfield, E. (1989) Cognition, construction of knowledge, and teaching. *Synthese*, 80, 121-140.

Vygotsky, L. S. (1962) *Thought amid language* (E. Hanfmann and G. Vakar, Eds. and Trans.). Cambridge, MA: MIT Press.

Vygotsky, L. S. (1978) *Mind in society: The development of higher mental processes* (M. Cole, V. John-Steiner, and B. Souberman, Eds.). Cambridge, MA: Harvard

University Press.

Vygotsky, L. S. (1986) *Thought and language* (Rev. ed., A. Kozulin, Ed. and Trans.). Cambridge, MA: MIT Press.

Vygotsky, L. S. (1987) *Thinking and speech* (N. Minick, Trans.). New York: Plenum Press.

Walkerdine, V. (1990) *Schoolgirl fictions.* New York: Verso.

Wells, G. (1986) *The meaning makers: Children learning language and using language to learn*. Portsmouth, NH: Heinemann.

Wells, G. (1993) Reevaluating the IRF sequence: A proposal for the articulation of theories of activity and discourse for the analysis of teaching and learning in the classroom. *Linguistics and Education,* 5, 1-37.

Wertsch, J. (1984) The zone of proximal development: Some conceptual issues. In B. Rogoff and J. Wertsch (Eds.), *Children's learning in the 'zone of proximal development'* (New Directions for Child Development 23, 7-18). San Francisco: Jossey-Bass.

Wertsch, J. (1985b) *Vygotsky and the social formation of mind.* Cambridge, MA: Harvard University Press.

Wertsch, J. (1991) *Voices of the mind: A sociocultural approach to mediated action.* Cambridge, MA: Harvard University Press.

Wertsch, J., and Stone, A. (1985) The concept of internalisation in Vygotsky's account of the genesis of higher mental functions. In J. Wertsch (Ed.), *Culture, communication, and cognition: Vygostkian perspective* (162-179). New York: Cambridge University Press.

Wolf, D., and Hicks, D. (1989) Voices within narratives: The development of intertextuality in young children's stories. *Discourse Processes*, 12, 329-351.

Wood, D., Bruner, J., and Ross, G. (1976) The role of tutoring in problem solving. *Journal of Child Psychology and Psychiatry* 17, 89-100.

Yackel, E., Cobb, P., Wood, T., Wheatley, G., and Merkel, G. (1990). The importance of social interaction in children's construction of mathematical knowledge. In T. J. Cooney (Ed.), *Teaching and learning mathematics in the 1990s* (12-21). Reston, VA: National Council of Teachers of Mathematics.

Yaroshevsky, M. (1989) *Lev Vygotsky* (S. Syrovatkin, Trans.). Moscow: Progress Publishers.

CHAPTER 2
Classroom assessment and the language of teaching
Harry Torrance and John Pryor

Introduction

One of the most important reasons for the complexity of classroom assessment is that it does not occur in isolation; it is accomplished within a social and educational context where a great number of apparently straightforward transactions are influenced not just by the circumstances of the moment, but by expectations and understandings deriving from much longer established and taken-for-granted practices. This chapter explores classroom assessment by considering the language in which it is accomplished and how it relates to the micro-sociology of the classroom. Here we demonstrate the complex dynamics of routine classroom assessment, in whole-class and small-group settings.

Studies of language in the classroom from many different points of departure have raised a number of different issues, but seem to agree that once the pupil's perspective is taken into consideration, a picture of great complexity emerges. In particular, the assumptions of those currently determining policy on assessment in schools in the UK, that teachers can easily interpret pupil behaviour and ask clear questions that elicit clear and discrete answers, are not well founded, as our data will demonstrate.

The central problem of classroom language is that it embodies both the form and the content of classroom life – what Bruner (1986:131) describes as 'the 'two-faced' nature of language'. Teachers and, especially, pupils have to achieve competence in both. Thus, the participants in classroom life have to understand their roles in relation to each other – who is allowed to speak, where and when – and the function that language plays in continually creating and re-creating these rules and expectations, as well as decoding and responding to the specific content of any particular question and answer sequence. The possibilities for misinterpretation are many and varied.

You could e.g confusion

Assessing in the context of whole-class teaching

Our data confirm the extent of this complexity and the opportunity for misunderstanding in even the most apparently straightforward of classroom assessment contexts. In the following transcript of a Year 2 whole-class maths lesson, for example, the teacher is revising work on tens and units before going on to extend the work by introducing the concept of rounding up to the nearest appropriate number [Year 2 children are aged 6-7 years]. The extract demonstrates the way in which questions are routinely asked of individuals, but in the context of 'teaching' the class; i.e.

* First published in Torrance, H. and Pryor, J. (1998) *Investigating Formative Assessment*. Buckingham: Open University Press.

questions are not simply and solely directed at the individual concerned, but serve other purposes with respect to keeping the class on task and moving the lesson along. Towards the end of the extract it also demonstrates how a simple misinterpretation of linguistic meaning can lead to a misjudgement of pupil understanding. In the extract the children are seated on the floor in a fairly tight group in one corner of the classroom, in front of a whiteboard on which the teacher is writing numbers. The transcript is presented in two columns: the left-hand column includes a description of the interaction (italicised) and the speech of the teacher and children, the right-hand column includes our commentary on the action – a first level of analysis. [Transcription conventions are explained in the Appendix.]

T picks up pen and begins to write the numbers 20, 40, 60, 80 spaced out across the top of the whiteboard.

T   here now these are –

About a third of the children raise their hands. T turns to face the class.

T   what I want to know is – if you know what all those <u>four</u> numbers are – so put your hand up if you can tell me what all <u>four</u> of those numbers are –

11:41

At this point most of the children have their hands up.

T OK – I want to know who knows all four of them – Becky	T wants to confirm that the class knows the numbers and to establish a basis for the rest of the lesson. T chooses a weaker pupil; if she gets it right T can be almost certain that the rest of the class also understand, so that the lesson can move on.
Becky twenty/forty/sixty/eighty	
T OK – good – put your hands down we've had the answer – next question	'OK – good': the first IRF sequence is safely completed; T draws a verbal line under the first interaction, the base is established.
is – I want to know how many tens there are – in all of those numbers –	T now moves on to the first real topic – tens and units.
About half the class raise their hands.	
T Martin –	T appears to have chosen Martin because he thought he was not paying attention. In addition, Martin is more of a barometer for the class than Becky – if Martin gets it right T can move on with confidence that most children are following with understanding; if not, some instruction will be in order.
Martin turns to face T.	
T I want <u>all</u> of them	
Some of the children with their hands up let them droop, most children keep them up.	
Martin TWO	
T which number	The Response is not satisfactory so T extends the sequence.
M all of them – two / two / two	Why does Martin say two? Does he really not understand tens and units? Has he been panicked by being picked unexpectedly and wants to please – any answer is better than no answer? He has been reminded that a correct answer will refer to all four numbers, but for whatever reason this does not provide sufficient scaffolding; so T takes him through the task number by number.
By this stage only a few hands are still raised.	
T No – so you're saying there's two tens there	
T half turns to the whiteboard and points to the figure 20. Children are gradually raising their hands so that around a half of them are now bidding.	

M   mm

Martin nods.

T   and two tens in that number

T points to 40.

M   mmm

Martin puts his head on one side

This is said with falling intonation, suggesting that Martin has little confidence in his answer.

T   how many in that number Martin
           how many > tens <

Nevertheless, focusing the question helps scaffold Martin's answer and he now seems to understand T's expectations.

M   > four < =

T   – right how many tens make sixty =

T points to 60

'right' – sequence complete, move on to the next IRF sequence.

M   – six

T   how many tens make –

T points to 80.

M   eight =

Having established a rhythm, from which T assumes the child now understands the nature of the task and the correct Response, the Feedback doesn't have to be explicit; simply moving on to the next question (Initiation) is sufficient to confirm the correct answer when used in conjunction with suitable gesture and intonation.

Although the hands of the other children have been drooping during this exchange it is only when this point is reached that a significant number take them down completely. The children's faces remain fixed on the board and the T.

T   = have you noticed – when you said
           eight – eight's there

T points to the 8 in 80

However, T seems concerned that Martin (and/or other members of the class) may only be recalling the numbers – six 10s are 60, eight 10s are 80 – rather than discerning the answer from what is written on the board and making the connection between tens and units, so he explicitly reiterates the point.

T   and when you said six there's a six
           there –

T points to the 6 in 60

T   did you notice when you said four –
           there's a four there _

T points to the 4 in 40

Martin   yeah > (**) < =

... *[inaudible, a few seconds]* ...

T   > the first number < tells you how
           many tens there are – so I'll put a
           little tee for tens –

Further scaffolding is provided for the whole class – the column is now to be headed 'T'.

T turns back to whiteboard and writes the letter T above the 8 in 80. He turns back to the class. All hands are now down except for Hannah's.

T   eighty has ~ > eight tens <

T cues class as he writes.

Cs   > eight tens <

T turns back to white board and writes the letter T above the 6 in 60.

T   sixty has > six tens <

Cs   > six tens <

T writes the letter T above the 4 in 40

Cs   forty has four tens =

T turns back to class

T   = shhh – right then – how many units – are there –

       'right then' – a 'framing move' – closure on the first part of the topic – another verbal line is drawn.

Faye raises her hand and is rapidly followed by several other children. T turns halfround and points to the 20.

T   in <u>this</u> number – how many units are there Faye =

       IRF begins again with 'how many units are there in this number?' The question is then focused on a specific individual but as part of the whole-class teaching strategy.

F   = none

Most of the hands go down but some remain up

T   = none – there's no units – Alice

C   > none <

A   > none <

       The Response is straightforward and correct. However, since we have moved on to a new part of the topic, T explicitly confirms the Response with definitive Feedback ('none – there's no units') before checking with another child.

This first extract of transcript, then, demonstrates very clearly the way in which individual children are selected to answer questions for reasons which go beyond simply gathering data on whether or not they 'know' the answer. The answers are utilised as part of the whole-class teaching strategy, both to continually establish and re-establish the teacher's control of the discourse – asking questions always puts the questioner in a powerful position – and to move the lesson towards the substantive goal which the teacher has in mind. The teacher then moves on to the next topic of rounding up:

T   OK that's the first question -now I'm just going to write some different numbers now and I just want you to watch – I'm going to write some different numbers – now – on here – OK

       'OK' – once again closure is announced, but closure does not lead immediately to moving on since T has to write more numbers on the white-board before announcing the next topic.

       'OK' – enunciated as a question, but of course T is not asking for the children's agreement, this is an instruction to be quiet.

T turns away from the class and begins to write random two-digit numbers spread haphazardly across the whiteboard. As he does so he hums. Children start to put their hands up.

C   (*I've got a)

This comment is whispered. T looks over his shoulder at the class ... [ ] ...

11:43

T   – shhh – just watch please OK – (**) to get a few more on –

       Again, 'OK' is enunciated as a question, but actually marks the instruction.

Cs remain quiet

... [T continues to write] ...

T turns back to face class

T OK now – we're going to do some <u>rounding up</u> – I'm going to write that on the – whiteboard for you – we're going to do some – <u>rounding up</u>

T writes words 'rounding up' in capitals above the random numbers. He turns back to the class.

11:44

T I'll explain – <u>rounding up</u> – you've got four numbers here – twenty – forty, sixty, eighty –

T is half turned to the whiteboard drawing circles round the numbers at the top of the board.

T I'm going to choose one of these numbers – I'll choose this number here

T points to the number 37 which is situated at the top right-hand side of the whiteboard about 5 cm from the number 80. He turns back to the class.

T that number's got three tens and seven units right – thirty seven – which number – is this nearest to –

A few hands go up.

T look at thirty seven – is it nearest to <u>twenty</u> or is it nearest to forty – is it nearest to <u>sixty</u> or is it nearest to <u>eighty</u> – which one of those four numbers is this nearest to – Ellen

By this stage most children in the class have raised their hands; many lower them when Ellen is nominated.

E erm eighty

T so you think that thirty-seven is nearest to eighty – OK – what do you think Alice

Ellen screws up her face.

A erm forty

More children begin to raise their hands.

T forty – what do you think Rachel

R twenty

'OK now' – another marker – now the topic can be introduced.

Ellen seems to have interpreted 'nearest' in terms of physical proximity to the next number written on the board, rather than in terms of the maths task at hand, rounding up. T misses this (though recognises it when reviewing the videotape later). Instead T notes the answer neutrally ('OK') but by immediately repeating the question to another child implies it is not correct.

T gets a satisfactory Response but does not close the sequence; his repetition of the question implies that yet another answer may be required. Rachel may or may not think 20 is correct, but she seems to have been persuaded that 40 is wrong.

T	you think it's nearest to twenty – what do you think Charles
Ch	forty
T	forty – what do you think Tim
Th	forty
T	forty – what do you think Kate
K	sixty
T	sixty – what do you think Elspeth
E	forty
T	forty – what do you think Christina
Ca	sixty
T	sixty – what do you think Miles
M	forty

By continuing to repeat the question T seems to want to establish by consensus what the correct answer is, rather than just telling Ellen she is wrong. Is T trying to be kind to Ellen? Or has T been so knocked off balance by such an 'obviously' wrong answer that a wide survey of class opinion is required?

Whatever T's intentions, the repeated question seems to be starting to confuse the children. Several children have answered 'forty' yet T is still asking the question – so perhaps 'forty' is wrong, let's try 'sixty'. Thus it may be that Kate and Christina, as with Rachel before them, think 'forty' is correct but are giving an alternative because 'forty' hasn't been confirmed.

The teacher goes on to survey class opinion on the matter by asking children to vote (by putting up their hands) on which number is 'nearest' to 37; the teacher then tries to settle the issue by employing a large tape measure (the class 'metre monster') and asking children to count the spaces from 20 to 37, 37 to 40, and so forth. At this point physical proximity of the numbers along the tape does come into play, implicitly, as the concepts of nearest appropriate number and nearest physical proximity are conflated. However, the origin of Ellen's misunderstanding is not uncovered or addressed. Overall the two extracts provide plenty of evidence of the continuous process of individual questioning which goes to make up so-called whole-class teaching. Both teachers and pupils – and assessment policy makers – have to be able to recognise that such question and answer sessions are as concerned with accomplishing the lesson as with assessing individuals. There is no sense in which teachers could treat such questions as 'items' in the sense of examination questions, and explicitly monitor and record the responses to them. At the same time, however, it is inevitable that teachers will come to cumulative judgements about who is making appropriate progress and who is not; who can be relied upon to give the correct answer when required, and who will be cooperative even when they are struggling to give the correct answer. This is the reality of day-to-day teacher assessment. It is also the case that in such whole-class teaching situations, misinterpretations such as those of Ellen cannot be explored in detail, as to spend time focusing on one child's responses would risk losing the attention of the majority of the class (cf. Wong 1995). This may lead to significant misjudgements about pupil understanding and achievement.

Ambiguous questioning in a small group

In fact, detailed assessment of individual pupils is much more likely to be planned for, and to occur, in the context of small group work. However, the size of the group does not escape the issue of linguistic structure and expectation, nor the problem of linguistic uncertainty and the possibilities for misinterpretation. In the following extract the teacher's intuitive employment of the phrase 'this one' introduces an element of ambiguity into a focus-group teaching and assessing session on number recognition with three reception class pupils. The teacher has initially used the story of the Three Bears, along with three toy teddy bears to introduce the topic of counting and number recognition, and is now distributing large tiles with the numbers 1, 2 and 3 written on them.

T   what number what number's that –

T holds up large tile with figure 1 written on it.

Cs   one

T   now you have the one

Hands tile to Jimmy revealing the number two tile.

... [a few seconds mumbling] ...

T brings forward the number two tile and looks at Seb.

T   what number's >that one<

Simon >umm<

T is looking at Seb and puts her finger to her mouth when Simon says 'umm'.

T   >do you (*know what that is)<

Simon um – three

T   it's a three you think –

T looks back at Seb

T   what number do you think it is Seb

Seb   um – two

T   two –

T looks back directly at Simon

T   it's a two –

T looks back at Seb

T   so you have the two

T gives the number two tile to Seb; number three tile is revealed. T closes Three Bears book and places it behind her on the floor. T turns to face Simon directly across the table.

T   what number's that one Simon

Simon er – (*four)

T   it's a – <u>three</u>

Simon three =

T   = that one's a three

T hands the tile to Simon.

Jimmy you don't know all your numbers

T   sorry – Jimmy – could you say that again – I didn't <u>quite</u> hear

Jimmy he dun't know about (*all of) his numbers

T   he doesn't know about all the numbers – well we can help him can't we ... [ ]

         ...

T grasps tile whilst still talking about the story of the three bears and, without a pause, starts to ask a question about the number on the tile (number one). The question seems to be addressed to the group in general and is now about recognising the symbol for one rather than counting the three bears.

There is no explicit acknowledgement of the correct answer, but distributing 'the one' seems to confirm it and constitute Feedback.

We have already had number 1, T now introduces the word 'one' to denote something other than the number 1.

An answer is clearly expected and Simon gives one, either not recognising, or ignoring, T's injunction not to speak. It is not correct but has he been influenced by the original task focusing on the three bears story book; would he expect to be shown the number three? Can we make a judgement about his capacity to count and recognise numbers? Whatever is the case, T repeats the question, and much more explicitly, so long as 'it' is correctly interpreted.

She is correcting Simon's mistake, presumably assuming that he cannot recognise the numbers two and three.

'the two' – not two bears, nor two tiles, but the tile with the '2' printed on it. What might Seb and Simon make of this phrase – two what?

Some sort of symbolic closure is taking place here. This is no longer a language activity – the book has been replaced by the number tiles.

T again uses the word 'one' in her question, this time while holding up the symbol for three.

T seems to be certain that Simon has said a wrong number, perhaps because he got it wrong last time, although it is not clear from the recording.

The confusion of one and three is compounded.

Two errors are generalised to 'all your numbers' (note personalising possessive). This comment does not seem to be kindly meant by Jimmy, and highlights the public context of much classroom assessment, even when exposure is only within a small group. And why does T apparently compound the problem by asking Jimmy to repeat his comment? Did T really not hear, or is this an example of a question whose locutionary force is different from its ostensible purpose; designed to give T the opportunity to draw the group together to help Simon – always presuming he needs help. This could be seen as a sympathetic gesture in the context of providing scaffolding for Simon, but does he think he is now the recipient of the group's pedagogical condescension?

Much later in the interaction, a noise disturbs the group and they look round to see the rest of the class being taken out of the classroom by the nursery teaching assistant. At this point Simon demonstrates that whether or not he has recognised the numbers on the tiles correctly, he certainly can count (in a more informal or authentic situation) though it is not clear if the teacher picks up on this:

T writes down. The door squeaks again -Seb, Jimmy and T look round.

Simon   (*) how many've we got there – one two three four five – that's all

Simon turns around and looks at the rest of the classroom. He points to each person in the classroom in turn.

Someone has left the room. Simon notices that there are only five people in the classroom (the fifth is the researcher). In a real context he has been able to demonstrate his knowledge and understanding of number up to five. Moreover, he has a notion of that being a relatively small number in the context of the whole class.

So opportunities for misapprehension and ambiguity are legion in infant school classrooms – and indeed many others. Possibilities for opportunistic 'authentic' assessment also exist, as with the example of Simon above, but making the most of them would require immense perspicacity from teachers and an orientation to the divergent possibilities of the infant classroom which a focus on National Curriculum attainment targets and statements of attainment, or even level descriptors, is unlikely to encourage. Our point is not that we wish to criticise these individual teachers – quite the reverse, when reviewing such extracts we can visualise ourselves making similar moves, they are the very stuff of routine teaching – but such ambiguous encounters are likely to carry consequences for individual children's learning, and they certainly demonstrate the need for caution when discussing the problems and possibilities of classroom assessment.

Thus, to reiterate, teachers' questions and pupils' responses will always be serving a number of different purposes and accomplishing a number of different functions at one and the same time. In particular, pupils constantly strive to interpret teachers' questions and make sense of what is being asked of them in the context of this interactive process, over and above what might be taken to be the obvious meaning of a particular question. Now this does not mean that all attempts at formative classroom assessment will necessarily founder, but it does mean that the process of accomplishing formative assessment is likely to be a good deal more complicated than presently acknowledged.

References

Bruner, J. (1985) Vygotsky: a historical and conceptual perspectives, in J. Wertsch (ed.) *Culture, Communication and Cognitive: Vygotskian Perspectives.* Cambridge: Cambridge University Press.

Wong, E.D. (1995) Challenges confronting the researcher/teacher: conflicts of purpose and conduct. *Educational Researcher*, 24(4): 22-8.

Appendix
Transcription conventions for classroom interaction

(*)	inaudible (probably one word)
(**)	inaudible phrase
(***)	longer inaudible passage (e.g. sentence)
(*Tuesday)	inaudible word, 'Tuesday' suggested by transcriber
–	short pause
disapp\	incomplete word
<u>these</u>	word emphasised
Bold	word pronounced with lengthened vowel and diphthong sounds
COME HERE	words said very loudly compared to other utterances of this speaker
=	rapid change of turn of speakers (used at end of the utterance of one speaker and beginning of next speaker's utterance)
>It's mine<	simultaneous speech
Italics	non-textual material (stage directions)
the/cat/sat	word-by-word enunciation with flat intonation (e.g. emergent reader)
T	teacher
T2	second teacher
C	unidentified child
Cs	unidentified children
Cl, C2	first child, second child etc.

rising intonation, slowing (invitation to other speaker to complete sentence)

9:42	time reading from video camera
... [J] ...	a few seconds of transcript omitted – extraneous material (e.g. interruption by another child) not relevant to point discussed in the chapter

CHAPTER 3
Guided participation, discourse and the construction of knowledge in Mexican classrooms
Sylvia Rojas-Drummond

Introduction

In this paper I will summarise two strands of research on the nature of guided participation taking place inside some Mexican classrooms. The first strand deals with the relationship between guided participation and pre-school children's capacity to solve logical and arithmetic-word problems competently and independently. The second strand analyses the relationship between guided participation and primary students' capacity to deal with functional literacy activities (comprehension, production and learning from texts).

The two strands of research were analysed using very similar methods. At the same time, however, they involved students of two different educational levels working on various knowledge domains and under two curriculum programs. These contrasts were selected to test the generality of results across different populations, knowledge domains and educational contexts.

In terms of theory, the studies contribute to our understanding of the dynamic relationships holding between interactive and discursive classroom practices, on the one hand, and developmental and learning processes in childhood on the other. At the same time, the studies offer some methodological tools to carry out fine-grained analyses of guided participation practices. Lastly, the studies contribute to educational practices by offering a detailed account of the types of interaction and discourse which, across two developmental levels, two curriculum approaches and various knowledge domains, were associated with better learning outcomes. This account can serve as a guide to help improve the quality of teaching-learning processes in the classroom.

This research has been greatly influenced by a sociocultural perspective. Thus, I will start by reviewing some key developments in the field which have influenced our work. Secondly, I will outline the methodological framework used in both strands of research to analyse interactive and discursive practices in the classroom. Thirdly, I will summarise the main findings of each of the two strands of research and the generalities that emerged by considering them in conjunction. And lastly, I will discuss the theoretical, methodological and educational implications of the studies presented.

*   First published in H. Cowie and D. van deer Aalsvoort (Eds) 2000 *Social Interaction in Learning and Instruction: the meaning of discourse for the construction of knowledge*. Oxford: Elsevier.

Theoretical background

Guided participation

According to the sociocultural perspective, during development social interaction between experts and novices and among various members of a community leads to the joint construction of zones of proximal development. This construction takes place through guided participation (Vygotsky, 1978; Rogoff and Wertsch, 1984; Rogoff, 1990). In this apprenticeship, children actively engage in cultural practices where adults initially model, guide and help regulate performance, while creating temporary scaffolds which provide bridges from the old to the new and support children's emerging abilities (Wood, Bruner and Ross, 1976; Brown and Reeve, 1987; Rogoff, 1990). Guided participation allows novices or 'newcomers' to move from an initial 'legitimate peripheral participation' (Lave and Wenger, 1991) to gradually increasing command and responsibility over the diverse activities and artefacts involved in particular cultural practices. As novices become more competent and independent in particular domains, they re-construct and appropriate the regulative functions that occurred socially. Progress towards competence and expertise results from a complex interplay between social factors (among others) and each child's own developmental processes and constructions. Thus, the child plays an active, constructive role in the overall process of guided participation, even as a novice (Saxe, Guberman and Gearhart, 1987; Rogoff, 1990; Elbers et al., 1992).

The role of scaffolding

One key question when trying to understand how guided participation leads to development of expertise refers to the nature of the interactions taking place between experts and novices, or among the various members of a community, and how this nature affects the emerging processes and outcomes. In this respect, the seminal work of Bruner and associates on the nature of scaffolding and its role in promoting development has contributed importantly to our understanding of Vygotsky's original conceptions of the dynamic interactions between learning and development. Similarly, this work has provided important insights for understanding how guided participation between adults and children can be pivotal in promoting progress when it is organised around zones of proximal development (Wood, Bruner and Ross, 1976; Vygotsky, 1978; Rogoff and Wertsch, 1984).

Bruner's pioneering work in the late '70s generated a wealth of literature on the nature of scaffolding and its role in promoting learning and development in various sociocultural settings. These settings include experimental situations (Wertsch et al., 1980), home environments (Saxe, Guberman and Gearhart, 1987), a wide variety of informal apprenticeship contexts (Rogoff and Lave, 1984; Lave and Wenger, 1991) and more formal educational contexts (Brown and Palincsar, 1989; Newman, Griffin and Cole, 1989; Moll, 1990; Nicolopolou and Cole, 1993; Brown and Campione, 1996). In the school context, several studies have focused on scaffolding as it takes place between adults and children (e.g. Hedegaard, 1996), among peers (e.g. Cowie et al., 1994) and through the mediation of artefacts such as computers (Wegerif and Scrimshaw, 1997). The literature describes how the patterns of relations between interactive practices and developmental and learning processes and outcomes are shaped by the specific contexts in which the practices take place. In spite of this specificity, studies consistently highlight the central role scaffolding plays within guided participation, and how it can foster development and learning when it is shaped to work within zones of proximal development. It is important to stress, however, that we conceive of scaffolding as a co-constructive process where novices and experts actively contribute to its unfolding, rather than as a uni-directional one shaped mainly by the adult (Elbers *et al.*, 1992; Renshaw and Brown, 1999).

Discourse and knowledge construction

Another key factor in understanding how guided participation gradually leads to increasing competence and independence is the role played by cultural artefacts in general, and linguistic signs in particular, as mediators of activity. Sociocultural theory has highlighted the central role played by cultural artefacts, and particularly language, in mediating social interaction and cognition throughout development (e.g. Vygotsky, 1962; 1978; Bruner, 1990; Bronckart, 1992; Wertsch, 1991, 1998; Wertsch, Del Rio and Alvarez, 1995; Cole, 1996). Through discursive interactions meanings are negotiated, allowing for increasing intersubjectivity, which is crucial for working in the zone of proximal development and towards appropriation of cultural practices (Rogoff, 1990). Similarly, social communication is gradually re-constructed as internal speech or voices of the mind (Wertsch, 1991, 1998), contributing importantly to problem-solving, knowledge construction and self-regulation, among other central cognitive functions.

Recently, the study of the role of language in mediated action has been extended by important work on the function of discourse in social interactions within various educational contexts and in diverse cultural groups (e.g. Wertsch, Del Rio and Alvarez, 1995; Coll and Edwards, 1996; Hicks, 1996). This work has highlighted the key role of discourse as 'a social mode of thinking', which can facilitate the guided construction of knowledge (Mercer, 1995). This work also reflects a growing tendency within sociocultural theory to consider encompassing units of analysis centred on mediated action in its sociocultural context (Wertsch, 1998). Similarly, recent efforts have been increasingly directed towards understanding how participants in learning communities engage in the social construction of knowledge and the re-creation of culture. In addition, recent studies have addressed the role of interaction and artefact mediation in weaving the course and outcomes of these cultural activities (e.g. Wertsch, Del Rio and Alvarez, 1995; Brown and Campione, 1996; Cole, 1996, 1998).

In conclusion, the literature highlights the importance of guided participation, and particularly the nature of the interactive and discursive practices taking place between experts and novices, as key factors to help understand the course and outcomes of development and learning. This research has been carried out in a great variety of sociocultural settings, and represents samples of situated practices from diverse developmental levels, knowledge domains, learning contexts and cultural groups. However, in the educational context, although the literature is abundant with very enlightening accounts of how guided participation and discursive practices take place in classrooms and other learning environments, the studies do not necessarily make links between the nature of these practices and the developmental and learning outcomes associated with them. At the same time, we need more fine-grained empirical accounts of how guided participation actually evolves in the everyday classroom activities. We also need more research on which particular aspects of expert-novice interaction and discourse can be associated with particular developmental and learning outcomes in the students, to understand these dynamic interactions more fully The field has also lacked adequate methodological tools to carry out these fine-grained analyses in situated learning contexts. The studies reviewed below attempt to contribute theoretically, methodologically and practically to understanding and promoting these processes in educational settings.

Methodological scheme for analysing classroom Interaction and discourse

In order to analyse interaction and discourse in the classroom, a methodological scheme was developed in conjunction with Neil Mercer from the Open University in the UK, and has since been refined and used in several studies of Mexican and British children, including the Mexican studies reviewed here. The scheme is concerned with analysis of interactive and discursive practices, particularly the function of talking and joint activity that take place between adults and children. Similarly, it focuses on the use of discourse as a 'social mode of thinking' (Mercer, 1995). Analysis of joint talk and activity in turn allows us to make inferences about what is taught and learned, as well as about the ideology of education enacted by the teachers and students through their routine talking and action. Thus, we analyse interaction at three interrelated levels: 1. the actual discourse taking place among the participants, 2. the actions and interactions accompanying these exchanges; and 3. the educational ideology or beliefs about the teaching-learning process which might be embodied in the participants' talk and actions. We consider this ideology in terms of five dimensions within which we can characterise some aspects of the teaching-learning process, and which are of particular interest to our work: (a) the extent to which learning is treated as a social, communicative process; (b) the extent to which teachers and students actively engage in the joint construction of knowledge; (c) the extent to which teachers focus on the processes of problem solving and reasoning and not only on fact acquisition; (d) the extent to which teachers give priority to the processes for learning and not only to products (task completion) and (e) the extent to which teachers help children achieve understanding and competence through scaffolding. This methodological framework is based on the considerable resources of prior relevant research, including our own. Our primary aim is to characterise teaching-learning practices and to distinguish, in the most concise way possible, between the education style of a teacher who provides more of a social-interactional, co-constructive, scaffolding approach to teaching and learning and one who enacts a more conventional, directive and transmissional approach. We can then relate these patterns to developmental and learning outcomes in the students.

In order to develop our methodological scheme, we originally drew on our own experience of qualitative analysis of classroom interactions and the findings of other researchers in many countries. This enabled us to generate a list of observable teacher and students' behaviours or Actions which might represent or embody each Dimension of interest. We also sought agreement within the research team on the pragmatic function(s) of each Action. The result of this iterative process was a tentative matrix of a variety of Actions which could be associated with each of the five Dimensions considered.

The next part of the procedure centred around a series of qualitative measures on the discourse taking place. These measures involve detailed analysis of discourse features, using methods developed by ourselves and colleagues in related research (e.g. Edwards and Mercer 1987; Mercer, 1995; Wegerif and Mercer, 1997: Wegerif, Rojas-Drummond and Mercer, 1999; Rojas-Drummond, Mercer and Dabrowski, 2001). Attention is given to the ways language is used, in context, as a means of pursuing classroom activities. This involves close consideration of video evidence and transcriptions to establish how the teacher and children engage in joint tasks. These activities enabled us to test and refine our hypotheses about the supposed functions of each Action and discursive feature considered, leading to some revision and refinement of the Dimension/Action matrix. The version of the matrix which emerged from the procedures described above is presented in Table 1.

To implement this methodology for analysing actual interactive episodes, we start with video-recordings from the episodes of interest. We transcribe them, adding notes on relevant contextual features. Then we carry out various qualitative analyses of the data in the fashion described above, and also examine the types of Actions and discursive exchanges displayed by the participants, guided by our methodological scheme. For this examination we identify, characterise and count the occurrences of all Actions and discursive exchanges in our complete set of recorded data, on the basis of our Dimension/Action matrix (attempting all the while to achieve satisfactory levels of inter-observer agreement). Reference to our detailed video transcriptions enables us to check the pragmatic function(s) of the Actions and discursive patterns under analysis.

The frequencies of Actions and discursive patterns obtained are inserted into the matrix appearing in Table 1. This enables us to draw a 'profile' for each particular set of participants, after weighing the tendencies evident in all the quantitative and qualitative measures obtained during the interactive and discursive episodes observed over time. These tendencies are then analysed for each of the five Dimensions considered in our scheme, in order to draw inferences about the pedagogical ideology embodied in the talk and actions of the participants. These pedagogic beliefs are derived from the overall interactive patterns observed, and are conceived of as flexible tendencies within continuums, rather than fixed dichotomic styles. Our characterisations allow various comparisons among teaching and learning practices. At the same time, the complementary use of qualitative and quantitative analyses enables us to make categorical comparisons without decontextualising the talk and action, thus overcoming a well-recognised weakness of most 'systematic observation' categorical schemes.

I will next provide a glimpse of what some of the Actions and discursive patterns look like when actually enacted, by offering four representative excerpts from teacher-student exchanges, extracted from each of the two lines of research to be presented in the next section (see Table 2). Each example includes a brief contextual description, the actual dialogue which took place (translated from Spanish) and the Dimensions and Actions coded for these exchanges according to our methodological scheme. The codes include a Roman numeral for the Dimension concerned, followed by a letter for the particular Action identified. (Please refer to Table 1 for identification of numerical and letter codes).

Notice that the discourse in both Official pre-school and primary examples (control groups) is mostly characterised by Initiation-Response-Feedback (IRF) sequences, of the type we term 'Loop IRFs'. These tend to close the exchange without necessarily taking the child's response much further. In contrast, the discourse of both High/Scope (H/S) and Cooperative Learning exchanges is characterised by 'Spiral IRFs', which carry students' responses to (potentially) higher levels of understanding and/or performance. Spiral IRFs are typically accompanied by a variety of co-constructive and scaffolding strategies, and the H/S and Cooperative Learning excerpts exemplify several types. Loop IRFs, on the other hand, are associated with a less co-constructive and scaffolded interactive style, as is apparent from contrasting both sets of excerpts. As will become evident from the studies to be presented, we have found the types of IRF observed (Loop versus Spiral) to offer a particularly sensitive and reliable indicator to help discriminate between the styles of teaching-learning practices under study.

Table 1: Dimensions and actions for describing how teachers and students enact the process of teaching and learning

Dimension I. Learning is an individual process vs. learning is a social-communicative process

A.   Using pupils as a resource or social-cognitive support for the activity of other pupil(s).

B.   Building knowledge from one to another in a chain, using the responses of previous pupils to direct the interactions with subsequent pupils.

C.   Organising group-work activities so that there are interchanges of viewpoints between pupils and/or sharing of responsibility in solving problems.

D.   Promotion of interactions between experts (teachers or pupils) and novices where they both participate in the task.

Dimension II. Knowledge must be transmitted by a teacher or discovered by individual learners vs. knowledge can be jointly constructed

A.   Using 'Spiral' Initiation-Response-Feedback (IRF) exchanges (take up on student's response to higher levels of understanding and/or performance), vs. only 'Loop' ones (simply close the interchange).

B.   Using reformulations, elaborations and/or recaps.

C.   Cued vs. direct elicitations of information/responses.

D.   Asking questions which explore pupils' levels of understanding.

E.   Promoting semiotic challenge to guide pupils towards higher levels of understanding.

F.   Negotiating meanings with pupils

G.   Making explicit the ground rules or demands of a task.

H.   Explicitly linking prior knowledge (from outside or inside the classroom) to the current activity.

Dimension III. Becoming educated essentially means acquiring facts vs. becoming educated includes learning ways to solve problems

A.   Using 'why?' questions to get pupils to justify answers or to reason and reflect.

B.   Using open questions.

C.   Eliciting problem solving strategies (e.g. analysing goals, planning, monitoring, error-correction, etc.) from the pupils.

D.   Eliciting goals and varied ways of solving problems from pupils.

E.   Constructing knowledge jointly with pupils.

Dimension IV. Priority is given to task completion (product) vs. emphasis placed also on the process of learning

A.   Recapping or reviewing learning with pupils.

B.   Emphasising the meaning or purpose of tasks.

C.   Emphasising or elaborating the process of arriving at a solution.

Dimension V. Learning is solely the responsibility of the learner vs. learning can be nurtured by a teacher

A.   Promoting the active participation of pupils.

B.   Exploring the initial level of pupils' understanding of tasks and materials.

C.   Reducing degrees of freedom to allow pupils to concentrate on certain key aspects of the task when the task is difficult.

D.   Using 'retreat and rebuild' exchanges (repair processes where pupils' mistakes are used by the teacher to reconstruct knowledge).

E.   Modelling of desirable actions, strategies and outcomes.

F.   Providing elaborated feedback on a pupil's response/approach to a problem.

G.   Gradually withdrawing expert support when pupil demonstrates competence.

H.   Making pupils' achievements explicit to them and/or other pupils.

Table 2: Excerpts of adult-children dialogues from preschool and primary strands of research

A.   Excerpts from Official and H/S Preschool Curricula in Arithmetic Reasoning Activities

(1)   *Excerpt from Official Curriculum*

Sequence 1. Counting vegetables

Context: Teacher in front of blackboard. Pupils in U-shaped table. Teacher has two sheets of paper on blackboard, one with sets of vegetables, the other with numbers. She is pointing at different sets with different number of vegetables and asking for corresponding number ...

Code: Dialogue:

Discourse	Action	Dialogue
IIA Loop		Teacher: Here is a set of what? (points at set of 1 vegetable). Students: Of 1. Teacher: Of one item.
IIA Loop		Teacher: Here is a set of how many? (points at set of 2). Students: Of 2 items. Teacher: Of 2 items.
IIA Loop		Teacher: Here? (points at set of 3). Students: 3. Teacher: Of 3 items.
IIA Loop		Teacher: (Points at set of 4). Students: 4 Teacher: Of 4.
IIA Loop		Teacher: (Points at set of 5). Students: 5
	VH	Teacher: And of 5. Good.
IIA Loop		Teacher: Now, do you all know what these are called? (points at numbers). Students: Numbers.
	VH	Teacher: Numbers, right? Good. ...You're going to relate the sets according to the number appearing on the right. OK? ... Nobody start yet. Nobody helps each other. Work on your own

(2)   *Excerpt from High/Scope Curriculum*

Sequence 2. Gathering apples

Context: Teacher and group of students playing a game with a dice, boards with a tree and ladder, and small toy apples. They have just finished taking turns in climbing up the ladder and bringing down certain number of apples each, according to numbers on dice ...

Code: Dialogue:

Discourse	Action	Dialogue
IIA Spiral	IC	Teacher: Let's see, let's see. Who brought down more apples? Omar: I did.
IIA Spiral	IID	Teacher: How many did you get down? Omar: 2.
IIA Spiral	IIE	Teacher: And how many were left in the tree? Gina: 4.
IIA Spiral	I B/ III C	Teacher: 4. Let's see, count them, Omar, to see if there are 4. Omar: 1,2,3,4,5.

Table 2: Excerpts of adult-children dialogues from preschool and primary strands of research (continued)

Code: Dialogue:

Discourse	Action	
IIA Spiral	VD	Teacher: Let's see. Count them again. Omar: 1...
IIA Spiral	VC	Teacher: Ah-huh (pointing). Omar: ... 2, 3, 4.
	VH IIIB/ IVA	Teacher: Yes, you see? 4 apples were left. That's it! ... Fine, ... Let's see, now, what did we learn in this game?

B.   *Excerpts from Primary Control and Cooperative Learning groups in reading comprehension activities*

(1)   *Excerpt from Control Group*

Sequence 3. Identifying main characters from a story

Context: Teacher standing in front of class, with book on hands, students with books opened. Students have just finished reading silently a story about 'Yacub Magrebi', a rich arab who had a dream about a treasure ...

Code: Dialogue:

Discourse	Action	
IIA Loop		Teacher: Who are the characters? And then we are going to reach some conclusions. For you, Aurelio, who are the characters of this story? Of this text? Aurelio: Ah ..., Yacub Magrebi, The Judge, ...
	VF VH	Teacher: Let's see ... Yacub Magrebi, he is the arab, right? Very good.
IIA Loop		Teacher: Who else? Aurelio: The Judge ... Teacher: The Judge.
IIA Loop I		Teacher: ... Aurelio: The thieves ... Teacher: The thieves ...
IIA Loop		Teacher: ... Aurelio: and the policemen.
	VH	Teacher: Very good.
IIA Loop		Teacher: And you, Pilar, for you who are the main characters there? Pilar: Yacub and The Judge.
	VH	Teacher: Yacub and The Judge, only two, fine.
IIA Loop		Teacher: And you Ernesto? Ernesto: Yacub, The Judge, and the thieves, that's it.
	VF	Teacher: The Judge, The Arab, and that mysterious character that he saw in his nightmare, his dreams, right? ...

Table 2: Excerpts of adult-children dialogues from preschool and primary strands of research (continued)

(2)   Excerpt from Cooperative Learning Group

Sequence 4. Clarifying ideas from a summary

Context: The group guide and the students are sitting in a circle. The students, in pairs, have written a summary of part of a text about characteristics of Vertebrates. The guide is reading aloud to the group a summary produced by one pair of students, and stops in one section ...

Code:		Dialogue:
Discourse	Action	
IIA Spiral	II D	Guide: Let's see, this is a difficult word. Who knows what metamorphosis is? Daniel: An illness.
IIA Spiral	IA/ IIF	Guide: (To all): Do you think that metamorphosis is an illness? David: No. Alejandro: No.
IIA Spiral	ID	Guide: What is metamorphosis? ... David: The development of a frog.
IIA Spiral	IIE	Guide: The development of a frog; yes. But, what does metamorphosis mean? Students: ... (no response from students).
II A Spiral	III C	Guide: Listen and pay attention to something. You all read the word 'metamorphosis', and why, if no one understood it, did no one ask for clarification?
	IV C	Remember that it is very important when we read to be checking if we understand or don't understand.
	VH	When we don't understand, what do we do?
	VH	Alejandro: Clarify it.
	VF	Guide: Clarify it, ask for help, right? Very good.
	IIB	So, then, what is metamorphosis? You told us well, David, it is how the frog develops, and the amphibians, right? But do you know what 'metamorphosis' means? That there is a *change* in development

In the next section I will present the two strands of research on preschool and primary school children respectively. After each presentation I will discuss results from each strand of research. Then, in the final section, I will provide an overall discussion of both strands of research in combination.

Summary of two strands of research
High/Scope (H/S) vs. official pre-school curricula

Method

In this strand of research we set out to analyse further some original findings from a previous longitudinal study on the development of independent problem solving capacities in Mexican pre-school children (Study 1: Rojas-Drummond and Alatorre, 1994). We carried out a follow-up study of the same children and teachers (Study 2: Rojas-Drummond, Mercer and Dabrowsky, 2001) to analyse more directly the nature of the guided participation taking place in the classroom that might have contributed to our original findings, using the methodological scheme outlined above.

The children and teachers (same for both studies) came in equal numbers from two pre-school settings: the H/S Curriculum (Hohmann, Banet and Weikart, 1979) and the official state curriculum. Both pre-school groups were equivalent in relevant socio-economic and educational measures, and included 5-6-year-old children and their respective teachers.

In essence, results of Study 1 had shown that at the end of the academic year the H/S children's performance on two dynamic assessment tests (arithmetic word-problems and figure-matching puzzles) was significantly more competent and more independent than that of their peers in the official curriculum. Further qualitative analysis of the arithmetic test revealed that at the end of the year the H/S children were able to solve most of the problems without any type of aid. In contrast, the official school children still relied mostly on the experimenter providing concrete and tangible representations of the elements involved in the problems, to achieve success. These patterns suggested that by the end of the year the H/S children had moved faster from potential to real levels of development, displaying appropriation of more sophisticated and self-regulated (that is, more independent and competent) problem-solving strategies.

Which factors can account for the differences found? Given the apparent homogeneity of the two populations, we argued that at least some aspects of the type of curriculum in operation were partly responsible for the H/S children's superior performance. Furthermore, on the basis of the sociocultural literature in the field, we speculated that part of the explanation might reside importantly in the nature of guided participation, particularly daily interactions and discourse between children and teacher, since it is these exchanges that actually enact the educational proposals of each curriculum.

In Study 2 we investigated this hypothesis in more detail. During Study 1 and parallel to the dynamic assessment, we had videotaped teacher-children interactions in activities around arithmetic reasoning for each of the four classes under study (two each for H/S and official curricula) several times throughout the year. This source of data became the focus of Study 2 in which we applied the methodological scheme described above to analyse all the exchanges recorded. Inter-observer reliability from a random sample of six representative sessions yielded an overall average score of 89.8%, with a range of 86-93%.

Results

Systematic comparisons between curricula for each Action were carried out after pooling frequency distributions across teachers and sessions for each curriculum. Statistical comparisons between curricula were performed for each of the 24 Actions allowing for quantitative comparisons. Most of the significant comparisons favoured the H/S curriculum (63%), while none favoured the official curriculum (Table 3).

An analysis of the Actions which yielded more highly significant results ($p < 0.001$ and $p < 0.01$) indicated that, in comparison with the official curriculum, the H/S teachers and students engaged significantly more frequently in the following types of interactions:

(a) At the discursive level, they displayed significantly more often Spiral IRFs (47% of all exchanges), which potentially take the students to higher levels of understanding and/or performance. In contrast, only 8% of Spiral IRFs were evident in the exchanges from the official curriculum (the other 92% were Loop).

(b) At the level of Actions, Spiral IRFs were translated into a variety of social-constructivist and scaffolding strategies, which also appeared significantly more often in the H/S exchanges: H/S teachers more frequently elicited problem-solving strategies in their students; reduced degrees of freedom, thereby allowing students to concentrate on certain relevant aspects of the activity; displayed 'retreat and rebuild' exchanges; modelled desirable actions; provided elaborate feed-back; used other students as a social-cognitive support for learning; explicitly linked prior knowledge to the current activity; emphasised the processes for arriving at solutions and made students' achievements explicit to the group (see Table 3).

Discussion

Besides the quantitative analyses carried out, we observed many interesting qualitative differences between the styles of teacher-student interactions between the two curricula. Overall, these observations qualified and reinforced the quantitative results obtained. In general, they revealed that the H/S teachers tended to be more consistent, explicit, systematic and comprehensive in the acting out of the strategies and behaviours considered under Actions in the system of analysis. At the same time, the specific tasks that the H/S teachers chose to promote mathematical reasoning tended to be more clearly directed towards advancing in that direction, and appeared to convey more functionality and meaningfulness, involving many more adequate games and group-work activities. Likewise, their scaffolding strategies, besides being much more prominent, tended to be more varied, sophisticated and more attuned both to the individual child and to the mastery of the tasks at hand.

Taken together, the quantitative and qualitative results of Study 2 suggested that H/S teachers and students, in comparison with those of the official curriculum, engaged in a style of interaction that synthetically could be characterised as follows:

(a) it tended more towards the social construction of knowledge through interaction and discourse among all participants; (b) it was more oriented towards the promotion of various processes of learning, problem-solving and domain-specific strategies and (c) teachers actively encouraged the above processes through a scaffolding style of guided participation. This style, which we term social-constructivist, was quantitatively and qualitatively more prominent in the H/S teachers and students than in the official curriculum ones. In contrast, the latter exhibited a style of interaction which entailed a more conventional, directive, transmissional, hands-off and product-oriented approach (termed directive-transmissional).

On the basis of the pooled results from Studies 1 and 2, we argue that at least part of the explanation for the H/S children's more developed and independent problem-solving strategies

Table 3: Comparisons between curricula that yielded significant results

	Comparisons	
Favouring	**Number**	**%**
H/S	15*	63
Official Curriculum	0	0
Neither	9	37
Total	24	100

* The 15 Actions which differed significantly (Chi Square tests for independent samples[1]) were: IIA, III C, VC, VD, VE, VF (p <0.001); IA, IIH, IVC, VH (p <0.01); IIB, IID, IIE, IIF IIIB (p < 0.05) (Table I for Dimension-roman and Action-letter codes).

1   The nature of interactive data does not meet the requirements of independence of observations of the Chi Square Test. However, given the nominal level of measurement, we did not encounter adequate alternative statistical tests within the non-parametric ones to deal with comparisons of this type of data. We decided to apply the test in spite of this limitation, to offer extra support to the claims made about the many apparent qualitative and quantitative differences we observed in the data.

(Study 1) may lie in the differential amount, and quality of interaction and discourse taking place in each curriculum (Study 1). In particular, the more social-constructivist, scaffolding style of interaction apparent among the H/S teachers and students might contribute to the children's faster movement from potential to real levels of development, and towards the appropriation of more competent and independent problem-solving and learning strategies. This, of course, is likely to occur in conjunction with some or all of the other components of the H/S curriculum. But we believe, based on the sociocultural literature previously reviewed, that the guided participation practices actually taking place between adults and children played a key role in this dynamics.

I will next move to the second strand of research mentioned in the Introduction, to provide further evidence for the relationship between particular styles of guided participation and certain developmental and learning outcomes. This research focuses on primary school children and the development of functional literacy.

Cooperative learning and promotion of functional literacy in primary classrooms

Method

Our line of research on the development of functional literacy has consisted of a series of longitudinal studies of teachers and children in Mexican primary schools (see review in Rojas-Drummond, Dabrowsky and Gomez, 1998). Two of these studies are the focus of the present report.

Here too, we undertook to analyse further some original findings from a previous longitudinal study on the development and promotion of functional literacy in Mexican primary school children (Study 1: Rojas-Drummond *et al.*, 1998). We set to analyse in more detail the nature of guided participation taking place in the classroom which might have contributed to our original findings (Study 2: Rojas-Drummond *et al.*, 2002).

Briefly, Study 1 entailed an investigation of 4th-graders (9 years old) and teachers from two equivalent public primary schools in Mexico City, assigned to an experimental or control condition. Experimental groups were exposed to a series of training sessions, following a socio-instructional programme for promoting functional literacy. Our programme was adapted from the cooperative learning or 'reciprocal teaching' methods developed by Brown and her collaborators (see Brown and Palincsar, 1989; Brown and Campione, 1996), and included cooperative learning teams working with a guide-experimenter in place of a teacher. Control groups followed their regular lessons from the Official curriculum.

In general, results from this first study showed that cooperative learning procedures were highly effective in promoting students' appropriation of declarative and procedural knowledge for comprehension, production and learning of narrative and expository texts. Further, qualitative analysis showed that the improvement in the experimental groups reflected more developed strategies to organise, synthesise and produce more cohesive and elaborated texts. These abilities did not seem to be dealt with directly or successfully within the regular classroom, since control groups did not show evident progress throughout the year in any of the discursive and learning parameters analysed.

We hypothesised that the above findings were at least partly due to the nature of the guided participation practices taking place during the cooperative learning sessions, in comparison with those commonly occurring within the regular classroom (the official curriculum). Therefore, we carried out a follow-up study of the same children and teachers, again in collaboration with Neil Mercer, to explain further the sources of our original findings (Study 2: Rojas-Drummond et al., 2002). Here, we analysed more directly the styles of interaction and discourse taking place in the classrooms of each experimental group, using the methodological scheme presented previously.

As part of our general method, all experimental sessions applying cooperative learning with expository texts had been videotaped, together with some regular control classes. These videos provided the basic source of data for Study 2. In particular, one team of six students and their guide were followed throughout nine sessions of cooperative learning in which work centred around expository texts from a natural science textbook. At the same time, control teachers and students were videotaped during regular classes, working around reading and learning activities.

All video transcripts were analysed systematically in qualitative and quantitative terms, using the methodological scheme described in the two previous sections.

Results

Similarly to the pre-school strand of research, we carried out statistical comparisons between the frequency distributions of Actions obtained for the two experimental groups, for each of the 24 Actions allowing for quantitative comparisons. Most of the comparisons (71%) were significant in favour of the cooperative learning group, while none favoured the control group (Table 4).

An analysis of the Actions which yielded more highly significant results ($p<0.001$ and $p<0.01$) indicated that participants in the cooperative learning groups engaged significantly more frequently in the following type of exchanges, in comparison with the control groups:

(a) At the discursive level, they displayed Spiral IRFs much more often (89% of all exchanges). In contrast, Spiral IRFs were almost non existent in the control group (only 2% in the total sample; the other 98% were Loop).

(b) At the level of Actions, Spiral IRFs were translated into a variety of social-constructivist and scaffolding strategies; these appeared significantly more often in cooperative group exchanges than in control group exchanges. Participants of the cooperative learning groups more often engaged in: using other students as a resource to support the ongoing activity, asking questions to explore a student's level of understanding, presenting challenges, negotiating meanings, making ground rules explicit, eliciting various problem-solving strategies, using 'retreat and re-build' exchanges, using reformulations and elaborations, emphasising a variety of strategies for arriving at solutions, revising a student's learning, emphasising the meaning or purpose of activities, reducing degrees of freedom to allow students to concentrate on key aspects of the task and providing elaborated feedback.

Discussion

A qualitative analysis similar to the one applied to pre-school data qualified and reinforced the quantitative results (as it did for the pre-school data). Overall, the style of interaction and discourse which emerged as typical of the cooperative learning activities could be characterised as follows: (a) It tended more towards social construction of knowledge; (b) it was more oriented towards guiding the construction of knowledge through a wide variety of supporting strategies; and (c) It tended to emphasise the acquisition of different types of strategies for problem solving, reasoning and learning in students.

In contrast, the typical interactive style of teachers and students of the official curriculum (control groups) tended to be more directive although less supportive: (a) teachers provided most of the information and dominated most of the talk; (b) however, their supportive strategies tended to be scarce and less varied, and (c) teachers tended to emphasise fact acquisition and task completion, at the expense of underlying problem-solving and other learning processes. This more 'directive-transmissional' approach is typical of primary practice in several official Mexican schools, as found in various studies (Mercado, 1997; Mercado *et al.* 1997).

Table 4. Comparisons between experiment groups that yielded significant results

	Comparisons	
Favouring	**Number**	**%**
Cooperative Learning	17*	71
Control Group	0	0
Neither	7	29
Total	24	100

*The 17 Actions which differed significantly (Chi Square tests for independent samples) were: IA, IIA, IID, IIE, IIF, IIG, III C, VD (p <O.OOI); IIB, IIID, IVA, IVB, VB, VC, VF, VH (p <0.01); VE (p <0.05) (Table I for Dimension-roman and Action-letter codes).

Taken together, the quantitative and qualitative analyses of interaction and discourse in each experimental setting suggest an overall pattern. The cooperative learning procedures tested seemed to foster a social-constructivist, scaffolding style of interaction, as previously defined. In contrast, as in official pre-school classrooms discussed previously, official primary teachers and students exhibited a style of interaction which tended more towards a directive-transmissional approach.

Combining results from the two cooperative learning studies reviewed we suggest that success of cooperative learning in promoting students' declarative and procedural knowledge (Study 1) is partly due to the differential amount and quality of the interactive and discursive practices taking place in each setting (Study 2). In particular, the more social-constructivist, scaffolding style of guided participation observed in the cooperative learning groups may partly account for the more competent performance displayed by the experimental students in declarative and procedural knowledge around functional literacy.

Taking the two strands of research together (involving pre-school and primary students respectively), the differences found between groups in each strand clearly reveal specific patterns, which result from the nature of the particular activities, educational programme and developmental level involved in each setting. At the same time, however, looking at both strands in combination there were consistencies in many of the Actions that resulted in a significant difference between curriculum groups in both strands. In particular, in comparison with the respective official curriculum groups, both the H/S and the cooperative learning groups engaged more significantly in the following types of Actions and discursive patterns: I. Actions which capitalise on other students to support learning; II. Discursive patterns which emphasise the joint construction of knowledge; III and IV. Actions which promote problem solving and learning processes; and V. A variety of scaffolding strategies to support these processes. (The specific Actions which yielded significant results across the two strands of research were: IA, IIA, IIB, IID, IIE, IIF, IIIC, VC, VD, VE, VF and VH. See Table 1.) These types of Actions therefore are the best indices in the reviewed studies for distinguishing between social-constructivist and directive-transmissional styles of interaction. At the same time, the occurrence of Loop *vs*. Spiral IRFs turned out to be a particularly sensitive discursive feature for discriminating between these interactive styles. Importantly, many other Actions rest upon these basic discursive structures.

The above findings corroborate some previous studies (see Mercer, 1995) where Spiral IRFs and various accompanying supportive strategies have been found to be key indicators of a social-constructivist, scaffolding interactive style. Mercer further argues that Spiral IRFs represent central discursive structures which can play a key role in promoting the guided construction of knowledge.

Our overall analyses further suggest that the social-constructivist practices observed in both strands of research, including those for the H/S and the cooperative learning participants, represent a substantial change from the typical styles of interaction and discourse in many Mexican official curriculum classrooms. This change can improve students' competence in activities related to problem solving and functional literacy.

Wertsch's (1991) analysis of cooperative learning within a Bakhtinian perspective further supports the present interpretation. He argues that in cooperative learning children gradually internalise the dialogic structure of the interaction. This process involves adopting the privileged role of asking questions and a more active interanimation of reader, writer, text and audience. Adopting these roles in turn results in a fundamental shift in the arrangement of voices that ventrilo-quate the speech genre of formal instruction. We believe similar changes went on in our co-operative learning groups in comparison with the typical interactions that prevail in many Mexican official primary classrooms. Also, related changes of roles, dialogic structures and arrangement of voices can be assumed to have taken place in the H/S groups in comparison to the typical practices of the official curriculum classes.

General conclusions on the two strands of research reviewed

Our analyses showed that the practices found in pre-school and primary settings differed in many respects related to the unique context under study. Nonetheless, consideration of the patterns emerging from both strands of research, which concerned various domains and two educational programmes (H/S and cooperative learning), yielded an array of interesting consistencies. In particular, the two strands suggest that a social-constructivist, scaffolding style of guided parti-cipation, as actually enacted in the everyday classroom practices of adults and children, can be associated with significant enhancement of various learning and developmental outcomes. These include the promotion of competence and independence in domains such as problem solving and functional literacy (that is, a tendency towards appropriation and self-regulation of general problem-solving strategies and domain-specific ones in the students). It is possible that students from the H/S and cooperative learning groups acquired not only better knowledge, but a different type of knowledge than their respective official curriculum peers (see Rogoff, 1994).

Our findings provide empirical support for certain sociocultural claims. Our research has high-lighted some of the mechanisms involved in key sociocultural constructs related to the nature of guided participation. These mechanisms include how social-constructivist and scaffolding inter-active and discursive practices promote learning and development. Our findings also allow us to underpin empirically, in situated educational contexts, some of the actual interactions and dis-cursive patterns that comprise some of these constructs.

Our results in general confirm and expand findings from previous studies of the relations bet-ween expert-novice guided participation and development of children's competence and independence (Wood *et al.*, 1976; Brown and Palincsar, 1989; Moll, 1990; Rogoff, 1990; Mercer, 1995; Wertsch *et al.*, 1995; Brown and Campione, 1996; Cole, 1996; Hedegaard, 1996). The studies also contribute to current sociocultural research by offering detailed accounts of how participants in learning communities achieve the social construction of knowledge through dis-cursive exchanges.

Regarding our methodological approach, we offer a practical tool for carrying out fine-grained analyses of everyday interactive and discursive practices in the classroom. I trust the presentation of data also conveyed some of the advantages which can arise from combining an array of quantitative and qualitative analyses. Here, the array yielded a fuller explanation of sociocultural phenomena related to interaction and discourse, in the context of teaching and learning practices (cf. Hammersley, 1994).

A weakness of this methodology, however, is that, although it deals with adult-student(s) inter-actions, analysis centres more fully on the adult. To address this limitation, in current studies we are adopting a more comprehensive approach which considers adult-child and child-child inter-actions and discursive exchanges in conjunction, and which takes fuller account of children's active contributions to the dynamics of the interaction. It thus analyses the role of all participants in weaving the course and results of the teaching-learning process (Rojas-Drummond *et al.*, 1999).

The studies presented can also point up techniques for improving the quality of the teaching-learning process taking place in the classroom. For example, teachers can be encouraged to reflect on their current practices and participate in designing and implementing new educational activities that benefit from a social-constructivist approach. Also, our methodological scheme includes actions that can be adapted to particular teaching contexts. We are at present involving primary school teachers and students in such experiences, with very promising results.

In addition, based on these and related findings, we are at present implementing educational programmes that capitalise on styles of interaction and discourse to promote learning and development. For this, we are creating complementary spaces within schools where participants of learning communities can engage in a diversity of social-constructivist practices. These practices include ludic and functional activities mediated by a variety of cultural artefacts. Our findings have led us to design and implement an ongoing project in primary schools. 'Learning Communities for the Social Construction of Knowledge' (Rojas-Drummond and LCC, 1998) was inspired by numerous educational developments emanating from sociocultural theory and practice, including the 'Fifth Dimension' proposal (Nicolopoulou and Cole, 1993; Cole, 1996; Cole and Brown, 1996-1997). As part of this current enterprise, we are implementing a 'double system of guided participation' which fosters social-constructivist, scaffolded and exploratory styles of interaction and discourse among all participants, including children, teachers and researchers (Rojas-Drummond *et al.*, 1999). So far, these types of programmes are offering valuable educational experiences which have shown to promote significantly learning and development of participants (e.g. Blanton *et al.*, Cole and Brown, 1996-1997).

In conclusion, the studies offer theoretical, methodological and practical contributions to sociocultural theory and educational practice. Along with many other researchers in the field, our contributions have resulted from our attempts to understand how participants of learning communities construct knowledge socially. We have also attempted to empower these participants with tools for enriching the course and outcomes of their cultural activities.

References

Blanton, W., Moorman, G., Hayes, B., and Warner, M. (1996) Effects of participation in the Fifth Dimension on school achievement. Technical Report 3. Fifth Dimension Project. Presented at the 2nd Conference of Socio-Cultural research: Vygotsky-Piaget Geneva, Switzerland.

Bronckart, J.P. (1992) El discurso como acción. Por nuevo paradigma psicolongüístico. *Anuario de Psicologa*. Univeridad de Barcelona, 54. 3-48.

Brown. A.L., and Campione. J.C. (1996) Psychological theory and the design of innovative learning environments: on procedures. principles and systems. In L. Schauble, and R. Glaser (Eds.) *Innovations in Learning New Environments for Education* (289-325). Mahwah, NJ: Lawrence Erlbaum.

Brown. A.L., and Reeve. R. (1987) Bandwidths of competence: the role of supportive contexts in learning and development. in L.S. Liben (Ed.). *Development and Learning: Conflict or Congruence?* (173-223). Hillsdale. N.J: Lawrence Erlbaum.

Brown. A.L.. and Palincsar A.S. (1989) Guided, co-operative learning and individual knowledge acquisition. In L. Resnick (Ed.). *Knowing, Learning and Instruction* (393-451). New York: Lawrence Erlbaum.

Bruner, J. (1990) *Acts of Meaning*. London: Harvard University Press.

Cole, M. (1996) *Cultural Psychology. A Once and Future Discipline*. Cambridge. MA: Harvard University Press.

Cole, M. (1998) Can Cultural Psychology help us think about diversity? *Mind, Culture and Activity*. 5(4), 291-304.

Cole, M., and Brown, C. (1996-1997) Using new information technologies in the creation of sustainable afterschool literacy activities. *Third Year Report to A.M. Foundation.* Laboratory of Comparative Human Cognition, University of California, San Diego.

Coll, C., and Edwards, D. (Eds.). (1996) *Teaching, Learning and Classroom Discourse.* Madrid: Infancia y Aprendizaje.

Cowie, E., Smith, P., Boulton, M., and Laver, R. (1994) *Cooperation in the Multi-Ethnic Classroom: The Impact of Cooperative Group Work on Social Relationships in Middle Schools.* London: David Fulton.

Edwards, D., and Mercer, N. (1987) *Common Knowledge: The Development of Understanding in the Classroom.* London: Methuen/Routledge.

Elbers, E., Maier, R., Hoekstra, T., and Hoogsteder, M. (1992) Internalisation and adult-child interaction. *Learning and Instruction*, 2, 101-118.

Hammersley, M. (1994) Questioning the qualitative and quantitative divide. Paper presented at the 1994 Annual Conference of the British Psychological Society.

Hedegaard, M. (1996) The zone of proximal development as basis for instruction. In H. Daniels (Ed.). *An Introduction to Vygotsky* (171-195). London: Routledge.

Hicks, D. (Ed.). (1996) *Discourse, Learning and Schooling.* Cambridge: Cambridge University Press.

Hohmann, J, Banet, J, and Weikart, D. (1979) *Young Children In Action.* Ypsilanti. the High/Scope Press.

Lave, J, and Wenger, E. (1991). *Situated Learning. Legitimate Peripheral Participation.* Cambridge: Cambridge University Press.

Mercado, R. (1997) El habla en el aula como vehiculo del proceso de ensenanza-aprendizaje en una escuela primaria de Mexico. Doctoral Thesis, Autonomous University of Madrid, Spain.

Mercado, R., Rojas-Drummond, S.M., Mercer, N., Dabrowski, E., and Huerta, A. (1997) La interaccion maestro-alumno como vehiculo del proceso de ensefiañza-aprendizaje en Ia escuela primaria. *Morphe*, 8-9(15/16), July 1996-June 1997.

Mercer, N. (1995) *The Guided Construction of Know/edge: Talk Amongst Teachers and Learners.* Clevedon: Multilingual Matters.

Moll, L. (1990) *Vygotsky and Education: Instructional Implications and Applications of Socio-Historical Psychology.* Cambridge: Cambridge University Press.

Newman, D., Griffin, P, and Cole, M. (1989) *The Construction Zone. Working for Cognitive Change in School.* Cambridge: Cambridge University Press.

Nicolopolou, A., and Cole, M. (1993) The Fifth Dimension, its play-world, and its institutional contexts: The generation and transmission of shared knowledge in the culture of collaborative learning. In E.A. Forman, N. Minnick, and C.A. Stone (Eds.). *Contexts for Learning. Sociocultural Dynamics in Children's Development.* New York: Oxford University Press.

Renshaw, P, and Brown K. (l999). Appropriation and resistance within collaborative learning activities. Analyses of teacher-student and student-student interaction based on Bakhtin's theory of voice. Paper presented at the European Association for Research on Learning and Development Conference. Goteberg, Sweden, 1999.

Rogoff, B. (1994). Developing understanding of the idea of communities of learners. *Mind, Culture and Activity,* 1(4). 209-229.

Rogoff, B., and Lave, J. (1984) *Everyday Cognition: Its Development in Social Context.* Cambridge, MA: Harvard University Press.

Rogoff, B., and Wertsch, J. (Eds.). (1984) Children's learning in the zone of proximal development. *New Directions for Child Development.* No.23, San Francisco: Jossey Bass.

Rogoff, B. (1990) *Apprenticeship in Thinking. Cognitive Development in Social Context.* New York: Oxford University Press.

Rojas-Drummond, S., and Alatorre, I (1994) The development of independent problem solving in pre-school children. In N. Mercer, and C. Coil (Eds.). *Explorations in Sociocultural Studies, VoL 3: Teaching, Learning and Interaction* (161-175). Madrid: Infancia y Aprendizaje.

Rojas-Drummond, S., Dabrowski, E., and Gomez, L. (1998) Functional literacy in Mexican primary schools: A research review. *Center for Language and Communications Occasional Papers*, 55, November. Milton Keynes: The Open University.

Rojas-Drummond, S., Hernandez, G., Velez, M., and Villagran, G. (1998) Cooperative learning and the appropriation of procedural knowledge by primary school children. *Learning and Instruction*, 8(1), 37-62.

Rojas-Drummond, S., and Laboratorio de Cognicion y Comunicacion (1998) Creando comunidades de aprendizaje en escuelas primarias en Mexico: Una perspectiva Sociocultural. *Educar*, 9. Guadalajara, Jalisco: Secretaria de Educacion Publica Mexico, 29-40.

Rojas-Drummond, S., Mercer, N., and Dabrowski, E. (2001) Collaboration, scaffolding and the promotion of problem-solving strategies in Mexican pre-schoolers. *European Journal of Psychology of Education* XVI, 2, 179-196..

Rojas-Drummond, S., Marquez, A., Rios, R., and Velez, M. (1999) The social construction of knowledge in learning communities: analysing and promoting adult-child and child-child interactions. Paper presented at the European Association for Research on Learning and Development Conference, Goteberg, Sweden, 1999.

Rojas-Drummond, S., Mercer, N., Velez, M., and Rios, R. (2002) Interaction, discourse and the promotion of functional literacy in the classroom. *Centre for Language and Communications Occasional Papers.* Milton Keynes: The Open University.

Saxe, J. Guberman, S., and Gearhart, M. (1987) Social processes in early number development. *Monographs of the Society for Research in Child Development.* (216), 52(2).

Vygotsky, L.S. (1962) *Thought and Language.* Cambridge, MA: MIT Press.

Vygotsky, L.S. (1978) *Mind in Society.* Cambridge, MA: Harvard University Press.

Wegerif, R., and Mercer, N. (1997) Using computer-based text analysis to integrate qualitative and quantitative methods in research on collaborative learning. *Language and Education*, 11(3), 271-286.

Wegerif, R., and Scrimshaw, P. (Eds.). (1997) *Computers and Talk in the Primary Classroom.* Clevedon: Multilingual Matters.

Wegerif, R., Rojas-Drummond, S., and Mercer, N. (1999) Language for the social construction of knowledge: comparing classroom talk in Mexican preschools. *Language and Education*, 13(2), 133-151.

Wertsch, J. (1991) *Voices of the Mind.* London: Harvester.

Wertsch, J. (1998) *Mind as Action.* New York: Oxford University Press.

Wertsch, J., Del Rio, P., and Alvarez, A. (Eds.). (1995) *Sociocultural Studies of Mind.* Cambridge: Cambridge University Press.

Wertsch, J., McNamee, G., McLane J., and Budwing, N. (1980) The adult-child dyad as a problem-solving system. *Child Development*, 51, 1215-1221.

Wood, D., Bruner, J, and Ross, G. (1976) The role of tutoring in problem-solving. *Journal of Child Psychology and Psychiatry*, 17, 89-100.

CHAPTER 4
A Vygotskian approach to evaluation in foreign language learning contexts
Andréa Machado de Almeida Mattos

Introduction

This paper reports on the results of a small-scale research project applying Vygotskian concepts to the evaluation of English as a Foreign Language, and suggesting that language assessment should be adapted to meet more 'real-life' learning situations. The study was initially based on an article by Richard Donato (1994), which used the concepts of zone of proximal development (ZPD) and scaffolding to demonstrate L2 acquisition through interaction in a social context. Schinke-Llano (1993: 123), describes the ZPDs as being 'the area in which learning takes place', while according to Lantolf and Appel (1994:10), Vygotsky described it as:

> the distance between the actual development level as determined by independent problem solving and the level of potential development as determined through problem solving under adult guidance or in collaboration with more capable peers.

Thus, for Vygotsky, the mental development of a child is distributed along stages: the child progresses to a more advanced stage when s/he is able to carry out alone certain tasks for which, in the previous stage, s/he would have needed the help of an adult (or 'more capable peer') to perform successfully. The term 'scaffolding' exactly describes the sort of help the child gets from the adult when s/he is not able to perform the task. Donato (1994: 40) explains the concept by saying that:

> in social interaction a knowledgeable participant can create, by means of speech, supportive conditions in which the novice can participate in, and extend, current skills and knowledge to higher levels of competence.

Donato demonstrates in his article that scaffolded help can be obtained through collaborative work among peers of the same level of competence in L2 acquisition settings, and not only through the unidirectional help of a more capable peer or expert, as the majority of research on scaffolding has shown.

Still following Donato, the present research also makes use of the concept of internalisation, which is explained in the following way:

> During problem solving, the experienced individual is often observed to guide, support, and shape actions of the novice who, in turn, *internalises* the expert's strategic processes (*ibid.* 1994: 37).[1]

* First published in *ELT Journal*, 2000 Vol 54/4, 335-345.

This research also used the notions of task and activity, as defined by Coughlan and Duff (1994:175), to show how different subjects interpret the proposed objective of the same task. These authors suggest that:

> a task is a kind of *behavioural blueprint* provided to subjects in order to elicit linguistic data. On the other hand an activity comprises the behaviour that is actually produced when an individual (or a group) performs a task. It is the process, as well as the outcome, of a task.

In other words, the task is what subjects are supposed to do, following previously defined objectives, in order to provide data for research in language acquisition. A task has its own objectives, which may have been proposed by the researcher or by a language teacher. However, different language learners may have their own interpretation of the objective proposed for a task. The activity, though, has no previously defined objectives, so in order to complete the task at hand, participants set their own objectives, which may be different from those intended by the researcher/teacher. Participants therefore act according to the activity they set for themselves, that is, according to their own objectives. Different participants may also act in different ways, precisely because they may have formed different interpretations of a task, and thus set different objectives for themselves, and engage in different activities. This point will be further clarified and illustrated through the data presented in this study.

A final issue examined in the present research is the presence of private speech in the data collected. Private speech is 'a means of self-guidance in carrying out an activity beyond one's current level of competence' (Donato 1994: 48). According to Schinke-Liano (1993:123), 'private speech represents an effort on the part of the individual to regain control of the task situation'.

Study design and procedures

As already stated, in the first instance this study is based on Donato's research on scaffolding, which demonstrated that when learners of a second language are working in co-operative tasks, they 'create a context of shared understanding in which the negotiation of language form and meaning co-occurs' (1994: 43). The two purposes of the study therefore, are (1) to find examples of scaffolding between subjects during the performance of a proposed co-operative task, and (2) to find evidence of language learning resulting from scaffolded interaction.

The present study employs a two-phase research design, in which each phase makes use of the same instrument: a picture-story by Mark Fletcher, specially designed to be photocopied and used as classroom resource material, and originally published in *English Teaching Professional* (see Appendix). During the first preparation phase, the researcher was not present, and subjects were asked to discuss the pictures together co-operatively in order to make up a coherent story. Subjects were given 15-20 minutes to finish the task, and were instructed not to memorise the story. They were also asked to speak in English as much as possible, and to avoid the use of their mother tongue. The purpose of this phase was to give them time to negotiate L2 form and meaning in free interaction, so that scaffolding could be observed. In the second, 'presentation' phase, which immediately followed the first one, each subject was asked to tell the story they had created to the researcher. The purpose of this second phase was to observe whether internalisation due to scaffolding during the preparation phase was evident. Both phases were recorded on an audio-tape, and subsequently transcribed. The protocols from these two phases constituted the data for this study.

The subjects were four volunteers whose English level of competence was around FCE[2] level. They worked in pairs during the preparation phase but were interviewed separately during the presentation phase. Subjects in each pair were well used to working collaboratively in previous learning situations, but neither pair knew the other. The names of the subjects have been changed.

Findings

The data were analysed for different types of evidence. In the case of protocols from the preparation phase, the analysis was aimed at finding examples of scaffolded interaction between subjects, while protocols from the presentation phase were analysed for examples of internalisation of the scaffolded passages present during the preparation phase. It was assumed, once again following Donato, that if a subject who had received help during the preparation phase was able to appropriately reproduce the scaffolded passage (word or phrase) during the presentation phase, this would constitute sufficient evidence to support the hypothesis that language development was taking place as a result of scaffolding.

Protocols from the preparation phase were also analysed for examples of private speech and for evidence of the development of different activities during the collaborative accomplishment of the same task.

Scaffolding

There are several passages in the data where scaffolding can be observed, and to illustrate the process some of them are presented and discussed below.

The first pair – Paulo and Sofia – engage in scaffolded interaction from the very beginning of their discussion, trying to help each other make sense of the pictures in order to create the story:

S: Here they are...[3] ahm... *Eu não sei...* [I don't know][4]

P: *Making[5]* ...

S: Yeah. *Making* vases. Ah... they are ...

P: And the ... the woman here is ... carrying the vase, and the guys and the men are ... uh making some wine.

These are the first protocols from Paulo and Sofia's preparation phase where they discuss pictures 1 and 2. It is possible to notice that Sofia is about to give up the task when she says '*I don't know*', but Paulo immediately pushes her on by helping her to figure out what the men in picture 1 are doing: 'making vases'.

When they discuss pictures 6 and 7, they exchange roles: it is now time for Sofia to help Paulo with words that he wouldn't have been able to provide alone:

P: Yeah. What's ...

S: And the vase was taken in this ah ...

P: Sheep [ship]

S: ... *sailboat*. Yeap.

P: To some place ...

S: No ... yep. And the boat ...

P: And . ... there was ... there were ahm ...

S: *Storm*, there was a *storm* ...

P: *Storm*, there was a *storm* and then ... every ...

S: ... the boat

P: ... sunk.

In picture 9, it is again time for Sofia to ask for help. Once more she is not able to understand what is going on in the picture and Paulo readily provides the answer:

S: Yeah. He brought the vase home and gave it to his wife.

P: No, no, not his wife. [laugh]

S: *Who's that?*

P: This is a *technician* that ahm ...

S: That ... yes.

P: ... was prepared to reconstr... reconstruct the ... rebuild the ...

S: The vase.

P: ... old stuffs. OK?

S: OK.

From these passages it is possible to conclude that Paulo and Sofia play different roles when collaborating to find the solution to the task. Sofia seems to be more advanced in terms of language knowledge, and therefore helps Paulo mainly by providing English words. Paulo, on the other hand, seems to be better prepared than Sofia in terms of problem-solving strategies. It is he who guides her through the pictures and helps her make sense of the drawings.

The second pair – Mariane and Gladys – also engage in scaffolded interaction from the very beginning of their discussion:

M: Three hundred ...

G: Three hundred B ... *before Christ.*

M: What?

G: *Before Christ.*

M: *Before Christ.*

G: Well, three men ...

M: Three ... men ...

G: ... making vases.

M: ... were making vases. Were making and drawing pictures on the vases.

G: Yes.

This pair seem to be at the same language level, so they really help each other wherever needed. Mariane calls Gladys's attention to her wrong use of the plural in the following passage (picture 8):

G: Many, many time later ... the shipwreck ... the ... divers ...

M: *A diver.*

G: ... the divers ...

M: *The diver*. It's only one.

Although scaffolded interaction proves to be, as will be demonstrated in the next section, an important tool for learning a foreign language, it may not always be successful. Sometimes it may also result in one learner providing the other with a wrong word or phrase. The following passage is a clear example of this so-called 'negative learning':[6]

M: What is it?

G: I think that is a... kind of car...

M: Ah!

G: and the men are ...

M: The material to do the vase: *barro.* Pronto! [that's it!] You do the vase with *barro*, but I don't know how to speak *barro* in English.

G: *Mu ... mug.*

M: *Mug?*

G: *M-u-g.* [spelling]

M: *M-u-g*: mug. OK.[7]

Internalisation

Following the analysis of scaffolding, protocols from the presentation phase were analysed in a search for examples of internalisation of the scaffolded passages observed during the preparation phase. All four subjects demonstrated some internalisation of the scaffolding they received. In Paulo's presentation, for instance, he appropriately uses the words he learnt with Sofia. The following is an example of an excerpt where he used a word he had learnt during his interaction with her:

And then, ahm ... the missing picture is this guy selling the vase to people that ... go to another places by, by *sailboats* and, maybe to sell some other things and then the vase was in this *sailboat* and the... the boat sunk and stayed under the sea for a long, long time (talking about pictures 5, 6, and 7).

Sofia, although more advanced than Paulo in her command of English, also internalised his strategic help. In the following excerpt from her presentation phase, she also uses words provided by him during their interaction:

This picture shows a man painting the vase and the one *making* vases, and the two ones, that was worn by this woman ... (talking about picture 1).

And last year it was found by this ... skindiver who took it to ... *an expert*, probably, who... evaluated the vase and found out that it was very ... valuable (talking about pictures 8 and 9).

Gladys received less help from Mariane during the preparation phase, and therefore internalised less, but she proved to be attentive when she talked about picture 8 in her presentation:

So, last year, now recently, eh ... there is a man, *a diver*, and he was found ... was looking for something and then he found many ... Well, many things in the ocean, like for example, the vase.

On the other hand, Mariane demonstrated more internalisation, precisely because she received more help. Here is an example:

> ... the three men, this three men eh ... took this material to the mens. And the others in the picture number one, made the vase and after... draw ... they ... draw them, and the time is three hundred *before Christ*, in Athens.

Unfortunately, Mariane also demonstrated that she had internalised the negative learning passage:

> This workers eh ... ca ... cought *mug* and some kind of grass, suppose, to ... make the vase. The *mug* to make the vase and the ... som ... and ... the kinds of grass to draw the vase (talking about picture 3).

Private speech

The passages where private speech was observed appropriately represent situations in which subjects were facing some difficulty in completing the task.

Sofia, who was not very good at working out the pictures, used private speech to try to find a coherent meaning to pictures 1 and 2:

> S: Someone made the vase here ... he painted the vase also,
>
> P: Yeah.
>
> S: ... then he gave this lady the vase. The lady ah ... *What did she do?* ... She
>
> P: She's carrying something in the vase.

Paulo also makes use of private speech during a scaffolding passage where Sofia tries to teach him the correct usage of the verb 'to sink', while they are discussing picture 7. However, the scaffolding was not successful, and Paulo did not reproduce the correct tense during the presentation phase.

> S: Storm, there was a storm ...
>
> P: Storm, there was a storm and then ... every ...
>
> S: ... the boat ...
>
> P: ... *sunk*.[8]
>
> S: ... sank. [correcting P]
>
> P: *Sssunk...*
>
> S: Sank.
>
> P: What? *Sink, sank, sunk...*
>
> S: Sink, sank, sunk.

(All the above was spoken at the same time by both speakers. P seems to be speaking to himself, while S seems to be trying to teach P.)

Same task/different activities

As discussed by Coughlan and Duff (1994), different subjects may make different interpretations of the objective proposed for a particular research task. This was clearly observed during Paulo and Sofia's preparation phase. As shown in the Appendix, the proposed task was a picture-story with a missing picture. Subjects were instructed to make up a story and to try to imagine what that missing picture could be.

Although Paulo and Sofia co-operated in trying to solve the same task, they were both observed to be setting different objectives of their own, and thus engaging in different activities. While Sofia was worried about finding the missing picture, Paulo was more worried about what for him was a much more important problem: understanding the time gap in pictures 2, 3, and 4. These different activities can be perceived through the following excerpts:

P: The whole history [story] is ...

S: ... a vase with a very interesting story.

P: ... seems to be very clear but this *from picture 2 to 3 and to 4,* I don't think we have a very clear history, I don't know ... uhm ... I think ah ... uhm... when the ... Greek ... eh ... people ... eh ... civilisation ... I ...

S: Are you sure they are grapes?

P: Uhm?

S: Are you sure these are grapes?

P: Oh, they are ...

S: Yeah, they are.

P: ... people that ... that are ... ahm... who works in the land ... to produce food. Land?

S: Yeah.

P: Yes. And he found the vase.

S: *The missing picture* ... is the one who shows this guy here giving the vase ... writing ... he's writing the story. That's the missing picture.

This excerpt represents the subjects' discussion after the missing picture, which came after they had finished discussing the whole story. Some minutes later, Sofia asks about the missing picture again, and Paulo says that it is not the important point:

S: What is the missing picture? The one who ...

P: The... guy... selling the, the vase to... to a ... to a guy that will send the vase to another ... country ... I don't know. But this is not the problem. The problem is from picture 2 to 3...

Towards the end of their discussion Paulo already considers that the task is finished, but Sofia once more asks the same question about the missing picture. At this point Paulo may even be sounding irritated, but unfortunately transcriptions don't reveal intonation traces:

P: And then ...

S: Then they gave it ...

P: That's it.

S: ... to the sailorman ...

P: *... a good history.* [story]

S: *So, what is the missing picture?*

P: The guy from picture 4... is selling the vase to ...

S: Someone who is in picture 6.

P: Yes!

Conclusion

From the reported findings, it is possible to derive some conclusions which are consistent with Vygotsky's view of language development. When applied to foreign language learning contexts, these conclusions may help to build a new approach to evaluation, based on Vygotskian principles, which will in turn provide a better setting for language learning and teaching.

First of all, the data collected and the subsequent analysis are consistent with Coughlan and Duff's distinction of task and activity mentioned at the beginning of this paper. In their analysis, these researchers illustrate that 'second language data cannot be neatly removed from the socio-cultural context in which it was created or collected' (Coughlan and Duff 1994: 190) and suggest that SLA[9] researchers should 'look more closely at the activity that surrounds the data they have collected, and use this information to shed light on otherwise anomalous results' (*ibid*. 191). Placing their suggestions in the field of second/foreign language teaching, rather than SL Research, it is possible to make a correlation between research tasks and learner evaluation tasks. Teachers all over the world have used tasks to evaluate language learners. Generally speaking, learners are evaluated on the basis of fixed or expected answers, and those who depart from this expectation usually receive low marks. Hopefully, the data analysis reported here will be a reminder to those teachers who adopt this kind of evaluation system: in performing the same proposed task learners might have different interpretations of the proposed objective, according to their own sociocultural contexts, and might decide to perform the task in a different way. It follows that teachers should try to evaluate their students on the basis of the activities they set for themselves, and not on the basis of previously set objectives, which might be external to their students.

There is another possible conclusion related to learner evaluation. Students have always been worried about tests, and many language learners are especially worried about taking oral tests. The procedure for data collection described here could well be used in such tests, since students are usually afraid of taking risks in front of the examiner, and feel frustrated with their inability to produce the language they are learning. Scaffolded interaction should, therefore, be used as preparation for oral tests in order to overcome learners' frustration, and to provide a safe ground for risk-taking. Donato (1994: 45) provided support to this view when he observed that 'frustration and risk were minimised by relying on the collective resources of the group'. Furthermore, such an approach to evaluation helps to destroy the idea that it is not possible to learn a foreign language from one's peers. As has been demonstrated, it is perfectly possible for an L2 learner to internalise, that is, to learn, what s/he has heard from another learner in a mutually collaborative situation.

Underhill (1987: 33) also suggests some techniques for oral tests which the learner is able to prepare in advance, on the following grounds:

> The learner has sufficient time before the test to prepare for the task and therefore brings to the test a good idea of what he will say. (...) A prepared oral test gives all the learners something to say without putting words into their mouths; it tests the ability to compose and pre-

sent statements with care and deliberation rather than the spontaneous self-expression of an interview-type test.

A final reason why teachers should adopt scaffolded interaction as preparation for oral tests is that students are used to spending at least a few minutes preparing their presentations during their daily lessons. If this is so, why not let them do the same for their tests? As a fellow teacher has recently pointed out at a local meeting, 'tests should be part of students' daily life, and not their tragedy' (Barata 1996).

Notes

1 Emphasis added.

2 First Certificate in English (Cambridge University Examinations Syndicate).

3 ... This symbol means there was a pause in speech.

4 [] This symbol means comments were added by the researcher. The original words have been translated into English.

5 Italics were used to call attention to the specific words commented on.

6 Although there is always a risk of negative learning, scaffolded interaction's advantages compensate for its drawbacks. Such advantages will be discussed in the Conclusion.

7 The correct word for 'barro' should be 'mud'.

8 It is possible to see (p.6) that Paulo still used the participle, instead of the past form of the verb, in his presentation phase.

9 Second Language Acquisition.

References

Barata, M. C. C. M. (1996) 'Como variar na hora de avaliar'. Paper presented at XIII *Semana de Estudos Germanicos,* UFMG: Belo Horizonte, Brazil.

Coughlan, P. and P. A. Duff. (1994) 'Same task, different activities: analysis of a second language acquisition task from an activity theory perspective' in J. P. Lantolf and G. Appel (eds.).

Donato, R. (1994) 'Collective scaffolding in second language learning' in J. P. Lantolf and G. Appel (eds.).

Fletcher, M. (1997) Treasure! (adapted from Picture Stories Please). *English Teaching Professional* 3/23.

Lantolf, J. P. and G. Appel (1994) 'Theoretical framework: an introduction to Vygotskian approaches to second language research' in J. P. Lantolf and G. Appel (eds.).

Lantolf, J. P. and G. Appel (eds.) (1994) *Vygotskian Approaches to Second Language Research.* Norwood, NJ: Ablex Publishing.

Schinke-Llano, L. (1993) 'On the value of a Vygotskian framework for SLA theory and research.' *Language Learning* 43/1: 121-9.

Underhill, N. (1987) *Testing Spoken Language.* Cambridge: Cambridge University Press.

Appendix

ONE-STOP LESSON

Treasure!

The Metropolitan Museum in New York has a superb addition to its priceless collection of Greek vases. At an auction in London yesterday it bought a vase with a very interesting history ...

Mark Fletcher

Photocopiable Teacher resource Materials · Adapted from 'Picture Stories Please'
Published By: ENGLISH EXPERIENCE. 25 Julian Road. Folkestone. Kent CT19 %HW. England

Issue Three April 1997 • ENGLISH TEACHING *professional* • 23

PART TWO
Literacy and learning

Introduction

Literacy is high on the educational and political agenda at national and international levels, being variously associated with individual cognitive development, employment opportunities and national economic success. However, literacy is a complex phenomenon and exactly what it meant by 'literacy' is hotly debated. Key questions explored in the chapters in this part are: what is meant by 'literacy' and 'being literate'? does being literate involve particular kinds of reasoning? is it more useful to talk in terms of literacies rather than literacy? what kinds of literacy should be taught in schools and formal educational contexts, and why? how can literacy be researched?

The first two chapters in this part illustrate two main approaches to literacy which can be broadly described as 'literacy as a cognitive skill' and 'literacy as social practice'. In chapter 5 David Olson, who has written extensively on cognition and literacy, argues that 'becoming literate' has specific and profound effects on ways of thinking, both for individuals and for societies. Olson argues that once literacy is part of a cultural tradition, it contributes to a particular way of thinking which is not then bound to the written mode but can, rather, be expressed through any mode. In the Western world, he argues, reasoning associated with literacy has given rise to what he calls 'scientific thinking'.

The chapter by Brian Street, an anthropologist who has carried out literacy research in a range of cultural contexts, illustrates what is often referred to as a 'social practices' approach to literacy. In contrast to Olson's focus on literacy and the mind, Street focuses on literacy as a fundamentally social phenomenon with literacies varying according to social-cultural contexts and embedded in relations of power. In this chapter Street aims to explore the relevance of a social practices approach to policies on literacy teaching. Street begins the chapter by describing the way in which debates about the teaching of literacy have been represented in the media around a series of either/or choices about teaching methods, for example, phonics *vs*. whole language, but, he argues, there is a need to move beyond this level of debate to explore the theoretical and ideological bases on which such distinctions are argued.

In Chapter 7, Catherine Wallace, a teacher and researcher in the area of English as a foreign language, focuses on the significance of what she refers to as 'literate English' in a global context. To a certain extent her notion of 'literate English' echoes Olson's notion of 'scientific thinking' with her emphasis on explicit reasoning. Wallace acknowledges the range of local literacy practices in people's lives but argues that there is a need to teach what she refers to as 'literate English' in the English as a foreign language classroom. However, Wallace differs from Olson in her emphasis on the need for the teaching of critical literacy alongside the teaching of literate

English. Her discussion of critical literacy is informed by the work of Paulo Freire (1970), who conceptualises literacy not just as reading the word but as 'reading the world'.

The final two chapters in this part of the Reader focus on research studies exploring children's literacy. Chapter 8 is by Eve Gregory and Ann Williams, who have carried out longitudinal research into the home, community and school literacy practices of minority language children in the UK. In this chapter they outline the research methodologies that they have used and the multilayered analysis they have developed, in particular their use of ethnography and ethno-methodology. Ethnography enabled them to explore what they refer to as the 'cultural grammar', that is, a set of rules that govern members' successful participation in local cultural practices. Ethnomethodology facilitated their exploration of the specific and detailed ways in which the participants construct cultural grammar or cultural knowledge through interaction. From their research they were able to identify, amongst other things, the different reading practices at home and at school, the specific ways in which siblings support younger learners' reading at home, and the different scaffolding strategies provided by teachers in classrooms.

The final chapter in this part of the Reader is by Gemma Moss, who has been researching the literacy practices of children and young people for some time. In this chapter Moss focuses on the ways in which the documented differential genre-preferences between boys and girls arises, by carefully documenting the literacy events in primary classrooms. Moss offers a framework for categorising different reading activities in the classroom at both empirical and theoretical levels. She draws on Bernstein's work on languages of description in empirical research, the 'language of enactment' and the 'language of explanation', and illustrates the development of such languages in her own research on gender and literacy.

CHAPTER 5
Literate mentalities: literacy, consciousness of language, and modes of thought
David R. Olson

The question I propose to address in this chapter is the role that writing played and continues to play in the evolution and development of the form or mode of thought, the mentality, if you will, that we in the West describe as scientific. I will conclude with some comments on how children acquire this more specialised model of thought.

Goody and Watt (1963) first suggested that the Greek invention of logic was a by-product of the invention of an alphabet. They argued that the existence of a permanent representation of speech allowed readers, unlike speakers, to reflect on the linguistic and logical properties of their own speech and so to detect the relations we continue to this day to describe as logical. While they were careful not to identify logic with rationality, they did infer that the invention of logic was an important step in the evolution of that formal mode of thought we dignify by the term *scientific.*

Although the hypothesis is entirely plausible, it suffers from a critical defect, namely, the lack of evidence. Three widely cited criticisms must be acknowledged. Lloyd (1979) showed that the evolution of analytic arguments evolved in the marketplace, in oral argument and counter-argument rather than in the private scrutiny of written documents. True, the Greeks could write, but there is little evidence that writing was the primary mode of discourse; writing was some-times used to record speech, but the primary mode of discourse remained oral. Even the notion of proof, Lloyd argued, had more to do with silencing the opposition than with strict logical deduction. Thomas (1992), in her more extensive analysis of ancient Greek literacy, found that literacy had many forms and functions, was intimately connected with oral discourse, and reflected as much as shaped Greek culture. As a result, it is impossible to state in any simple and direct way how literacy contributed to classical Greek thought.

Second, Scribner and Cole's (1981) widely cited study of the uses and consequences of literacy among the Vai of Liberia compared three groups of subjects: those who were schooled and literate in English, those unschooled but literate in Vai, an indigenous syllabic script, and those who had neither been to school nor were literate in Vai. To their dismay, being literate in Vai had little effect on cognitive performances, while being schooled in English had marked effects. Greenfield (1983), in reviewing the book, expressed the general view by saying that the Scribner and Cole volume 'should rid us once and for all of the ethnocentric and arrogant view that a single technology suffices to create in its users a distinct, let alone superior, set of cognitive pro-cesses' (p.219).

*   First published in D. Olson and N. Torrance (eds.) 1996 *Modes of Thought: explorations in culture and cognition.* Cambridge: Cambridge University Press. 141-151.

Third, no satisfactory basis has been found for clearly distinguishing the oral from the written because writing has been related to speaking in so many different ways. Writing is sometimes used to record speech; other times it provides a written script for subsequent oral performance. Writing, until recently at least, has been closely tied to speaking. Finnegan (1988), among others, has noted the complete interdependence of the two, and Carruthers (1990) has shown that even in a highly literate society, the monastic society of the late medieval period, scholars did their thinking and composing almost exclusively in oral form. Even Saint Thomas Aquinas is said to have composed his magisterial *Summa* by dictating orally to a fleet of scribes. The boundary between the oral and the written, like the distinction between oral and literate cultures, therefore, has been blurred considerably.

My suggestion is that the focus on the modality of expression, the oral and the written, may have obscured a more important underlying fact, namely, how writing and the literate tradition contributes to the formation of a set of concepts about language that have turned out to be extremely important in the evolution of what we think of as scientific thought. The virtue of the hypothesis is that it escapes the criticisms mentioned earlier. It is not critical that Aquinas did his composing orally so long as he did it in terms of the categories and distinctions evolved for creating and interpreting written texts. And it does not matter that those competent in the Vai script showed few of the capabilities of those schooled in English, for only the latter explicitly marked the metalinguistic distinctions that were tested for. And it does not matter that the Greeks did their disputations in the agora so long as those arguments could be scrutinised in literate terms, specifically, in terms of their 'actual linguistic meanings' as Epicurus insisted (Long and Sedley, 1987).

Actual linguistic meanings

Lloyd (1990) pointed out that some forms of argument, especially those of syllogism, axiomatic deductions, and proof, depend upon the univocal meanings of expressions. Yet the concept of 'actual linguistic meanings' like the concept of 'literal meaning' is extremely difficult to analyse. Lloyd (1990) points out that Aristotle's conception of natural science necessarily excluded the metaphorical: 'metaphors... are disastrous in scientific explanations and they make a nonsense of syllogistic' (p.22). Metaphor, while acceptable in poetry and rhetoric, took on a pejorative tone when applied in science. But what is that 'actual linguistic meaning'? It cannot be identified with intended meaning because either literal or metaphorical meaning could be intended. Furthermore, no meaning is free from metaphor.

Yet it is useful to distinguish the literal from metaphorical if for no other reason than to use these categories to criticise one's own and other's arguments. Lloyd (1990) puts it this way: 'it is evident that where *there are no such explicit categories as these*, statements of ideas and beliefs are less liable to a certain type of challenge' (p.25). One such challenge was that leveled at Empedocles, who claimed that the salt sea is the sweat of the earth. Aristotle dismissed the claim, arguing that while that may make good poetry, it made poor science. An important part of writing is the invention and learning of devices for indicating how a statement is to be taken; literal and metaphorical ways of taking an utterance are importantly different. But such a distinction is neither absolute nor universal.

Seventeenth-century writers such as Galileo and Thomas Brown drew an equivalent distinction between speaking strictly and speaking roundly or 'largely' (Olson, 1994, p.270) in order to reconcile biblical texts with the newly discovered facts of nature. When the Bible said, or at least implied, that the earth was at the centre of the universe with stars arrayed above it, that was taken as speaking largely. The correct relations could be expressed in careful language, preferably mathematics.

In our own time, Grice (1989) usefully distinguished 'sentence meaning' from 'speaker's or utterer's meaning,' the former a meaning expressed by lexicon and syntax, the latter a meaning intended by a speaker and conveyed sometimes by what is said and sometimes by what is not said. We recall Grice's famous, if invented, example of the music reviewer who wrote 'Miss X produced a series of sounds that corresponded closely to the score of 'Home Sweet Home.' ' The listener would ask him or herself why had the reviewer said all that instead of simply *sing*; the answer is presumably to indicate some striking difference between Miss X's performance and the activity usually described as *singing*. The listener may infer that 'Miss X's performance suffered from some hideous defect' (Grice, 1989, p.37).

Now my hypothesis is simple: Literacy has a distinctive influence on how language, in particular meaning, is conceptualised. The meaning tied to the form of an expression is the literal meaning; the form of an expression is what is brought into consciousness by writing and literacy. Criticism of an argument in terms of its form is therefore a literate form of thinking. Epicurus' talk of 'actual linguistic meanings' marks him as literate.

Some caveats. Literacy, being able to read and write, is not responsible for bringing 'language into consciousness' in any general sense. Each aspect of language comes into consciousness to the extent only that one has a model or theory or concept for representing that aspect of language. Furthermore, some other activities bring aspects of language into consciousness just as well as writing does – rhyme and alliteration are cases in point. Distinctions between 'straight' and 'crooked' speech (Feldman, 1991), between story and song, or between questions and statements are marked in many, perhaps all, languages, written or not. Hence, my suggestion is rather that writing brings some distinctions into consciousness, among them, the notion of literal meaning. I will elaborate this hypothesis by appeal to some historical data and some experimental data of my own and others.

The invention of writing systems

The implications of writing for cognition have been overlooked, in part because of a faulty theory of writing. The Aristotelian assumption, accepted until quite recently, is that writing is the transcription of speech. That assumption has informed the histories of writing as well as the theories of reading. Some recent writers, Harris (1986) prominent among them, have suggested that the Aristotelian view is based on an anachronism. To assume that writing is putting down speech assumes that the writers already have a concept or concepts of speech that they try to honour in their script. Historical evidence is just the opposite. Early scripts show no sign of an awareness of language as a series of sentences, words or sounds. Earliest scripts represented, for example, 'three sheep' with three tokens, one for each sheep, rather than two tokens, one for each word (Schmandt-Besserat, 1992). The inference is that writing represented things, not words; the discovery of a word was, and continues to be, for children growing up in a literate society, one of the great cognitive achievements. Again, this may require a qualification. Words, as lexical entities, are part of the cognitive competence of speakers. What is to be learned is a concept of word, a concept that includes not only 'sheep,' but also 'three' and 'what.' This is the concept that was and is so difficult to achieve. The very idea that speech could be inventoried in the way that objects can be inventoried is a remarkable insight indeed.

A similar story can be told, indeed has been told (Olson, 1993; Sampson, 1985), for the discovery of the phoneme as represented by a letter of the alphabet. The problem was not one of representing sounds by letters, but of coming to hear words as composed of constituents that could be represented by letters. Again the story is complex and not completely relevant here, but simplifying brutally, we could say that rather than the alphabet being a product of the 'genius' of the Greeks, it was the simple product of attempting to use a Semitic script, a script well suited to represent Semitic languages, to represent the Greek language, for which it was ill suited, with the consequent attempt to 'hear' Greek in terms of the categories provided by the letters of the script. The uninventoried sounds discovered by the Greeks were what we now think of as the vowels. We shall see how this works when we consider how children learn to spell.

The upshot of this story is that the history of writing is not one of learning to transcribe speech, but rather of learning to 'hear' and think of language in terms of the categories and distinctions provided by the writing system. The history of writing is, in large part, the history of bringing speech into consciousness. Not all aspects of speech, of course, but at least those aspects marked in the writing system. Sentences, words and phonemes are such aspects. (Illocutionary force is not well represented by an alphabetic writing system, and recovery of force has remained one of the largely unresolved aspects of language, a point that figures centrally in Olson, 1994.)

I want now to turn to some of the experimental data on consciousness of language as it develops in children, again to show that ways of thinking about language are influenced in important ways by familiarity with a script. Again, a caveat is in order. Since Levy-Bruhl (1926), at least anthropologists have been leery of the comparisons between adult members of traditional (sometimes unlettered) cultures and child members of literate Western cultures. And rightly so; the assumption invites domination and sometimes conquest. But corresponding changes have occurred in our thinking about cognitive development. We no longer think of conceptual development simply as an unfolding, but rather we see children as constructing for themselves many of the same concepts that we recognise as having been constructed historically. Among them are some particular concepts of language to which I now turn.

Children's metalinguistic development

Consider first children's knowledge of phonemes. Phonemes are subsyllabic constituents of speech. To be a speaker is to 'know' in some sense the phonology of the language. Isolating phonemes and knowing about phonemes is quite a different thing, for that involves bringing phonemic constituents into consciousness and turning these constituents into objects of reflection. It is the relation between knowledge about phonemes and writing systems that concerns us here.

The traditional assumption, the one traceable to Aristotle's view that writing is transcription, and one still common in some theories of reading, is that as children know the phonology of their language, the problem in reading is learning how to express that knowledge with letters of an alphabet. The problem with the traditional view is that there is no basis for saying that speakers know *about* their phonology independently of the scripts invented for representing speech. Harris (1986) pointed out that the Greek inventors of the alphabet never succeeded in developing a phonological theory for the simple reason that they mistakenly took the alphabet as that theory, ignoring phonological distinctions not represented by the alphabet. An example in English is the distinction between long and short /a/. *At* and *ate* differ only in the length of the vowel yet both are expressed by the same letter form *a*. To claim that a letter was invented to 'represent' an otherwise known sound involves an anachronism; rather it was the invention of the letter that allowed the sound to be heard *as a sound*. The letter invites the formation of a new equivalence class.

Complexities of the relation between sounds and letters have led some 'whole language' writers to claim that reading can proceed without regard to the relations between phonology and alphabet by focusing on the 'meaning.' Left unanswered, however, is what precisely they are making sense of. In my view, what they are making sense of when they learn to read is how writing relates to speech.

I shall mention two lines of evidence that indicate how writing systems influence the perception of speech. Some two decades ago, Read (1971) examined children's invented spellings, that is, how children who did not know 'correct' spellings made up spellings for words. Notable among his findings were the following invented spellings, characteristic of most of the children he studied:

day DA lady LADE feel FEL

and

bait, bet, bat BAT

but also

igloo EGLIOW fell FALL

He interpreted the findings as indications of children's implicit phonological knowledge, which surely it must be. But the evidence may be viewed in another way, namely, as a matter of analysing one's speech in terms of the categories offered by the writing system.

Consider how this would work. The children all knew the alphabet, that is, the names of the letters and how to draw them. Their task, as they saw it, if I may be so bold as to speak for these preschool children, was to interrogate their pronunciation of words in terms of the letter names they knew. Thus, knowing the letter *a* was called /a/, they listened to their pronunciation of such words as *day* and *lady* and hearing that sound represented it by *a*, producing DA and LADE. The same is true for all so-called tense vowels for which the name of the letter corresponds to the sound it represents. So too for *bait, bet,* and *bat,* for which the sound of the letter name /a/ is closest to the vowel sound in the word and so is written as *a* to produce BAT in all three cases.

The more complex are children's inventions for so-called lax vowels, the short *a, e, i, o,* and *u.* These are the sounds that the letter supposedly represents, rather than simply the letter name. It is the difference between *hat* and *hate* or between *beet* and *bet*. Whereas adult spellers use *a* for both long and short /a/ as above, children inventing spellings write the short /i/ with an *e* so that *fish* is spelled FES and the short /e/ with an *a* so that *fell* is spelled FALL, and so on. As Read points out, children detect the phonetic relationship, the similarity in sound, rather than the phonemic relationship. In my terms, the children hear their speech in terms of a similarity relation between the names of the letters and the sounds in their speech.

The relation between speech and writing may be stated more generally. It is that the alphabet provides a model, a set of constituent forms and sounds, in terms of which the children analyse their speech. The units of speech they detect are not the phonemes of the language, but rather the sounds corresponding to the names of the letters. The writing system provides a model for speech and thereby brings that speech into consciousness. Note that it is not that one becomes conscious of one's speech generally, but rather that one comes to hear one's speech as composed of those constituents represented by the alphabet. Incidentally, this would help to explain the well-known fact that knowledge of the alphabet is a good predictor of children's progress in learning to read.

One criticism that may be leveled against the more general claim that learning an alphabet is learning a model for the sound patters of one's speech is that these findings may be simply 'developmental,' that is, a characteristic that children grow out of rather than a reflection of a particular form of knowledge. This possibility has been ruled out by recent cross-cultural findings.

It is well known that people familiar with an alphabet 'hear' words as composed of the sounds represented by the letters of an alphabet. People tend to think that there are more sounds in the word *pitch* than in the word *rich*, although linguists assure us that there are not (Ehri, 1985). Similarly those familiar with an alphabet are able to delete the sound /s/ from the word *spit* to yield /pit/ or to add an /s/ to /pit/ to make the word *spit*. Morais, Bertelson, Cary, and Alegria (1986) and Morais, Alegria, and Content (1987) found that Portuguese fishermen living in a remote area who had received even minimal reading instruction were able to carry out such segmentation tasks, whereas those who had never been exposed to the alphabet could not. Similarly, Read, Zhang, Nie, and Ding (1986) found that Chinese readers of traditional character scripts could not detect phonemic segments, whereas those who could read Pinyin, an alphabetic script representing the same language, could do so. Thus, to learn to read any script is to find or detect aspects of one's own implicit linguistic structure that can map onto or be represented by that script. In this way, the script provides the model for thinking about the sound structure of speech. The model provides the concepts that make these aspects of speech conscious.

Knowledge of phonology may have little impact on thinking. I detailed it only because it shows in a clear way how the writing system brings an aspect of speech into consciousness. I want now to show that writing serves the same role in bringing meaning and, in particular, sentence meaning into consciousness. To anticipate our conclusion, it is an awareness of sentence or linguistic meaning that gives literate thinking its particular properties.

Members of traditional cultures have been shown to treat alternative expressions having the same sense as being 'the same.' In contrast, members of literate cultures tend to use the stricter criterion of verbatim repetition as being 'the same' (Finnegan, 1977; Goody, 1987). The very notion of *verbatim*, according to the wording, is medieval in origin, suggesting that the concept is a relatively modern one.

Some recent work on children's understanding of the relations between 'what is said' and 'what is meant' has shown that preschool children have particular difficulties with just this set of concepts. Hedelin and Hjelmquist (1988) showed preschool children a collection of animals including a black dog and a white dog, all of which were fed in turn except for the white dog, which remained standing outside the barn. Children were told to pass on to the newly arriving zookeeper the message 'The dog is hungry.' The children successfully relayed the message. Then the zookeeper asked, 'Did you say the white one was hungry?' to which children under five replied, 'Yes,' whereas those over five replied, 'No.' These findings are similar to those reported earlier by Robinson, Goelman, and Olson (1983).

Our research (Torrance, Lee, and Olson, 1992) tested preliterate children on their ability to distinguish a verbatim repetition from a paraphrase. We asked children, the youngest of which were three years of age and the oldest, ten, to make judgments as to whether or not 'Teddy Bear' should be awarded a sticker on the basis of how well Teddy responded to various requests. In one series of trials Teddy's task was to say *exactly* what a story character, Big Bird, had said when he came into the kitchen. These were the verbatim trials. In a second series of trials, Teddy's task was to say what Big Bird wanted – he did not have to use the same words. These are the paraphrase trials. Practice trials involving correction preceded the experimental trials. In each trial the child was asked to judge whether or not Teddy got it right and so deserved a sticker. If so, the child was given the privilege of rewarding Teddy with a sticker or saying 'No sticker, Teddy'. Needless to say, children delighted in their role as judges.

As predicted, children under five years succeeded with the paraphrase items while failing the verbatim item. What they found difficult was to withhold a sticker from Teddy when Teddy was to say the same words, for example, 'Big Bird is hungry,' but had actually said, 'Big Bird wants food'. Thus although they can repeat a sentence from an early age, only when they are about six – becoming readers in Canadian schools – do they succeed in rejecting paraphrases when asked exactly 'what was said'. Interestingly, the pattern can be reversed if one uses well-practiced nursery rhymes in which wording becomes the critical factor. On these trials, children succeed on the verbatim items, correctly rejecting paraphrases. However, they now fail the paraphrase items; they fail to acknowledge that the paraphrase expresses the same meaning as the original expression.

Although it remains to be shown, the distinction between verbatim repetition and paraphrase, we suggest, is not merely 'developmental,' that is, something that will be overcome with age. Rather, we suggest that it reflects a new consciousness of the semantic properties of language, the notion of fixity of wording that comes from reading and otherwise dealing with written texts.

Thinking

Unlike knowledge about phonology, knowledge about 'actual linguistic meanings,' that is, the meaning tied to the actual linguistic form, the 'very words,' does have implications for the evolution of a literate mode of thought.

The relations between writing, literal meaning, logical form, deduction and proof are, it goes without saying, extremely complex. But is seems safe to say that logical proof depends upon the form of an expression, not its content. Deciding on the truth of a belief on the basis of evidence is presumably universal to the human species, if not to lower creatures. But deciding on the validity of an argument depends upon judgments of necessity holding between words and statements. Proof involves the notion that something follows necessarily from what was said. It requires some distinction between an inference and an implication. But if something is to be derived from a statement (rather than the situation described), some means must be available for preserving and referring to that statement. This is where, by hypothesis, writing comes in; writing is 'closed' (Barthes, 1977) in a way that speech is not. The implication is seen as following from the statement as fixed and as distinguished from its paraphrase.

Fixity is not enough. Proof requires the meaning to be fixed as a literal meaning as well. Metaphor is incompatible with proof. Proof assumes literal meaning. Logic and literal meaning seem to be mutually defining. Literal meaning is that meaning for which rules of logic hold. To return to Lloyd (1990, p.22): 'metaphors... are disastrous in scientific explanations and they make a nonsense of syllogistic.'

Systematically applied, this way of taking expressions results in a new genre, scientific or philosophical discourse. Such discourse is not only intended to be taken literally, it tends to control how it is taken by restricting the type of speech acts involved to a single type, namely, assertives. Expressions not even labelled as assertives are known to be such by their position in the genre.

These rules do not easily apply to ordinary expressions, for ordinary expressions may not specify how they are to be taken, whether as statements, promises, predictions, or the like. To illustrate, an utterance such as 'Dinner is at eight' could be taken as a statement, a promise, an invitation, or even an admonition – if one were late.

Implication depends upon how utterances are taken. Consciousness of the fact or possibility that utterances can be taken literally – according to the very words – is at the heart of literate thinking.

That ways of taking utterances determines how we reason from them is nicely shown in some research by Cheng and Holyoak (1985). Adult subjects were to judge the truth of a logical rule by testing examples against that rule. However, subjects' responses tended to reflect their interpretation of that rule. Although intended as a logical premise *If p, then q*, subjects tended to translate it into a pragmatic statement suitable for granting permission. Thus in testing the validity of the rule 'If one is to drink alcohol, then one must be over eighteen,' subjects were likely to think of two implications, one valid, namely, *p only if q (one can drink alcohol only if one is eighteen)*, and one invalid, namely, *if q (one can), p* (if eighteen, then one can drink alcohol). The latter, although congruent with a permission statement, makes the logical error of treating the conditional as a biconditional.

But not all ways of taking utterances are available to everyone. The option of taking utterances literally according to the very form of the expression seems itself to be a literate enterprise. Consider the famous studies of reasoning among the unlettered peasants of Uzbekistan in the 1930s. A sample from one of the interviews is as follows:

> In the far North, where there is snow, all bears are white. Novaya Zemlya is in the far North and there is always snow there. What colour are the bears there?

> To which a non-literate subject, not untypically, responded: 'I don't know... There are different sorts of bears, (Luria, 1976, pp.108-109)

Luria called such responses failures to infer from the syllogism. In general, when subjects had no knowledge of the facts alleged in the story, they were unwilling to draw any inferences from it; if the alleged facts contradicted their beliefs, they based their conclusions on what they knew rather than on what the questioner has intended as the premise.

Of course, there is nothing wrong with such reasoning. The problem comes from the researcher failing to indicate how to take the statements in the story. He intended it as a premise; the subject took it as hearsay. But that is not the whole story. The legacy of Western literacy is the ability, on occasion, to take utterances literally according to the narrow meaning of the words employed.

Taking an expression literally was not a problem only for Luria's illiterate subjects; it is a problem extensively discussed in the anthropological literature. Since Levy-Bruhl, anthropologists have been puzzled by some expressions that seem to be characteristic of at least some traditional societies: 'Twins are birds' of the Azande or 'Corn is deer' of the Huichol. Western literate cultures provide two mutually exclusive ways of taking such expressions as literal or as metaphorical. The problem is that these options seem not to be available in traditional societies. But why should members of another culture be forced to choose between the alternatives valued in our culture? This is a theme carefully developed in Lloyd (1990) and Frye (1982).

Perhaps the conclusion is that it is never possible to deal with expressions in ordinary language as if they were verbal formulae. For that reason, science has increasingly come to rely on mathematics and other formal models. But that does not take away from the point that a consciousness of the verbal form and its attendant sentence meaning is what allows discourse to achieve the explicitness and formality distinctive of modern science and the distinctive mode of thought that it entails.

Furthermore, it is this role that underwrites the importance of literacy in education. In this context, literacy is to be thought of as a particular way with words, their meanings, and their roles in expressions and not merely as the ability to inscribe. The very meaning of literacy has to, indeed already has begun to, change.

References

Barthes, R. (1977) *Image-music-text* (S. Heath, Trans.). Glasgow: Fontana Collins.

Carruthers, M. J. (1990) *The book of memory: A study of memory in medieval culture.* Cambridge: Cambridge University. Press.

Cheng, P., and Holyoak, K. (1985). Pragmatic reasoning schemas. *Cognitive Psychology,* 17, 391-416.

Ehri, L. C. (1985). Effects of printed language acquisition on speech. In D. R. Olson, N. Torrance, and A. Hildyard (Eds.), *Literacy, language, and learning: The nature and consequences of reading and writing* (pp. 333-367). Cambridge: Cambridge University. Press.

Feldman, C. F. (1991) Oral metalanguage. In D. R. Olson and N. Torrance (Eds.), *Literacy and orality* (pp. 47-65). Cambridge: Cambridge University. Press.

Finnegan, R. (1977) *Oral poetry: Its nature, significance, and social context.* Cambridge: Cambridge University. Press.

Finnegan, R. (1988) *Literacy and orality: Studies in the technology of communication.* Oxford: Blackwell.

Frye, N. (1982) *The great code.* Toronto: Academic Press.

Goody, J. (1987) *The interface between the oral and the written.* Cambridge: Cambridge University. Press.

Goody, J., and Watt, I. (1963) The consequences of literacy. *Contemporary Studies in Society and History,* 5, 304-345.

Greenfield, P.M. (1983) Review of 'The psychology of literacy' by Sylvia Scribner and Michael Cole. *Harvard Educational Review,* 53, 21 6-220.

Grice, P. (1989) *Studies in the way of words.* Cambridge, MA: Harvard University. Press.

Harris, R. (1986) *The origin of writing.* London: Duckworth.

Hedelin, L., and Hjelmquist, E. (1988) Preschool children's mastery of the form/content distinction in spoken language. In K. Ekberg and P. E. Mjaavatn (Eds.), *Growing into the modern world.* Trondheim: University of Trondheim, Norwegian Centre for Child Research.

Levy-Bruhl, L. (1926) *How natives think.* London: George Allen and Unwin. (Original work published 1910.)

Long, A. A., and Sedley, D. N. (1987) *The Hellenistic philosophers.* Cambridge: Cambridge University. Press.

Lloyd, G.E.R. (1979) *Magic, reason and experience.* Cambridge: Cambridge University. Press.

Lloyd, G.E.R. (1990) *Demystifying mentalities.* Cambridge: Cambridge University. Press.

Luria, A.R. (1976) *Cognitive development: Its cultural and social foundations.* Cambridge, MA: Harvard University Press.

Morais, J., Alegria, J., and Content, A. (1987). The relationships between segmental analysis and alphabetic literacy: An interactive view. *Cahiers de Psychologie Cognitive,* 7, 415-438.

Morais, J., Bertelson, P., Cary, L., and Alegria, J. (1986). Literacy training and speech segmentation. *Cognition,* 24, 45-64.

Olson, D.R. (1993) How writing represents speech. *Language and Communication,* 13(1), 1-17.

Olson, D.R. (1994) *The world on paper: The conceptual and cognitive implications of writing and reading.* Cambridge: Cambridge University. Press.

Read, C. (1971) *Pre-school children's knowledge of English phonology.* Harvard Educational Review, 41(1), 1-34.

Read, C. A., Zhang, Y., Nie, H., and Ding, B. (1986) *The ability to manipulate speech sounds depends on knowing alphabetic reading.* Cognition, 24, 31-44.

Robinson, E., Goelman, H., and Olson, DR. (1983) Children's relationship between expressions (what was said) and intentions (what was meant). *British Journal of Developmental Psychology*, 1, 75-86.

Sampson, G. (1985) *Writing systems.* Stanford, CA: Stanford University Press.

Schmandt-Besserat, D. (1992) *Before writing.* Austin: University of Texas Press.

Scribner, S., and Cole, M. (1981) *The psychology of literacy.* Cambridge, MA: Harvard University Press.

Thomas, R. (1992) *Literacy and orality in ancient Greece.* Cambridge: Cambridge University Press.

Torrance, N., Lee, E., and Olson, D. (April, 1992) The development of the distinction between paraphrase and exact wording in the recognition of utterances. Poster presentation at the meeting of the American Educational Research Association, San Francisco, CA.

CHAPTER 6
The implications of the 'New Literacy Studies' for literacy education
Brian Street

The Literacy Debate

My 'problem' stems from the anthropological observation that a visiting Martian might be surprised at the extent to which arcane debates about literacy, language and learning appear in the public domain in contemporary British and American society. Popular newspapers and tabloids as well as the quality press, and also television and radio seem full of accounts by 'experts' of their own piece of the struggle over the meanings of literacy and in particular the acquisition of literacy: phonics *vs.* whole language, code-based *vs.* meaning-based reading, cognitive and situated models of literacy; student-centred *vs.* whole-class teaching. Although my own interest has mainly been in the uses rather than the acquisition of literacy, and my own part in the debate has been about social practices associated with reading and writing rather than psycholinguistic conflicts over the grapheme/phoneme relationship, I am intrigued by the way in which these debates have taken on a social character of their own.

Those in other niches of the intellectual horizon may go a lifetime without their debates splashed across full-page spreads of *The Sunday Times* (10 April 1994), *The Independent* (7 February 1993), etc., so it is a matter of intellectual and social history why this should be the case with respect to literacy and language in education. That this may appear common sense to some – 'literacy is the basics, the ground on which other social practices in modern society rest' – attracts my attention even more. What counts as common sense in one culture and in one era may indeed be arcane or ideologically fundamental in another. And there have certainly been many times and places where the view of literacy represented in the newspaper headlines of the late 1990s has not been the received wisdom.

So what is the Literacy Debate? I do not intend to outline it in detail here, as my concern is more with alternative models, but Wray (1997) has recently provided a clear summary of the issues. According to Wray the debate can be traced back through a quarter of a century, 'yet still appears to centre around two polarised positions: Chall (1967) set the terms of the debate as being on the one hand between those who advocated a code-based approach to teaching reading and on the other those who emphasised the place of meaning' (Wray, 1997, p.161). This basic divide seems to remain, even where the terms may have shifted somewhat, to conflicts between 'phonics' and whole language/'real books', (Goodman, 1996; Willinsky, 1990; Meek, 1991); the role of phonics in the UK National Curriculum (Raban, 1996; Beard, 1993); whether written alphabetic knowledge is best learned 'naturally' (Willinsky, 1990) or through formal delivery (Ofsted,

* First published in *English in Education*, 1997, Vol. 31, No.3, 45-59.

1996); and to a distinction between 'autonomous' and 'ideological' models which I suggested in 1985 and which has recently been adapted for teachers in adult literacy programmes (Fiedrich, 1996, reprinted in *Literacy across the Curriculum*, 1997).

Many researchers, including Wray himself, have tried to propose a 'balanced' approach and most teachers probably combine the use of 'real' materials and learning for meaning with workshop-type sessions on particular problems of the phoneme/grapheme relationship. Nagy and Anderson (1997) have recently argued on theoretical grounds that phonemic awareness requires both practice in 'natural' conditions and some explicit instruction. Research suggests that 'it should be considered an outcome, rather than a cause, of learning to read' (p.2): they resolve what appears a paradox in the Literacy Debate by postulating 'a reciprocal relationship' between phonemic awareness and learning to read: although the concept of phoneme is essential to the alphabetic insight, letters provide a scaffold for the development of this difficult concept. 'It is the process of beginning to learn to read that draws the child's attention to letters, sounds and their relation-ships, enabling the insight which unlocks the system' (*ibid.* p.2). In other words, formal learning of the phoneme/grapheme relationship – what is popularly known as phonics – is not enough: learners also learn through practice and use. But neither is practice and use sufficient, as some whole-language proponents suggest: some formal learning is also necessary. This, then, is the sense in which language and learning theory lead to a balanced approach.

Some recent balanced approaches, however, may not be quite as evenhanded as the term sug-gests. A recent book that claims to offer 'balanced perspectives' provides an object lesson in how ideological arguments are disguised behind the supposedly detached and neutral discourse of the autonomous model of literacy (Street, 1995). Roger Beard (1993, p.1) cites favourably Chall's (1967, 1983) claim that 'overall, code-emphasis approaches produce better results in the teaching of early reading'.

According to Beard, this is 'not a surprising conclusion because the English writing system is an alphabetic one ...', thereby apparently rejecting the 'balanced' view of the character of alphabetic systems put forward by Nagy and Anderson above. Although the book claims to provide a balanced approach to the phonics (or code-emphasis) and whole-language (or meaning-emphasis) approaches, it is quite clear that its editor and the selection of chapters lean towards the former: the term balance here does not refer to the balance of articles in the book, which mainly privilege a phonics and skills-based approach, but indicates that this book is intended to balance the influence of the whole-language and child-centred view, which has clearly held sway for too long. This notion of balance represents probably the dominant discourse in current policy documents (LTF, 1997; TTA, 1997), which frequently claim that research shows a phonics approach to be best and blames falling standards of literacy on the strength of the whole-language, meaning-based movement of the 1970s and 1980s.

The debate itself, then, is almost always loaded, despite the frequent claims to scientific know-ledge, objectivity and common-sense truths about the nature of language and literacy. The debates and the discourses in which they are represented need both locating and explaining. In this paper I shall attempt to apply to it some insights from recent anthropologically oriented views of literacy, that are coming to be known as the New Literacy Studies (NLS). I will firstly explain what the term NLS refers to, detail some of the theoretical ground and understandings of language and literacy on which NLS stand and pursue the implications of these new ap-proaches for the problem posed. Finally, I will suggest ways in which educational policies around curriculum and teaching may be affected by these developments. This is not so much to resolve the debate as to shift the ground on which we consider issues of language and literacy in the first place.

New understandings of language and literacy

The New Literacy Studies (Gee, 1991; Street, 1984, 1993a and b) consist of a series of writings, in both research and practice, that treat language and literacy as social practices rather than technical skills to be learned in formal education. The research requires language and literacy to be studied as they occur naturally in social life, taking account of the context and their different meanings for different cultural groups. The practice requires curriculum designers, teachers and evaluators to take account of the variation in meanings and uses that students bring from their home backgrounds to formal learning contexts, such as the school and the classroom. The New Literacy Studies emphasise the importance of 'culturally sensitive teaching' (Villegas, 1991) in building upon students' own knowledge and skills (Heath, 1983; Heath and Mangiola, 1991).

The new research and practice are based upon new ideas about the nature of language and literacy. In turn, the research has reinforced and developed these ideas (Collins, 1995). There are two major tenets to this new thinking: a) the notion of 'social literacies'; b) that language is 'dialogic'.

Social literacies

This phrase (Street, 1995) refers to the nature of literacy as social practice and to the plurality of literacies that this enables us to observe. That literacy is a social practice is an insight both banal and profound: banal, in the sense that once we think about it it is obvious that literacy is always practised in social contexts and that even the school – however artificial it may be accused of being in its ways of teaching reading and writing – is also a social construction. The school, like other contexts, has its own social beliefs and behaviours into which its particular literacy practices are inserted. The notion is, in this sense, also profound in that it leads to quite new ways of understanding and defining what counts as literacy and has profound implications for how we teach reading and writing. If literacy is a social practice, then it varies with social context and is not the same, uniform thing in each case.

I have described this latter view as an 'autonomous' model of literacy: the view that literacy in itself has consequences irrespective of, or autonomous of, context. In contrast with this view, I have posed an 'ideological' model of literacy, which argues that literacy not only varies with social context and with cultural norms and discourses regarding, for instance, identity, gender and belief, but that its uses and meanings are always embedded in relations of power. It is in this sense that literacy is always ideological – it always involves contests over meanings, definitions and boundaries and struggles for control of the literacy agenda. If that is true, then it becomes harder to justify teaching only one particular form of literacy, whether in schools or in adult pro-grammes – or at least the justification needs to be made explicit. If literacy is seen as simply a universal technical skill, the same everywhere, then the particular form being taught in school gets to be treated as the only kind, as the universal standard that naturalises its socially specific features and disguises their real history and ideological justifications. If literacy is seen as a social practice, then that history and those features and justifications need to be spelled out and students need to be able to discuss the basis for choices being made in the kind of literacy they are learning.

Recently there has been some elaboration of key concepts in this field, such as the notion of 'multiple literacies'; literacy events and practices; social, community and individual literacies; and I will briefly indicate the issues and outline my own position. One of the major tenets of the New Literacy Studies has been that literacy is not a single, essential thing, with predictable consequences for individual and social development. Instead there are multiple literacies that vary with time and place and are embedded in specific cultural practices.

Examples of variation in literacies have included Heath's (1983) account of three literacies associated with three communities in the Piedmont Carolinas (Roadville, Trackton and Maintown literacies); my own (Street, 1984) account of three literacies in an Iranian village (schooled literacy, Qoranic literacy and commercial literacy; Barton and Padmore's (1991) account of 'community literacies' in the north of England; descriptions of schooled and *sub rosa* literacies amongst adolescents in the US by Shuman (1986), Camitta (1993) and Bennet and Sola (1994); and Besnier's (1996) analysis of the literacies associated with sermons and with letter-writing in Nukulaelae. Recently, concern has been expressed regarding this pluralisation of literacies. Wagner (personal communication) argues that this creates a new reification in which each literacy appears a fixed and essential thing. I have argued that there is a danger of associating a literacy with a culture where current anthropological perspectives suggest fragmentation and hybridity in both domains (Street, 1993c). Kress (1997) sees the claim for plurality of literacies as paradoxical for NLS since it implies a stability in each literacy that such researchers explicitly reject:

> This paradox only exists if in the first place we assume that language is autonomous, unaffected by the social, and therefore stable. If we assume that language is dynamic because it is constantly being remade by its users in response to the demands of their social environments, we do not then have a need to invent a plurality of literacies: it is a normal and absolutely fundamental characteristic of language and of literacy to be constantly remade in relation to the needs of the moment; it is neither autonomous or stable, and nor is it a single integrated phenomenon; it is messy and diverse and not in need of pluralising. (p.115)

Although I agree with Kress in principle, and indeed this argument reinforces the point I am making here about dynamic models of language and literacy, I think that for strategic reasons it has been important to put forward the argument regarding plurality. I have found, particularly in development circles, where agencies present literacy as the panacea to social ills and the key ingredient in modernisation, the dominant assumption has been of a single autonomous literacy that is the same everywhere and simply needs transplanting to new environments. In order to challenge this view and to focus on the specificity and dynamic character of literacy, the notion of multiple literacies has played an important role. Indeed, a recent Unesco document for an international conference to rethink approaches to literacy in development has accepted this view and the strategic and practical implications are immense (Unesco, 1997). Whilst formally and for research purposes we might be better working with the concept of literacy practices – which I have argued elsewhere is more robust and sensitive to local variation – at the national and international levels of policy and strategy we still need to characterise the dynamic and culturally varied quality of literacy practices by referring to the plurality of literacies.

There is, however, another sense in which the plurality of literacies has come to be used and here I agree fully with Kress. He argues that this second sense comes from the metaphorical extension of the concept of literacy to other domains of social life, such as computing, politics, etc. One even hears of emotional literacy. Apart from glib and lazy rhetorical usages, Kress also sees these extensions as flawed in that they fail to see language as just one of many modes of communication.

> Because it is seen as the only real mode, as the most highly developed, the one that sustains thought and rationality, all other modes of communication, or for that matter, all cultural systems, have to be described as being literacy. This devalues the term, so that it comes to mean nothing more than 'skill' (as in keyboard skills) or competence. It also prevents the possibility of examining the actual function of other systems as systems in their own right. (Kress, 1997, p.115)

This then raises the question of the boundaries of what is included under the term literacy, which Kress and I would agree is a multiple and complex of phenomena, including print, text as block, letters, text as genre, letters as sound, media layout, etc. I would just add that recent debates about multi-literacies (cf. New London Group, 1996) seem to imply a similar reduction of the concept of literacy to a given channel – in this case the 'multi' in multi-literacy seems to refer to whether the particular literacy is in the visual, media or print domain, as though each were a separate literacy. I would prefer to think of literacies as some complex of these domains that varies with context, so that the mix of visual, print and other aspects depends upon cultural and contextual features. Computer literacy, for instance, is not a new single literacy but involves different uses of oral and literate channels in different situations: there is no one phenomenon called computer literacy and the term can be misleading in both research and policy terms.

I have preferred for research purposes, if not immediately for policy purposes, to work with the concept of literacy practices. This term enables us to specify the particularity of cultural practices with which uses of reading and or writing are associated in given contexts. Within a given cultural domain there may be many literacy practices, i.e. not one culture and one literacy. By literacy practices I mean not only the observable behaviours around literacy – Heath's 'literacy events' – but also the concepts and meanings brought to those events and which give them meaning. Strictly speaking, then, the literacies referred to above – Heath's three Piedmont communities and their different literacies; the Iranian village literacies; community literacies in the north of England; schooled and out-of-school literacies; etc. – are best thought of as literacy practices. It is sometimes clumsy to refer to, for instance, 'schooled literacy practices', especially in contexts where policy makers and the media are still working with an autonomous model of literacy that scarcely gives credence to out-of-school literacies anyway. There the specification of the dynamic, culturally-specific and valued character of local literacies still requires the pluralisation, despite Kress and others' reservations. But *in situ*, when one is dealing with the particular forms of reading and writing and their meanings to different groups of people, the concept of literacy practices becomes the key term.

From this perspective one may ask what are the literacy practices at home of children whose schooled literacy practices are judged problematic or inadequate. From the school's point of view those home practices may represent simply inferior attempts at the real thing; from the researcher's point of view those home practices represent as important a part of the repertoire as different languages or language varieties. Viewing them as literacy practices can help both perspectives to address exactly what such literacy involves and, from a pedagogic point of view, what is there to be built upon if the aim is to help such people to add dominant literacy practices to their linguistic repertoire.

Again, however, there is a terminological confusion. For some the term literacy practices is taken to refer to what teachers and pupils do in school, i.e. schooled literacy practices, the practice of classroom literacy. When I have asked people on literacy training courses, from countries such as Bangladesh and Namibia, to describe the literacy practices in their area and consider their implications for educational policy, the answer has frequently been in terms of what happens during the literacy campaign, the literacy practice of the classroom. For research purposes, and in the long term I would argue for policy purposes, it is helpful to keep these two meanings distinct: whilst literacy practice may traditionally refer to classroom behaviours, literacy practices allow us to adopt a broader and more culturally relative perspective and thereby to see and value varieties of literacy practices that we might otherwise miss and that would certainly remain marginalised through such lack of attention.

Dialogic language

New theories of language closely associated with those regarding social literacies, focus upon the nature of language as a continually negotiated process of meaning making as well as taking. In this research tradition, it is viewed as always a social process, as interactive and dynamic (Volosinov, 1973: Hymes, 1977; Halliday, 1978). For Bakhtin (1981), language is both centrifugal and centripetal, in the sense that users are always struggling to extend its boundaries and meanings as well as working within prescribed limits; and it is dialogic in the sense that it is always in dialogue – language, even when employed silently by single individuals, is always part of a social interaction, whether with imagined others or with the meanings and uses of words that others have employed at other times and places. As Bakhtin states, 'words come saturated with the meanings of others'. Again this view of language might appear commonsensical at one level – we all know that languages vary, whether that means the differences between French and English, or at a more local level between different dialects, creoles and patois. But the implications of this stance, like that of 'social literacies', are at the same time profound. If language is always contested, negotiated and employed in social interaction, then the appropriateness of particular uses and interpretations have likewise to be opened to debate: it becomes impossible to lay down strict and formal rules for all time and the authority of particular users – whether teachers, grammarians or politicians – becomes problematised. We all, as it were, take possession of language again rather than being passive victims of its entailments.

It is on this tradition in the study of language that Kress is calling when he argues, as we saw above, that 'language is dynamic because it is constantly being remade by its users in response to the demands of their social environments'. Similarly, theorists in the New Literacy Studies have tended to root their ideas about reading and writing, as aspects of language, in broader linguistic theories of a dialogic and constructivist kind. Gee (1991), one of the leading exponents of NLS, describes a case study of sharing time in US schools as frequently built upon dominant theories of language that the authors cited above are challenging:

> sharing time, as a literacy building activity, is based solidly on ... a myth: the view of language (deeply embedded in our language and our culture) that meaning is something that is packaged in nice little bundles (words and sentences) and conveyed down a little tube-like channel to someone else who simply undoes the package and takes out the morsel of meaning. (p.93)

In contrast to this atomised view of language that corresponds to the *autonomous* model of literacy, Gee poses a view of language that corresponds more closely to the *ideological* model of literacy and to the notion of language as dynamic expressed by writers like Bakhtin, Kress, etc.:

> In fact, language is always something that is actively constructed in a context, physically present or imagined, by both speaker/writer and hearer/reader through a complex process of inferencing that is guided by, but never fully determined by, the structural properties of the language. (*ibid.*)

The implications of this view of language are only just being felt in applied studies (cf. the work and publications of the British Association for Applied Linguistics (BAAL), e.g. Graddol, 1993). With respect to education, and schooling in particular, these perspectives have recently been conveyed through the notion of Critical Language Awareness (Fairclough, 1995), which argues that learners should be facilitated to engage in debates about the nature and meaning of language, rather than be treated as passive victims of its 'structural properties'. This includes learning some metalinguistic terms, but a more inclusive set of such terms, learned for a different purpose, than those often put forward by state institutions, such as the recent TTA proposals for language in the Initial Teacher Training curriculum (TTA, 1997). It is to the basis of these dominant views of language, expressed in popular media and through state institutions, that I now turn, to discuss the implications for research and practice of the new, dialogic and social interpretations of language outlined above.

The implications for research and practice

The implications of this for research and practice are considerable. Both researchers and prac-titioners – and many of the best people in this field do both these days (Cochran-Smith and Lytle, 1993) – acknowledge the fears and desires that come with investigating and reflecting on lan-guage and literacy in these ways: we are not just neutral observers, but social beings already inscribed with culturally influenced manifestations of the deeper fears and desires that influence all human life (see Street, 1997 for a fuller exposition). The fears and desires associated with dialogic and social interpretations of language and literacy have been largely associated with a reactionary and self-interested élite, afraid of the disorder and indiscipline that they associate with such open-ended theorising. It is to these fears and desires that the newspaper headlines about 'illiteracy', 'falling standards' and social breakdown are pandering. But progressive educators have their own fears and desires, built into the process of learning and studying them-selves. The desire to privilege the dialogic, contestable and social nature of language and literacy, to live with diversity, still entails its own struggle: it is the struggle of all Utopian movements, with the order and constraint within which freedom and variation are possible. Utopian desires too are tempered by the reality that social life, including language and literacy practices, is patterned and persistent even amidst its rich diversity.

One way of adjusting this patterning to the flux, ambiguity and uncertainty that our research and our teaching experience honestly tell us we must face when dealing with language and literacy is through theory: to make explicit the theory on which our actions are based, and to follow through the implications of that theory, is to provide for order and authority without descending to authoritarianism. Advocates of the NLS may have felt that their approach has meant going against the grain, challenging dominant 'ways of knowing' (Baker *et al.*, 1996): but it may be that the grain is not simply that of a dominant society with which they can feel romantically in

conflict but that of their own deepest desires and fears. We all have to live with the psychological and social consequences of the new theories.

What, then, are the practical consequences for educationalists of recognising these principles and difficulties? I would like to conclude by spelling out a provisional check list of the principles on which the application of NLS to education in general and to literacy in particular would be based, in the hope of stimulating further debate. Specific proposals for curriculum, pedagogy and assessment would follow:

a) Literacy is more complex than current curriculum and assessment allows.

b) Curricula and assessment that reduce literacy to a few simple and mechanistic skills fail to do justice to the richness and complexity of actual literacy practices in people's lives.

c) If we want learners to develop and enhance the richness and complexity of literacy practices evident in society at large, then we need curricula and assessment that are themselves rich and complex and based upon research into actual literacy practices.

d) In order to develop rich and complex curricula and assessment for literacy, we need models of literacy and of pedagogy that capture the richness and complexity of actual literacy practices.

What teaching methods are appropriate to this new understanding of literacies remains open to debate: there is no necessary one-to-one relationship between a specific theory of literacy and a specific teaching method, although NLS does point in some directions that challenge current orthodoxies. For instance, teaching, whatever form it takes (e.g. whole-class; student-centred; phonics-based; 'real' books) has to be able to take account of the variation in literacy practices amongst students and to give value to their different backgrounds and the different literacies they employ in their home contexts. An emphasis on real uses of literacy and attention to the contexts of use appears more likely to follow from these tenets than a focus on artificial or formal features of supposed universal literacy. From this perspective the issue of standard English is not so much 'for or against' as recognising that the justification needs to be presented to students themselves and that they need to be able to discuss alternative varieties of language use and learn when it is appropriate to use them (cf. Fairclough, 1995), rather than simply reject them altogether from the classroom. This position corresponds to recent work on the role of argument in the science class-room (Driver *et al.*, 1994; Mitchell, 1996), so the issue is not just one for English teachers.

The emphasis from this perspective, then, is on appropriateness, a key concept in the ethno-graphy of communication (cf. Hymes, 1977), rather than on a pure concept of correctness that dominates much formal thinking on language and literacy. The NLS, then, do not eschew the focus on standard or deny the value of grammar and whole-class teaching: they intervene in those debates at a different level than the simple polarities set up in current media representations. Because they are rooted in research as well as practice, NLS imply a teaching method that likewise facilitates for students and teachers alike the development of provisional models that help them to describe, observe and analyse different literacies rather than just learning and teach-ing one literacy as given. In Heath's terms (1983), teachers and students become 'ethnographers', exploring the various meanings and uses of literacy in the social context of the school and its surrounding communities: 'schooled literacy' becomes one amongst many of the literacies with which they engage (Street and Street, 1991).

Recognition of 'the richness and complexity of actual literacy practices' has provided the basis for a number of new approaches to classroom practice, of which I will cite just a few examples from other countries which I hope will elicit responses regarding similar research and develop-ment here. Heath and Mangiola (1991) were commissioned by the National Education Associa-tion in the USA to develop a classroom text that would help teachers address 'the literacy needs of the culturally and linguistically diverse students who now populate our schools'. The resulting text offers detailed case studies of 'successful cross-age tutoring programs' where students who had been failing and dropping out were trained to tutor young elementary students in reading. The dramatic success of such programmes in terms of teacher attitudes and pupil improvement in literacy skills was put forward as a model for teacher research collaboration in the area of language and literacy diversity and it would be fruitful to explore the possibilities of adapting the model to the UK situation.

In South Africa, a recent research project has investigated the everyday literacy practices of people in the Cape area – activists in 'settlements; farm workers; taxi drivers; election officials; elderly township residents' (Prinsloo and Breier, 1996). Using the evidence of variation and complexity, the researchers have argued that the new education framework needs to be loosened at the edges to facilitate entry to those previously denied formal education: for many whose lifelong learning of language and literacy had made them competent communicators, the new formal requirements of bureaucracy and of education are creating marginalisation and 'illiteracy' – as with many Unesco-type Literacy programmes it is often the arrival of the programme itself, with its autonomous model of literacy, that creates the 'illiteracy' about which the media then agonises. The research on everyday literacy practices in this project is now being used as the basis for a new, facilitating curriculum and pedagogy.

Similarly, a current 'Community Literacy' project in Nepal, funded by the Overseas Development Administration (ODA), is proposing to commence with research into actual uses of literacy in different communities as a basis for considering proposals for teaching and learning (Rogers, 1994). Eschewing the traditional dependence on primers – basic text books, frequently uniform across a whole country – the project instead emphasises 'real' materials – the actual texts, whether posters, signposts, labels and wrappers, religious documents, letters, development messages, political propaganda, etc. that constitute the literacy environment. The literacy programme will be based upon proposals by non-governmental organisations (NGOs) for locally based uses of such materials to facilitate learning rather than on a national, uniform primer-based campaign.

In Australia, likewise, tutors and researchers are cooperating to develop literacy courses that build upon local meanings and uses. In one instance (Black and Thorp, 1997) a single literacy class in Sydney, Australia revealed a remarkable complexity of language choices amongst students that presented a significant challenge to tutors: one student from Afghanistan, for instance, switched between Farsi, Pashto, English and Arabic, employing two scripts according to context and function; another spoke five languages, including different dialects of Chinese, and likewise switched between scripts – in this case the roman alphabet and the Chinese logographic – according to situation. A research project in Brisbane, Australia similarly explored the complexity of home and school literacies, in this case focusing more on locality and class than on language and ethnicity (Freebody *et al.*, 1995). A team of researchers funded by the Department of Education studied 'everyday literacy practices in and out of schools in low socio-economic urban communities', observing in close detail the linguistic behaviour around texts both at home and at school in order to establish the relationships between them. Important implications were drawn out for pre-service and in-service programmes, notably attuning teachers more to local literacies and challenging dominant stereotypes about children's ability to learn and use literacy. For the purposes of this article, a major finding that challenges the romantic perception of NLS as simply a way to critique dominant practices is that

> With respect to the home-school relationship, our findings do not lead to any grounds for privileging home versus school literacy practices. Rather they lead to recommendations concerning the more effective mutual recognition of these practices in both sites. (*ibid.*, p. xxii)

These examples suggest a challenge for educators in the UK likewise, where the new theories of language and literacy outlined above have been well understood for over a decade (Brookes and Hudson, 1982). For instance, research into community literacies has been conducted by a team of researchers from Lancaster University and their work has been particularly influential in adult literacy work (Barton and Ivanic, 1991; Barton and Hamilton, 1998). But the combination of ethnographic-style research into everyday literacy practices and constructive curriculum development and pedagogy that is beginning to characterise the adult field in many parts of the world has not, I suspect, penetrated so deeply into the school or into teacher training in the UK. Indeed, the present media and policy representations of literacy have made this harder by drawing upon tropes rooted in less culturally sensitive models of language and literacy. The task, then, appears to be twofold: to challenge the dominant representations of literacy; and to develop collaborative research projects that look at the actual literacy practices of both home and school, with a view, as Freebody (1995) states, to 'effective mutual recognition of these practices in both sites'. For the data thus collected to be fed into teacher training programmes and into curricula and pedagogy requires no little change in dominant representations. If this article has contributed in a small way to such a change, it will have served its purpose.

References

Baker, J., Clay, C. and Fox, C. (eds) (1996) *Challenging Ways of Knowing in English*, Mathematics and Science. London: Falmer Press

Bakhtin, M. (1981) (trans. M. Holquist and C. Emerson) *The Dialogic Imagination*. Austin: University of Texas Press

Barton, D. and Hamilton, M. (1998) *Local Literacies*. Routledge: London

Barton, D. and Ivanic, R. (1991) *Writing in the Community*. London: Sage

Barton, D. and Padmore, S. (1991) 'Roles, networks and values in everyday writing', in *Basic Skills Agency* (1997) International Numeracy Survey. London: Basic Skills Agency (BSA)

Beard, R. (ed.) (1993) *Teaching Literacy: Balancing Perspectives*. London: Hodder and Stoughton

Black, S. and Thorp, K. (1997) *Literacy Practices and Linguistic Choices*. NSW: Northern Sydney Institute of TAFE

Brookes, A. and Hudson, R. (1982) 'Do linguists have anything to say to teachers?', in Carter, R. (ed.) *Linguists and the Teacher*. London: Routledge

Camitta, M. (1993) 'Vernacular writing: varieties of literacy among Philadelphia high school students', in Street, B. (ed.) *Cross-cultural Approaches to Literacy*. Cambridge: Cambridge University Press

Chall, J. (1967) *Learning to Read: the Great Debate*. New York: McGraw Hill

Chall, J. (1983) *Stages of Reading Development*. New York: McGraw Hill

Cochran-Smith, M. and Lytle, S. (1993) *Inside-Outside: Teacher Research and Knowledge*. New York: Teachers College Press

Collins, J. (1995) 'Literacy and literacies', in *Annual Review of Anthropology*, 24, 75-93

Driver, R., Asoko, H., Teach, J., Mortimer, E. and Scott, P. (1994) 'Constructing scientific knowledge in the classroom', in *Educational Researcher*, 23, 7, 5-12

Encyclopaedia of Education. Oxford: Pergamon, 3453-9

Fairclough, N. (ed.) (1995) *Critical Language Awareness*. London: Longman

Fiedrich, M. (1996) *Literacy in Circles?* (Working Paper no.2). London: Action Aid

Freebody, P. et al. (1995) *Everyday Literacy Practices in and out of School in Low Socio-Economic Urban Communities*. Brisbane, Australia: Department of Education

Gee, J. (1991) 'The narrativisation of experience in the oral style', in Mitchell, C. and Weiler, K. (eds) *Rewriting Literacy: Culture and the Discourse of the Other*. New York: Bergin and Garvey, 77-102

Goodman, K. (1996) *Ken Goodman on Reading: A Common-sense Look at the Nature of Language and the Science of Reading*. Ontario, Canada: Scholastic

Graddol, D. (ed.) (1993) *Language and Culture*. Clevedon: Multilingual Matters/BAAL

Halliday, M. (1978) *Language as Social Semiotic*. London: Edward Arnold

Heath, S.B. and Mangiola, L. (1991) Children of Promise: Literate Activity in *'Linguistically and Culturally Diverse Classrooms'*. Washington DC: National Education Association

Heath, S.B. (1983) *Ways with Words*. Cambridge: Cambridge University Press

Hymes, D. (1977) *Foundations in Sociolinguistics*. London: Tavistock

Independent on Sunday (1993) 'Illiterate England', 7 February, p.19

Kress, G. (1996) 'Internationalisation and globalisation: rethinking a curriculum of instruction', in *Comparative Education*, 32, 2, 185-96

Kress, G. (1997) *Before Writing: Rethinking the Paths to Literacy*. London: Routledge

Kress, G. and van Leeuwen, T. (1996) *Reading Images: The Grammar of Visual Design*. London: Routledge

Lea, M. and Street, B. (1997) 'Student writing and faculty feedback in HE: an academic literacies approach' (unpublished MS)

Literacy Across the Curriculum (1997) 'Two different theoretical approaches to literacy and their implications for adult literacy programs', LAC, 12, 3, 4-5

Meek, M. (1991) *On Being Literate*. London: Bodley Head

Mitchell, S. (1996) *Improving the Quality of Argument in Higher Education.* School of Education, Middlesex University Report and Evaluation Series

Nagy, W. and Anderson, R. (1999) 'Metalinguistic awareness and literacy acquisition in different languages', in Wagner, D., Venezky, L. and Street, B. (eds) *Literacy: An International Handbook.*

New London Group (1996) 'A pedagogy of multiliteracies: designing social future', in *Harvard Educational Review,* 66, 1, 60-92

Oakhill, J., Beard, R. and Vincent, D. (eds) (1995) 'The contribution of psychological research', special issue of *Journal of Research in Reading*, 18, 2

Prinsloo, M. and Breier, M. (eds) (1996) *The Social Uses of Literacy.* Amsterdam: J. Benjamins

Rogers, A. *et al.* (1994) *Using Literacy: A New Approach to Post-literacy Materials.* ODA Technical Report

Sola, M. and Bennett, A. (1994) 'The struggle for voice: narrative, literacy and consciousness in an East Harlem school', in Maybin, J. (ed.) *Language and Literacy in Social Practice.* Buckingham: Open University Press

Shuman, A. (1986) *Storytelling Rights: the Uses of Oral and Written Texts by Urban Adolescents.* Cambridge: Cambridge University Press

Street, B. (1984) *Literacy in Theory and Practice.* Cambridge: Cambridge University Press

Street, B. and J. (1991) 'The schooling of literacy', in Barton, D. and Ivanic, R. *Writing in the Community.* London: Sage, 143-66

Street, B. (1993a) *Cross-Cultural Approaches to Literacy.* Cambridge: Cambridge University Press

Street, B. (ed.) (1993b) 'The New Literacy Studies', special issue of Journal of Research in Reading, 16, 2

Street, B. (ed.) (1993c) 'Culture is a verb', in Graddol, D. (ed.) *Language and Culture.* Clevedon: Multingual Matters/ BAAL, 23-43

Street, B. (1995) *Social Literacies: Critical Approaches to Literacy in Development*, Ethnography and Education. London: Longman

Street, B. (1996a) 'Social literacies', in Edwards, V., Corson, D. and Corson V. (eds) *Encyclopaedia of Language and Education.* Netherlands: Kluwer Academic Publishers, 161-86

Street, B. (1996b) Review of International Adult Literacy Survey, in *Literacy across the Curriculum*, 12, 3, Winter, 8-15. Montreal: Centre for Literacy

Street, B. (1996c) 'Academic literacies', in Baker, J., Clay, C. and Fox, C. (eds) *Challenging Ways of Knowing in English, Mathematics and Science.* London: Falmer Press

Street, B. (1997) 'Hobbesian fears and utopian desires: the implications of 'New Literacy Studies' for education' (paper to cross-London seminar in Language and Literacy, King's College London, May,

The Sunday Times (1994) 'The dangers of illiteracy', 10 April, p.10

Unesco (1997) Working Paper for International Workshop on Literacy, *Education and Social Development: the Making of Literate Societies.* Hamburg: Unesco

Villegas, A.M. (1991) *Culturally Responsive Teaching.* Princeton: ETS

Volosinov, V.N. (1973) *Marxism and the Philosophy of Language.* Orlando: Academic Press

Whorf, B. (1959) *Language, Thought and Reality.* Cambridge, Mass.: MIT Press

Willinsky, J. (1990) *The New Literacy: Redefining Reading and Writing in Schools.* London: Routledge

Wray, D. (1997) 'Research into the teaching of reading: a 25-year debate', in Watson, K., Modgill, C. and Modgill, S. (eds) *Education Dilemmas: Debate and Diversity*, Vol.4: 'Quality in Education'. London: Cassell

Recent proposals for literacy in UK schools

Committee for Linguistics in Education (CLIE) (1997) 'Recommendations to the Teacher Training Agency', in BAAL *Newsletter*, 55, Spring, 17-19

Literacy Task Force (LTF) (1997) *A reading revolution: how can we teach every child to read well?* Preliminary report of the LTF published for consultation, February

Teacher Training Agency (TTA) (1997) *Initial Teacher Training: Consultative Document,* February

CHAPTER 7
Local literacies and global literacy
Catherine Wallace

The future of English as a global language seems assured. Although there are other world languages, only English is used transnationally, with a majority of its users now those for whom it is a second language (Graddol, 1999). In response to this expansion, and going against the grain of mainstream values and discourses, many teachers and scholars have wished to defend and valorise the local over the global. Vernacular speech or literacy is set against standard, institutionalised and mainstream language varieties. 'Little' languages are seen like little people as needing to be defended. At the same time, there is a strong implication that the local offers the best means for the expression of 'authentic' identity and political resistance on the part of subordinated groups. In this chapter I wish to challenge some of these assumptions. I want to argue that, as teachers of English, our best response to the global future of English is not resistance to the language which provides us with a living, nor even an apologetic defence, but a rethinking of what *kind* of English best serves the needs of its users for the twenty-first century.

Literacy and literacies

Just as local or indigenous languages are privileged over English in critiques of linguistic imperialism, so local and vernacular literacies are favoured in much of the current work in literacy, particularly the research carried out under the auspices of what has come to be known as the New Literacy Studies. This has investigated not mainstream, institutionalised literacy in languages of high national and international prestige such as English, but local, vernacular literacies. These vernacular literacies may be in languages other than English as documented, for instance, in Martin-Jones and Bhatt (1998). Or they may take place in English but for local, everyday purposes. In each case literacy is seen not as something possessed as a skill but as something done or performed as a contextualised practice (Barton, 1994; Baynham, 1995). Local literacies operate in private domains, such as family life, as opposed to public ones, such as the media and education (Wallace, 1988). The interest in documenting the everyday literacy practices of children and adults is reflected in a number of recent titles, such as *City Literacies* (Gregory and Williams, 2000) and *Local Literacies* (Barton and Hamilton, 1998).

The preference for seeing literacy as context dependent and situationally contingent has led to the now widely preferred pluralisation of literacy. Gee (1990: 153) claims: 'Literacy is always plural.' Rather than a single monolithic literacy we have multiple literacies: school sanctioned literacy becomes just 'one of a multiplicity of *literacies* which take place in people's lives, in different languages, in different domains and for a variety of purposes' (Gregory and Williams, 2000: 11). The challenge to an overarching, universal literacy came originally from Brian Street

* First published in D. Block and D. Cameron (Eds) (2002) *Globalisation and Language Teaching*, London: Routledge.

in his influential book *Literacy in Theory and Practice* (Street, 1984). This first proposed a difference between not literacies as such but two major conceptualisations of literacy: *autonomous* and *ideological* literacy – autonomous suggesting that one is talking of a universal skill or aptitude, being able to read and write; to combat this technicist, skills-based view of literacy the ideological view has it that literacy is a social construct, taking on complex cultural and ideological meanings and diverse forms in specific settings. Hence the widely preferred plural form.

Street's original characterisation was a powerful one. It offered an important challenge to a hitherto exclusively Western understanding of literacy, as well as developing an awareness of cross-cultural differences in literacy practices, which Gregory and Williams (2000) draw on in their account of culturally distinctive literacy practices of language minority children and the implications for schooling in the mainstream. However, the continuing preference for conceptualising literacy both as plural and as broadly autonomous or ideological in orientation, presents several problems. First, the emphasis on the multiple character of literacies may trivialise and relativise their significance; there is a danger that in emphasising parity we may fail to acknowledge those power relations which are so strongly associated with certain literacies, as opposed to others, most evidently school literacy. Certainly, power is a central theme in New Literacy Studies discourse, but the implications are not clearly followed through. For instance, does school sanctioned literacy, often linked to English, offer perceived or real advantages? Is its power merely symbolic? Moreover, the emphasis on discreteness in statements such as: 'Practices each require different skills ... learned in different ways' (Gregory and Williams, 2000: 9) leads one to wonder how far this knowledge has the potential to cross boundaries, how far it might be put to productive use in a range of settings, including school. Indeed in many of the ethnographic studies, though Gregory and Williams's book is a notable exception, educational or school literacy gets scant mention.

Finally, the autonomous/ideological characterisation has led to a tendency to see autonomous literacy as necessarily and exclusively represented in educational contexts. Street and Street (1995), for instance, appear to equate schooled literacy with autonomous literacy. It is taken for granted that schooled literacy in the sense of classroom literacy instruction is constructed and practised largely as neutral technology, with reading 'taught as a set of skills which can be broken into parts and taught and tested' (Barton, 1994: 162). Certainly much of the discourse in recent documents such as the British National Literacy Strategy seems to favour a view of literacy as involving the unproblematic teaching of skills, with little contextualisation of practice, and little acknowledgement in the case of bilingual learners that they may have distinctly different literacy experiences and different language repertoires, including understandings gained from knowledge of the vernacular or home language. However, schooling does not need to be interpreted in this manner. It is not that teaching and learning decontextualises so much as it, in Bernstein's (1996) terms, *re*contextualises, reshaping everyday experiences and knowledge. Although school and home are different domains, it is not the case that school focuses necessarily on skills-based work and out of school contexts on more creative, more 'authentic' activities. There is a danger of' taking a romantic, over-celebratory attitude to contingent, everyday and out-of-school literacies; after all, in many out-of-school cultural contexts literacy will be perceived as the learning of skills or routines of the 'listen, learn, and repeat' kind, documented as one literacy practice of three Roadville parents in Heath's (1983) study of the literacy practices of three communities in the United States. At the same time school literacy practices can be misrepresented as inevitably and inherently mechanistic. The job of educators is to acknowledge the differences, to build bridges between the domains of school and everyday life, but not necessarily by privileging the primary literacies of learners, nor by taking a narrow view of school literacy as skills-based.

Notions of primary and secondary kinds of knowledge, experience and identity are suggested by Gee's (1990) characterisation of primary and secondary Discourses, where he uses the term Discourse to mean 'ways of being in the world' – that is, more than just language, but ways of displaying membership of a particular social group. Schooling is a Secondary Discourse, as opposed to the Primary Discourse of early social settings. As children move from home to school they move from familiar domestic worlds which are part of their primary socialisation to take on other identities, ways of behaving and ways of using language. Literacy is part of this. As Gee (1990: 153) puts it: 'Literacy is mastery of, or fluent control over, a Secondary Discourse.'

Halliday (1996:353) characterises this shift less in terms of identity than of knowledge: he describes the difference between everyday life and school as being between what he calls primary and secondary knowledge: the latter is more heterogeneously constituted and specific to educational settings. Similarly, Bernstein (1996) talks of vertical and horizontal literacies. The latter are segmental and embedded in ongoing practices and directed to specific goals, and are often acquired through apprenticeship. It is these local and contingent literacies which have been investigated ethnographically in the studies described earlier. Vertical discourse and its associated literacy is scaffolded in schools and learned rather than acquired or picked up on the job. It is not that school literacies are inferior attempts at 'the real thing' (cf. Street and Street, 1995: 106) – they are qualitatively different. Schooled language, which is literate-like rather than necessarily delivered through the medium of print, is, as I argue more fully later in this chapter, a code for learning and for wider communication rather than for day-to-day use. Nor is it the case that primary knowledge, including, most importantly, knowledge of home languages and literacies, is to be discarded; rather it is rearticulated among a greater diversity of voices and experiences, which accompany the move into secondary socialisation. It takes on some of the characteristics of written language; it is 'construed out of the dialectic between the spoken and the written' (Halliday, 1996: 353). Cummins and Swain (1986) make a similar point in talking about the shift from embedded, primarily oral language towards disembedded, written or literate-like language that educational development in school represents. The question then arises as to how one supports the entry of learners who are skilled in vernacular literacies into the more elaborated, vertical discourse required for success in school or other educational settings. For language minority children, moreover, this shift or switch may involve not just a new language variety but a new language code, frequently English.

A further difficulty with the major focus in the New Literacy Studies on practice and practices in non-school settings is a relative neglect of process and processing. This is partly because of a wish to diversify literacy not merely in terms of domains but also in terms of media. An important point of difference between Gee and Halliday, for instance is that Gee does not wish to privilege print over other kinds of technologies. Therefore the linear processing unique to print is of less interest. Halliday, however, takes the view, which I follow here, that the specific features of print literacy offer particular educational advantages:

> The written world is a world of things. Its symbols are things, its texts are things and its grammar constructs a discourse of things, with which readers and writers construe experience. Or rather, with which they reconstrue experience, because all have been speakers

and listeners first, so that the written world is their secondary socialisation. This is critical for our understanding of the educational experience ... the language of the school is written language. (Halliday, 1996: 353)

It will be seen that Halliday continues to use the terms 'readers' and 'writers' in orthodox ways, to refer to the interpreters or producers of continuous print texts. There has been a diminished interest, in much of the social and anthropological literacy literature at least, in print literacy. *Reading* is not included in the glossary to an influential new collection of papers on literacy, *Multiliteracies* (Cope and Kalantzis, 2000). And yet social subjects in a common-sense way continue to see themselves as readers and writers, and to value skill in these activities. Print is still the medium we mainly deal with, albeit in different forms – email and hypertext being the most obvious ones. And for many language minorities in Britain whose primary socialisation will be in their home, community language, the written world of secondary socialisation is in English.

Literate English and critical literacy

I want to push the case for literacy further by arguing not just for the unique role of print literacy, but also for the value of sustained engagement with written text; to claim, moreover, unpalatable though it may be in a relativist age, that some texts are more linguistically and cognitively challenging than others, and that it is particularly important that such texts should be made available in English to a wide range of students. For foreign and second language learners that means access not so much to the oral everyday English favoured by many contemporary teaching approaches but to English language literacy.

Nakata, writing from a postcolonial perspective, comments thus on the demand for English literacy on the part of Torres Strait Islanders:

At present when Islanders call for English literacy we are told we need literacy in one of our traditional languages first. Why do we need to read and write in our first language which is after all still a robust oral tradition? Simply because it works in French Canada! This standpoint assumes that learning English at school cancels out children's previously acquired and ongoing acquisition of their first language competencies and communicative patterns. (Nakata, 2000: 112)

Nakata's point here about the vitality of local languages echoes Halliday's about a distinctive 'written world of secondary socialisation' which is not threatening to the mainly oral world of primary socialisation. It also meshes with the argument made by Joseph Bisong (1995) who proclaims the ethnolinguistic vitality of Nigeria's indigenous languages, which are not threatened, he claims, by English, because of the differing functions which local and global languages fulfil.

I would wish to extend the scope of Nakata's point to include not just English literacy but *literate English*, meaning the *kind* of English (which may also be spoken) most like formal written English such as we encounter in broadsheet newspapers, quality novels and non-fiction texts. It is important to say what I am not talking about here: I am *not* talking about standard or of native speaker English. It is irrelevant for my argument here that one can, often only with some effort, identify a speaker as Russian or Danish or Ghanaian. Indeed the still ongoing debate on what kind of English to teach in terms of say British or American – or Nigerian or Singaporean – now seems a rather arid one, because the kind of English we admire for its elegance and eloquence is frequently not produced by those whose first language it is. It is a supranational global English which does not necessarily emanate in any direct way from the centre, as suggested in over-polarised accounts of centre versus periphery English; it will clearly demonstrate a whole range of functions but as a Secondary Discourse it is most powerful when used discursively rather than experientially. In the terms used by Habermas (1979) it is *constative speech* in that it carries with it obligations to provide grounds for what is said. Transnational English will need not to be reduced or simplified, as some accounts of its role as a lingua franca seem to suggest, but on the contrary to be elaborated to take account both of its likely expository function in formal settings, and of the reduction in shared world knowledge that is associated with transcultural exchanges.

Apart from its role in argument, 'literate English' is valuable in talk for learning in classrooms. Clegg (1992) drawing on the work of Gordon Wells, calls this *literate talk* – not just for content learning but for learning more about language itself, testing the limits, especially for L2 learners, of what they can do with their language. As Clegg (1992: 17) puts it, this involves students 'try-ing to get a foothold in new cognitive territory'. Literate talk – or literate English, defined to in-clude oral and written language – is language which is not spontaneous but planned. It is more elaborated than informal speech, makes explicit its grounds and provides a useful bridge into expository written language. It is talk which is exploratory, where 'partners engage critically but constructively with each other's ideas' (cf. Mercer, 1996), as opposed to the spontaneous and fluent speech which tends to be favoured in the foreign and second language classroom. More-over it is not just in structure that the language is more complex, which may after all be a matter of empty elaboration, of mere verbiage, as Labov (1972) pointed out in his well-known defence of the logic of non-standard English. For this reason a term used by Granville *et al.* (1998) is helpful. They talk of the need for an 'enriched English', in the process of making a case for the role of good quality English teaching as subject (rather than medium) in post-apartheid South Africa. A pedagogy for an 'enriched' English will clearly need to attend to the complex manner in which structure, content and function inter-relate in the production of effective, literate English.

It should be emphasised that there is nothing inherent in English as a *language* which makes it more suitable than any other language for this role. As Granville *et al.* point out, it is rather that English has developed extensive resources as a result of its dominance across many domains of use. It is English, with its global reach, which is likely to take on public functions as opposed to the private and solidary functions of vernacular languages and literacies. Elaborated to fulfil this role, literate English, for both centre and periphery users, faces outwards rather than inwards. As Nakata (2000: 112) says with reference to the Torres Strait Islanders: 'An English education will enable us to negotiate our position in relation to these outside influences' – but the point has wider implications

To summarise, I want to defend the position of global literate English as what Chew (1999) calls 'an international auxiliary language'. The kind of English serving this function will not neces-sarily be standard in form. There will inevitably be, usually minor, regional variations phono-logically, lexically and syntactically, but functionally it will be elaborated to serve global needs, the most crucial one, as argued later in this chapter, being as a tool for resistance.

Global English will inevitably be differently inflected in different contexts. Language minority children in English medium schools will draw on different resources and have different im-mediate needs from adult EFL learners. But the commonalities will be more significant than the differences. Literate English is part of vertical rather than horizontal discourse. While local languages and literacies tend to serve horizontal, contingent and solidary functions, global English spans a wider range of contexts, and has universal applicability and resonance.

The value of the studies done by literacy ethnographers is not in doubt; teachers need an understanding of the full range of students' identities and languages. However, our business as language educators is ultimately with the wider picture, with forms of language which have currency beyond the particular and contingent, which will prepare our students for the unpredictable futures of the era of fast capitalism; which will offer tools to resist not English itself but meanings which are frequently conveyed through English, often via powerful genres such as news and advertising and, as evidenced by its position as a major export industry for Britain, the English Language Teaching global textbook (see Gray, 2002).

Pennycook (1994) acknowledges a 'writing back' role for English, whereby English is refashioned to serve the aesthetic and political purposes, particularly in postcolonial contexts, of new generations of users. These new users participate in the dismantling of the colonial legacy of English. This is also the spirit of Pierce's (1989) proposal, writing in the context of South Africa, by which the citizens of post-apartheid South Africa opt not for the replacement of English as a lingua franca by an indigenous language, but for a new kind of English – Pierce calls it 'people's English' – inflected with different kinds of meanings. The principle that one can draw variously on the resources of a single language, reshaping the discourses which have established its hegemony, is very much linked to critical discourse analysis and critical literacy, which I turn to next.

If *literacy* and *global* are terms fraught with difficulty then so is the term *critical* in general and *critical literacy* in particular. A major figure in critical literacy studies was Paulo Freire (1972), who saw the power of literacy as a way of reflecting back to learners their own lived experience, not in a direct and immediate way but systematised and amplified through dialogue, as part of the educational process. What critical educators who follow a broadly Freirean ideology share, is a belief in the empowering potential of literacy, a potential which is articulated in different ways: for Lankshear *et al.* (1997) critical literacy is powerful to the extent that it offers a vantage point from which to survey other literacies. It achieves this through acting as a secondary Discourse in Gee's terms and thereby providing a metalanguage, a language to talk about not just literacy itself, as a form of social and cultural practice, but about features of texts and aspects of the reading and writing process. Critical reading involves gaining some distance on our own production and reception of texts; we are not just involved in an ongoing way in these as we process or interpret texts but we also take the opportunity to reflect on the social circumstances of their production, on why they come to us in the form they do, and on the variable ways their meanings may be received in different cultural contexts. Thus, in gaining a degree of distance on what we typically take for granted, we may become aware of what other discourses might replace the ones actually present; how else might this text have been written? At the same time, we are encouraged to ask what other ways there are of reading a text beyond our own currently preferred one, or that favoured by the writer.

The ability to engage in this level of critical analysis is not easily achieved. It will elude many native speakers of a language. However, the indisputable power of English as a global language necessitates a high level of critical literate English if it is to serve the 'writing back' or 'talking back' role of resistance. This is not provided by an instructional *lingua franca* model of English which restricts communication to immediate, utilitarian contexts. Edward Said, when visiting a

Persian Gulf university in 1985, observed that students following the English programme proposed to end up working for airlines or banks in which English was the lingua franca. This view...

> all but terminally consigned English to the level of a technical language stripped of expressive and aesthetic characteristics and denuded of any critical or self-conscious dimension. You learned English to use computers, respond to orders, transmit telexes, decipher manifests and so forth. That was all. (Said, 1994: 369)

Global English teaching and the ELT Profession

I have proposed that English language teaching, like globalisation itself, does not need to be seen to bring only negative consequences. This is not to deny that English language teaching agencies, in particular some international publishers, have sometimes quite explicitly taken a market view of English language teaching as a commodity. There is some justification for the view expressed by Phillipson and Skuttnab Kangas (1999) that Eastern Europe has become the new postcolonial world (Gray, 2002). Asked to comment on recent English language teaching projects in Eastern and Central Europe, Widdowson talks of there being 'rather too much of people coming in from outside 'bringing in the good news' with scant knowledge of local traditions of scholarship and education' (Widdowson, quoted in Thomas, 1999: 125). However, our resistance as language teachers need not be to the teaching of the language itself so much as to the grosser kinds of cultural and linguistic imperialism which continues to characterise some ELT discourse and practices. The reductive thrust of this, as argued above, fails to make available to learners an English which can serve the writing back or talking back function of critique. The answer, however, is not to throw in the towel but to do the job better, whether as language teachers or as teacher educators.

If we accept the need to deal with the realities of the globalisation of English in the broad ways outlined above, what more specific implications arise in terms of the kinds of second language learners we teach in different contexts and the way we might draw on, adapt or reject prevailing methodologies and materials?

One effect of a general ideological preference for specificity and localisation is the identification of subgroups of learners, the development of specific competences of the kind noted by Said, and a consequent proliferation of specialist fields in English Language Teaching: ESP, EAP and, particularly in British ELT discourse, the long-standing division between EFL and ESL. While the EFL/ESL divide makes sense in school contexts, where children of immigrant or refugee families are receiving their schooling through the medium of English rather than learning it as a subject in the curriculum, in some adult learning contexts in Britain the value of the distinction is more dubious. It is based on outdated and essentialist assumptions that there are two clearly defined groups: One being short-stay students, mainly from European countries, and the second, refugees or asylum seekers who are judged to have different educational needs, even though these same students may in an earlier era have found themselves in the EFL 'European' group. In a recent study of one London Further Education college, Cooke (2000) found that the so-called ESL learners are currently likely to be asylum seekers or refugees from many parts of the world. They are assumed, in many instances quite wrongly, to have low educational levels and consequently judged to have literacy problems. Moreover, their supposed literacy needs are addressed with competence-based instruction and assessment, a clear example of Street's autonomous literacy pedagogy at work. The EFL 'European' group in the same college study with a standard global textbook, which is reductive in a different way, offering what we might call the three Ds view of consumerist EFL culture, *dinner parties, dieting* and *dating*, and reflecting the preoccupations of the textbook writers rather than their likely readers. Indeed, as Gray (2002) also notes, one of the ironies of the so-called global textbook is its typically narrow and parochial discourse. Consequently neither the group designated EFL nor that designated ESL is offered quality English language teaching provision, which, I am arguing here, is educationally demanding, rooted in literate language and designed to prepare students for longer term and relatively unpredictable needs as continuing learners and users of English.

In overseas contexts learners may be in EFL settings or in postcolonial periphery settings. Canagarajah (1999) documents the bizarre situation in which learners in Sri Lanka are, in the guise of following communicative approaches, frequently working with old texts long abandoned in centre contexts, and which even in their heyday were gross caricatures of the ways of life they claimed to represent. Canagarajah (1999: 87) notes: 'What we cannot tell is whether the authors and publishers of [American Kernel Lessons] and similar courses understand how little relation their subliminal messages bear to the life of students and teachers in periphery contexts'. One could add that these messages bear little or no relation to the lives of anyone anywhere. In the next section 1 take a closer look at how far contemporary favoured methodologies are able to offer access to global literate English of the kind argued for here.

In ESL school contexts literacy and literate talk have received more attention than in typical adult ESL and EFL contexts. Clegg (1996:3) makes a plea for other than merely narrowly defined linguistic goals in the education of ESL children. 'The main point of their learning English as an additional language is so that they can use it for their cognitive, academic and curricular development'. However, in many English language teaching contexts favoured methodologies take a more restricted view of communicative ability. These methods or approaches cluster under the broad umbrella of communicative language teaching (CLT). CLT has been under attack for some time on the grounds that – as interpreted in actual ELT materials if not applied linguistics texts – the goal tends to be talk for its own sake; simply talking is enough, and it is immaterial *what* you talk about. Pennycook (1994: 311) refers to the phenomenon as the 'empty babble of the communicative language class'.

In spite of the recent challenge by Pennycook, and others such as Cope and Kalantzis (1993) who also question the dominant progressivist ideology, versions of communicative language teaching are still not seriously challenged, in particular the premise that the goal of language teaching is to enable communication with native speakers in natural, everyday environments. This resonates with the emphasis in the New Literacy Studies described earlier: everyday, lived experience is perceived as more legitimate or authentic than what Gee (1990) has called 'contrived educational settings'. As I note in Wallace (2001: 213) educational settings are *necessarily* contrived; it is the job of teachers to contrive situations for learning. The teacher's skill is demonstrated though the manner in which the classroom can offer learning opportunities not readily available in everyday life situations. Admittedly this goal becomes obscured in some progressivist language teaching methodologies. A major one is Task Based Learning, for some time now the most popular methodological offshoot of CLT. Like CLT, it is also experientially grounded in the everyday worlds of learners and concerned with the achievement of immediate outcomes, such as solving a problem or carrying out instructions. It is, claims Kramsch (1995: 48) 'characterised by its local treatment of local problems through local solutions'.

We need, in short, to question the contribution of Communicative Language Teaching and Task Based Learning to the development of what I have called literate English, in so far as both prepare learners to deal with small-scale, day-to-day encounters between friends or intimates in familiar settings such as at parties, school or the workplace, or to engage in everyday trans-actions. We might expect to have moved right away from the following objective for EFL pro-grammes offered by Van Ek, with reference to the Threshold Syllabus of the 1970s, which nonetheless continues to inform much current methodology and materials: 'the learners will be able to survive (linguistically speaking) in temporary contacts with foreign language speakers in everyday situations whether as visitors to the foreign country or with visitors to their own' (Van Ek, 1976: 24-5).

What might alternatives to CLT or TBLT look like? What are feasible ways of promoting a global critical literacy through the medium of English? What options are available to those who do not wish merely to translate the shallow preoccupations of British and American popular culture on to the world stage? Several scholars, most notably Pennycook (1994) and Canagarajah (1999), have proposed critical pedagogy as a necessary underpinning to any English Language Teaching project which wishes to address the global reach of English. However, there are different inter-pretations of critical pedagogy. Some emphasise humanistic learner-centredness (e.g. Kanpol, 1994). Others acknowledge the dangers of a romantic over-celebratory approach to the validation of learners' experiences: 'we must resist the somewhat misleading tendency in critical peda-gogical circles to romanticise student opposition and minority discourses as being always libera-tory and progressive' (Canagarajah, 1999: 97). Nonetheless Canagarajah is learner-centred to the extent that he supports the need for teachers to 'unravel the hidden cultures of their classrooms and students' (Canagarajah, 1999: 193), and believes 'that pedagogies of resistance need to be rooted in the everyday life of our students' (1999:194). I take a different view: that we should acknowledge and respect but not appropriate or incorporate the underlife, as Canagarajah calls it, of our students; that it is not our role to nurture those sites; that the concerns of teachers should be less with personal or local empowerment than with a longer-term challenge to social inequity in a wider sense (Wallace, 1999).

Practically, such a critical pedagogy involves addressing issues which may resonate locally but which have global implications; in terms more specifically of *language* teaching, it means developing literate English as a priority. This is not an imposition from the centre; it requires not the acquiescence of subordinated groups but their participation, if English is to be constantly re-created to serve emancipatory rather than oppressive goals. An attenuated, reduced English can-not serve this purpose. Literate English is also creatively more flexible than the restricted, horizontally embedded English of CLT. In other words the critical and creative use of English which Canagarajah rightly calls for is the end point rather than the starting point of critical peda-gogy.

A key factor in the students' progress to critique and creativity by way of literate English is their ability and willingness to resist. Canagarajah (1999: 182) notes the necessary role for reflective resistance in view of his observation of the 'largely non-reflective' ways in which students 'display their strategies of linguistic appropriation'. This relates to a distinction first made by Giroux (1983) between *opposition* and *resistance*. Opposition can be seen as an instinctive, un-reflected upon response to domination; resistance as a considered, reflected upon, rational stance, where earlier instinctive responses have been subjected to analysis.

The goal then is to lead students from opposition to resistance, from knee-jerk hostile response to reflective, considered judgement. For Canagarajah the route is pluralised English, which he sees as 'standard grammars and established discourses being infused with diverse alternate grammars and conventions from periphery languages' (1999: 175). My proposal favours not pluralism but universality. I would argue, reconfiguring the role of hybridity and pluralisation, that vernacular codes, which will be in local varieties and languages, possibly not written, not elaborated – to serve wider needs, will be multiple and shifting, while English as a global literate language will expressly serve the purpose of embracing a range of settings; it requires greater stability as a 'syncretic' language, to take a term used by Searle (1983), that binds diverse periphery and centre communities together. Once this is established, as noted above, it can be put to critical and creative use, challenging and dismantling the hegemony of English in its conventional forms and uses.

To turn instinct into reflectiveness, opposition into resistance, means forging English as a critical analytical tool which is elaborated to serve those purposes. In terms of currently favoured teaching methodologies, it means a radical rethinking of both Communicative Language Teaching and Task Based Learning, at least as both of these tend to be translated into current teaching material. It means teaching a kind of language which is not for immediate use, not to be taken out into the streets and the clubs, but which can serve longer-term needs.

The proposal I want to consider here, necessarily briefly, centres around print literacy and literate talk and comes broadly under the auspices of Critical Language Awareness (e.g. Fairclough, 1992). The purpose of Critical Language Awareness is to make language itself the object of critical scrutiny – both language as social practice and language as social process, evidenced in the reading and writing of texts. In the course of learning about these social practices and processes learners are made aware of how language might be differently shaped to meet needs beyond those which are closest and most familiar to them. Practically speaking in the classroom this involves the provision of a wide range of text genres, frameworks for analysis and opportunities for talk around text (Wallace, 1992).

The teacher may start with analysis of texts brought into the classroom by herself or the students; however, ultimately the aim is to encourage students to respond to texts within wider contexts of use. This means being aware of the placing and meaning of texts in a range of settings beyond the classroom. The text is necessarily recontextualised within the classroom and takes on cultural meaning by being brought into a pedagogic setting by students or teachers. Canagarajah (1999) describes the way commercial English language texts can be appropriated by students to their own ends. But *any* text, designed as pedagogic or coming from an everyday source, can be made use of in a range of ways within the classroom. Indeed the point of critical language study is to read texts in different ways, to subject everyday texts to other than everyday readings. An example of the kind of response I have in mind occurs in this 'think aloud' reading of an article about Singapore by a Japanese student of mine on a Critical Reading course, as she reacts to the way in which oriental people are exoticised in popular news and magazine articles: 'I don't like this article so much because I think in this kind of text generally speaking I think the British people, and other European people, seem like they are looking at Far Eastern people in some different way – as if looking at some complete strangers, like people who's mad or who act beyond their comprehension.'

We are familiar with the idea of 'text as linguistic object', in English Language Teaching, where texts are gutted for linguistic structure. Indeed much reading instruction has traditionally taken this form. We can equally see texts as *cultural* objects or artefacts in the sense that they embody the values and belief systems of the societies and communities from which they arise, as my student observed in the case of the text about Singapore. Moreover, it is clearly advantageous to examine not just texts in standard English but in a range of forms, genres and discourses. In particular it is revealing to look at texts across linguistic and cultural boundaries, for instance at the way genres are interpreted in different cultural settings. This macro awareness of texts can then be refined by more micro analysis of specific linguistic and discoursal selections of the kind promoted in Critical Discourse Analysis (CDA) approaches (cf. Wallace, 1992).

Critical literacy and literate talk are mutually reinforcing in the sense that talk around texts offers opportunities to check out our own preferred readings against those of others. Such talk also creates the occasion for multiple interpretations of texts, each of which can be argued through, defended, modified or abandoned in discussion with others. This is when literate talk is both put to work but also is enhanced in the course of critique. It is talk which is literate in the sense that, as I noted earlier, like formal modes of writing it makes its case explicit and the grounds for claims are open to scrutiny by others. In this sense it is constative in Habermas's (1979) terms. It involves not talk as social action, doing things with words, which has prevailed in the foreign language classroom, but 'the acquisition and development of more complex conceptual structures and cognitive processes' (Wells and Chang-Wells, 1992: 55).

In the CLA classroom students are encouraged to deploy literate talk in critiquing a range of texts. One way of doing this is to offer opportunities for students to first rehearse in small group discussion their contributions to subsequent public debate, where views are shared and reconsidered in a wider forum, thus allowing space for more extended, planned discourse than is usually available to students in communicative language classrooms, where short-burst informal talk is privileged. It will be argued that foreign language learners have these abilities well developed from their first language. This is often true. However, such learners then welcome the opportunity, denied them in most language classrooms, to exercise their discursive abilities at the same time as developing literate English.

Conclusion

My defence is not of English but of a particular kind of literate English. This more widely contextualised form of English, often in written form but also used in formal spoken contexts, coexists with vernacular literacies, with each occupying distinct domains. For its users, literate English offers a form of secondary socialisation into the world of global English. We need to ensure that this world is not exclusively represented by the Murdoch press or CNN or the commodified worldview of the ELT textbook; but that learners of English as a foreign and second language can participate in its critique and recreation. Modes of resistance to English are available through English, but a critically nuanced literate English. We resist global tyranny with global means. For today's world we might reverse Van Ek's counsel of twenty-five years ago to say that the need today is to help our learners to deal with 'ongoing contacts with a world community of intellectuals, most of whom will not be native speakers of English, in the public arena beyond the national boundaries either of their own country or any other, English speaking one'.

References

Bakhtin, M. (1986) *Speech Genres and Other Late Essays*, C. Emerson and M. Holquist (eds), trans. V W McGee, Austin: University of Texas Press.

Barton D. (1 994) *Literacy: An Introduction to the Ecology of Written Language*, Cambridge: Blackwell.

Barton, D. and Hamilton, M. (1998) *Local Literacies*, London: Routledge.

Baynham, M. (1995) *Literacy Practices*, London: Longman.

Bernstein, B. (1996) *Pedagogy Symbolic Control and Identity,* London: Taylor and Francis.

Bisong, J. (1995) 'Language choice and imperialism: a Nigerian perspective', *ELT Journal* 49, 2: 122-32.

Canagarajah, A.S. (1999) *Resisting Linguistic Imperialism in English Teaching*, Oxford: Oxford University Press.

Chew. P. C. (1999) 'Linguistic imperialism, globalism and the English language', in D. Graddol and U. Meinhof (eds) *English in a Changing World*, Guildford: AILA.

Clegg, J. (1992) 'The cognitive value of literate talk in small-group classroom discourse', *Thames Valley Working Papers* 1:1-22.

Clegg, J. (ed.) (1996) *Introduction in Mainstreaming ESL: Case studies in Integrating ESL Students into the Mainstream Curriculum*, Clevedon: Multilingual Matters.

Cooke, M. (2000) 'Wasted opportunities: a case study of two ESOL programmes in a Further Education College in central London', unpublished MA dissertation, Institute of Education, University of London.

Cope, B. and Kalantzis, M. (1993) *Cultures of Schooling: Pedagogies of Cultural Difference and Social Access,* Basingstoke: Falmer Press.

Cope, B. and Kalantzis, M. (eds) (2000) *Multiliteracies: Literacy Learning and the Design of Social Futures*, London: Routledge.

Cummins, J. and Swain, M. (1986) *Bilingualism in Education*, London: Longman.

Fairclough, N. (1992) *Discourse and Social Change*, Cambridge: Polity Press.

Fairclough, N. (1995) *Critical Discourse Analysis,* London: Longman.

Freire, P. (1972) *The Pedagogy of the Oppressed*, London: Penguin.

Gee, J. (1990) Social Linguistics and Literacies: Ideology in Disco urses, Basingstoke: Falmer Press. Gee, J. P, Hull, C. and Lankshear, C. (1996) *The New Work Order: Behind the Language of the New Capitalism*, Boulder, CO: Westview Press.

Giroux, H. (1983) 'Theory of reproduction and resistance in the new sociology of education: a critical analysis', *Harvard Educational Review* 3, 53: 257-93.

Giroux, H. (1992) *Border Crossings: Cultural Workers and the Politics of Education*, New York: Routledge.

Graddol, D (1999) 'The decline of the native speaker', in D. Graddol and U. Meinhof (eds) *English in a Changing World,* Guildford: AILA.

Granville, S., Janks, H., Mphahlele, M., Reed, Y., Watson P, Joseph M. and Ramani, E., (1998) 'English with or without g(u)ilt: a position paper on Language in Education Policy for South Africa', *Language and Educational Development* 12, 4: 254-72.

Gray, J. (2002) The Global Coursebook in English Language Teaching in D. Block and D. Cameron (eds) *Globalisation and language teaching*, London: Routledge.

Gregory, E. and Williams, A. (2000) *City Literacies: Learning to Read across Generations and Cultures*, London: Routledge.

Habermas, J. (1979) *Communication and the Evolution of Society*, London: Heinemann.

Halliday, M. A. K. (1996) 'Literacy and linguistics: a functional perspective', in R. Hasan and C. Williams (eds) *Literacy in Society,* London: Longman.

Heath, S. B. (1983) *Ways with Words*, Cambridge: Cambridge University Press.

Kanpol, B. (1994) *Critical Pedagogy: An Introduction*, London: Bergin and Garvey.

Kramsch, C. (1995) 'The applied linguist and the foreign language teacher: can they talk to each other?', in G. Cook and B. Seidlhofer (eds) *Principle and Practice in Applied Linguistics*, Oxford: Oxford University Press.

Labov, W. (1972) 'The logic of non-standard English', in P. P. Giglioli (ed.) *Language and Social Context*, Harmondsworth: Penguin.

Lankshear, C., Gee, J.P., Knoebel, M. and Searle, C. (1997) *Changing Literacies*, Buckingham: Open University Press.

Martin-Jones, M. and Bhatt, A. (1998) 'Literacies in the lives of young Gujerati speakers in Leicester', in A. Durgunoglu and L. Verhoeven (eds) *Literacy Development in a Multilingual Context: Cross-cultural Perspectives*, Mahwah, NJ: Lawrence Erlbaum.

Mercer, N. (1996) 'Language and the guided construction of knowledge', in G. Blue and R. Mitchell (eds) *Language and Education*, Clevedon: Multilingual Matters/BAAL.

Nakata, M. (2000) 'History, cultural diversity and English language teaching', in B. Cope and M. Kalantzis (eds) *Multiliteracies: Literacy Learning and the Design of Social Futures*, London: Routledge, pp. 106-20.

Pennycook, A. (1994) *The Cultural Politics of English as an International Language,* London: Longman.

Pennycook, A. (1998) *English and the Discourses of Colonialism*, London: Routledge.

Phillipson, R. and Skuttnab-Kangas, T. (1999) 'Englishisation: one dimension of globalisation', in D. Graddol and U. Meinhof (eds) *English in a Changing World*, Guildford: AILA.

Pierce, B. N. (1989) 'Toward a pedagogy of the possible in the teaching of English internationally: people's English in South Africa', *TESOL Quarterly*, 23,3: 401-20.

Said, E. (1994) *Culture and Imperialism*, London: Vintage.

Searle, C. (1983) 'A common language', *Race and Class* 25, 2: 65-74.

Street, B. (1984) *Literacy in Theory crnd Practice*, Cambridge: Cambridge University Press.

Street, B. and Street, J. (1995) *The Schooling ofLiteracy in Social Literacies,* Longman: London.

Thomas, D. (1999) 'Culture, ideology and educational change: the case of English language teachers in Slovakia', unpublished PhD thesis, Institute of Education, University of London.

Van Ek, J. A. (1976) *Significance of the Threshold Level in the Early Teaching of Modern Languages*, Strasbourg: The Council of Europe

Wallace, C. (1988) *Learning to Read in a Multicultural Society: the Social Context of Second Language Literacy*, Hemel Hempstead: Prentice-H [all.

Wallace, C. (1992) 'Critical literacy awareness in the EFL classroom', in N. Fairclough (ed.) *Critical Language Awareness*, London: Longman.

Wallace, C. (1999) 'Critical language awareness: key principles for a course in critical reading', *Language Awareness* 8, 2: 98- 110.

Wallace, C. (2001) 'Critical literacy in the second language classroom: power and control', in B. Comber and A. Simpson (eds) *Negotiating Critical Literacies in Classrooms*. Mahwah, NJ: Lawrence Erlbaun.

Wells, G. and Chang-Wells, G. L. (1992) *Constructing Knowledge Together: Classrooms as Centers of lnquiry and Literacy*, Portsmouth NIH: Heinemann.

Chapter 8

Investigating family literacy histories and children's reading practices in London's East End

Eve Gregory and Ann Williams

Introduction

The teacher goes over to where Shuma sits and says 'Choose one of these books. Quietly read through the book. If you don't know a word, write it down.' She points to the book as she repeats, 'Write the words down. OK?' The child nods...

Shuma has not understood the task – she writes down the words she does understand. 'No, honey, I don't want you to write down the words you know, but the ones you don't understand', the teacher says with emphasis, 'OK?... so that I can help you.' Another child comes along to show some words and stands a couple of minutes to show her. Soon after, Shuma approaches and asks permission to play on the computer. 'Well, I'd like to see what you've done first', states the teacher. However, some confusion arises and Shuma does go off to the computer. (Rashid: 1996)

The extract from Nasima Rashid's notes describes just one incident in a school day for five year old Shuma and her friends learning in their East London primary class where all the children speak English as an additional language[1]. When Shuma comes out of school, she enters a very different world...

Everyone sits on the mat swaying to the sound of their own voice. Although on initial appraisal the noise level seems high, little of this is idle chatter. It is the express wish of the teachers that children read aloud, partly to assist their learning, but more importantly so that Allah can hear. Children are encouraged to develop a harmonious recitation in unison with the gentle rocking to and fro which accompanies the reading, as they are told that Allah listens to his servants and is pleased if they take time to make their reading meaningful... 'Now, repeat after me', the teacher solemnly requests. 'kalimah tayyiba... la ilaha ilallaho... Mohammadan rasolallahe'[2]. He tells them to look at him as they repeat... I leave the room on the third recitation of the prayer and notice that the children have not wavered at all; they remain seated on the floor as they have done for the last hour and a half. (Rashid, 1996)

Although many linguistic minority children will experience such contrasts, little recognition has been given in Britain to cultural differences in learning practices. A number of factors might be responsible for the lack of research in this area. Since the debate on linguistic and cognitive deficit or difference (Bernstein, 1971, Labov, 1972), researchers and teachers have been anxious to emphasise similarities rather than differences in language use in the homes of different social classes (Wells, 1981, Tizard and Hughes, 1984). A second reason may stem from the strong

* Adapted from 'Family literacy history and children's learning strategies at home and at school: perspectives from ethnography and ethnomethodology' *Studies in Educational Ethnography*, 1998 vol. 1: 19-46.

British tradition of child-centredness in Early Years education, grounded in Piagetian child development theory which focuses on the child as an individual rather than as a member of a cultural or ethnic group. Finally, recent government policy in Britain stresses the need to promote a 'common culture' (Tate, 1995) which will 'iron out' cultural differences between groups. This aim is reinforced in practice by the English National Curriculum which hardly acknowledges the learning practices of different minority groups. 'Equality of opportunity', a promise made in the Education Act of 1988, is currently interpreted as 'the same provision'. In practice, this means that both school and home-school literacy programmes are generally designed for the 'common' (English) culture.

As a consequence, teachers in Britain are unable to call upon a corpus of research studies on the literacy and learning practices of different cultural groups in the British context to inform their classroom practice. The British experience contrasts with that of the USA where there is a long tradition of research investigating continuities and discontinuities between home and school learning practices (Scollon and Scollon, 1981, Heath, 1983, Rogoff, 1990, Volk, 1994, Reese and Gallimore, 1995, Duranti and Ochs, 1996), the learning styles of different cultural groups and the effect of awareness of these on teaching styles (Au, 1980, Michaels, 1986). Nevertheless, some recent studies in Britain are beginning to reveal the rich variety of literacy practices of minority groups which may remain unknown to their children's teachers (Barton and Hamilton, 1992, Saxena, 1994, Gregory, 1994 and 1996, Gregory and Williams, 2000b). The ethnographic study outlined below aims to contribute to this growing fund of knowledge, to compare the literacy and learning practices of monolingual Anglo British and Bangladeshi British families with those of their children's teachers and, further, to investigate the transfer of learning strategies by young children from home to school and vice versa. Ultimately, the research aims to provide data showing whether and how a child's home learning strategies and home/school interaction might be theorised as part of the school learning process.

Background

The poor literacy and numeracy achievement of young children from economically disadvantaged families in British schools has been well documented over the past 20 years (Chazan and Williams, 1978, Ofsted, 1996) and public debate has been renewed since the introduction of the National Standard Attainment Tests in 1992 (Ofsted, 1996). The performance of children of Bangladeshi British origin has recently been highlighted as particularly low (Select Committee to the House of Commons, 1986/7, Ofsted, 1996). The government's response to poor achievement has resulted in considerable investment in Basic Skills Programmes through ALBSU (1993). Programmes currently in use in Britain rest on a firm belief in the intergenerational effects of literacy and numeracy failure. Their evidence is based on data from the National Child Development Study whose sample was drawn from those born in the UK between 3rd and 9th March, 1958. However, this cohort excludes most families from many ethnic minority groups, the majority of whom did not enter Britain in large numbers until the 1960s. Therefore, although the intergenerational factor is presented as a generalised conclusion (ALBSU, 1993), it has so far not been substantiated through empirical studies across cultural groups.

Family literacy programmes which provide the 'double bonus' of helping parents and children have been promoted as a model which is 'truly generational' (Brooks et al, 1996, p.6) for developing literacy skills in Britain. However, such programmes have been criticised for ascribing 'literacy impoverishment' to economically disadvantaged families and ignoring the considerable scope and variety of existing literacy practices of both majority and minority communities (Barton and Hamilton, 1992, Williams, 1997). Cross-cultural studies of cognitive development, conducted mostly in USA, have highlighted differences in the ways in which caregivers guide children's learning (Rogoff, 1990). Both groups of researchers suggest that important questions need to be explored as to the literacy practices of diverse cultural groups and the relationship between these home learning practices and children's cognitive strategies at school. Our project started then with the following set of research questions.

Research questions

- What place do literacy activities have in the out-of-school lives of five year old inner-city children and their parents?

- To what extent do family practices and literacy histories shape children's strategies in early literacy lessons in mainstream school?

- In what ways do children restructure their home learning patterns during the initial period in school and what role does the teacher play in this?

- What influence do 'schooled' learning practices have on the learning patterns of the family over time?

- What knowledge do teachers bring of families' literacy practices and how do they use this in their teaching?

The research presented here formed part of a longitudinal study running from 1992 to 1998 which investigated the literacy practices of both present and past generations of families who had close links with two primary schools in the East End of London (Gregory and Williams, 2000a). The one year study described in this paper was conducted between September 1994 and July 1995[3].

Methodology

The research used both qualitative and quantitative methods in a multi-layered analysis which combined both ethnography and ethnomethodology.

Layer 1: Ethnography

Ethnography was important in its aim to identify the 'cultural grammar' or set of rules which members need to know in order to become competent members of the group. The role of the researchers was to be both insiders and outsiders. As teachers themselves, they shared many of the experiences of the participants, spending considerable time in homes and classrooms and accompanying the families on shopping or other visits. At the same time, their task was to remain 'strange' in order to make explicit to outsiders what was common knowledge within the group. Ethnographic methods including participant observation, interviews with caregivers, children, teachers and community class teachers enabled us to give a detailed account of the literacy practices taking place in homes, communities and classrooms and to examine patterns of difference and similarity between groups.

Layer 2: Coding the Teaching Strategies

A quantitative analysis was carried out of the teaching strategies used by classroom teachers, caregivers and siblings when reading with the young children. Strategies were identified following the method described by Campbell (1981) and Hannon, Jackson and Weinberger (1986). They were coded and quantified in order to compare teaching styles across the three sets of teachers: mainstream teachers, caregivers and siblings.

Layer 3: Ethnomethodology

An ethnomethodological approach using Conversation Analysis was used to provide an account of turn-taking between adult/older sibling and child (Sacks, Schleghoff, and Jefferson, 1974, Heap, 1985). This finely-tuned analysis demonstrated how participants built upon each others' contributions to create 'cultural knowledge'. The aim was to show how adult or older sibling and child situated themselves in the reading session and how both parties participated in the teaching and learning through interaction and negotiation.

Design of the study

Sample

Two groups of children: seven Bangladeshi British children and six Anglo monolingual English children, were recruited from two primary schools only 500 yards apart in the East End of London. The Bangladeshi British children came from a Year 1 class, but changing demographic patterns in this part of the capital meant that we were unable to find sufficient monolinguals in the Year 1 classes and had to recruit children from Year 2. After discussions with the class teacher and the head teacher, the parents of the Anglo monolingual children were contacted by letter and follow up phone calls were made after parental consent had been obtained. In the case of the Bangladeshi British group however, different procedures were followed. After discussions with the head teacher, the parents were visited in their homes by the Bangladeshi British researcher, who explained the project to them. Letters in both Bengali and English with details of the project were sent out and parental consent for the children to take part in the project was obtained. We refer below to the teacher working with the monolingual English children as Teacher 1 and her colleague working with the Bangladeshi British children as Teacher 2.

Data

A member of each family, in most cases the mother, was interviewed once a term. In the Bangladeshi British families the father was sometimes present. In the case of one monolingual English family the father was present at all interviews and the grandparents were also present on one occasion. Each interview lasted between one and two hours. Interviews with the monolingual English mothers were carried out in the home, the parents' room in the school, the school refectory or a local cafe and all were recorded on a portable tape-recorder and transcribed by the research officer. The Bangladeshi British mothers were interviewed in their homes by the Sylheti[4] speaking research officer who made detailed field-notes in English immediately after interviews.

One morning a week throughout the school year was spent in classroom observation and field-notes written up.

The data for each child consisted of:

* one/two recorded reading sessions with the class/group teacher (in the case of the children in Reading Recovery[5] one session with the specialist teacher)

- one audio recording of the child reading at home with a parent or older sibling
- one audio recorded interview between the child and a researcher
- three interviews with a parent of each child
- field-notes on each child participating in a variety of classroom reading activities
- field-notes from each Bangladeshi British child's Bengali and Qur'anic class

Data on the general history of the area and changing migration patterns were collected through secondary sources.

Analysis

The data analysis was conducted using the method of multi-layering (Bloome and Theodorou, 1987). This approach enabled us to combine three layers of analysis, the focus moving from the outer layer or the social context, through a middle layer in which we examined and quantified the strategies used by teachers, parents and children, to an inner layer in which ethnomethodological techniques were used to examine in detail the roles of teacher and child in individual reading interactions.

Layer 1: The Ethnographic Analysis

Patterns of similarity and difference were sought between:

- demographic characteristics of each group
- the literacy histories and current reading practices of the two groups of children, their parents and teachers
- parents' and teachers' views of the role of the school and the family in children's reading development
- the children's reading in different domains

Layer 2: Coding the Teaching Strategies

Teacher/child, parent/child and sibling/younger sibling reading sessions were examined and a list of strategies used by the 'teachers' to facilitate the reader's progress through the text was drawn up[6]. Work by Campbell (1981) and Hannon, Jackson and Weinberger (1986) was used to identify a preliminary set of strategies. Close examination of our data revealed twelve distinct teaching strategies which we grouped under two broad headings:

Modelling strategies whose aim was to teach the child to be a 'good reader'

Scaffolding strategies which concentrated on the text itself and were used to help the reader decode the text

MODELLING STRATEGIES

1 Teaching opening and closing moves

Nadia: (aged 6 reading with Aisha, aged 5) *Shall we read who it's by? By Franklin M. Bradley. Illustrated by Holly Keller.*

2 Imparting knowledge about books

T1: *We've just reached the middle. How do I know this is half way?*

I could tell roughly by the story or perhaps I could tell by the number of pages but I'm just going to do this... That's the middle... How do I know? Look!

Child: *Oh because there are staples there.*

3   Positive feedback

T2: *Well done*

4   Negative feedback – no examples in teachers' transcripts, but fairly frequent in the texts of Nadia and the parents.

Aisha (reading):   *So play nicely Bo...*

Nadia: *No, see that says 'boy'. You just put an 's' on the end*

5   Text-to-life interactions

T2: *Do you like jelly-beans? No? Have you had them before? Well I like them.*

6   Language development

T1: *...wearing her of the rabbit holes?*

Child: *...off the rabbit holes*

T1: *Does that make sense?*

Child: *wear ...he*

T1: *So if her dad is speaking to her and is telling her about rabbit holes, tree roots and... what's he doing he's ... warn...*

Child: *He's warning her...*

SCAFFOLDING STRATEGIES

1   Providing text

Susie (reading):   *Wilbur bur...*

Mum: *Turned*

Susie: *turned ... turned... through...*

Mum: *three...*

2   Phonic strategies

T1: *....Do you remember? If you see a letter E and the letter A together ... can you remember the sound?*

Child: *edie... eddie...*

T1: *beady... beady... beady eye...*

3   Breaking down words – no examples of this in the teachers' transcripts but frequently used by Nadia and caregivers

Aisha: *You'd...*

Nadia: *Look. See that says 'bet'*

Aisha: *...bet*

Nadia: *And that says 'er'. Put them together and they make..?*

Aisha: *Better ... play nicely*

4   Establishing meaning

T1:   *Heads... How do you know head?*

Child: *Because look...* (points to picture)

T1:   *You noticed that in the picture already. Well done*

5   Pausing and prompting

T1:   *Give Sarah a chance to think. Sarah, what is it?*

Child: *daughter*

T1:   *daughter*

6   Insisting on accuracy

Sibling: *It's...*

Ahmed: *It's a 'whobber'. Meg...*

Sibling: *Mog*

Ahmed: *Mog catched a fish*

Sibling: *No, caught*

Ahmed: *caught a fish*

All reading sessions were analysed and the 'teacher's' moves were allocated to one of the twelve categories of strategies. The number of moves in each category was expressed as a percentage of total 'teacher' moves in each reading session. It was then possible to compare the relative frequency of use of all the strategies across three sets of 'teachers': parents, school teachers and the siblings. In addition, a reading session in which one project child, Nadia, read with Aisha, a younger child, was analysed, thus providing insights into the types of strategies the young readers had learned from their 'teachers'.

Layer 3: Ethnomethodological Analysis

Conversation analysis or 'talk-in-interaction' (Sacks, Schleghoff and Jefferson, 1974) was then used to show how joint cognitive activity also termed 'scaffolding' (Mercer, 1994) or 'guided participation' (Rogoff, 1990) took place. The transcriptions revealed that the Bangladeshi British siblings used a series of intricate and finely tuned strategies to support the young readers as they struggled with the text. As the younger child's proficiency increased, the support was gradually removed until the child was able to read alone. We were able to identify the following stages in the siblings' support of their younger siblings' reading:

1   *Listen and repeat*: the child repeats word for word after the older sibling

2   *Tandem reading*: the child echoes the sibling's phrases and 'joins in'

3   *Chained reading*: the sibling starts and the child continues until s/he needs help again

4   *Almost alone*: the child initiates reading and reads until s/he encounters an unknown word which is then supplied by the sibling

5   *The recital*: the child reads the complete text.

Results

Layer 1: Demographic data

The data collected included information on the parents' employment and accommodation, the educational background of the parents and the child's position in the family.

FAMILY BACKGROUND

Table 1: Bilingual children and their families

	Position in Family	Father's Occupation	Mother's Education	Mother's Occupation	Accommodation
Uzma	4/5	Restaurant-owner	Grade 5*	housewife	flat
Maruf	5/5	Shop worker	Grade 5	housewife	double flat
Shima	5/5	Unemployed	Grade 5	housewife	house
Shuma	2/4	Waiter	to age 15	housewife	flat
Akhlak	9/11	Unemployed	Grade 7	housewife	flat
Henna	3/4	Unemployed	Grade 4	housewife	flat
Shanaz	2/3	Factory owner	Grade 5	housewife	flat

*Grade 5: these mothers have completed primary education in Bangladesh. Shuma's mother was educated in UK and left school at age 15.

Table 2: Monolingual children and their families

	Position in Family	Father's Occupation	Mother's Education	Mother's Occupation	Accommodation
Susie	1/1	Policeman	Age 16	Childminder	Flat
Sally	3/3	Publican	Age 16	Works in family pub	week – flat weekend – house
Anne Marie	1/1	Builder	Age 16	Insurance clerk	house
Naomi	2/2		Age 16	Unemployed	flat
Richard	3/3	Unemployed	Age 16	Access course	flat
Stewart	2/2	Plumber	Age 16	Playleader in children's playground	flat

---

Four factors contributed to differences in the children's home literacy practices. First, the different pattern of employment between the two groups highlights the relative isolation of Bangladeshi British families living in this area in comparison with the monolingual Anglo families. No Bangladeshi British mother was in employment outside the home, in contrast with all but one of the monolingual mothers whose work or studies demanded literacy skills outside the home. Three out of seven Bangladeshi British fathers were unemployed and the remaining four fathers were employed in the immediate area with colleagues from the same country of origin. Second, the education histories of the Bangladeshi British mothers meant that, although literate in Bengali, only one was able to read or write English. This contrasted with the mono-lingual mothers, three of whom had GCE passes. Third, the cramped accommodation of the Bangladeshi British families meant that they did not have room for the array of educational toys found in some of the monolingual family homes. Finally, in contrast to the monolingual children, the Bangladeshi British children had a number of older siblings living at home who played a significant role in the children's reading development.

Literacy histories and current reading practices of parents and teachers

Each group looked back on very different memories of learning to read and now associated read-ing with very different purposes and materials. The two mainstream school teachers remember learning to read at home and in school as pleasurable. Both still read for enjoyment when they had time although Teacher 2 distinguished between challenging or 'good' books and other kinds of material.

The monolingual mothers, in contrast, all made a clear distinction between school reading and home reading. Their overriding memory of school was of truanting, bullying by other pupils, a lack of encouragement by their teachers and their subsequent feelings of having 'missed out' in some way on education. Two mothers spoke of having been dyslexic. However, all had happy memories of early reading outside school, mainly because their parents 'provided lovely books', comics or literacy materials. One spoke of attending Hebrew classes which she really enjoyed 'because you could relate to people'. Five out of the six mothers still loved reading and spent considerably more time than the teachers engaged in a variety of literacy activities such as informal book discussions or pub quiz groups, acting as chairperson for the local Residents' Association as well as being crossword or autobiography addicts. In contrast with Teacher 2, no mothers mentioned 'educational' or 'good' books. Reading was seen purely as a pleasurable activity and was often a joint or social affair.

For all the Bangladeshi British mothers, learning to read had a serious purpose, usually asso-ciated with religion. As children in Bangladesh, most had attended Mosque and Bengali schools. Reading any kind of fiction had been strongly discouraged by parents. Five of the seven mothers had left school by the end of class 5 (aged 11), the average age for girls to leave school in Bangladesh. In contrast with the monolingual Anglo group, limited schooling was accepted by these women as inevitable. The strong association of reading with learning the Qur'an remained with them throughout adult lives. (The Arabic word for 'reading' (qara'a') also carries the mean-ing 'learning by heart' (Wagner, 1993, Baynham, 1995)). Although one woman borrowed Bengali novels from the library, reading generally meant 'reading the Qur'an'.

Pleasure was reserved for news-telling ie meeting with friends and neighbours to exchange news, ideas and views, a regular occurrence in the women's lives. Both reading and news-telling were group activities.

Our findings, therefore, indicate very different interpretations of reading and experiences of schooling by the three groups. These findings reflect those of recent studies in the USA of cultural models of education held by different groups (Reese and Gallimore, 1996; Williams and Gregory, 2001).

Adults' perceptions of the role of the school and the family on children's reading

Both teachers indicated that the parents' role was to listen to their children reading, using the PACT materials (Parents and Children Together: a home reading scheme) and felt that some parents were not strict enough about using them. The teachers' perceptions of their own role, on the other hand, differed greatly. Teacher 1 felt that the teaching of reading was very much her responsibility. She was very experienced and had developed her teaching methods 'by observing and working with children, rather than adhering to any one particular orthodoxy'. Observations and recordings of Teacher 1 throughout the year demonstrated a close link between her aims and practice. In contrast, Teacher 2, working with the Bangladeshi British children, thought parents should take a more active role in their children's reading, a view which contrasted sharply with that held by the parents themselves, who believed that teaching reading was the responsibility of the school teacher. Teacher 2's views reflected her own childhood experiences of reading as a pleasurable activity and she consequently wanted parents to enjoy reading with their children. Neither teacher seemed to be fully aware of the scope of reading practices their pupils were engaged in outside school.

All the parents, without exception, were keen for their children to benefit from the educational opportunities they themselves felt they had missed and they provided all they could to foster their young children's reading development. Nevertheless, the teacher was held to be the expert and parents viewed their own role as merely complementing hers. Neither group of parents had a clear idea of how reading was taught in school; nor were they too sure what the teachers expected of them at home. The Bangladeshi British parents assumed that the English teacher would use the same teaching methods as were used in the Bengali and Qur'anic class and judged their children's progress accordingly. Although the monolingual English parents felt equally unclear about teaching methods, they appeared less concerned, possibly because all were extremely pleased with their children's progress, which they attributed to Teacher 1's 'brilliance'. Both groups of parents wanted more work to be sent home; the PACT reading books taken regularly by children were not generally regarded as serious homework.

The children's reading practices in different domains

Common to all the children except the two monolingual English speaking boys was that less time was spent on school reading taken home than on other reading and literacy activities. Apart from this, the out-of-school literacy activities of the two groups differed in terms of context, participants, purpose, scope and materials (see Tables 3 and 4).

The monolingual children read mostly in informal contexts and for enjoyment using a whole variety of books, comics and other materials. Reading could be an individual or a social activity, as for example during 'playing schools' sessions where the girls modelled themselves on their teacher. A distinction must be made between the girls, and the boys of this group who rarely read at all outside school. In contrast, the Bangladeshi British boys and girls learned in both formal contexts, ie learning standard Bengali using primers and learning to read the Qur'an in Arabic (Williams and Gregory, 1999), and in informal contexts, learning to read English using books from school. The principal difference between the two groups was that in the Bangladeshi British homes, it was the older siblings rather than the parent who read with the young children.

There were both similarities and differences in the organisation of reading in the two school teachers' classrooms. Both schools had a policy of quiet reading. Both used a combination of dif-

TABLE 3 Literacy – related activities at home and in the community: Bangladeshi British children

Type of Practice	Context	Participants	Purpose	Scope	Materials	Role of Child	Language
Qur'anic class	formal: in classrooms or in someone's living room	group of 1 – 30 mixed age-range	religious: to read and learn the Qur'an	approx. 7 hours a week	Raiel (wooden book stand) Preparatory primers or Qur'an	child listens and repeats (individually or as group); practises and is tested	Arabic
Bengali class	formal: in classrooms or in someone's living room	group of mixed age range. Can be children of one family up to group of 30	cultural: to learn to read, understand and write Standard Bengali	approx. 6 hours a week	primers, exercise books, pens	child listens and repeats (individually or as group); practises and is tested	Standard Bengali
Reading with older siblings	informal: at home	dyad: child + older sibling	homework: to learn to speak and read English	approx. 3 hours a week	English school books	child repeats, echoes, predicts and finally answers comprehension questions	English
Videos/Television	informal: at home	Family group	pleasure/ entertainment		TV in English; videos (often in Hindi)	child watches and listens. Often listens to and joins in discussions. Sings songs from films	Hindi and English

TABLE 4 Literacy – related activities at home and in the community: English monolingual children

Type of Practice	Context	Participants	Purpose	Scope	Materials	Role of Child	Language
Playing School	informal: at home	group or individual	play	frequently (girls)	blackboard, books, writing materials	child imitates teacher and/or pupils	English
PACT (Parents And Children Together: Home reading scheme)	informal: at home	parent/child dyad	homework: to improve child's reading	daily	school reading book	child reads and is corrected by parent using scaffolding or modelling strategies	English
Comics, fiction, non-fiction	informal: at home	individual or dyad (parent or grandparent/child)	pleasure	frequently	variety of comics, fiction, non-fiction books	child as expert with comics or books; as interested learner reading adult non-fiction, magazines etc.	English
Drama class	formal	group	pleasure and to learn skill	2 hours a week	books: poetry and plays	child performs in group; recites as individual	English
Computers	informal	individual or in dyad with friend or sibling	pleasure	frequently	computer games	active participant	English
Video/Television	informal	family group or individual	leisure/ entertainment	daily	TV/ videos	child listens and watches; discusses with others	English

ferent reading schemes and other materials, colour-coded for difficulty and both had purchased sets of books which the children could read in groups, according to ability. However, Teacher 1 (working with the monolingual group) worked almost entirely through group reading or shared reading with the whole class, whilst Teacher 2 (with the bilingual children) listened to the children individually. As a consequence, the groups read for considerably longer with Teacher 1 than the individuals with Teacher 2. Teacher 1 also spent longer explaining tasks and discussing expectations with the whole group. An immediate explanation for the unequal amounts of time spent on reading might be that the Anglo monolingual children who read in groups were in Year 2, while the Bengali British children who read individually were in Year 1. Nevertheless, we noted that all these young children were able to concentrate for longer periods during their community classes than was expected of them in mainstream school.

Layer 2: Teaching strategies

Transcripts of recorded reading sessions in different contexts revealed very different patterns of interaction between the participants. We began to examine these by coding the teaching strategies used by:

1) Teacher 1/children in class group reading sessions (Teacher 1 always worked with groups of children)

2) Teacher 2/individual child

3) older Bangladeshi British sibling / child at home

4) monolingual Anglo mother/ child at home

5) child/younger child in school.

Community classes were not included as audio recording was not permitted. Nevertheless, we were able to observe that the pattern of *Listen, Repeat, Practise, Test* ran through all the Bengali and Qur'anic classes and has been recorded in other studies (Wagner, 1993).

Prompted by observations of Qur'anic classes where teachers all used a single strategy – providing text – in contrast with the English teachers who used a variety, our coding differentiated between what we refer to as 'modelling' and 'scaffolding' strategies. Our initial hypothesis was that

a) all the English reading sessions in mainstream school would be characterised by a pattern of modelling strategies in contrast with the Qur'anic and Bengali classes where scaffolding (ie text based) strategies would dominate[7]

b) the monolingual English children would be less accustomed to scaffolding strategies than their Bangladeshi British counterparts and would be more disposed to adopt the modelling strategies of their English teacher.

Our results however pointed to a similar pattern emerging from all reading interactions, with the exception of those of Teacher 2. The strategy of providing text was the main strategy used by all 'teachers' except Teacher 2 (see figures 1, 2 and 3).

We had expected strategies used by the Bangladeshi British older siblings to reflect those of their community classes and these did consist largely, though not uniquely, of providing text. However, this strategy also figured extensively in the teaching of the caregivers, the monolingual child, Nadia, teaching Aisha, and was the most common strategy during the group reading sessions of

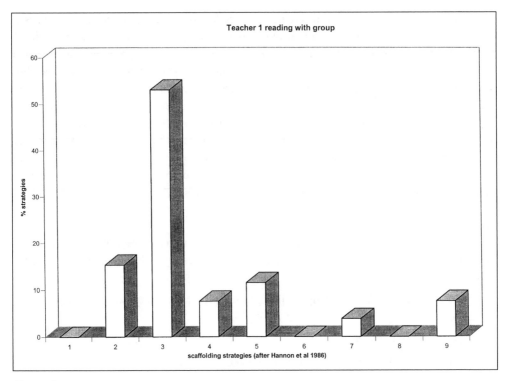

Figure 1

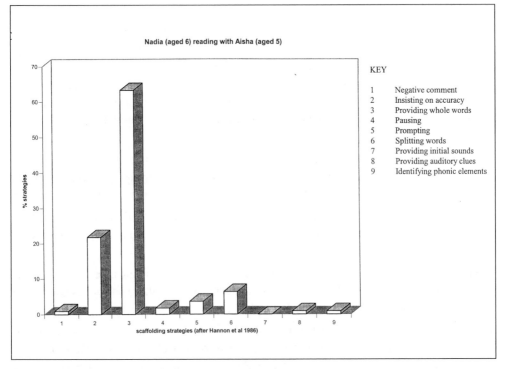

Figure 2

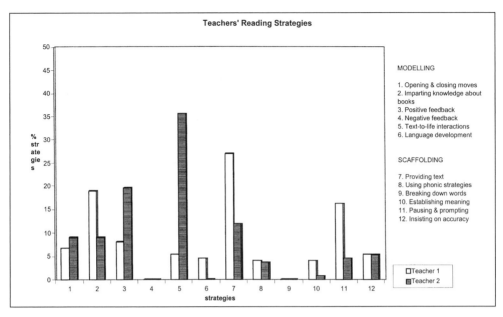

Figure 3

Teacher 1. In contrast, this strategy was seldom used in the reading sessions between children and Teacher 2. Figures 1 and 2 also highlight the similarity between the teaching of Teacher 1 and that of Nadia. Teacher 2's work on the other hand differ from that of both the Qur'anic teacher and the older siblings in that her preferred strategy was making text-to-life comments (fig.3). Although both teachers used a variety of scaffolding and modelling strategies, Teacher 1's lessons revealed a balance of approaches whereas those of Teacher 2 with the bilingual group, consisted mainly of modelling strategies, which her pupils would not have encountered in their community class lessons.

Layer 3:'Teacher'/child interaction in different domains
a) Reading with Siblings
In Layer 3, ethnomethodological analysis of transcripts of children and siblings reading together revealed the extent to which guided participation takes place in reading interactions. Analysis of the reading sessions between the Bangladeshi British children and their older siblings revealed an intricate and finely-tuned scaffolding which was gradually removed as the child's proficiency developed. This resulted in a form of syncretism, or blending, whereby the siblings gradually grafted mainstream school strategies onto the pattern of providing text familiar to the young children from their Qur'anic classes.

The older siblings' teaching was characterised by sustaining a fast-flowing pace, providing a firm scaffold (repetition or echoing only gradually giving way to prediction by the learner), demanding a high level of accuracy through frequent correction, allowing – perhaps expecting – the child to repeat a correction before continuing, a lack of evaluation and a lack of text-to-life comment during the readings.

Strategies observed in the reading behaviour of the younger siblings included echoing words and phrases, repeating word-by-word or phrase-by-phrase, sometimes anticipating the next word(s), repeating a word after being corrected before continuing and not hesitating about joining in. All the interactions were characterised by a high number of exchanges between participants, with no breakdown in communication.

The extract below is typical of a reading session between Bangladeshi British siblings. It illustrates the first stage in the siblings' scaffolding strategies, *Listen and Repeat*.

Child	Older sibling
	1 The postman
2 The postman	*3 It was Tum's birthday*
4 was ....birthday	*5 Ram made*
6 Ram made	*7 him a birthday card*
8 him a birthday card	

b) Reading with mainstream school teachers

Transcripts of reading sessions recorded in both mainstream school classrooms were then examined to see whether evidence of the home patterns of interaction between the Bangladeshi British siblings could be found in school reading sessions. The reading interactions between Teacher 2 and her Bangladeshi British pupils showed the teacher giving a different type of support. Her approach was characterised by making many text-to-life references and repeating the last word the child read rather than allowing the child to repeat after her. Excerpts show how this last practice resulted in the reversal of the repeat move used by the siblings, and gave rise to truncated interactions quite unlike the fast flow of reading the child had experienced at home.

Child	Teacher 2
	1 O.K. Point to the words like
	you did last time
2 (There) string	*3 string*
4 string. On the upstairs	*5 upstairs*

The group reading sessions of Teacher 1, in contrast, revealed the use of many strategies which characterised the Bangladeshi British sibling/child interaction. We could trace the fast flow of reading, repeating text, echoing, insisting on accuracy and other strategies familiar from interaction between siblings at home. Interestingly, however, in Teacher 1's reading sessions it was mostly the other children in the group who provided this support and the teacher who orchestrated the whole.

(Teacher 1 is reading with a group which includes children of Bangladeshi British, African Caribbean, African and Anglo monolingual origin. It is Child 1's turn to read)

1   Child 3   *daughters! daughters!*

2   Child 1   *help*

3   Child 2   *because*

4   Child 1   *because it gave him a...*

5   Child 2   *change*

6   Child 3 *chance*

7   Child 1 *chance to have a quick smoke. They were very...*

8   Child 4 *close*

9   Child 1 *close. One...*

Thus, far from discovering considerable differences between school-oriented and non-school-oriented groups documented in previous studies (Scollon and Scollon, 1981, Heath, 1983) we found remarkable similarities in both the strategies and in the finely-tuned 'scaffolding' of the Bangladeshi British siblings and parent-teachers, child-teachers and one of the mainstream school teachers.

Conclusion

Findings from this study suggest that ethnography and ethnomethodology can be combined to provide a dynamic framework within which to analyse child/adult or child/child reading inter-actions. The ethnographic approach presented in Layer 1 allowed us to investigate the social context and the different interpretations of reading brought by children from home and community literacy experiences as they enter school. Layers 2 and 3 highlight the effects of different interpretations of teachers' (be they school-teachers, caregivers or older siblings) strategies during the child's first years in school. The ethnomethodological approach which was a finely-tuned analysis of interaction permits us to trace both successful and truncated exchanges. It also permitted us to highlight the syncretism, or blending of strategies taking place as older siblings combined mainstream school and community class teaching strategies in their work with their younger brothers and sisters. The small scale of the study however means that the results should be seen as preliminary and be interpreted rather as providing an overview of the strategies used by different kinds of teachers than as a controlled comparison of methodologies. Nevertheless, the combination of approaches can be seen as a powerful tool in analysing discourse in educational contexts in the homes and classrooms of the many cultural groups who make up our society.

This research was supported by the Economic and Social Research Council from 1994-1995 (R 000 22 1186). We should like to acknowledge the assistance of Jane Mace, co-director in this project and Nasima Rashid, research officer, the families and schools and particularly the two teachers in whose classrooms the research took place. Our thanks are also due to Hayat al Khatib for her assistance with translation from Arabic into English.

References

ALBSU (1993) *Parents and their Children: The Intergenerational Effect of Poor Basic Skills*, London: Adult Literacy and Basic Skills Unit

Au, K. (1980) Participation structures in a reading lesson with Hawaiian children: Analysis of a culturally appropriate instructional event. *Anthropology and Education Quarterly,* 17: 115-152

Barton, D. and Hamilton, S. (1992) *Literacy in the Community.* Final Report of ESRC Project R 000 23 3149

Baynham, M. (1995) *Literacy Practices: Investigating Literacy in Social Contexts.* London: Longman

Bernstein, B. (1971) 'A sociolinguistic approach to socialization with some reference to educability' in Hymes, D. and Gumperz, J. (eds) *Directions in Sociolinguistics.* New York: Rinehart and Winston

Bloome, D. and Theodorou, E. (1987) 'Analysing Teacher-Student and Student-Student Discourse' in (eds) Green, J., Harker, J. and Wallat, C. *Multiple Analysis of Classroom Discourse Processes*, Norwood, N.J.: Ablex

Brooks, G. *et al* (1996) *Family Literacy Works: The NFER Evaluation of the Basic Skills Agency's Demonstration Programmes.* London: The Basic Skills Agency

Campbell, R. (1981) An Approach to Analysing Verbal Moves in Hearing Children Read, *Journal of Research in Reading*, 4, (1), pp 43-56

Chazan, M. and Williams, P. (1978) *Deprivation and the Infant School*. Oxford: Basil Blackwell

Duranti, A. and Ochs, E. (1996) *Syncretic Literacy: Multiculturalism in Samoan American families*. California: National Center for Research on Cultural Diversity and Second Language Learning

Gregory, E. (1994) Cultural Assumptions and Early Years' Pedagogy: the effect of the home culture on minority children's interpretation of reading in school. *Language, Culture and Curriculum*, Vol 7, No 2, pp 114-125

Gregory, E. (1996) *Making Sense of a New World: Learning to Read in a Second Language*. London: Paul Chapman Publishing

Gregory, E. and Williams, A. (2000a) *City Literacies: Learning to Read across Generations and Cultures*. London: Routledge

Gregory, E. and Williams, A. (2000b) *Work or Play? Unofficial literacies in the lives of two East London communities*. In M. Martin Jones and K Jones (eds) Multilingual Literacies Amsterdam: John Benjamins

Grimes, B. (1992) *Ethnologue: Languages of the World*. Dallas, Texas: SIL

Hannon, P., Jackson, P. and Weinberger, J. (1986) Parents' and teachers' strategies in hearing young children read, *Research Papers in Education*, 1, (1), pp 6-25

Heap, J. (1985) Discourse in the introduction of classroom knowledge: reading lessons. *Curriculum Inquiry*, vol 16, no 1

Heath, S.B. (1983) *Ways with Words: Language, life and work in communities and classrooms*. Cambridge: Cambridge University Press

Labov, W. (1972) *Sociolinguistic Patterns*. Philadelphia: University of Philadelphia Press

Mercer, N. (1994) 'Neo-Vygotskyian Theory and Classroom Education' in (eds) Stierer, B., and Maybin, J. *Language, Literacy and Learning in Educational Practice*. Clevedon: Multilingual Matters for O.U.

Michaels, S. (1986) Narrative presentations: an oral preparation for literacy with first graders, in Cook-Gumperz, J. (ed) *The Social Construction of Literacy*. Cambridge: Cambridge University Press

National Child Development Study – see ALBSU (1993)

Ofsted (1996) *The Teaching of Reading in 45 Inner London Primary Schools*, (ref. 27/96/D5) London: Ofsted

Rashid, N. (1996) Field notes from a visit to a Qur'anic class in the London Borough of Tower Hamlets

Reese, L. and Gallimore, R. (1996) *Ethnotheories and Practices of Literacy Development Among Immigrant Latino Parents*. Paper presented at the American Association for Educational Research Conference, New York, 8-12 April 1996

Rogoff, B. (1990) *Apprenticeship in Thinking: Cognitive development in social contexts*. Oxford: Oxford University Press

Sacks, H. Schleghoff, E.A. and Jefferson, G. (1974) A simplest systematics for the organisation of turn-taking for conversation, *Language* 50/4, pp 696-735

Saxena, M. (1994) 'Literacies among Panjabis in Southall' in (eds) Hamilton, M., Barton, D., and Ivanič, R., *Worlds of Literacy*. Clevedon: Multilingual Matters

Scollon, R. and Scollon, B.K. (1981) *Narrative, Literacy and Face in Interethnic Communication*. Norwood, N.J.: Ablex Pub. Corp.

Select Committee to the House of Commons (1986/7) *The Achievement of Bangladeshi Children in School*. London: HMSO

Tate, N. (1995) Final speech at International Conference *Supporting Additional Language Learners*. London: April 1995

Tizard, B. and Hughes, M. (1984) *Young Children Learning*. London: Fontana

Volk, D. (1994) A case-study of parent involvement in the homes of three Puerto Rican kindergartners. *The Journal of Educational Issues of Language Minority Students*, Vol. 14, Fall, pp 1-25

Wagner, D.A., (1993) *Literacy, Culture and Development. Becoming Literate in Morocco*. Cambridge: Cambridge University Press

Wells, G. (1981) *Learning Through Interaction*. Cambridge: Cambridge University Press

Williams, A. (1997) 'Investigating Literacy in London: three generations of readers in an East End family' in E. Gregory, (ed) *One Child, Many Worlds: Early Learning in Multicultural Communities*. London: Fulton

Williams, A. and Gregory, E. (1999) Home and school reading practices in two East End communities. In A. Tosi and C. Leung (eds) *Rethinking Language Education: from a Monolingual to a Multilingual Perspective*. London: CILT

Williams, A. and Gregory, E. (2001) Siblings bridging literacies in multilingual contexts. *Journal of Research in Reading*, vol 24: 3

Notes

1   This is a term recently adopted in UK to refer to children who speak a language other than English at home.

2   ... There is no god but one god... Muhammed is the messenger of God..

3   Gregory, E. Mace, J., Rashid, N. and Williams, A. *Family Literacy Histories and Children's Learning Strategies at Home and at School*. ESRC funded project 1994 – 1995, (R 00022 1186).

4   Dialect of Bengali spoken in Sylhet, in Eastern Bangladesh. Approximately 70% lexical similarity with Bengali (Grimes 1992).

5   Reading Recovery: a programme devised by Marie Clay and used in British schools in the 1990s to provide one-to-one tuition for beginning readers who were experiencing difficulties with initial reading.

6   It was not possible to audio tape Bengali and Qur'anic classes.

7   The teaching of reading in the UK during the 1980s and early 90s was characterised by the use of meaningful texts and high quality books rather than text-based phonic approach.

Chapter 9

Analysing literacy events: mapping gendered configurations of readers, texts and contexts

Gemma Moss

Introduction

This paper draws on data collected as part of the Fact and Fiction Research Project, funded by the ESRC between 1996-1998, which set out to explore the gender differentiation of reading in the primary years in the UK from a literacy as social practice perspective. The project focused on the 7-9 age group – the point at which children begin to develop as independent readers – and concentrated on their use of fact and fiction texts in different social settings. Data was collected in four different primary schools. In each case study site the project team[1] documented how reading in school was structured through the literacy events which constituted the curriculum; and by using interview, questionnaire and photography, examined how children made sense of their experience as readers both in and outside school.

Quantitative research of long standing shows a remarkably consistent pattern to boys' development as readers: they do less well than girls; they read less than girls; they are more likely to nominate a preference for non-fiction (Barrs, 1993). In some quarters, reflection on the potential interrelationship between these facts has led to calls for greater emphasis on non-fiction in the primary reading curriculum, on the assumption that a change from narrative to non-fiction texts would better meet boys' existing interests and would represent a turn away from a supposedly feminised primary curriculum built around narrative, in which the main role models as readers are provided by a largely female teaching staff, something which is also seen as acting to the detriment of boys.

Such a perspective accepts differences in genre-preferences between boys and girls as given, and asks few questions about why or how such preferences arise. By contrast, this project sought to give a social account of genre-preferences by treating texts as always embedded in literacy events, social encounters which would themselves fundamentally structure who would get access to which kinds of texts on what basis, thus mediating the content of the text for the reader. From this perspective, gendered preferences for this kind of text over that kind of text would be intimately connected to the social contexts in which particular texts circulate, as much as to the texts themselves. The project set out to explore the gender differentiation of reading at this level through a focus on literacy events. In the process, it evolved a set of analytic tools in relation to the data which were used to map out how different combinations of readers, texts and contexts created different orientations towards what it means to read and to be a reader in school settings, and the consequences this had for the gendering of reading.

In effect the project treated texts, readers and the immediate context for reading as the resources from which a given literacy event would be composed. Each set of resources would bring its own 'meaning potential', to borrow Halliday's phrase (Halliday, 1978), but the extent to which that meaning potential was realised would depend on the interaction between elements in a given case, their re-working this time round. In this respect the resources any one individual could muster would be played out in relation to the resources made available through the social structuring of the event as a whole and the social constraints, and social histories from which it was constituted. Concentrating on the dimensions of text, context and reader present in any one literacy event created the means to identify common patterns in the literacy events observed across the four case study sites, and identify salient continuities and differences between them. This in turn led to the formation of an analytic matrix which helped further refine both data collection and analysis. At the same time looking at text, contexts and readers through the lens of the individual literacy event provided a powerful means of constituting these elements together as the object of enquiry. Within linguistics, and indeed ethnography, these are traditionally handled separately, using different kinds of analytic tools. Part of the aim of the project was precisely to overcome this methodological divide.

Literacy events *in situ*: tracking down texts, contexts and readers

The commitment of the project was to document literacy events by recording which texts were being used by which readers in which contexts. Readers here didn't mean just which individuals but also how they were designated for the duration of the literacy event. In some classrooms, for instance, children would be ability-sorted for particular curriculum activities, and as a result be given different texts to work with. Sometimes this would also involve them re-locating to a different part of the classroom or the school. By logging the particular combination of texts, contexts and readers in the literacy events which took place, the project aimed to show how far and in what ways fact and fiction texts were being differentiated through use, and the role the school played in this.

Data collection began with classroom observation designed to log whatever reading took place during the course of the school day. The kind of text that was involved, be it book, writing on the board, worksheets, even the register, was noted along with who was involved in the act of reading, in what kind of context. The term 'context' encompassed the talk which accompanied the text, the physical setting for its use, and the kind of activity which it led to, that is to say, both the material and discursive space in which the text was embedded.

Two things were immediately striking: first, there was considerable variation in the literacy events composed and orchestrated by the teacher. There was a lot of reading going on over the course of the school day – indeed one could argue that the school curriculum is largely constructed through an on-going sequence of literacy events – but what happened around texts often took different forms, involving the mobilisation of different kinds of resources. There was no single school literacy being enacted. Secondly, there were regularities involved in that variation. There were common ways of doing things, common expectations about how things would be done. The fact that the project started observations at the beginning of the school year made this clear, as the teachers often explicitly inducted their new charges into the requisite classroom knowledge about which resources belonged in which context and what was to be done with them. 'When it is Art, you will need your red sketch book and your 2b pencil. This is where you will sit.' Through their designation of the appropriate use of space, time and resources, teachers marked out and choreographed different kinds of literacy events with different consequences for reading. Movement from one part of the room to another – from the mat to the tables, for instance – would signal a different order of social relations, a different conceptual take on the task in hand, and a different focus for activity. Whilst watching the construction of the new, it was also possible to observe ways of doing things with texts which children were already familiar with, school-wide practices which they brought with them unchanged to the new setting. For instance, in School 1, Bluebird, the Year 3 class were explicitly inducted into the structured way of organising reading time known in the school as Everybody Reading In Class (ERIC). In Year 3 this involved a carousel of activities: teacher reads to whole class; children read in pairs; children read in small groups; children read silently on their own; children read non-fiction. All this was new to the class so, turn by turn, the teacher explained the routines which would allow this kind of activity to happen later on in the year with a minimum of teacher intervention. This involved knowing which books you should be using when, and what the expectations were about where children would sit, whether they should listen or read aloud and so on. Whilst I and they learnt about this together, I also observed things happening which no-one had spoken about, but which everyone else seemed already to understand and expect. The child who under her own steam left the class-room and returned about ten minutes later with a book I hadn't seen her with before, apparently without anyone having told her to do so, turned out to be returning a reading scheme book to the place outside the classroom where they were kept and picking up another one, a routine already familiar to her from a previous year.

Doing ethnography or building a language of description

Ethnographic traditions have evolved largely through the use of a particular range of techniques designed to elicit and preserve ways of knowing and acting which belong to the researched. The assumption is that these ways of knowing and acting may differ from the researcher's and, to be fully understood, should be studied without pre-judging their value or efficacy, but rather by treating them on their own terms. Whatever the particular techniques employed, and the intensity with which they are used (Bloome and Green, 1996), such an approach inevitably places a premium on the ways in which the researched describe things for themselves, or any other means by which they make visible the key conceptual distinctions which underpin what they do.

In many ways the Fact and Fiction project was precisely working within this tradition. Its focus on literacy events was designed to identify how the boundary between fact and fiction texts was marked in and through the social interactions in which reading in school was embedded. In the first instance this meant paying close attention to which texts were getting into which contexts for which readers. The expectation was that this would help reveal what different kinds of reading were going on, and what criteria were in place which differentiated between them. But the phrase 'different *kinds* of reading' already takes us on from individual literacy events. It suggests a way of aggregating some literacy events together as representing the same thing, while at the same time discriminating between them and other literacy events which are representing something different. Ethnographic traditions are often far less clear on precisely how this process of cate-gorisation, and thereby generalisation, happens through the research activity, let alone the prin-ciples which will lead to it being done well rather than badly.

In this respect, the Fact and Fiction project turned to the work of Basil Bernstein, and his view of the crucial role that 'languages of description' play in the research process. In an essay entitled

'Research and Languages of Description', Bernstein (1996) described the ethnographic endeavour in these terms:

> In the classical ethnographic position, the researcher has first to learn the language of the group or society and know the rules of its contextual use. From here on, the researcher is developing reading rules (of recognition and realisation) to grasp how members construct their various texts or manage their contexts. The researcher here is modelling the member's recognition and realisation rules, or the strategies of practice these rules constrain. (p137-8)

Ethnographers would have little difficulty in sharing this view of the point of their endeavour. What Bernstein goes on to do is highlight the central role which the language used to describe the empirical object of the research plays in both the analysis and the theory-building which are part and parcel of the research process. The key metaphor that Bernstein employs for this is that the researcher's language of description acts as a translation for, rather than a simple reduplication of, the language of the researched. The act of translation constructs the tacit model which underpins and generates the specific performance or text of the researched.

> If the researcher fails to construct the model s/he is marooned in the specific contexts and their enactments, is in no position to appreciate the potential of the meanings in that particular culture, and thus its possible enactments. Without a model, the researcher can never know what could have been and was not. Without a model, the researcher only knows what his/her informants have enacted. S/he is fixed in their temporal and spatial frames. (*Ibid*, p138)

Any such model needs to operate on two levels, or in Bernstein's terms via two languages – one concerned with the delineation of the immediate empirical object (the language of enactment), one with the generative principles which enable it to do its work (the language of explanation)[2].

> Principles of description construct what is to count as empirical relations and translate those relations into conceptual relations. A language of description constructs what is to count as an empirical referent, how such referents relate to each other to produce a specific text, and translates these referential relations into theoretical objects or potential theoretical objects. (*Ibid*, p136)

The researcher's language of description must therefore always go beyond the language of the researched but must do so in a principled way which makes transparent and exposes the inner workings of the culture, by translating what is (the particular instance) into what might be (the other potential instances which could be generated from the same set of principles). It is precisely this difference between the language of the researcher and the language of the researched, grounded in their respective functions, which ultimately enables the researcher to be held to account, and the validity of the language of description created in this way to be tested out (Moss, 2001).

Grouping literacy events: commonalities and variation

What does this mean in practice? On the Fact and Fiction project, classroom observation provided detailed accounts of individual literacy events, in each case documenting the text involved, who its readers were and the context in which the reading seemed to be taking place. Such accounts also provided evidence of the language used on the ground by participants to describe particular aspects of the events they were involved in, and/or the texts associated with them. This was important information, which helped steer the course of the research by delineating salient contrasts made at the local level. For instance, one of the research activities which the team instigated at the start of the project was to try and log who was reading what during quiet reading time. Whatever its actual name, and the precise way in which this activity took place, sooner or later in each school site children would be given the opportunity to choose freely from a range of books in class one they could settle down to read to themselves. During this time the researchers would circulate frantically, trying to jot down the individual titles particular readers had chosen. The logic of the exercise was to find out whether more boys than girls were reading non-fiction at these times. What frequently happened was that the researcher would approach a particular child with the question 'What are you reading?', at which point the child would put down their book and go and find, or gather up a different text altogether, with the words, 'I'm reading this.' In fact what they were showing us was a different category of text, known on the ground as their reading book.

A reading book has a precise definition, not in terms of the type of book it is, but in terms of the contexts it is associated with. It can be fiction or non-fiction (though we documented far fewer of the latter in this role, and those almost exclusively from reading schemes). It can come from home, or from the school or class library, or from reading stock designated for this specific pur- pose (schools varied in the degree they restricted what could count as a reading book and the per- centage of pupils controlled). A reading book is meant to travel home, though it may not neces- sarily be read there (schools differed in their expectations on this point, as did parents and chil- dren in their willingness to undertake this task). But you absolutely must have it when an adult in authority asks you to read aloud, be they classroom helper, parent or teacher. Moreover, to enable such an event to pass off successfully in school, the book has to be seen to match the reader's perceived level of proficiency. Those who struggle to read their 'reading book' on the appointed occasion can be interrupted mid-text and sent off to change it for one more closely matched to their ability. Reading aloud to a figure of authority in this kind of context leads to a public evaluation of reading competence. This is signalled by the way in which such judgements are noted down in the home reading book in which the child logs the book they are reading, and in the teacher's records.

Reading for proficiency

In the account given above, the categorisation employed at local level for a particular kind of book led the researchers to follow the text, as it were, into its designated contexts of use, noting the social relations between participants embedded in those contexts, the kinds of activity they were associated with and, finally, the particular orientation towards literacy these produce. We came to call the literacy events which produced and confirmed the peculiar status of the reading book 'proficiency encounters' and the orientation towards literacy which such encounters em- bodied as 'reading for proficiency'. Whilst such encounters could take place in a variety of settings – home, school – involve a variety of participants in the role of assessor – parent, parent helper, classroom assistant, teacher – and include pupils designated poor or able readers; whilst they might encompass a wide range of texts, elicit different kinds of attention from the assessor, and different kinds of questions for the reader – focusing on decoding skills, comprehension or even enjoyment – at heart what united these different kinds of performance was an emphasis on the evaluation of individual competence, which framed reading clearly as publicly assessed work, for which the individual can absolutely be held to account, in a context where relations between reader and listener are unequal. Whatever the criteria in play, judgements about the individual reader's proficiency would be passed. It is hard to think of any other area of the curriculum where such sharply individualised judgements are routinely made on the basis of a particular performance. There is a kind of calling to account here which simply doesn't happen elsewhere. At root this tells us a good deal about the prime importance this society attaches to the acquisition of literacy.

'Reading for proficiency' groups together a series of literacy events which are driven by the same set of underlying principles. It can account for what they share and also allow for where and how they are differentiated amongst themselves. The formulation makes it possible to draw the line. Paired reading and group reading undertaken in the absence of the teacher are not proficiency encounters, although the reading which goes on may include some of the same techniques (sustained reading aloud of a given chunk of text by one individual, with others free to correct mistakes, and sometimes comment on the performance). They do not qualify because relations between participants are equal, no formal or public record will be made of the individual performance, and no consequences will follow for the standing of the individual reader.

This kind of chunking of literacy events, not by a single dimension but rather through a combination of the texts with which they were associated, and their function, the relations between readers which they engendered and the choreography of the context in which they took place, led the project to identify two other fundamental orientations to literacy which seemed to underpin both the variation and commonalities in the events documented across all four sites.

Reading for choice

The kind of literacy events which constitute this category are well represented by the carousel of activities organised at Bluebird School as ERIC time. Elsewhere they could most easily be recognised under the label 'quiet reading time'. Whilst proficiency encounters emphasise the relative standing of individual readers and their progress in becoming accomplished readers, reading for choice slots are geared to a different set of priorities, in which the act of selecting this text rather than that becomes more salient and is re-framed in terms of the readers' personal motivation and investment in the content of the text. Whilst the schools varied enormously in terms of the range of texts they made available and the structuring of the opportunities for their use, reading for choice slots consistently show children gaining access to a greater variety of texts during these times, as well as exercising greatest freedom over what they then do with them. In these respects, reading for choice seems to operate as time out from the disciplined working practices of the rest of the school curriculum, precisely because children are at least partially encouraged to direct this activity for themselves. Criteria for assessing the outcome of such activity are often diffuse and predicated on levels of personal engagement in the activity, rather than any concrete end product. Provided children keep to the general rules of classroom behaviour, teacher monitoring of what goes on is light.

As with reading for proficiency, the events which constitute reading for choice are recognised by teachers, children and parents as an integral part of the school reading curriculum. Taken together, this is where schools publicly exercise their responsibilities for teaching reading and developing readers, statutory duties specified as part of the school's role in England and Wales through the National Curriculum. In all the sites these two ways of doing reading were present side by side. But they by no means accounted for all of the reading going on in class. The bulk of reading observed took place according to quite different ground rules, which set it apart from the official reading curriculum.

Procedural reading

Whilst reading for proficiency and reading for choice are clearly delineated as part of the reading curriculum, procedural reading, from the point of view of participants, simply forms the background to some other curriculum activity or administrative task. This is reading at the service of something else, reading to get (other) things done. Reading of this kind plays a crucial role in steering curriculum delivery, but does so according to different ground rules from those outlined above. The most obvious texts associated with procedural reading are worksheets, textbooks and writing on the board. Thus they are predominantly non-fiction, often non-narrative, and designed in the first instance to be the focus of joint activity between teachers and pupils. Teachers introduce these texts to the class and take prime responsibility for making them accessible to pupils, by reading them aloud and/or explaining them before they hand them over. If pupils find that they are struggling with the reading, they can expect to ask for and receive help from the teacher or other pupils, for the end product of procedural reading is not the reading itself but something else – some other kind of output, be it in the form of a spoken or written text. The individual child's performance will be judged against this second text, not the act of reading *per se*. In this way, procedural reading becomes a collective effort, in which the level of individual competence of any one reader is not seen as a bar to working with the text.

The tripartite split: variation across sites

At the broad brush level the distinctions made here held fast across all the case study sites, although the relative weightings given to one way of reading over another varied between schools. They do not quite account for everything: for instance, one of the schools had a religious affiliation, which meant that prayers and religious observance formed a key part of the daily routine. These literacy events took on a different character because reading the texts in these contexts involved saying the words aloud, and together, often drawing on memory, rather than any written document. The oral text thus created took precedence over the written form from which it stemmed. In some respects, this practice seemed to spill over into other parts of the curriculum. Oral texts created in this way had a prominence in the daily routine of the classroom not found elsewhere. Even so, the tripartite split identified above still held good in relation to the bulk of curricular activity.

On the one hand, the categorisation of the data into **Reading for Proficiency**, **Reading for Choice** and **Procedural Reading** delineates the empirical objects of study. At the same time, the distinctions made here also create the basis upon which to begin to compare and contrast within cases as well as between them. For instance, literacy events designed to deliver reading for choice can be constructed in different ways. A similar curriculum slot, performing the same function but in a different setting, and mobilising different resources, can still turn out differently. The strong and well-motivated initial categorisation allows for a subtler subsequent analysis in which the potentially contradictory pull of different elements within any one event can be fully explored. This is shown below through comparison of the ways in which quiet reading time was managed in each of three sites.

Reading for choice: three contrasting instances

Every case study site included quiet reading time as part of its weekly activities. However, as the instances outlined below show, this could be managed in a range of ways and have different effects.

Reading for choice the pupil way

In School 4 quiet reading time happened alongside morning and afternoon registration, and was interrupted by routine administrative tasks, such as taking the register and notices. Reading could be substituted by finishing off homework or other classroom writing. This meant the majority of the children could well be doing other things besides reading. The books available for use during this time – the class library – were by and large not the books children could borrow to take home. With the exception of about five titles, they were all fiction, mostly chapter books. Non-fiction texts were kept in a central reference library for use in topic work. The most popular books in use during this slot were the few picture books in the stock. These had the advantage of being easy to read in one sitting. Some of the boys had smuggled in favourite non-fiction books from the school reference library which, although they were technically not supposed to borrow, they kept in their trays so could hold over to the next classroom reading session. Otherwise books were expected to be returned to the class library when the time was up. In fact, most of the class library books went unread: the length of texts didn't fit the amount of the time available to read them in. Many children simply sat with their reading books in front of them, mainly from reading schemes. Provided they were quiet, not much actual reading needed to go on.

In School 1, quiet reading had its own slot on the curriculum, alternating with paired reading, group reading, and the class reader. The class library contained a wide range of texts of different lengths and requiring different kinds of attention: fiction, non-fiction, pupil-made, a newspaper. It occupied a different space, separate from the main classroom and away from the teacher's gaze. Pupils could congregate on the comfy chairs and soft cushions or lounge on the floor, as they gathered to change books or stayed to read. The official injunction was to read silently, but quiet talk was tolerated and friends would often look at books together. Books with a strong visual element – picture books, puzzle books, some kinds of non-fiction – were often used in this way. Sometimes the class would be asked to talk about their reading at the end of the session, but more often they would pack away and then return to the business of the curriculum proper by con-gregating on the mat in front of the teacher. The children could make use of this same space and resources whenever they had finished work earlier than others in the class. When a sufficiently large number of children were making use of the facilities, the teacher would draw the curricular activity to a close and bring all the children together again to start the next lesson sequence.

Comparing schools

Both schools have a curriculum slot nominated as quiet reading in which notions of range and choice play a part. Yet the overall effect was different. Notionally speaking, children in both sites were free to choose what to read for themselves. During this slot they were also much freer to move around the class than they at other times, ostensibly because of the need to change books. They could also choose much more freely where they sat, and whether to read alone or with others. In these respects quiet reading time had the character of self-directed activity. This in itself set it apart from much of the rest of the curriculum. Once quiet reading time was over the teacher would take back control of the agenda again, allotting tasks, directing the pace, orchestrating the round of activities. These contrasts in both sites establish quiet reading time as time for play, rather than time for work. Yet in school 4, partly because of the mismatch between the resources and the context for their use, partly because reading competed with other activities reading remained low profile rather than being the sole focus. The occasion didn't function to underline what reading is or to build a collective sense of its possibilities. By contrast in school 1 range and choice were more than just rhetorical flourishes, they were materially underpinned. At the same time the kind of devolution to the level of individual responsibility seen here was part of a range of teacher strategies used elsewhere in the curriculum. It was part and parcel of how teachers managed the classroom. Consequently, with the resources to back it up, the specific responsibility individuals have for directing their own reading became much more highly visible and well defined.

Reading for choice the teacher way

An example from School 2 shows a different means of implementing reading for choice. Here choice of texts was largely managed by the teacher. Range was her expectation of what the class would cover at her direction, rather than what they would choose for themselves. At first during quiet reading time children would be allotted a turn with a particular genre – from distinct collections of information books, poetry, plays, topic books and (story)tapes – and told to choose from the basket where that collection was kept. Later they were restricted to their current reading books – the ones they would take to proficiency encounters. In this classroom, choice then became the range of texts the teacher taught during English curriculum time. Below are extracts from field notes taken whilst the class were doing joke books as part of English:

> T: This morning we are going to be looking at jokes. In your reading groups you are going to be looking at these [photocopies] and a couple of books from the book box. You can swap them around. Think about which one is the funniest

> T: *I've gone round,.. most people have found their favourite joke,.. you were reading them beautifully... Just bring your favourite joke, sheet or book, and we'll read some of them on the carpet*

Here the activity of reading is dominated by the teacher's stated purposes and the point she is leading them to: the written outcome from the reading – a class joke book. Yet along the way the teacher continues to frame individual activities in terms of pupil choice. Pupils have to choose their favourite joke, even if that means no more than choosing between so many jokes on a photocopied page, where none is more interesting than the others. They read a range of texts in order to select from the many. In contrast to the quiet reading times outlined above, this occasion remains strictly teacher controlled. Yet there is an oscillation between teacher talk which frames the activity as monitored work and teacher talk which frames the children's activity as self-motivated fun.

In part what this occasion points to is the potential hybridity of different literacy events. Different elements within them can pull different ways. In this instance teacher judgement on how well individual readers are doing is never far away. '*You were reading them beautifully*', edges the encounter towards a proficiency frame; whilst the end point of the activity – a class joke book – evokes the routines of classroom work, and a procedural frame. Yet the request is to find and pool individual favourites, to stake a claim for oneself through the choices one has exercised, whilst the texts themselves suggest fun, not work, as the agenda.

From the project perspective, the key analytic task is not so much to arbitrate between the combinations of different elements within particular literacy events as to map out how they interact. Placing this incident in the category Reading for Choice highlights a number of key contrasts which run through the data as a whole: the extent to which teachers visibly manage the reading curriculum from the centre or, sometimes by sleight of hand, devolve that management to the periphery; the extent to which reading is cast as work or play (see also Solsken, 1993); the extent to which reading is conducted as a collective or individual activity; the extent to which reading itself is backgrounded or foregrounded; and the different subjectivities which are formed as a result. Re-defining this data as 'reading for choice the teacher way' as opposed to 'reading for choice the pupil way' in the presentation above, highlights some of these distinctions. Again, the language used to group the data together is chosen deliberately to point to the underlying structural features which, taken as a whole, seem to delineate reading in school. In these respects, the terminology is part of the analysis.

Analysing how literacy events pull different ways

Once the categories are in place, they can be used to steer further comparisons. Reviewing the data as a whole it is possible to observe the oscillations and, indeed, tension between different elements within a single literacy event, and the ways in which they seem to sometimes pull in different directions. Sometimes the tensions are greater than at others. On the whole, literacy events which revolve around reading for proficiency show most homogeneity across the different sites and their boundaries are most clearly defined. Literacy events which revolve around reading for choice show maximum variation, within sites as well as between them and in the extent to which the principles which inform this way of reading permeate other areas of the curriculum. (The project data includes instances from one site where the ground rules for reading for choice seemed to underpin reading topic books in history, for instance.) In an attempt to examine these variations more thoroughly, the project established an analytic matrix to guide closer scrutiny of individual literacy events and to build up a more complex picture of activity in any one site. This involved returning to those literacy events which had been identified as representing a procedural, proficiency or choice axis and then reviewing in more detail the relationship between texts, readers and contexts within them.

From the project perspective, texts, readers and contexts are the semiotic resources which are drawn on in particular literacy events. The semiotic potential encoded in the resources of text, reader or context, may or may not be fully realised, and this in part depends on how the various resources interrelate, the extent to which they reinforce each other or pull in different directions. To give an example, all the classrooms the project documented included a soft area, however vestigial, often close to the class library or book corner, usually carpeted and containing at least one comfy chair, maybe fabric drapes. This setting was most strongly associated with reading for choice. Often, this area would only become available to children during quiet reading time, when they would be allowed to lounge on beanbags, recline on a comfy chair or simply spread out on the carpet. The setting encouraged pupils to, as it were, take time out from the rigours of proper lessons where they had to sit up straight and pay attention and adopt a quite different bodily posture. The material and physical resources of the setting, through their invocation of the comforts of a well-furnished front room, reinforce notions of reading as (domestic) leisure, even if practically speaking they can only do so in a token way: there are never enough chairs for everyone. But their potential to do this may not be fully realised: imagine the same setting used for a

The Fact and Fiction Matrix

Context	Procedural	Procedural	Proficiency	Choice	Choice
Curriculum slot	History topic – Ancient Greece	History topic – Ancient Greece	– Science/ reading to helper	– Finishing work	– English
Location	Seated at the tables	Freedom to move around the classroom	– two chairs at a table in the quiet reading area	– bean bags and comfy chairs in the 'soft' area containing the class library, adjoining the classroom proper	– tables
Activity, official/unofficial	With the textbook page open, children listen as the teacher reads from the text, then pauses to explain and add to the passage before going on	Using the topic books in class to compile information about the Greek gods, for writing up as a Fact File/Get the best books quick before they go and find the good bits	– child opens her reading book and reads aloud while adult helper corrects any mistakes. The child stops when asked	– finding a book to read/browsing and chatting with friends whilst choosing books from the kinder box	– finding a passage to read out loud/ browsing and chatting
Discursive orientation	'Today we're going to find out about Alexander the Great'	'Some of you know lots about this already, more than I do. Find out as much as you can'	- 'Can I have your home reading book to just write in it, darling? Well done, E. Next? Um, N'	– 'If you've finished your work, you can go to the kinder box'	– 'The reason I've asked you to do this is that we're going to put our favourite jokes into a book'

Notes

1   The Fact and Fiction project was based at the University of Southampton and funded by the ESRC. The Project team consisted of Dr Gemma Moss and Dena Attar.

2   In the 1996 essay Bernstein refers to L1 and L2 as the internal and external language of description respectively. In conversation he used the terms language of explanation for L1 and language of enactment for L2. I am reproducing these terms here, as I find them helpful.

Readers

	School 4 Year 4	School 1 Year 5	School 1 Year 3	School 1 Year 3	School 2 Year 3
Formation	The teacher is the main reader; the children listen together, whilst sharing one book between two.	The pupils are the main readers, working in friendship groups, mainly single sex	– Parent helper and child	– Children who have finished their work	– Whole class, sharing text with partners on their tables, mixed-sex
Access	Equal access to the same text	Unequal access to a range of texts, some of which the children have brought in themselves	– regulated access to texts. The child must bring their reading book and their home reading record book. If the reading book is too hard they may be asked	– unequal access	– unequal access to the selection of texts given to each group by the teacher. (More girls than boys
ended up			to change it		with the photocopied texts.)
Subject identity	Children as novices	Children as experts	– child as novice, subject to scrutiny	– subject identity regulated by peers, not teacher	– positioned by the teacher in between being good pupils and working well, and having fun

Text

	School 4 Year 4	School 1 Year 5	School 1 Year 3	School 1 Year 3	School 2 Year 3
Textual characteristics	Historical narrative; double spread; verbal text, with sub-headings and some images.	Various, most non-fiction, with relatively high ratio of image to verbal text, using double-spread	– picture book, narrative fiction + handwritten record	– Wide range: fiction, non-fiction, picture books	– Joke books
Text as material object	Paperback, stapled folio	Most hardback, bound folio	– large quarto hardback + school exercise book	– non-fiction, mostly hardback large quartos; fiction mostly small format paperbacks; only series fiction, hardback; picture books, hard and paperback	– some photocopies of double spreads; some paperbacks including stapled folios
Text's use category	Textbook	Topic books	– reading book + reading record book	– class library	– Joke books
Text location/source	Teacher's desk	Display table, pupil's trays and topic shelf	– kinder box via bookbag + bookbag	– the kinder box	- basket, labelled Joke Books
	School 4 Year 4	School 1 Year 5	School 1 Year 3	School 1 Year 3	School 2 Year 3

one on one proficiency encounter, with the child in the comfy chair sitting up straight and reading aloud to the teacher while the teacher assesses the child's performance. Within a given literacy event, temporary alliances between elements happen through the mobilisation of resources this time round. All the different elements within a given literacy event can fall the same way, reinforcing each other, or they can begin to pull in different directions. Part of the aim of the project was to begin to explore these dimensions. That meant looking much more carefully at the semiotic potential of the resources in use and what happened as they stacked up in a particular literacy event. The sample analysis of key literacy events provided in the matrix below gives an idea of the scope of the analytic endeavour.

The ways in which text, context and readers are configured, separately, and then in combination, is laid out in sequence within the matrix. The vertical columns represent individual literacy events, documented in the project field notes, here grouped under the headings of procedural, proficiency, choice; and stemming from different school sites, as indicated at the bottom of the chart. The rows deal in turn with context, readers and text. The sub-categories represent different aspects of texts, contexts and readers which seemed to have an impact on how reading was realised within a given event. The matrix itself in this respect shows the move precisely from the individual instance to the conceptual formation of its constituent parts, and thereby the generative principles which produce that instance.

Gender differentiation and the reading curriculum

The initial impetus for this enquiry, outlined above, was to examine how fiction and non-fiction texts are embedded in the school literacy curriculum, as part of a broader investigation examining the social construction of gender-differentiated genre preferences. One unexpected finding from the project data was the strength of the proficiency frame round reading in school, and the extent to which this permeates children's use of fiction texts. Whilst the principles which embody reading for choice remain strong at the rhetorical level, both in teacher talk about their practice and as part of official documentation on the curriculum, it was harder to find it fully operationalised on the ground.

Many of the texts in use in school underline the link between reading and proficiency. They do so as material objects, through their use of typeface and layout, and through the ways in which they combine verbal text and pictures. This is particularly true of fiction texts. Children's publishers differentiate and segment fiction texts according to proficiency levels, using agreed standards: the bigger the type face, the larger the spaces between the lines of type, the higher the proportion of picture to text, the easier the book will be to read. Libraries and bookshops sort and store their fiction collections by similar criteria: picture books, read-alones, junior fiction, will be housed on different shelves. Together they construct a reading ladder, and, by implication, the reader's place on it. Children, like grown-ups, can distinguish an easy book from a hard book because of the way it looks. The fiction books they choose to read thus also spell out their place on the proficiency ladder to others. The fact that in many classrooms weaker readers are often restricted to reading scheme books which spell out these distinctions even more clearly serves only to underline the point.

By contrast, very few non-fiction texts surface in proficiency encounters. The rare exceptions in the project data stem mainly from reading schemes – in some classrooms non-fiction texts were only officially made available in the context of task driven, procedural reading. Yet non-fiction texts remained popular choices, particularly amongst weak boy readers, when they could choose what to read for themselves. Even in classrooms where non-fiction was hard to come by and no official provision was made, they would still surface during quiet reading time.

Closer examination of the non-fiction texts weaker boy readers preferred revealed a highly motivated selection of texts with a number of shared features. First, they were highly visual. Page layouts were constructed on a double spread, with the visuals leading the written text. What print there was often amounted to no more than an individual heading and accompanying paragraph, related to the image but relatively free-standing of the rest of the verbal text on the page. Paragraphs could therefore be read in any sequence, with the visuals steering the selection individual readers make. Second, unlike the bulk of fiction texts, the most popular non-fiction texts eschewed carefully graded point size of typeface as a way of signalling the level of proficiency of their intended readership. Instead the range of typefaces used varied according to the prominence given to the verbal text on the page: large typefaces for headings; smaller for sub-headings; smallest for the individual paragraphs which accompanied the visual images. The bulk of the print on the page would be in a point size most normally associated in fiction with adult readers. This immediately set these texts apart from much of the rest of the book stock the school provided, and indeed caused some concern amongst many of the teachers in whose classrooms these materials circulated, as they weren't sure how far the verbal text matched the reading proficiency of the children in the class, let alone those who seemed to make a beeline for them. Finally, such texts were almost always large, bound hardbacks – again in distinct contrast to the predominantly paper-back, small size fiction texts or the stapled, soft-backed reading scheme books.

Non-fiction texts as material objects and in terms of their internal characteristics (i.e. their layout and visual style) signal adults as their intended readership. At the same time, they give weaker readers plenty to do with them, precisely because it is possible to steer round them using visual images alone, only browsing the headings and short paragraphs. For the weakest readers the pictures act as prompts for them to announce what they already know. They can spend time on them without having to pay any attention to the written text.

Approaching children's genre preferences through the range of social contexts for reading which frame texts in school suggests a new way of understanding their choices. In the project data, weaker girl readers were quite happy to go along with teacher judgements about their proficiency as readers but many of the weaker boy readers were not. During quiet reading time, weaker girl readers often chose to spend time on fiction texts which were well within or even below their competence, turning this kind of reading into a collaborative exercise in which they helped each other through the pages. Weaker boy readers often did everything they could to avoid spending time on text, in the hope of disguising to their peers their low status as readers. Low proficiency rankings seemed to conflict more with their sense of self-esteem. Weaker boy readers were in flight from negative proficiency judgements in ways in which girls were not. Non-fiction texts gave them somewhere to go. Indeed, precisely because of the role of visual rather than verbal text, they provided one of the few arenas where more and less able boys could meet on the same level: weaker boys could muster their expertise in response to such a text, without having to stumble through the print to identify what is going on. This is an advantage in relation to boys' status politics. It works less well in terms of making their reading progress. One net result of the strategies they employ is that they spend less time on verbal text (Moss, 2000). The kind of visual competences some of the weaker boy readers showed in steering their way round non-fiction texts have their place. But alone, they are not enough.

Implications for research

The project data reported on here were collected in order to identify how schools distinguished between fact and fiction texts through the range of literacy events which constitute the curriculum. As Bernstein comments, 'Qualitative procedures usually generate complex, multi-layered and extensive texts, for which there are rarely ready made quick fix descriptors' (Bernstein, 1996, p 135). The Fact and Fiction project was no exception to this rule, and swiftly amassed a vast amount of detailed fieldstones which somehow needed transforming into a manageable shape. For Bernstein the right kind of transformation takes place as the researcher develops the language of description for the objects of study, in ways which can bring into view the conceptual relations which underpin them. Developing the language is therefore a fundamentally theoretical act. The distinction between the terms the researcher uses and the language of the researched provides the means to test out the robustness of the theorisation, to see whether or not it brings into light something new (Moore, 2001). If the Fact and Fiction project has been successful, it is in making visible key distinctions embedded in the school literacy curriculum which drive and shape what individual teachers and pupils do, in ways that provide a basis for better understandings, as well as possible interventions and re-working of that curriculum in the interests of greater gender equity. Building a language of description in accordance with Bernstein's prescription is in these respects seen as a development of but also complimentary to other work on the ethnography of literacy.

References

Barrs, M. (1993) *Reading the Difference.* London: CLPE

Bernstein, B. (1996) *Pedagogy, Symbolic Control and Identity.* London: Taylor and Francis

Bloome, D. and Green, J. (1996) 'Ethnography and Ethnographers of and in Education: A situated perspective' in J. Flood *et al* (eds) *A Handbook for Literacy Educators.* New York: Macmillan

Halliday, M. (1978) *Language as Social Semiotic.* London: Arnold

Moss, G. (2000) 'Raising boys' attainment in reading: Some principles for intervention' in *Reading* Vol 34(3), 101-106

Moss, G. (2001) 'Bernstein's language of description: some generative principles' in *Social Research Methodology: Theory and Practice.* Vol 4(1), 17-19

Moore, R. (2001) 'Basil Bernstein: Theory, models and the question of method' in *Social Research Methodology: Theory and Practice.* Vol 4(1), 13-16

Solsken, J. (1993) *Literacy, Gender and Work in Families and in School.* New Jersey: Ablex

PART THREE
Discourse and identity

Introduction

In response to broader paradigm shifts within the social sciences, there has been a shift in the field of language studies from a concept of identity as a set of relatively fixed individual internal attributes, towards a more fluid notion of identity as socially constructed. Researchers have become increasingly interested in how people try out, negotiate and perform aspects of their identity through dialogues and interactions across different areas of their lives. Responses and feedback from others are important within this process and identity thus becomes more of an interactive concept, referring both to how one sees one's position and meaning in the world and also to how one is identified by others. Alongside this more fluid interactive notion of identity is the recognition that in social life language is not a neutral, transparent medium but both reflects, and is involved in, the construction of systems of values, beliefs and social practices. The term 'discourse' is increasingly used to signal this conception of language as social and ideological practice, and the construction of identities through discourse is seen as closely related to institutional structures and wider power relationships.

The chapters in Part 3 are all based on research studies in specific educational settings, ranging across India, South Africa, Britain and the United States. The first two chapters (Bucholtz and Maybin) provide detailed micro-level studies of students' talk with each other. In the first part of Mary Bucholtz's chapter she argues that the introduction of practice theory into sociolinguistics is an important development and that the community of practice provides a useful alternative to the speech community model, which has limitations for language and gender researchers. In presenting her own research on talk and identity among North American High School girls, Bucholtz shows how identities were shifting, performed and struggled over through language. She uses the more ethnographic, activity-based approach of the community of practice model in order to examine how a minority community of teenage girl 'nerds' negotiate gender and other aspects of their identities through practice. Extending this model, identities can be explained as the outcome of positive and negative identity practices rather than as fixed social categories.

Janet Maybin also focuses mainly on students' informal talk among themselves, drawing on Bakhtinian ideas to examine how 10-12 year-olds report and take on other voices from teachers, books, worksheets and each other in their talk. She suggests that children use other voices strategically to invoke particular intertextual links and that they reproduce or frame these voices in various ways that indicate their own evaluative position in relation to that of the imported voice. The patterning of voice reproduction in students' informal talk, as well as in their dialogues with teachers, which she briefly discusses, suggest that students are orientating towards institutional constructions of knowledge and authority, though with some instances of resistance. In this way they actively participate in their own induction into schooled values, practices and identities.

The next two chapters look at discourse in classrooms where students and teachers confront racial, ethnic, socioeconomic and linguistic diversity and where this diversity becomes an important part of curriculum work.

Kris Gutiérrez, Patricia Baquedano-López and Carlos Tejeda draw on their long-term experience of ethnographic work and discourse analysis in US bilingual classrooms to argue that diversity and difference, which are often seen as problematic for teaching, can be transformed into powerful building blocks for learning. They are particularly interested in hybrid language and schooling practices which bridge home and school to produce what they call 'Third Spaces', which provide children with zones of proximal development. Gutiérrez *et al* use examples of classroom discourse from a dual immersion second and third grade classroom to show how the reconfiguring of student identities and classroom knowledge in Third Spaces enable students to engage more constructively with learning in a renegotiated classroom curriculum.

In Chapter 13, Carolyn McKinney reviews the idea of critical literacy, and how it has been used in teaching different age groups of students in Australia, Britain and South Africa. Critical literacy pedagogy encourages students to examine the ways in which texts convey particular ideological messages and position people in various ways, the resources people have to resist such positionings and how wider social processes shape language use and interpretation. While it has often been assumed that such an approach will empower students, McKinney suggests that critical literacy work in South Africa reveals a more complex situation, raising questions about the theoretical assumptions underpinning conceptions of critical literacy and about its pedagogic applications. She uses case study material from her own research with South African university students to suggest that critical literacy work is closely tied up for students with desirable and undesirable identities and that such work needs to be sensitive to the micro-politics of the classroom as well as to students' wider social, cultural, political and historical contexts.

In the final chapter in this section, Vai Ramanathan is also concerned with broader historical processes and their impact on institutional practices and student identities. Ramanathan argues that a hierarchical relationship on a global level between inner and outer circle English speakers is reproduced in the relationship between more and less powerful social groups within India. She focuses on the way in which institutional practices in tertiary education serve to sustain an unequal relationship between middle class students with easy access to English and lower caste students who attended Gujarati-medium schools and have to contend with English at tertiary level. Institutional practices of streaming, the use of Hindi and Gujarati in class and an emphasis on grammar rather than communicative English all serve, she suggests, to cut lower caste students off still further from proficiency in English and from the jobs and futures they desire.

CHAPTER 10
'Why be normal?': language and identity practices in a community of nerd girls
Mary Bucholtz

In sociolinguistics, social theory is rooted in the concept of the speech community. As a language-based unit of social analysis, the speech community has allowed sociolinguists to demonstrate that many linguistic phenomena previously relegated to the realm of free variation are in fact socially structured. Thus Labov (1966) showed that the linguistic heterogeneity of New York City can be quantitatively analysed as the patterning of a single speech community, despite differences in New Yorkers' language use based on sociological variables such as age, social class and gender.

Nonetheless, because the concept of speech community is indigenous to sociolinguistics, it is not connected to any larger social theory. This theoretical isolation, along with the fact that the speech community defines the social world in strictly (socio)linguistic terms, has meant that sociolinguistic theory has largely stood apart from theoretical advances in related disciplines. Meanwhile, within sociolinguistics, the concept of the speech community has been hotly contested and continually revised as researchers have uncovered the limitations of previous definitions.

The speech community presents special difficulties for researchers in the sociolinguistic subfield of language and gender. The disciplinary autonomy of theory based on the speech community is unproblematic for traditional sociolinguistic research, which uses social information to account for linguistic phenomena such as sound change. But when sociolinguists reverse the direction of analysis – asking instead how linguistic data can illuminate the social world, as language and gender researchers seek to do – then connections to social theory beyond linguistics become imperative. Moreover, the speech community model, which was designed to analyse sociolinguistic phenomena at a macro level, is often inappropriate and inadequate for the kinds of questions currently being asked in language and gender scholarship. Central among these is the question of identity: How do speakers use language to project their identities as gendered beings? And how are gender identities interwoven with other social parameters?

This article draws on a theory of community and identity that avoids the problems associated with the speech community model. The new framework, the community of practice, emerges from **Practice Theory**, an approach that has currency in such disciplines as sociology, anthropology, and education. The connections of the community of practice to these recent developments in other fields allow sociolinguists to offer more fully theorised social explanations than were possible with the earlier model. In addition, the community of practice overcomes many of

* First published in *Language in Society* 28, 203-223. Cambridge University Press 1999.

the faults that sociolinguists have found with the speech community, and it therefore has wide applicability to the field's central questions. The theory's broad range of use is especially evident in language and gender studies – because, unlike the speech community, the community of practice was introduced into sociolinguistics specifically to address issues of gender.

In this article, I build on the theory of the community of practice to develop its potential as an analytic tool for the sociolinguistic investigation of gendered identities. The framework is applied to a social identity, that of the nerd, which has remained out of bounds in traditional sociolinguistic research based on the speech community. This identity is analysed within the community of practice framework because only this concept permits us to draw on the linguistic and social information necessary to understand the production of nerd identity. I argue that nerd identity, contrary to popular perceptions, is not a stigma imposed by others, but a purposefully chosen alternative to mainstream gender identities which is achieved and maintained through language and other social practices.

Language and practice theory

The idea that the social world is best viewed as a set of practices is not new. Praxis is a foundational concept of Marxism, and more recently Giddens (1979) has offered a practice-based account as a way out of the impasse created by social structure, on the one hand, and personal agency on the other. Given the focus of practice theory on enduring social activity, it was perhaps inevitable that it should soon come to view language as a central object of social analysis. Outside linguistics, this perspective has been most fully articulated by the French sociologists Pierre Bourdieu (1978, 1991) and Michel de Certeau (1984). Both Bourdieu and de Certeau understand language in relation to other social practices, and both scholars view language as a social phenomenon, rather than merely as an abstract formal system.

For Bourdieu, the starting point of practice is **habitus**, the set of dispositions to act (e.g. speak, walk, read, or eat) in particular ways which are inculcated in each individual through implicit and explicit socialisation. These dispositions are linked to particular social dimensions such as class and gender. Habitus is also tied to the body via **hexis**, the individual's habitual and socially meaningful embodied stances and gestures, and through other aspects of physical self-presentation. Language is merely one practice in which habitus is embedded, and through which the individual becomes socially locatable to observers. Thus non-linguistic social practices and language should be approached in analogous ways. As Bourdieu observes (1991:89),

> Not only are linguistic features never clearly separated from the speaker's whole set of social properties (bodily hexis, physiognomy, cosmetics, clothing), but phonological (or lexical, or any other) features are never clearly separated from other levels of language; and the judgement which classifies a speech form as 'popular' or a person as 'vulgar' is based, like all practical predication, on sets of indices which never impinge on consciousness in that form.

Bourdieu here offers two important methodological insights to sociolinguists: first, that non-linguistic practices may carry important linguistic information (and vice versa); and second, that a complete sociolinguistic analysis must examine multiple levels of language simultaneously. Yet, as a theorist, Bourdieu is less useful to sociolinguists, and especially to language and gender scholars. His insistence on the unconsciousness of practice reflects a general attenuation of agency within his theory. Although speakers are not bound by their habitus, which is inflected by the particular context in which it occurs, the tendency is to act in accordance with what has been naturalised as appropriate. Bourdieu sees the individual, then, more as a product of social structure than as a free agent. Practice at the local level, especially linguistic practice which is embedded in the class habitus of the standard and the non-standard, is primarily in the business of reproducing existing social arrangements.

For de Certeau, by contrast, the individual is much more agentive, because the focus of investigation is subversion as well as reproduction of the social order. De Certeau makes the link between language and other social practices even more explicit than did Bourdieu before him. De Certeau sees all social practices, both linguistic and non-linguistic, as similar in their social effects. But where Bourdieu considers practice to be a reproduction of social structure, de Certeau views it as an appropriation, an act of agency. The point, then, is to understand how culturally shared resources (such as language) are made to serve the specific social needs of individuals. These needs may enforce the social status quo, but they may just as easily challenge or revise it.

A third theory of practice has been developed within anthropology by Ortner (1996), who criticises earlier scholarship on the grounds that it fails to take seriously the practices of women. Making the female agent central in the project of practice theory, Ortner constructs a framework that has room for both structure and agency. Although language is not a guiding concept in Ortner's work as it is for Bourdieu and de Certeau, she views structure itself as textual in nature – the 'field of a linguistic system', in de Certeau's words – within which an individual act of speaking operates. Thus a complete analysis of gender, and especially of language and gender, cannot focus on texts alone. As Ortner argues (1996:2),

> Studies of the ways in which some set of 'texts' – media productions, literary creations, medical writings, religious discourses, and so on – 'constructs' categories, identities, or subject positions, are incomplete and misleading unless they ask to what degree those texts successfully impose themselves on real people (and which people) in real time. Similarly, studies of the ways in which people resist, negotiate, or appropriate some feature of their world are also inadequate and misleading without careful analysis of the cultural meanings and structural arrangements that construct and constrain their 'agency', and that limit the transformative potential of all such intentionalised activity.

The possibility – and the reality – of such unified analyses within language and gender studies is offered by the community of practice framework. More than any previous approach in sociolinguistics, the community of practice allows researchers to examine, in a theoretically adequate way, both the actions of individuals and the structures that are thereby produced and reproduced, resisted and subverted.

Gender, the speech community, and the community of practice

Ortner's introduction of a feminist perspective was a relatively late development in practice theory in anthropology and sociology. Likewise, the theory of the community of practice, which emerged from education (Lave, 1988, Lave and Wenger, 1991, Wenger, 1998), was not applied to gender until it was imported into linguistics by Eckert and McConnell-Ginet in a highly influential survey article (1992). As an alternative to the speech community – a central analytic tool of sociolinguistics – the community of practice requires language and gender scholars to rethink traditional notions of community, identity and gender. However, Eckert and McConnell-Ginet do not offer an explicit critique of the speech community; although that concept has been widely debated (see Hudson, 1980, Williams, 1992), its particular limitations for language and gender research have not been systematically addressed. I suggest six ways in which the speech community has been an inadequate model for work on language and gender:

(a) Its tendency to take language as central.

(b) Its emphasis on consensus as the organising principle of community.

(c) Its preference for studying central members of the community over those at the margins.

(d) Its focus on the group at the expense of individuals.

(e) Its view of identity as a set of static categories.

(f) Its valorisation of researchers' interpretations over participants' own understandings of their practices.

Language vs. social practice

The speech community has been defined in many ways, but every definition posits language as a primary criterion of community. What is taken as shared may be the linguistic system (Bloomfield, 1933:42-56); or shared linguistic norms (Labov, 1972, Guy, 1988); the pattern of variation (Milroy, 1992); or only a set of sociolinguistic norms (Romaine, 1982). The emphasis may be less on the linguistic system, and more on shared interactional settings and norms (Hymes, 1974, Dorian, 1982, Silverstein, 1996). But in every case, the focus remains on language. Even many scholars who advocate a more interactional approach understand **interaction** to be a pre-eminently linguistic concept. Other forms of mutual engagement – that is, all non-linguistic aspects of social activity – are marginalised or ignored.

By recognising practice – the social projects of participants – as the motivating context for linguistic interaction, the theory of the community of practice makes activity much more central to sociolinguistic analysis. Just as importantly, whereas the speech community model understands language as fundamentally disembodied – as detachable from the physicality of speakers – the community of practice quite literally reincorporates language into the physical self. In this regard, it echoes Bourdieu's concept of hexis – a crucial connection for feminist researchers, for whom the specificity of the gendered body is a theoretical starting point.

Consensus vs. conflict

Another aspect of the traditional model that has received a great deal of criticism is the idea that the speech community is constituted around shared sociolinguistic norms. This definition was first proposed by Labov (1972) and was taken up by many subsequent researchers. The postulate that speakers agree on and uphold certain linguistic forms as normative, regardless of differences in social background, assumes a consensus model of society that is at odds with a long-standing tradition of social theory. Several sociolinguists have critiqued the Labovian definition of the speech community on these grounds (e.g. Rickford, 1986, Milroy, 1992). Moreover, the invocation of 'norms' obscures the fact that these are successfully imposed ideologies favouring the interests of the powerful (Bourdieu, 1991). This arrangement has long been recognised by scholars of language and gender who have worked to combat views of women's language as deficient in comparison to men's (see Cameron, 1992:42 ff.)

Central vs. marginal members

The language of norms also presumes that some members of the speech community are central and others are marginal, and that it is the central members who are of interest. To be sure, the structured heterogeneity of the speech community improves on earlier models by recognising the existence and systematicity of heterogeneity; however, speakers who do not share the same norms (for example, because they are recent immigrants or transplants from other regions) are excluded from the community.[1] Thus, despite the model's emphasis on heterogeneity, the focus is in fact on what speakers share. Marginal members rarely enter the analysis, and when they do, they remain at the margins; their linguistic practices are used primarily to demonstrate how they fall short of central membership. Language and gender researchers are acutely aware of the problems with this approach. Because women may be defined, implicitly or explicitly, as marginal to the vernacular speech community, they may be underrepresented or simply mis-represented (cf. Morgan, 1999). Speakers whose identities differ from those of the wider com-munity – especially those whose gender identities do not conform to community norms – are likewise omitted or obscured in research within this paradigm.

The expectation of consensus in speech community norms also requires that the system be closed to outside influence. The possibility of interaction between speech communities is not important in the model.[2] Hence researchers seek sameness, not difference; difference (e.g. in language use) is contained by interpreting it as sameness at an underlying level (e.g. in shared sociolinguistic norms). With this emphasis on analysis of the group as an autonomous system, phenomena resulting from linguistic and cultural contact (Pratt, 1987) may be overlooked. For example, the focus on the internal workings of the speech community does not accommodate investigations of gendered interaction across cultural groups.

Groups vs. individuals

Related to the problem of homogeneity in the speech community model is its privileging of the group over the individual as the unit of analysis. In such an approach, the role of the individual is merely to instantiate the practices of the group. Individual actions result less from choice and agency than from a social order that impinges on individuals from above. The traditional model's strong preference for structure over agency means that individual variation, or style, is inter-preted as the mechanical outcome of structural forces such as situational norms. A more agentive view locates style in personal choices concerning self-presentation (Johnstone, 1995, 1996, Johnstone and Bean, 1997). This perspective, which also admits structural constraints on the individual, is well suited for gender studies, given the field's longtime recognition that individuals make purposeful choices in the face of the limitations imposed on them by social structures. As Ortner notes above, one of the benefits of practice theory is its ability to cope with both aspects of women's (and men's) lives.

Identity categories vs. identity practices

The structural perspective is a static perspective, one in which the social order remains largely unaltered. Changes in the practices of its inhabitants have the effect of keeping the system in equilibrium. Nowhere is this more evident than in the speech community model's implicit theory of identity: Individuals are viewed as occupying particular social identities throughout their lives by virtue of their position in the social structure. Such an analysis is particularly problematic for researchers of language and gender. The concept of identity is central to gender-oriented research, but the version offered by the speech community framework contradicts basic insights of recent feminist theory. Contemporary feminists view identities as fluid, not frozen; they note that, although identities link individuals to particular social groups, such links are not pre-determined. Instead, identities emerge in practice, through the combined effects of structure and agency. Individuals engage in multiple identity practices simultaneously, and they are able to move from one identity to another. This process is not entirely unconstrained; speakers may end up reproducing hegemonic identities more often than resisting them, as suggested by Holmes (1997). It is also important, however, to call attention to the previously unacknowledged flexibility of identity formation.

Top-down vs. bottom-up

For the specificity of identity to become visible, it must be examined from the point of view of the individuals who enact it. Such a vantage point is not available within the speech community model, which privileges the analyst's interpretations over those of participants. Indeed, the speech community itself is an analytic construct which may fail to correspond to its putative members' own perceptions. Nonetheless, many analyses are carried out under the belief that the linguist has access to elements of speakers' reality that are not available to the speakers themselves.

An alternative to this top-down paradigm is **ethnography**, an approach that is participant- rather than analyst-driven. Where the speech community framework is skeptical of speakers' perspectives on their own practices, ethnography makes local interpretations central to the analysis. Gender does not have the same meanings across space and time, but is instead a local production, realised differently by different members of a community; thus an ethnographic orientation yields particularly fruitful results for language and gender research.

Nerds, gender, and the community of practice

The inadequacies of the speech community model for scholars of language and gender are overcome in the theory of the community of practice as articulated by Eckert and McConnell-Ginet 1992, 1995.[3] Rather than investing language with a special analytic status, the community of practice framework considers language as one of many social practices in which participants engage. By defining the community as a group of people oriented to the same practice, though not necessarily in the same way, the community of practice model treats difference and conflict, not uniformity and consensus, as the ordinary state of affairs. The inherent heterogeneity of the community of practice also brings marginal members to the forefront of analysis. One reason for this shift to the margins is that some peripheral members are recognised as novices, as in Lave and Wenger's original formulation (1991). More importantly, however, the community of practice, unlike the speech community, may be constituted around any social or linguistic practice, no matter how marginal from the perspective of the traditional speech community. Likewise, by focusing on individuals as well as groups, the theory of the community of practice integrates structure with agency. And because identities are rooted in actions rather than categories, the community of practice model can capture the multiplicity of identities at work in specific speech situations more fully than is possible within the speech community framework. Such nuanced description is also facilitated by Eckert and McConnell-Ginet's intrinsically ethnographic approach to language and gender research. The remainder of this article draws on the above characteristics of the community of practice to demonstrate the theory's utility in the investigation of an understudied social identity as it emerges locally in a high-school setting.

Eckert (1989a) offers an account of the social organisation of a typical suburban US high school. She found that students' social worlds and identities were defined by two polar opposites: the Jocks (overachieving students who oriented to middle-class values) and the Burnouts (under-achieving students who were bound for work, rather than college, at the end of their high-school careers). Yet the dichotomy that separated these students also united them in what can be under-stood as a single community of practice, since the ultimate goal of members of both groups was to be *cool*. The difference lay in how each group defined coolness.

Not all high-school students, however, share the Jocks' and Burnouts' preoccupation with coolness. A third group, the nerds, defines itself largely in opposition to cool students – whether Jocks, Burnouts, or any other social identity. Nerds stand as the antithesis of all these groups, a situation that Eckert succinctly captures in her observation, 'If a Jock is the opposite of a Burn-out, a nerd is the opposite of both' (1989a:48). But despite the structural significance of the nerd in the organisation of youth identities, few researchers have examined its implications, and those who have tried have fallen far short of the mark in their analyses. Thus the sociologist David Kinney, in a rare study of nerds (1993), argues that, in order to succeed socially, nerds must undergo a process of 'recovery of identity' that involves broadening one's friendship network, participating in extracurricular activities, and heterosexual dating: in short, they must become Jocks. Another scholarly treatment (Tolone and Tieman, 1990) investigates the drug use of nerds in an article subtitled 'Are loners deviant?' – in other words, are nerds really Burnouts?

What both studies overlook is that being a nerd is not about being a failed Burnout or an in-adequate Jock. It is about rejecting both Jockness and Burnout-ness, and all the other forms of coolness that youth identities take. Although previous researchers maintain that nerd identity is invalid or deficient, in fact nerds, like Jocks and Burnouts, to a great extent consciously choose and display their identities through language and other social practices. And where other scholars tend to equate nerdiness with social death, I propose that nerds in US high schools are not socially isolated misfits, but competent members of a distinctive and oppositionally defined community of practice. Nerdiness is an especially valuable resource for girls in the gendered world of the US high school.

Elsewhere (Bucholtz, 1998) I describe the social identity of the nerd and detail the phonological, syntactic, lexical, and discourse practices through which nerd identity is linguistically indexed. Here I propose a framework for the classification of such practices. These linguistic indices are of two kinds: **negative identity practices** are those that individuals employ to distance them-selves from a rejected identity, while **positive identity practices** are those in which individuals engage in order actively to construct a chosen identity. In other words, negative identity practices define what their users are *not*, and hence emphasise identity as an intergroup phenomenon; positive identity practices define what their users *are*, and thus emphasise the intragroup aspects of social identity. The linguistic identity practices of nerds in the present study are shown in Table 1.

The negative identity practices listed here work to disassociate nerds from non-nerds, and es-pecially from cool teenagers. Each of these practices, which mark nerdy teenagers as avowedly uncool, constitutes a refusal to engage in the pursuit of coolness that consumes other students. Meanwhile, all the positive identity practices listed contribute to the speaker's construction of an intelligent self – a primary value of nerd identity. These linguistic practices also have non-lin-guistic counterparts in positive and negative identity practices of other kinds (see below).

TABLE 1. Linguistic identity practices of nerds at Bay City High School.

Linguistic Level	Negative Identity Practices	Positive Identity Practices
Phonology	Lesser fronting of (uw) and (ow)*	
Phonology	Resistance to colloquial phonological processes such as vowel reduction, consonant-cluster simplification and contraction	Employment of superstandard and hypercorrect phonological forms (e.g. spelling pronunciations)
Syntax	Avoidance of nonstandard syntactic forms	Adherence to standard and superstandard syntactic forms
Lexicon	Avoidance of current slang	Employment of lexical items associated with the formal register (e.g. Greco-Latinate forms)
Discourse		Orientation to language form (e.g. punning, parody, word coinage)

*In Bucholtz (1998) I offer a fuller discussion of the phonological and syntactic patterns of nerds. The present article focuses primarily on lexicon and on discursive identity practices. The variables (uw) and (ow) are part of a vowel shift that is characteristic of California teenagers (Hinton et al. 1987, Luthin 1987). It is stereotypically associated with trendy and cool youth identities.

But linguistic practices can often reveal important social information that is not available from the examination of other community practices alone. For example, Eckert and McConnell-Ginet 1995 apply the theory of the community of practice to Eckert's study of Jocks and Burnouts. Linguistic analysis revealed that the two groups were participating at different rates in the Northern Cities Vowel Shift, with the most innovative vowels being those used by the 'Burned-Out Burnout girls', the most extreme adherents to this social identity. Eckert and McConnell-Ginet's finding runs counter to the sociolinguistic tenet that 'in stable variables, women use fewer nonstandard variants than men of the same social class and age under the same circumstances' (Chambers, 1995:112). The researchers argue that the vowels employed by the Burned-Out Burnout girls are resources through which they construct their identities as tough and streetwise; unlike the boys, who can display their toughness through physical confrontations, female Burnouts must index their identities semiotically, because fighting is viewed as inappropriate for girls. Thus Burnout girls and boys share an orientation toward toughness in their community of practice, but the practice of toughness is achieved in different ways by each gender. By viewing language as equivalent to other social practices like fighting, Eckert and McConnell-Ginet are able to explain the ethnographic meaning of the Burnout girls' vowel systems, and to show how, as symbolic capital (Bourdieu, 1978), language can acquire the empowering authority of physical force itself.

Nerds, of course, attain empowerment in very different ways than either Burnouts or Jocks. One of the primary ways they differ from these other, more trend-conscious groups is through the high value they place on individuality. Compared to both Jocks and Burnouts – who must toe the subcultural line in dress, language, friendship choices, and other social practices – nerds are somewhat less constrained by peer-group sanctions.

For girls, nerd identity also offers an alternative to the pressures of hegemonic femininity – an ideological construct that is at best incompatible with, and at worst hostile to, female intellectual ability. Nerd girls' conscious opposition to this ideology is evident in every aspect of their lives, from language to hexis to other aspects of self-presentation. Where cool girls aim for either cuteness or sophistication in their personal style, nerd girls aim for silliness. Cool girls play soccer or basketball; nerd girls play badminton. Cool girls read fashion magazines; nerd girls read novels. Cool girls wear tight T-shirts, and either very tight or very baggy jeans; nerd girls wear shirts and jeans that are neither tight nor extremely baggy. Cool girls wear pastels or dark tones; nerd girls wear bright primary colours. But these practices are specific to individuals; they are engaged in by particular nerd girls, not all of them.

The community of practice model accommodates the individuality that is paramount in the nerd social identity, without overlooking the strong community ties that unify the nerd girls in this study. The community of practice also allows us to look at nerd girls in the same way that Eckert and McConnell-Ginet (1999) view the Burnout girls: as speakers AND social actors, as individuals AND members of communities, and as both resisting and responding to cultural ideologies of gender.

Identity practices in a local nerd community

To illustrate the value of the community of practice framework, I will focus on a single social group that displays the nerd social identity. Nerds at the high school in my study constitute a single community insofar as they engage in shared practices, but this identity is divided into particular social groups whose members associate primarily with one another, and these groups form their own communities of practice. In communities of practice, unlike speech communities, the boundaries are determined not externally by linguists, but internally through ethnographically specific social meanings of language use. As suggested above, ethnographic methods therefore become crucial to the investigation of communities of practice.

The ethnographic fieldwork from which the data are taken was carried out during the 1994-95 academic year at a California high school that I call Bay City High. The social group of nerd girls that is the focus of this discussion is a small, cohesive friendship group that comprises four central members – Fred, Bob, Kate, and Loden – and two peripheral members, Carrie and Ada. (Ada does not appear in the data that follow.) All the girls are European American except Ada, who is Asian American. The same group also formed a club, which I will call the Random Reigns Supreme Club.[5]

Random Reigns Supreme is more properly described as an anti-club, which is in keeping with the counter-hegemonic orientation of nerd identity. It was created by members in order to celebrate their own preferences, from Sesame Street to cows to Mr. Salty the pretzel man. Members emphasise the 'randomness' of the club's structure. It is not organised around shared preferences; instead, any individual's preferences can be part of the club's *de facto* charter, and all six members are co-presidents. This structure contrasts with the corporate focus and hierarchical structure of most school clubs, which bring together people who are otherwise unconnected to perform a shared activity (Eckert, 1989a). The Random Reigns Supreme Club centres around members' daily practices, not specialised activities. It has no goals, no ongoing projects, and no official meetings. Nevertheless, members proudly take their place among the corporate clubs in the pages of the school's yearbook. The girls' insistence on being photographed for the yearbook has a subversive quality: The photo publicly documents the existence of this otherwise little-recognised friendship group, and demands its institutional legitimacy on par with the French Club, the Backpacking Club, and other activity-based organisations. Like their yearbook photograph, the language used by the girls not only marks their nerd identity but also expresses their separation from outsiders. As shown by the following examples (taken from a single interaction), the details of interaction are important and contested resources in defining a shared oppositional nerd identity within the club's community of practice.

Positive identity practices

As indicated above, many positive identity practices in which nerds engage contribute to the display of intelligence. The community value placed on intelligence is reflected in non-linguistic identity practices oriented to the world of school, books and knowledge. This orientation is amply illustrated in the following.[6]

(1)	1	Carrie:	Where where do those seeds come from?
	2		(points to her bagel)
	3	(laughter)	
	4	Bob:	[Poppies.]
	5	Fred:	[Sesame plants.]
	6	Carrie:	{But what do they look like?} (high pitch)
	7	Fred:	I have no idea. hh
	8	Bob:	Sesame:.
	9	Carrie:	[Is anybody-h]
	10	Fred:	Ask me (.) [tomorrow.]
	11		I'll look it up for you. h
	12	Carrie:	h Is anybody here knowledgeable about (.)
	13		the seeds on top of bagels?/
	14	Fred:	/Sesame.
	15	Bob:	They're sesame?
	16		They're not sunfl-?
	17		No,
	18		of course they're not sunflower.
	19	Loden:	Yeah,
	20		[What kind of seeds are–]
	21	Carrie:	[Because sunflower are those whopping ones?]
	22	Bob:	[Yeah.
	23		Yeah.
	24		I know.]
	25	(laughter)	

Carrie's question in line 1 creates the conditions for intellectual display. Although the humour of the question is acknowledged through laughter (line 2), it receives immediate, serious uptake from two participants, Bob and Fred (lines 4-5). Carrie's subsequent question (line 6), however, forces an admission of ignorance from Fred (line 7).

Because knowledge is symbolic capital within the nerd community of practice, Fred's admission results in some loss of face. She recovers from this (minor) social setback by invoking the authority of a reference book (*I'll look it up for you,* line 11). In this way Fred can safely assure her interlocutor that, although she does not yet know the answer, she soon will. She is also able to one-up Bob, who has misidentified the bagel seeds (line 4) and continues to show some scepticism about Fred's classification of them (*Sesame:,* line 8). Fred tracks this indirect challenge for five lines, through her own turn and Carrie's next question; rather than continuing to participate in the series of adjacency pairs that Carrie has initiated (lines 12-13), she responds to Bob (line 14). Fred thus succeeds in displaying both actual knowledge, about the type of seeds under discussion, and potential knowledge, about the appearance of sesame plants.

Claims to knowledge are, however, often disputed in this community of practice. After Bob provides an incorrect answer to Carrie and receives a correction from Fred, she continues to exhibit doubt about Fred's knowledge (line 15). She offers a second incorrect identification of the seeds in line 16, but this time she interrupts herself and self-corrects (lines 17-18), in an effort to prevent further other-correction. She does not succeed, however; and when Carrie explains why Bob is mistaken, the latter overlaps with her, offering three quick acknowledgments that are designed to cut off Carrie's turn (lines 22-24).

This passage shows several deviations from the preference organisation of repair in conversation (Schleghoff *et al.,* 1977), according to which self-initiation and self-repair are preferred over initiation and repair by another. Bob twice initiates dispreferred repairs of Fred's turns (lines 8, 15), and she even begins to carry out the repair itself in line 16. When Bob initiates a repair of her own utterance through self-interruption in the same line, Carrie performs the repair despite Bob's efforts to prevent her from doing so (lines 21-24). The frequent apparent violations of repair organisation suggest that, in this community of practice, self-repair is preferred only by the speaker; the listener's positive face (the desire to be viewed as intelligent) wars against and often overrides consideration of the speaker's negative face (the desire not to be viewed as unintelligent).

Bob's loss of face in ex. 1 leads her, in ex. 2, to initiate a new conversational direction:

```
(2)  26    Bob:      They come from trees.
     27              They have big trees and they just
     28              [ra:in down seeds]
     29              [(laughter)        ]
     30    Carrie:   [No they don't.  ]
     31              Uh uh.
     32              Why would little tiny seeds [come from– ]
     33    Fred:                                [{into  baskets.}]  (smiling  quality)
     34              Ye:p,

     35              [({I've been there.})] (smiling quality)
     36    Carrie:   [No:.   ]
     37    Loden:    [No:.   ]
     38    Bob:      [[Little tiny leaves come from trees,  ]]
     39    Fred:     [[And the whole culture's built around it,]]
     40              like in: some countries,
     41              All they do is like the women come out and they have ba(h)skets on
     42              th(h)eir h(h)eads and they st(h)and under a [tree,]
```

Bob jokingly provides an authoritative answer to Carrie's question (lines 26-28) and thereby skillfully shifts attention from her own lack of knowledge to Carrie's. Fred eagerly joins in with the parody of scientific discourse, amplifying on the theme while supplying invented anthropological details that invoke the didactic style of a typical high-school classroom or public television documentary (33-35, 39-42). Such teasing episodes are frequent in this friendship group. But more importantly, this exchange is a collaborative performance of nerd identity: the participants collude in sustaining the frame of an intellectual debate, even as laughter keys the talk as play. Nerd identities are here jointly constructed and displayed.

In ex. 3, Carrie – who up to this point has mostly provided opportunities for others to display their nerd identities, rather than participating herself (but see below) – shifts the topic, which she sustains for the rest of the interaction:

(3)	43	Carrie:	[My-]
	44		You sound like my crusty king,
	45		I'm writing this (.) poem because I have to like incorporate these
	46		words into a poem, and it's all about-
	47	(interruption, lines omitted)	
	48	Fred:	So what about this king?

Carrie's discussion of a class assignment returns to a central value of nerdiness: school. The topic is sustained for 56 lines and 26 turns; and although it is interrupted immediately after Carrie introduces it (line 47), Fred prompts her to return to the subject several minutes later (line 48). Carrie's enthusiastic description of her poem – and the eager participation of others in this topic – is rare among students with cool social identities, but it is quite common among nerds, for whom academic pursuits are a central resource for identity practices.

At the same time, however, Carrie's selection of subject matter for her poem, with its mildly scatological – or at least 'gross' theme (line 80) – is playfully subversive of school values and emphatically counter to traditional feminine topics, as ex. 4 illustrates:

(4)	49	Carrie:	He's like (.) has this (.) castle,
	50	(xxx:	Is he xxx king?)
	51	Carrie:	No–
	52		Yeah,
	53		he is.
	54	Loden:	hh
	55	Carrie:	He has this-
	56		(He has this castle right?
	57		except it's all crusty,]
	58		(rustling of lunch bag, clanging of aluminum can)
	59	(Fred:	Uh huh.)
	60	Carrie:	And so he lives on a boat [in the moat.]
	61	Bob:	[A crusty–]
	62	(Fred crushes her aluminum can)	
	63	Kate:	Who: a!
	64	(quiet laughter)	

65	Bob:	Is it really [crusty?]
66	Carrie:	[He's-]
67		And so like the- like because- the people are trying to convince
68		him that like he should stay in the castle and he's all,
69		('No, it's crusty!'] (high pitch, tensed vocal cords)
70		[(laughter)]
71	Carrie:	[('I'm in the moat!']] (high pitch, quiet)
72		right,
73	Bob:	What's wrong with [crusty castles?]
74	Carrie:	[And so-]
75		Well,
76		Would [you want to live]=
77	Kate:	[Crusty (castles).]
78	Carrie:	=in a castle full of crust?
79		{[ɨəɨ]} (noise of disgust and disapproval)
80	Kate:	How gross.]
81	Bob:	[I mi:ght.]
82	Carrie:	Huh?

Bob here enters into the unfeminine spirit of Carrie's narrative, even outdoing Carrie with her repeated insistence on her own immunity from 'gross' subjects like crustiness (lines 73, 81). A competitive tone is also evident in the multiple challenges she issues to Carrie throughout the latter's narrative (lines 65, 73). As questions, these challenges echo Carrie's earlier questions (lines 1, 6, 12-13); but whereas Carrie's appeared to be genuine information-seeking questions, Bob's are not. Carrie's recognition of this fact is shown by her failure to respond at all to the first question, and by her answering the second question with an equally challenging question of her own (*Would you want to live in a castle full of crust?*, lines 76, 78). Bob's face-threatening response (*I mi:ght*, line 81) perpetuates the jocular-combative tone. In ex. 5, however, this combativeness becomes not a shared resource for joint identity construction, but a marker of social division. The positive identity practices that dominate in the earlier part of the interaction are replaced by negative identity practices, as community members experience a threat not only to their face but also to their identities.

Negative identity practices
Example 5 is a continuation of Bob's face-threatening questions to Carrie. This final series of questions is unified through a shared template (*like + ADJ + crust*); their syntactic similarity emphasises that they are designed as a series, and it thus produces an effect of unremitting interrogation.

(5)	83	Bob:	What kind of crust?
	84		Like,
	85		bread crust?
	86	Carrie:	Like
	87	Bob:	Like [eye crust?
	88	Carrie:	[crusty crust.]
	89		Like {boo:ts y} (high pitch, tensed vocal cords)

90		crust.
91	(laughter)	
92	Bob:	Oh.
93		Well,
94		Maybe if it's bootsy,
95		I don't know.
96	Fred:	{ Boot[sy!]) (falsetto, sing-song)
97	Kate:	[(coughs)]
98	(laughter)	

These questions display Bob's nerd identity through her use of puns on the word *crust* (lines 85, 87). Punning, as a discourse practice that orients to linguistic form, is characteristic of nerds' discourse style (see Table 1). Carrie's refusal (line 88) to participate in Bob's punning thus constitutes a negative identity practice – one which, moreover, indexes a rejection of nerd identity as it has been constructed through preceding interactional practices. The refusal is made more evident by her exploitation (lines 86, 88-90) of Bob's syntactic template. By conforming to the syntactic form of Bob's turn, while failing to conform to the discourse practice of punning, Carrie separates herself from Bob at a point when the latter is fully engaged in nerdy identity practices.

This analysis is confirmed by Carrie's choice of upgraded adjective in line 89. *Bootsy* is a slang term with a negative evaluative sense; it is not used by other members of the Random Reigns Supreme Club. The introduction of youth slang into a group that explicitly rejects such linguistic forms is part of a strongly negative identity practice, and the reactions of Carrie's interlocutors are correspondingly negative: Bob's response (lines 92-95) jokingly concedes the point, while underscoring that Carrie has violated the rules of nerdy argument by appealing to the authority of cool youth culture. Fred's mocking repetition of the term (line 96) demonstrates that the use of slang is itself worthy of comment. With Carrie's narrative entirely derailed – it never becomes clear how it is connected to the earlier discussion – she soon afterward moves away from the group.

The complex interaction presented above reveals Carrie's peripheral status in this community of practice. As a non-core member, she moves between friendship groups – in fact, the interaction occurred when Carrie approached the core group in the middle of lunch period. Carrie's social flexibility has made her a cultural and linguistic broker for the Random Reigns Supreme Club, whose members become aware of current youth slang in large part through contact with her. Hence many slang terms that circulate widely in the cool groups are labelled by club members as 'Carrie words'.

Yet Carrie also demonstrates her ability and willingness to participate in the group's positive identity practices. She does so most obviously by engaging in sound play in recounting her poem (*crusty king*, line 44; *a boat in the moat*, line 60). More significant, though, is the subtle shift in her speech practices at the beginning of the interaction. Thus Carrie's question *Is anybody here knowledgeable about (.) the seeds on top of bagels?* (lines 12-13) draws on the formal register through her choice of the word *knowledgeable*. Among nerds, this register projects a speaker's persona as smart and highly educated. But the use of the formal register is strategic, not a mechanical result of membership in a particular social category. This point is supported by the fact that Carrie employs the nerd identity practice only after she asks two related questions in colloquial register (lines 1,6). Her unwillingness to overlap her turn with Fred's (lines 9, 10) further suggests that the question is a performance of nerdiness, not just a manifestation of it; she does not produce her utterance until she is assured of an attentive audience. That is, Carrie is simultaneously displaying and commenting on nerd practice – showing her awareness of nerdy linguistic forms, and announcing her willingness to enter a nerdy interactional space by carefully gauging her utterance to match the group's practices. Thus Carrie's performance of nerdiness places her within the community of practice; but her use of slang, as the other members are quick to let her know, moves her outside it. Such adjustments at interactional boundaries may reflect adjustments at community boundaries.

Conclusion

Because all the participants in the above exchange are middle-class European American girls from the same California city, the traditional sociolinguistic perspective would classify them un-problematically as members of the same speech community. Such an analysis would overlook the details of greatest interest to language and gender researchers: the performances of identity, and the struggles over it, which are achieved through language. However, by viewing the inter-action as the product of a community of practice, we can avoid this problem, as well as others associated with the speech community model.

The ethnographic method brings into view the social meanings with which participants invest their practices. These meanings emerge on the ground in local contexts; thus what it means to display academic knowledge, or to use slang, depends not on fixed identity categories but on where one is standing. Nor do participants necessarily agree on the meanings of their actions; nerdiness, like all identities, is a contested domain in which speakers struggle both over control of shared values, via positive identity practices (Who's better at being a nerd?), and over control of identity itself, via negative identity practices (Who counts as a nerd?). Such conflicts reveal the heterogeneity of membership in the community of practice – its constitution through the work of central and peripheral members alike. In this project, the interactional choices of specific individuals matter. Thus Carrie's identity is on display – and at risk – in a way that Loden's, for example, is not. These actions must be seen as choices, not as the outputs of interactional algorithms. While some practices reproduce the existing local social structure (as does Carrie's use of the formal register), others undermine it (e.g. her use of slang). Likewise, some nerdy practices (such as being good students) comply with the larger social order, while others (such as rejecting femininity) resist it. Linguistic practices, moreover, have no special status in this process. Instead, they work in conjunction with other social practices to produce meanings and identities. Bob's interactional work to distance herself from hegemonic femininity, for instance, is part of her overall participation in anti-feminine practices and her non-participation in feminine practices, as evidenced also by her physical self-presentation.

For sociolinguists, the community of practice represents an improvement over the speech com-munity in that it addresses itself to both the social and the linguistic aspects of the discipline. As a well-grounded framework with currency in a number of fields, practice theory in general, particularly the community of practice, revitalises social theory within sociolinguistics. What is more, it does so at a sufficiently general level to accommodate multiple dimensions of social analysis – including both structure and agency, both ideology and identity, both norms and inter-actions. The community of practice also provides an avenue for a more complete sociolinguistic investigation of identity. Although introduced for gender-based research, the community of practice has never been restricted to the analysis of a single element of identity. Indeed, it lends itself to the simultaneous investigation of multiple aspects of the self, from those at the macro level – like gender, ethnicity and class – to micro-identities like Jocks, Burnouts or nerds. The framework also allows for the study of interaction between levels of identity. The concepts of positive and negative identity practices, as proposed in this article, are intended as one way to develop the potential of the community of practice in this arena.

In addition to its benefits for social analysis, the community of practice offers an integrated approach to linguistic analysis. By understanding all socially meaningful language use as practices tied to various communities, the model enables researchers to provide more complete linguistic descriptions – along with social explanations – of particular social groups. Moreover, the community of practice provides a way to bring qualitative and quantitative research closer together. Because both kinds of linguistic data emerge from practice, both can be included in a single analysis. This richly contextualised approach to both language and society is one of the great strengths of the community of practice as a sociolinguistic framework.

Notes

* My thanks to Janet Holmes, Chris Holcomb, Stephanie Stanbro, and members of the Ethnography/ Theory Group at Texas A&M University for comments on and discussion of the ideas in this article.

1 The work of Barbara Horvath on immigrants in Sydney's speech community (Horvath, 1985, Horvath and Sankoff, 1987) has done a great deal to correct this omission.

2 Santa Ana and Parodi's model of nested speech communities (1998) is a recent attempt to address this problem.

3 A fuller discussion of the advantages of practice theory for language and gender research is provided by Bucholtz 1999.

4 Eckert 1989b calls this simple formulation into question; see also Labov (1990) for a response.

5 Though this is not its actual name, it preserves the flavour of the original. All other names are pseudonyms chosen by the speakers.

6 Transcription conventions are as follows:

.	end of intonation unit; falling intonation
,	end of intonation unit; fall-rise intonation
?	end of intonation unit; rising intonation
–	self-interruption
…	length
underline	emphatic stress or increased amplitude
(.)	pause of 0.5 seconds or less
(n.n)	pause of greater than 0.5 seconds, measured by a stopwatch
h	exhalation (e.g. laughter, sigh); each token marks one pulse
( )	uncertain transcription
( )	transcriber comment; nonvocal noise
{ }	stretch of talk over which a transcriber comment applies
[ ]	overlap beginning and end
/	latching (no pause between speaker turns)
=	no pause between intonation units

The transcript emphasises sequential organisation in order to highlight speakers' orientation to one another. It excludes phonological detail that is necessary for a complete analysis of nerd identity performance.

References

Bloomfield, Leonard (1933) *Language.* New York: Holt.

Bourdieu, Pierre (1978) *Outline of a theory of practice.* Cambridge and New York: Cambridge University Press.

Bourdieu, Pierre (1991) *Language and symbolic power.* Cambridge, MA: Harvard University Press.

Bucholtz, Mary (1998) Geek the girl: Language, femininity, and female nerds. In Natasha Warner *et al.* (eds.), *Gender and Belief Systems: Proceedings of the Fourth Berkeley Women and Language Conference,* 119-31. Berkeley: Berkeley Women and Language Group.

Bucholtz, Mary (1999) Bad examples: Transgression and progress in language and gender research. In Mary Bucholtz *et al.* (eds.), *Reinventing Identities.* New York: Oxford University Press.

Cameron, Deborah (1992) *Feminism and linguistic theory.* 2d edn. New York: St. Martin's Press.

Chambers, I. K. (1995) *Sociolinguistic theory.* Oxford: Blackwell.

Certeau, Michel de (1984) *The practice of everyday life.* Berkeley: University of California Press.

Don an, Nancy C. (1982) Defining the speech community to include its working margins. In Suzanne Romaine (ed.), *Sociolinguistic variation in speech communities,* 25-33. London: Arnold.

Eckert, Penelope (I 989a) *Jocks and Burnouts: Social categories and identity in the high school.* New York: Teachers College Press.

Eckert, Penelope (1989b) The whole woman: Sex and gender differences in variation. *Language Variation and Change* 1:245-67.

Eckert, Penelope and McConnell-Ginet, Sally (1992) Think practically and look locally: Language and gender as community-based practice. *Annual Review of Anthropology* 21:461-90.

Eckert, Penelope and McConnell-Ginet, Sally (1995) Constructing meaning, constructing selves: Snapshots of language, gender, and class from Belten High. In Kira Hall and Mary Bucholtz (eds.), *Gender articulated: Language and the socially constructed self,* 459-507. London: Routledge.

Giddens, Anthony (1979) *Central problems in social theory: Action, structure, and contradiction in social analysis.* Berkeley: University of California Press.

Guy, Gregory R. (1988) Language and social class. In Frederick J. Newmeyer (ed.), *Linguistics: The Cambridge survey, vol.4: Language: The socio-cultural context,* 37-63. Cambridge and New York: Cambridge University Press. 37-63.

Hinton, Leanne, *et al.* (1987) It's not just the Valley Girls: A study of California English. *Berkeley Linguistics Society* 13:117-28.

Holmes, Janet (1997) Women, language and identity. *Journal of Sociolinguistics* 1:195-223.

Horvath, Barbara (1985) *Variation in Australian English: The sociolects of Sydney.* Cambridge and New York: Cambridge University Press.

Horvath, Barbara and Sankoff, David (1987) Delimiting the Sydney speech community. *Language in Society* 16:179-204.

Hudson, Richard A. (1980) *Sociolinguistics.* Cambridge and New York: Cambridge University Press.

Hymes, Dell (1974) *Foundations in sociolinguistics: An ethnographic approach.* Philadelphia: University of Pennsylvania Press.

Johnstone, Barbara (1995) Sociolinguistic resources, individual identities, and public speech styles of Texas women. *Journal of Linguistic Anthropology* 5:183-202.

Johnstone, Barbara and Bean, Judith Mattson (1997) Self-expression and linguistic variation. *Language in Society* 26:221-46.

Kinney, David A. (1993) From nerds to normals: The recovery of identity among adolescents from middle school to high school. *Sociology of Education* 66:1.21-40.

Labov, William (1966) *The social stratification of English in New York City.* Washington, DC: Centre for Applied Linguistics.

Labov, William (1972) The reflection of social processes in linguistic structures. In his *Sociolinguistic patterns,* 110-21. Philadelphia: University of Pennsylvania Press.

Labov, William (1990) The intersection of sex and social class in the course of linguistic change. *Language Variation and Change* 2:205-54.

Lave, Jean (1988) *Cognition in practice: Mind, mathematics, and culture in everyday life.* Cambridge and New York: Cambridge University Press.

Lave, Jean and Wenger, Etienne (1991) *Situated learning: Legitimate peripheral participation.* Cambridge and New York: Cambridge University Press.

Luthin, Herbert W. (1987) The story of California (ow): The coming-of-age of English in California. In Keith M. Denning *et al.* (eds.), *Variation in language: NWAV-XV at Stanford,* 312-24. Stanford, CA: Department of Linguistics, Stanford University.

Milroy, James (1992) *Linguistic variation and change: On the historical sociolinguistics of English.* Oxford: Blackwell.

Morgan, Marcyliena (1999) No woman, no cry: Claiming African American women's place. In Mary Bucholtz *et al.* (eds.), *Reinventing identities.*

Ortner, Sherry (1996) *Making gender: The politics and erotics of culture.* Boston: Beacon.

Pratt, Mary Louise (1987) Linguistic utopias. In Nigel Fabb *et al* (eds.), *The linguistics of writing: Arguments between language and literature,* 48-66. New York: Methuen.

Rickford, John R. (1986) The need for new approaches to social class analysis in sociolinguistics. *Language and Communication* 6:3.215-21.

Romaine, Suzanne (1982) What is a speech community? In Suzanne Romaine (ed.), *Sociolinguistic variation in speech communities,* 13-24. London: Arnold.

Santa Ana, Otto, and Parodi, Claudia (1998) Modelling the speech community: Configuration and variable types in the Mexican Spanish setting. *Language in Society* 27:23-51.

Schegloff, Emanuel; Jefferson, Gail; and Sacks, Harvey (1977) The preference for self-correction in the organisation of repair in conversation. *Language* 53:361-82.

Silverstein, Michael (1996) Encountering languages and languages of encounter in North American ethnohistory. *Journal of Linguistic Anthropology* 6:1 26-44.

Tolone, W. L., and C. R. Tieman (1990) Drugs, delinquency and nerds: Are loners deviant? *Journal of Drug Education* 20:2.153-62.

Wenger, Etienne (1998) *Communities of practice.* Cambridge and New York: Cambridge University Press.

Williams, Glyn (1992) *Sociolinguistics: A sociological critique.* London: Routledge.

CHAPTER 11

Voices, intertextuality and induction into schooling
Janet Maybin

> Our speech...is filled with others' words, varying degrees of otherness or varying degrees of our-own-ness, varying degrees of awareness and detachment. These words of others carry with them their own expression, their own evaluative tone, which we assimilate, rework and re-accentuate. (Bakhtin, 1986: 89)

> Reported speech is speech within speech, utterance within utterance, and at the same time *speech about speech, utterance about utterance.* (Volosinov, 1986: 115)

Introduction

In this chapter I shall examine the ways in which 'other voices' in 10-12 year-old school children's informal talk are invoked to make particular intertextual links. I shall suggest that these links are used strategically and collaboratively by the children in their on-going construction of meaning. A large literature on intertextuality (the use of links and references to create a dialogue between texts) has developed since Kristeva first introduced the term into French criticism in the late 1960s through her discussion of Bakhtin's work (Moi, 1986). In research on the importance of intertextuality for meaning-making in educational contexts, most research has been concerned with students' reading or writing. Where researchers have addressed students' experience of oral voices or discourse, this has been in relation to their reproduction in students' written texts (eg Dyson, 1987, Short, 1992, Kamberelis and Scott, 1992, Scollon *et al*, 1998). I would suggest however that students' oral discourse itself is a particularly interesting site for looking at intertextual referencing. Far from being only about the 'here and now' as was once argued by writers contrasting speech with writing (eg Goody and Watt, 1968, Olson, 1977), talk provides a medium where a web of complex links to other conversations and other contexts is constructed between participants and exploited for a range of speaker purposes. One of the ways in which intertextual links are set up and manipulated in oral discourse is through speakers' taking on and reporting of other people's voices. In the data I collected on children's informal talk in school, this kind of intertextual referencing was important across a range of contexts. I shall look briefly in this chapter at the reproduction of other voices in teacher-student dialogue, but focus mainly on children's use of other voices in school-orientated talk among themselves which occurred in the course of carrying out classroom tasks and participating in school activities. I shall suggest that this talk, which is often ignored in educational research on classroom language, reveals complex and interesting uses of intertextual referencing and has its own particular importance for children's induction into educational discourses and schooled identities.

Bakhtin, Volosinov¹ and reported voices

Bakhtin (1981) argues that the words we use always bring with them connotations from the previous contexts of their use. This is particularly clearly the case when we report someone else's words which create an intertextual link with other conversations and other contexts. Certain aspects of these other conversations and contexts are highlighted through the voice and brought into play in the current conversation. For example, we may report someone's voice in telling an anecdote to call up a particular scenario or repeat an authoritative voice to lend weight to our argument. The associations a voice brings with it and the authority it invokes become an essential part of meaning-making in the reporting context.

Not only are the nature, content and associations of the reported voice important to this meaning-making, but so also is the particular way in which the voice is framed and reproduced by the reporting speaker. Volosinov (1986) draws a distinction between two main ways of reporting another voice. In linear reporting, the words are reproduced verbatim, and the boundaries between the reporter's voice and the reported voice are clearcut. In the pictorial style, however, the reported speech is infiltrated with the reporter's speech, and boundaries are not so clear. He suggests that the reporting mode is linked both to the nature of the voice being reported (authoritative voices tend to be reported in the linear style) and to prevailing ideological practices within a society (the linear style being associated with authoritarianism). Within the pictorial style, Volosinov identified further mixed styles of reporting speech where the reporting and reported voices merge in more subtle variations of direct and indirect discourse. These are used to particular effect by novelists, for instance when the reader can sense the author's irony behind a particular character's speech, or when the mood or perspective of a character spills over into the narrator's voice. For Volosinov, the central clue to the meaning of reported speech. either in literature or in everyday talk, lies in the ways in which a speaker frames and reproduces the reported voice in relation to their own purposes within the reporting context.

Bakhtin (1984) develops these ideas further into a typology of different ways of reproducing voices. Central to both Bakhtin and Volosinov's work is the idea that language use is never neutral but always reflects a particular evaluative position or moral perspective. They distinguish between cases when a reported voice is associated with the same evaluative position as the speaker and when it is not and are particularly interested in how a speaker manages different kinds of relationships with the voice they are reporting. Drawing on Bakhtin's 1984 typology, I have found the following categories useful:

a. *Quotation*, direct or indirect, where voices are reported which may or may not express a similar evaluative perspective to the speaker. Here, as in 'linear reporting' the boundaries between the reporting and reporting voice are clear. In oral discourse, however, speakers are not usually expected to quote the exact words of the person they are reporting, unless these are central to the point being made. Rather, they reproduce something close (or not so close) to what a speaker said, in a way which fits in with their current conversational purposes. To take an example from my data, when a student quotes his head teacher 'he's the one who done it and Mr. Perry goes, em he should have been punished as well', the student may not be quoting Mr. Perry's exact words but the phrase 'he should have been punished as well', clearly conveys Mr. Perry's moral perspective. This reported perspective, together with Mr. Perry's authority, are used by the student to strengthen his own position.

b. *Imitation*, which I divide into *repetition*, a fairly ritual and formulaic echoing of something another speaker has said, which sometimes occurs in teacher-student dialogue, and *appropriation*, where the speaker does not simply repeat someone else but takes on the given words and makes them their own, to suit their own communicative purposes. In relation to the example above, the student could have reproduced Mr. Perry's words, or perhaps a key phrase, without acknowledging that he is quoting him. In this case he would have, as it were, appropriated Mr. Perry's voice and reproduced it, together with Mr. Perry's moral perspective, as if it were his own.

c. *Stylisation*, where a voice is reproduced as if it were one's own but with 'a slight shadow of objectification' so that we hear the speaker's voice overlaid with another different voice (Bakhtin, 1984:189). A third strategy of the student referred to above might have been to reproduce a phrase from Mr. Perry without explicitly acknowledging its source but with some kind of slight stylistic change to signal that another voice is involved. Again, the evaluative positions of the speaker and the reported voice coincide.

d. *Parody,* where stylistic devices are also used to signal the voice as 'other', but in this case the evaluative perspective of the speaker and the parodied voice are in opposition. This produces an explicitly 'double-voiced' utterance where there is a kind of struggle between two opposing positions or perspectives. On occasion in my data children parodied teachers' voices, often to express their frustration or boredom with a school procedure.

e. *Hidden polemic*, where a speaker's words are strongly shaped in opposition to an absent voice. One could imagine the boy referred to as guilty in the student's comment above strongly protesting his innocence to his friends, implicitly arguing against the headteacher's perspective.

Bakhtin stresses that in the flow of communication such categories are overlapping and dynamic, and may merge into each other. There is a tendency in *imitation* and *stylisation* to bring two voices together into one, while the tension between opposing positions in *parody* and *internal polemic* tends to drive the voices apart. In the discussion below I shall not look at *internal polemic*, which was not as easily identifiable as cases where a second voice is more explicitly expressed within an utterance. I shall examine examples of students' use of repetition, appropriation, stylisation, parody and quotation and explore the implications of the intertextual relationships which are invoked by these discursive strategies. I shall suggest that in school-oriented talk among themselves, students use this form of intertextual referencing as part of their active participation in the process of being inducted into school procedures and discourses.

The data

The analysis below draws on data from an ethnographic study of language practices in two classes of 10-12 year old school children, each in a different school in neighbouring white, monolingual, working class communities in southern England. I focussed particularly on their use of informal talk to explore and construct knowledge and identities. The study included three and a half weeks' observation and continuous tape-recordings of talk across the school day (using a radio microphone and small cassette recorders), followed some weeks later by 30-60 minute interviews with children in friendship pairs. The interviews covered topics which had cropped up in the continuous recordings, children's out of school literacy practices and their other interests and preoccupations. The continuous recordings of children's talk together with my observation notes and the children's interviews enabled me to identify recurring themes and patterns in their talk, to build up dialogical and contextualising information in relation to particular conversation extracts and to track some uses of reported voices within and across conversations (Maybin, 1998). My analysis of the transcripts of children's talk is informed by my initial ethnographic observations of their daily life in school while I recorded their talk, and by the experience of transcribing the tapes and noting prosodic features which were often a vital clue to the evaluative function of an utterance.

In the discussion below I shall use the term 'voice' rather than 'discourse' because, although I want to emphasis the social and contextual associations which are imported along with a voice, I also want to note the specificity of voice reproduction in my data and the significance of particular voices and their transformation for children's 'ideological becoming'. I shall start by briefly pointing to some patterns of intertextuality in teacher-student dialogue, and then discuss the nature and significance of voice reproduction in students' school-orientated talk among themselves.

Teacher-student dialogue

A number of researchers of classroom language have pointed out that a recurring feature in teacher/student dialogue is the way in which teachers pick up on students' responses to their questions and appropriate and transform their words to shift these responses into schooled frames of reference and the genres of specific subject disciplines (eg Wertsch, 1991, Mercer, 1992). In my own data, the authoritative texts which tend to guide social behaviour within the classroom and set the frame for what counts as worthwhile knowledge are the teacher's voice and the textbook or worksheet. There is a hierarchical set of intertextual relationships where the teacher quotes, explains and appropriates the voice of written text and appropriates and rephrases student responses to shift students into school discourses. To give a couple of simple examples of this rephrasing from my data, on one occasion a teacher reformulates a student's response 'none' into the appropriate mathematical term 'nought' as she takes the class through a calculation she is writing on the board and on another occasion she takes up and rephrases the student term 'beach' as 'coastline' when helping students to read a map in a geography lesson. Students, on the other hand, tend to directly repeat key words or phrases from the teacher in class discussion, or to take on her voice as it were in filling in the gaps she creates for student responses in her explanatory and directing monologues (Maybin, 1999). These gaps sometimes required the students to respond by importing her voice from a previous context, for example when she asked 'What did I tell you about how to write the decimal point?' or 'What do you do if the table where you want to sit is full?'. These patterns of repetition and appropriation occurred both in dialogues about learning tasks and in dialogues about classroom organisation and children's behaviour, suggesting that hierarchical patternings of intertextual referencing are important in both academic and institutional disciplining.

Peer talk

Reproducing authoritative voices

In children's informal peer talk there is much more evidence of students appropriating voices from teachers and worksheets and making them their own, in order to direct and their own and other students' activities and to manage behaviour. For instance, when Mr Sinclair announced before reading a short story to the assembled school: 'You've got to concentrate a bit more than usual'. Gary whispered to the boys sitting next to him who were fidgeting: 'Shh, we've <u>got to concentrate!</u>'[2] And in the French class when Martie said to Gary 'Got to get this right, Gary', Gary replied using the words which their teacher had earlier addressed to himself: '<u>You don't have to get it exactly, just do your best</u>'. Again, Linda rephrases Mrs. Kilbride's instruction 'Copy it out nice and neat' to another student: 'Kieran, if you've drawn your thing in your book, <u>you're allowed to copy it out</u>'. Similarly, Tracy reformulates a worksheet instruction:

Extract (1)

Tracy	(reading) 'Find Scout Hall again. It is in the grid square B two. What shape shows it on the map?'
Jodie	That it? No, no.
Tracy	What shape? <u>You've got to name the shape.</u>

These appropriated voices invoke institutional procedures which are used to define meaning and procedures in a child's current activity. The children's own purposes are merged with the institutional purpose they invoke, their orientation towards the institutional perspective often signalled through the use of modality, either repeated from or added to the reproduced voice. In Vygotskian terms, the taking on of the voice of a teacher, textbook or worksheet, represents a stage between the original exchange and the internalisation of educational dialogue, which children may use to direct their future actions in the classroom. When children internalise voices and dialogues, they are also internalising cultural and social aspects of the institutional order and in this sense, 'the history of the process of the internalisation of social speech is also the history of the socialisation of children's practical intellect' (Vygotsky, 1978:27). Through their intertextual orientation to the authoritative voices of teachers and worksheets, Gary, Tracy and Linda are expressing a commitment to institutional authority, framed by the modal phrases 'got to', 'have to' and 'allowed to', which position themselves as obedient students. This is one way in which children induct each other into institutional roles and procedures, through repeating or rephrasing instructions about how you should sit still and listen in assembly, evaluate your work, or interpret worksheet questions.

Invoking an authoritative voice may also help children to pursue their own personal social goals. For example, ten year-old Julie appeals to the many teacher exhortations in the data about making sure work is carefully, neatly and fully completed and that children should not rush their work in order to win an argument about who has finished their writing first. The term 'finished' and the phrase 'never took your time' invoke teacher voices from previous occasions, and the school ground rule that rushed work does not count as properly finished.

Extract (2)

Julie	We've almost finished
Student	So have we
Julie	You ain't <u>finished</u>
Kirsty	Some people have already <u>finished!</u>
Sharon	Yea, look, they've <u>finished!</u>
Julie	(*To student Sharon has indicated*) What's that? You never took your time on yours!

While the appropriation of authoritative voices by Gary, Linda and Tracy explicitly invokes the dominant institutional perspective, this perspective is also implicitly invoked in the appropriation of authoritative voices to support personal discursive goals, as in Julie's use of the term 'finished'. From a Foucauldian point of view, all these uses of authoritative voices are part of the more diffuse institutional processes, through which 'power reaches into the very grain of individuals, touches their bodies and inserts itself into their actions and attitudes, their discourses, learning processes and everyday lives' (Foucault, 1980:39). Implicit orientation towards institutional perspectives, as well as the explicit invoking of procedures to guide action, confirms institutional practices and discourses.

However, there are also occasions when children directly challenge the authority of a particular voice. In these cases the imported voice is strongly grammatically or paralinguistically framed. For example, Melissa uses indirect reported speech to complain to Nicole that Mrs. Kilbride has given inconsistent instructions: 'First Miss tells us you've got to do a draft, right, then she tells us we've got to do it again on the same piece of paper'. And when Gary asks Mrs. Kilbride if he can explain about a computer programme in a school assembly, Darren assumes an exaggeratedly bored sounding flat intonation to mutter a parody to Gary of what he predicts will be Mrs. Kilbride's response: 'Yea and you tell about how you define it, and then how you draw it and how you, how you write it and how you look at it and how how how you (..)' Thus Darren signals his own distance from the propositional content of the (preformulated) reported speech, and his lack of commitment to school literacy practices. Tape recordings of the explicitly double voiced discourse of parody record Darren's assumed boredom simultaneously with his 'pre-voicing' of Mrs. Kilbride's instructions.

Children may also quote a teacher's voice from a particular context in making evaluative comments to each other about the teacher as a person. Teachers are often discussed in terms of how effectively they manage to control the class, while still maintaining good relations with students. Through children's evaluations of individual teachers as strict, funny, nasty or soft, institutional roles and specific relationships are negotiated and evaluated in relation to each other (see Gannaway, 1984). For instance, Julie and Kirsty have a fond respect for Miss Potts who combines strictness with humour. Miss Potts has just made a joke to the class and Julie turns to Kirsty, who is sitting next to her:

Extract (3)

Julie	D'you remember that time when we had to make words out of thingy and I said 'cod' and she said (*measured tone*) 'You cod be right!'
Kirsty	(*laugh*) Yes
Julie	She, she might be a bit strict but
Kirsty	/She is funny
Julie	Yes I know, she goes (*posh voice*) 'Oh I'm beautiful!'

Here, Julie responds to Miss Potts' joke by recalling similar occasions in the past which illustrate her humour, through direct quotation. The evaluative point Julie wants to make is emphasised in 'Oh I'm beautiful!' through her parody of Miss Pott's voice, first in the measured tone and then in the posh accent. However, in contrast to the example of Darren's oppositional parody of Mrs. Kilbride, Julie is here reporting Miss Pott's own parody of herself, as part of her appreciation of Miss Pott's sense of humour.

Reframing and transforming microcontexts

In the classrooms where I collected my data, children spent large amounts of time working through worksheet or teacher-initiated activities, sitting alongside one or more friends engaged in the same activity. Getting the work done, sometimes collaboratively, was combined with a certain amount of discreet social activity among students while the teacher worked her way around the individuals requesting her help. One of the ways in which students transformed a 'doing work' frame (Goffman, 1974, 1981) into a more playful or socially orientated frame, was through the introduction of other voices, for instance starting a 'he said, she said' kind of social anecdote, or often, in the case of the girls, by singing snatches of popular songs together, *sotto voce*. Stylisation of a particular word or phrase could also reframe an event, as the next example shows. Two eleven year-old friends, Kevin and Kieran, are writing answers to a worksheet called 'Finding positions'. The worksheet shows a grid plan of a zoo with drawings of different animals and buildings in the various grid squares. It gives students a list of grid references (A1, E2 etc) to which they have to match features shown on the plan and then a list of animals and buildings for which they have to find the grid references. For most of the half hour during which they worked on this worksheet, Kieran took the lead and often voiced his answers aloud to help Kevin, who initially found it difficult to understand what he was meant to do. Towards the end of the session Kevin had become more confident. In the extract below, Kieran (the more able student on this occasion) stylises the word 'wolves' which is the answer required for one of the grid references, and Kevin attempts to extend this playful frame further a few minutes later.

Extract 4

Kieran	Have you gone to the reptiles yet, A1?
Kevin	No, not yet.
	(pause)
Kieran	*(voice conveying mock fear)* 'wolves' Kieran playful stylisation
Kevin	Toilets, you end up at the toilets on E2!
	(pause)
Kieran	Reptiles. Where's the reptiles?
Kevin	Bottom corner
Kieran	Oh yea, A1. That done!

A few minutes later:

Kieran	Done that. *(reading)* 'Where do you find the, where do you find them, a, shop.'
Kevin	*(vocalising his own answer)* D3
Kieran	Find the shop
Kevin	*(story voice)* 'The lions'. Kevin playful stylisation I'm writing 'You end up dead in the lions'cage' *(giggle)*
Kieran	There ain't no lions Kieran responds in worksheet frame
Kevin	Oh, oh yea, I done that (puts on voice again) Kevin repeats stylisation 'end up dead in the lions' cage!' *(giggle)*

Kieran   You would be, there.   *Kieran responds in 'real life' frame*

The stylisations of 'wolves' and 'end up dead in the lions' cage' invoke a playful context of imaginary fierce animals, as a kind of humorous intertext for the pen and paper work of the boys' worksheet activity. Children often held a playful frame for a number of minutes alongside the business of getting their work done, dipping occasionally into play and then returning to the worksheet. Such playful frames are usually fleeting and fragile, as students need to be able to revert back to 'doing work' within a few seconds, if they see the teacher heading in their direction. In this case Kevin responds to Kieran's stylisation of 'wolves' with his own more extended suggestion 'end up dead in the lions' cage'. Kieran, however, switches back to the task frame in his answer 'There ain't no lions', meaning that, although there was a drawing of lions on the zoo plan, they didn't count as a correct answer to any of the worksheet questions. Then, when Kevin repeats his stylisation, Kieran invokes what might be called a 'real life' frame, 'You would be, there'. This extract illustrates the importance of the response in confirming the meaning of an utterance. Kevin wants to play but Kieran reverts back to a 'doing the worksheet' and then a 'real life' frame, thus cutting short the development of the playful exchange which Kevin has attempted twice to initiate.

While students often used intertextual voices to turn work into play, they could also be used in the other direction, to transform an informal exchange into work. Kirsty and Julie had collected a live snail as part of a scavenging hunt in the school grounds and were asked to draw and write about it and their other findings for a classroom display. Just before this they had looked at a library book about snails with a parent helper, who had read out passages about snails' teeth, eyes and tentacles [antennae] and tried to help the girls identify these on the snail they had collected. Julie and Kirsty were sitting chatting together while Julie drew the snail. It had by this time become something of a pet, nicknamed 'Sleepy' by the girls, who took turns in looking after it. Abruptly, Kirsty commented on Julie's drawing:

Extract (5)

Kirsty   Is that meant to be a snail?

Julie   Yea

Kirsty   I can't see its (*slight emphasis*) tentacles

I cannot say categorically that Julie recognised the word 'tentacles' as an intertextual reference, but there are frequent examples in the data of children importing an authoritative voice to help pursue social goals (as in the example of 'finished', earlier above). Using the word 'tentacles' which invokes two authoritative voices (the library book and the parent helper), potentially gives considerable force to Kirsty's comment. It also brings with it generic connotations of the earlier interaction, when the parent helper encouraged the girls to examine the snail through the eyes of the library book, as it were, and to view it in terms of technical details about teeth, eyes and tentacles. This intertextual reference therefore invokes a schooled genre which constructs what the snail is through the lens of an authoritative text. The 'looking after Sleepy' frame is transformed into the 'doing work for a school display' frame, which Kirsty uses to authenticate her less positive evaluation of Julie's drawing. This strategic use of intertextual references is so apparently automatic in children's talk that the cognitive processing involved must happen at a relatively unconscious level, suggesting that the use of intertextuality to make evaluative meanings is a deeply engrained part of these children's thought and language.

Speakers often evoke a new context directly, or use a particular linguistic feature to cue or rekey it, in order to position themselves more powerfully within an encounter (Goffman, 1981). In the examples above Kevin tries to reestablish a more egalitarian playful relationship with his friend after half an hour of following his lead in the worksheet activity and Kirsty attempts to undermine Julie's work (they often competed with each other). It could also be argued that the transformed frames rekey aspects of the children's identities. Kevin attempts to foreground his identity as Kieran's playmate, rather than the identity of struggling student. And in importing the frame of the library book activity into a context where the girls are casually chatting, Kirsty highlights Julie's identity as a 'student' who therefore will have to answer to school criteria in the evaluation of her drawing.

Intertextual referencing is again used strategically in a struggle between speakers in the final example below, which again involves Kieran from example (4), this time sitting working near Melissa and Nicole. Melissa is teasing Kieran and claiming that he cried on his first day to school. The Warehouse mentioned in the extract is the local youth club.

Extract (6)

Kieran	(*Melissa is flicking Kieran's hair with her pencil*) Stop that, or I'll punch you	
Melissa	Oh yea then, come on then, come on then	
Kieran	No I'm not going to waste my time	
Melissa	Do you remember the first day you come to school and <u>you was crying</u> because your mum was going to leave you? Yea?	1st parallel context
Nicole	Yea and do you remember I was frightened down the Warehouse?	2nd parallel context
Melissa	No	
Nicole	The first day you brought me over and I, <u>you goes (*aggressive tone*) 'Yea I could beat you up and all these kids as well'. But I never cried</u>	2nd parallel context
Kieran	<u>I never cried</u>	1st parallel context
Melissa	Yes you do, you were hiding behind the table	1st
Kieran	That's a lie	1st
Melissa	That was you	1st
Kieran	Was it hell	1st
Nicole	(imitating a teacher's authoritative voice) <u>Kieran, will you sit down and get down to your work!</u>	Reframing of current exchange

Where are we now? Miss, can you help me?

Melissa evokes the first parallel context to the current exchange, Kieran's first day at school, through reporting his voice 'you was crying' and Nicole evokes the second parallel context, her first day at the youth club, through evoking an exchange with Melissa where she is, by implication, much more courageous than Kieran: 'you goes (*aggressive tone*) 'Yea I could beat you up and all these kids as well'. But I never cried.' Although this second parallel context is not referred to again after the brief exchange between Melissa and Nicola, it has created a powerful intertext for the continuing exchange between Melissa and Kieran and the evaluation of Kieran's purported behaviour. Nicole's comments about going to the Warehouse can be interpreted as part of a conversation with Melissa where she is recalling a shared experience but also as a way of indirectly telling Kieran 'I had a much more frightening first day but, unlike you, I didn't cry'. The conflict between Kieran and Melissa escalates until Nicole defuses the situation by invoking the teacher's voice '<u>Kieran, will you sit down and get down to your work</u>', following this immediately by calling the teacher over to help her. Nicole's stylised teacher's voice transforms the conversational frame from 'winding up Kieran' to 'doing maths'. While transforming the frame may be partly motivated by an anxiety to hide the off-task nature of their conversation, or by a desire on Nicole's part to bring in an adult before the argument gets too out of hand, it also re-keys the interaction between the children, enabling Nicole to reclaim a dominant position in relation to Kieran, and also to reinstate herself within the conversation.

This kind of informal talk between children, with its rapid refootings and frame transformations, is characterised by Bakhtin as inwardly persuasive discourse, which he describes as contemporaneous, semantically open and intensely dialogic: 'it is not so much interpreted by us as it is further, that is, freely, developed, applied to new material, new conditions; it enters into inter-animating relationships with new contexts. More than that, it enters into an intense interaction, a *struggle* with other internally persuasive discourses' (Bakhtin, 1981 p 345-346). Bakhtin contrasts internally persuasive discourse with authoritative discourse (in my data the knowledge of textbooks, mediated by teachers) which is semantically fixed and can only be transmitted and received, not negotiated and transformed.

Conclusion

I have examined one aspect of intertextual referencing in children's informal talk: their use of other people's voices. The nature and authority of the voice, the content of what is reported and the associations which a voice brings with it are all central to meaning-making in the reporting context. So too is the management of the voice by the reporting speaker, who may use a range of discursive strategies, described by Bakhtin (1984) as quotation, imitation, stylisation, parody and hidden polemic. I have divided 'imitation' into two categories, repetition and appropriation. There is a clear hierarchy of voice reproduction in teacher-student dialogues in my data, where students repeat what teachers say and teachers repeat and appropriate the voices of textbooks, and also appropriate and transform the voices of students. Participation in these dialogues is an important part of students' induction into particular kinds of institutional relationships and procedures as well as into educational discourses and the particular patterning of repetition and appropriation in my data reflects the fairly traditional authority structure in my research context.

In informal talk among themselves the students used a wider range of reporting strategies. They appropriated authoritative voices from teachers, textbooks and worksheets and used these to guide their attention and activity (example 1). This kind of appropriation serves to instantiate institutional practices, relationships and identities, as well as to scaffold students' engagement in classroom tasks and learning. Appropriated voices may also be used for children's own personal goals (example 2), while still reflecting the speakers' orientation towards schooled sources of authority. This institutional orientation also frequently underpins students' criticisms of individual teacher's actions (for example Mrs. Kilbride's unclear instructions) and their evaluations of teachers as people (Miss Potts in example 3). Thus children can be seen as actively and collaboratively participating in their induction into school practices and taking on the associated relationships and identities. Occasionally, however, children in my data contest the voices they take on. In these cases they clearly (grammatically or prosodically) mark their distance from the evaluative perspective of the voice they are reproducing, for example in Darren's parody of Mrs. Kilbride's instructions for producing work to display in assembly.

Within the strongly dialogic, fluid nature of children's informal talk, intertextuality is closely woven into the ongoing process of meaning-making in communication. Speakers slip rapidly between different interpretative frames, transforming work on a maths problem into play (example 4), switching attention from informal chat onto a school task (example 5), or holding a number of frames simultaneously for strategic purposes (example 6). New frames produce new evaluative criteria and new positionings and identities for the participants, and may transform the meaning and significance of their activity. In this sense what might count as text and intertext are each interpenetrated by the other so that they become intricately intertwined within the reporting context. As Volosinov puts it: 'the speech being reported (the other person's speech) and the speech doing the reporting (the author's speech) exist, function and take shape only in their interrelation, and not on their own, the one apart from the other. The reported speech and the reporting context are but the terms of a dynamic interrelationship'. (Volosinov, 1986:119).

Focusing on reported voices in informal talk highlights the ideological and evaluative nature of reproduced discourse which Volosinov argues is central to its communicative function. The intertextual referencing discussed in this article is strategic and evaluative in terms of students' individual goals, and it also functions ideologically because the sources of authority invoked by children to pursue individual goals are embedded within the institutional practices and discourses of schools and classrooms. In this sense children's intertextual referencing articulates the relationship between the interactional order of their informal dialogue and activity and the institutional order of schooled knowledge and authority.

Transcription conventions
/ indicates where another speaker interrupts or cuts in

Comments in italics and parentheses clarify unclear references, or paralinguistic features eg he (*ie her Dad*), (*laughter*)

Underlining identifies references to intertextual voices.

In representing children's voices in the transcripts, I have recorded their non-standard grammatical expressions as accurately as possible, but not their non-standard pronunciation of particular words. In order to make the transcripts more readable, I have added some written punctuation. Names of people and places have been changed, to protect anonymity.

Notes
1   While there is some controversy about whether works published under Volosinov's name were in fact written by Bakhtin, I shall refer to the works by their published authorship.

2   See end of the chapter for transcription conventions. References to other voices are underlined.

References

Bakhtin, M. (1981) 'Discourse in the novel' in *The Dialogic Imagination* by M. Bakhtin, pp 287-422. Austin: University of Texas Press

Bakhtin, M. (1984) *Problems of Dostoevsky's Poetics*. Manchester: Manchester University Press

Bakhtin, M. (1986) *Speech Genres and other late essays* (ed Caryl Emerson and Michael Holquist). Austin: University of Texas Press

Dyson, A. H. (1987) 'The value of 'Time off Task': young children's spontaneous talk and deliberate text', *Harvard Educational Review*, 57(4) 396-420

Foucault, M. (1980) (ed Colin Gordan). *Power/Knowledge: Selected Interviews and Other Writings* 1972-9. London: Harvester Press

Gannaway, R. (1984) 'Making sense of school' in *Life in School: the Sociology of Pupil Culture* by M. Hammersley and P. Woods (eds), 191-203. Milton Keynes: Open University Press

Goffman, E. (1974) *Frame analysis*. Harmondsworth: Penguin

Goffman, E. (1981) 'Footing' in *Forms of talk*. Oxford: Basil Blackwell

Goody, J. and Watt, I. (1968) 'The consequences of literacy' in J. Goody (ed) *Literacy in Traditional Societies*. Cambridge: Cambridge University Press

Kamberelis, G. and Scott, K.D. (1992) 'Other people's voices', *Linguistics and Education*, 4(3-4), 359-403

Lindstrom, L. (1992) 'Context contests: debatable truth contests on Tanna (Vanuatu)' in *Rethinking Context: language as an interactive phenomenon* by A. Duranti and C. Goodwin (eds), 101-124. Cambridge: Cambridge University Press

Maybin, J. (1998) 'Children's voices: talk, knowledge and identity' in *The Sociolinguistics Reader Vol 2 Gender and Discourse* by J. Cheshire and P. Trudgill (eds), 278-294. London: Edward Arnold

Maybin, J. (1999) 'Framing and evaluation in 10-12 year old school children's use of appropriated speech, in relation to their induction into educational procedures and practices' in *TEXT*, Vol 19(4)

Mercer, N. (1995) *The Guided Construction of Knowledge: talk among teachers and learners*. Clevedon: Multilingual Matters

Moi, T. (ed) (1986) *The Kristeva Reader*. Blackwell: Oxford

Olson, D. (1977) 'From utterance to text: the bias of language in speech and writing' *Harvard Education Review*, 47(3), 257-281

Scollon, R., Tsang, W. K., Li, D., Yung, V., Jones, R. (1998) 'Voice, appropriation and discourse representation in a student writing task', *Linguistics and Education* 9(3): 227-250

Short, K. (1992) Researching intertextuality within collaborative classroom learning environments, *Linguistics and Education* 4, 313-333.

Volosinov, V. N. (1986) (trans. L. Matejka and I. R. Titunik) *Marxism and the Philosophy of Language*. Cambridge, Mass: Harvard University Press

Vygotsky, L. (1978) (ed. Cole, M. *et al*) *Mind in Society: the Development of Higher Psychological Processes*. Cambridge, Mass: Harvard University Press

Wertsch, J. (1991) *Voices of the Mind*. London: Harvester Wheatsheaf

CHAPTER 12

Rethinking diversity: hybridity and hybrid language practices in the Third Space

Kris D. Gutiérrez, Patricia Baquedano-López and Carlos Tejeda

Our long-term ethnographic work in formal and nonformal learning contexts has helped us see the changing and shifting nature of learning communities and their variant responses to these shifts. In this way, contexts for development are neither necessarily benign nor unproblematic, and, instead, can be characterised by their diverse, conflictual and complex nature. Some learning communities try to ignore, resist, and suppress these changes, whereas others recognise these points of disruption as the building blocks for potential learning. In our earlier work, we have illustrated how points of tension and conflict in various learning activities can lead to a transformation in the activity and the participation and discourse practices therein. These transformations can lead to productive literacy learning.

We have conceptualised such particular discursive spaces as the Third Space in which alternative and competing discourses and positionings transform conflict and difference into rich zones of collaboration and learning (Gutiérrez, Baquedano-López, and Turner, 1997; Gutiérrez, Rymes, and Larson, 1995). Thus, the construct of the Third Space has been productive in helping us understand the complexity of learning environments and their transformative potential. From the perspective of activity theory, the Third Space might also be considered an expanded activity (Engeström, 1999) in which the object of activity is extended and the activity itself reorganised, resulting in new opportunities for learning. Like Engeström, we also view these expanded activities, or third spaces, as zones of proximal development (Vygotsky, 1978). In contrast to the less problematic ways in which zo-peds are so often described, we want to highlight that zo-peds are also disharmonious and hybrid spaces. (See Griffin and Cole, 1984, for more discussion on zo-peds as sites of contestation.)

Our analysis of Third Spaces has shown that learning contexts are immanently hybrid, that is, polycontextual, multivoiced and multiscripted. Thus, conflict, tension and diversity are intrinsic to learning spaces. We have examined these tensions by studying the competing discourses and practices, the official scripts and counterscripts, of the various social spaces of learning communities. By attending to the social, political, material, cognitive and linguistic conflict, we also have documented these tensions as potential sites of rupture, innovation and change that lead to learning (Baquedano-López, Alvarez and Gutiérrez, 1998; Engeström, 1987, 1990, 1993; Newman, Griffin, and Cole, 1989). Here we define an activity system as social practice(s) that includes the norms, values, division of labour, the goals of a community, and its participants' enduring dispositions toward the social practice (Gutiérrez and Stone, 2000). In this article, we provide a situated analysis of one classroom community, where a purposeful use of hybridity and

---

* First published in *Mind, Culture and Activity*, 2000, Vol 6(4), 286-303.

diversity stimulates the transformation of activities into robust contexts of development. Diversity here not only includes racial, ethnic, socioeconomic and linguistic diversity, but also diversity in the mediational tools, roles, and the activity systems themselves. Hybridity and diversity, then, are not problematic but rather are viewed as important cultural resources in children's development (Cole, 1998). Hybridity and diversity serve as the building blocks of Third Spaces.

Our sustained presence as participant observers in urban schools contexts has helped us recognise the complexity of the networks of relations and activity systems that exist and emerge in classrooms. Using ethnographic and discourse analytic methods, we have studied the social practices of the teaching and learning of literacy, their microprocesses, and their relationship to other activity systems. This approach affords analyses across and within various levels of activity. These analyses also make visible the overlapping, interwoven and hybrid nature of social phenomena.

Although hybridity in learning contexts is ubiquitous, a focus on the hybrid nature of activity systems and their language practices helps make visible developmental spaces that may have been ignored previously. For example, in many classroom communities, teachers may not recognise nor have the training necessary to see diversity and difference and the resulting hybridity as resources for creating new learning spaces. Although such an understanding can inform practice in any learning community, it can be particularly productive in ethnically, racially and linguistically diverse learning communities where difference as a resource is not an organising principle of instruction. Thus, we propose hybridity both as a useful lens, a theoretical tool for understanding the inherent diversity and heterogeneity of activity systems and learning events, as well as a principle for organising learning. Utilising multiple, diverse and even conflicting mediational tools promotes the emergence of third spaces, or zones of development and thus expands learning (Engeström, 1987).

Hybridity

The concept of hybridity is not new; it already has become a useful term for problematising identity, particularly in postcolonial work on borderlands (Anzaldúa, 1987; Arteaga, 1994; Becquer and Gatti, 1991; Bhabha, 1994; Gómez-Peña, 1996; Lipsitz, 1994, 1998; Shohat and Stam, 1994; Valle and Torres, 1995). In particular, this body of work captures the struggle of translation and difference in contexts where cultural and linguistic practices, histories and epistemologies collide. Such translation, in which people negotiate what is known, for example, local cultural knowledge and linguistic registers, occurs when people attempt to make sense of their identity in relation to prevailing notions of self and cultural practices. This same complexity and struggle, as we have argued, is found in other contexts of cultural contact, particularly urban classroom settings. Here Anzaldúa's (1987) work on borderlands and identity formation is particularly useful in explaining hybridity. The description of her own learning experiences where difference, especially linguistic hybridity, was suppressed and devalued illustrates the normative practices that often still exist today.[1]

Our contribution here is to unpack the construct of hybridity as a new way of making sense of diversity in learning contexts. Hybridity exists at multiple levels of learning environments. The classroom, for example, is constitutive of multiple and connected activity systems, that is, it is polycontextual. We have termed these varied social spaces, or activity systems, the official and unofficial spaces of learning contexts. Although these spaces also are characterised by their

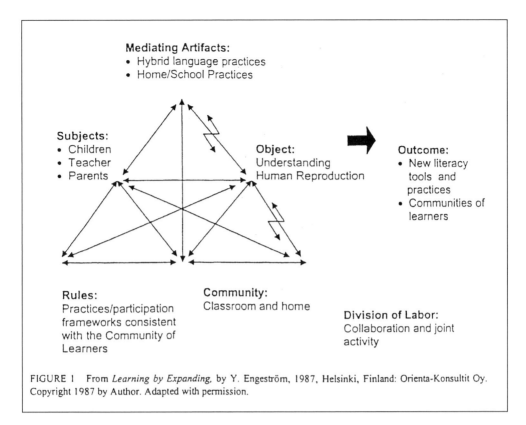

Mediating Artifacts:
- Hybrid language practices
- Home/School Practices

Subjects:
- Children
- Teacher
- Parents

Object:
Understanding
Human Reproduction

Outcome:
- New literacy tools and practices
- Communities of learners

Rules:
Practices/participation frameworks consistent with the Community of Learners

Community:
Classroom and home

Division of Labor:
Collaboration and joint activity

FIGURE I   From *Learning by Expanding*, by Y. Engeström, 1987, Helsinki, Finland: Orienta-Konsultit Oy. Copyright 1987 by Author. Adapted with permission.

various and often oppositional discourses and social practices, they are also mutually constitutive and transformative. In all cases, these tensions in activity rupture the normative practice, and new hybrid activities emerge. However, some classroom communities resist the transformation, whereas others opportunistically view these emergent activities as potentially fruitful contexts of development. We have conceptualised these improvisations as Third Spaces and argue that these learning zones are promoted and sustained by hybrid language and schooling practices that bridge home and school (Moll and Greenberg, 1990). Figure 1 illustrates how the mediating artifacts of hybrid language and home/school practices transform activity and literacy learning.

We will use one of our research sites to illustrate a hybrid activity system as represented in Figure 1. *Las Redes* (Networks), our afterschool computer club, is both a formal and nonformal learning context, influenced by the cultural practices of the elementary school and community in which it is located and by the University that helps organise it. Moreover, unlike in most formal contexts for learning, play and learning are built into the collaborative computer gaming activities in which adults and children participate. Further, hybridity at *Las Redes* is manifest in the coexistence, comingling of, and contradictions among different linguistic codes and registers in the course of everyday activity. Although these hybrid language practices are most visible in this setting, such language practices are always present, though not always legitimised and utilised, in formal learning contexts. The practices of this afterschool club, then, strategically incorporate the local knowledge of home and school and, in doing so, reorganise the roles, participation frameworks, and division of labour; in short, the social organisation of learning in this setting results in new activities and outcomes (Gutiérrez, Baquedano-López, and Alvarez, in press; Gutiérrez, Baquedano-López, Alvarez, and Chiu, 1999; Vasquez, 1994).

Such transformation, however, is not limited to informal learning contexts like *Las Redes*. We will illustrate the ways in which hybrid activity and hybrid language practices serve as triggers of transformation or expansion for literacy learning in one dual immersion elementary school classroom. In the following sections, we provide an ethnographic portrait of the community, the classroom, and a focal activity that spans six weeks.

The community

Bell Elementary School is a large elementary school located in the working-class sector of an economically and racially segregated section of an affluent, large West Coast city. This particular neighbourhood is largely Latino, working poor, and immigrant. Bell, the neighbourhood school, is a two-way Spanish immersion language magnet school created by the district in response to a mandate to desegregate its schools. The school and, thus, the classroom student population reflected this mandate and included many students from the surrounding neighbourhood and a number of middle-class Anglo and African American children whose parents had elected to enroll them in this magnet school. There was a range of proficiency in Spanish and English among the children. Some native Spanish speakers were proficient in English, and, similarly, some native English speakers were Spanish proficient. The proficiency was due, in part, to the children's continued enrolment in the same school for one or more years and, in some cases, with the same teacher.

The teacher of this combined second- and third-grade class, the focus of this study, had been teaching for two years and was theoretically grounded in cultural-historical theories of learning and development and Freirian pedagogies. We had been documenting this teacher's development since her pre-service experience at our university. In particular, we had been examining how this teacher employed cultural-historical and Freirian theories to create communities of learners similar to those put forth by Rogoff (1994). In her own words, the teacher, Ms. Rivera, described her practice:

> I guess you should know that I am a teacher that is guided by theory. My teaching is informed by my beliefs about learning, and I believe that learning is a social process. Therefore, I try to set up everything that happens in the classroom to occur socially. I am also guided by what I believe to be a critical pedagogy, a critical theory in which I don't want (interrupts herself) One of my goals is to give voice to the children, but not only voice, but to break the power structures of society, not to reproduce them; but to create a brand new structure in which they have the power so that not only does it create independence and self-esteem, but that they feel that they have what it takes to succeed in life, not only academically but in every area of their life. (A. Rivera, personal communication, February 1995)

Guided by these theories, the day-to-day practices of this classroom in this language magnet school provided multiple opportunities for students to have ongoing access to each other's linguistic, cultural and cognitive resources, and these practices had consequences that extended beyond the classroom walls (Gutiérrez, Baquedano-López and Turner, 1997). Moreover, the teacher's bicultural knowledge facilitated these practices. The teacher, fully literate in both Spanish and English, was a native of Mexico but was educated primarily in the United States. Her ability to use a range of registers, including formal and colloquial Spanish with her students and their parents, served to link home and school effectively. The hybrid culture of this classroom community was thus a fertile ground for Third Spaces.

Hybridity in the classroom

Ms. Rivera's Spanish immersion classroom is illustrative of a formal learning context in which hybridity is salient. We use representative data of sustained classroom activity in one particular elementary school classroom that we observed for over three years to explain how conflict and diversity become catalysts for curricular change, individual learning, and the larger activity system. In this learning context, its hybrid culture was actively mined in the ways the teacher and children consciously and strategically utilised their own linguistic repertoires and created new contexts of development; these hybrid language practices fostered language and literacy development. These hybrid language practices, however, were neither disconnected nor random. Instead, these practices were intimately connected texts, strategically used, and were the outcome of a hybrid activity system in which home and school were consciously bridged. Similar to practices represented in the work on Funds of Knowledge (Moll, 1998), the local practices, knowledge, and beliefs of both the local community and of the classroom and school community were brought to bear in everyday classroom practices.

Acceptance and use of diverse, alternative texts and codes, ways of participating, sharing expertise, and mediating literacy learning were part of the normative practice of this community of learners (Rogoff, 1994). Diversity, in this context, was a resource. As we will illustrate shortly, even unauthorised side talk, movement, and spontaneous interaction and collaboration, were unproblematic and redefined as part of the normative practice in this community. In other words, this particular classroom community was flexible and open to student behaviours that in other learning contexts might be considered inappropriate or forms of counterscript. Talk, interaction, reading, writing, and sharing in a variety of codes and registers here were considered the means to productive learning. Moreover, the teacher and the children placed a high value on respecting the language, social practices, and beliefs of the classroom community and its individual members. Classroom learning activities included teacher mini-lectures, reading and writing texts, and classroom discussion of topics generated by both teacher and students.

The hybrid culture produces a third space

To understand how hybrid cultures animate third spaces, let us look at the ontogenesis of an activity that stimulated a transformation in Ms. Rivera's classroom. We had observed that there were already multiple activity systems interacting in this learning context. Some children and the teacher participated regularly in the official space, in a sanctioned and legitimate curriculum; simultaneously, children often engaged in counterscript in the unofficial spaces of the classroom. In many classrooms, these resulting moments of conflict and tension would have been ignored or suppressed, with the children's attention redirected to the official curriculum. But in this classroom, such momentary friction among students or between students and teacher became the impetus for reorganising classroom activity.

One particular morning, conflict, triggered by a student calling another student a 'homo,' challenged a principle rule of this community of practice, the expectation of mutual respect. In the course of addressing this conflict, a series of student questions about homosexuality and human reproduction erupted. Ms. Rivera recalls:

> This unit was something that really happened out of a conversation with the children. Some children started calling others names. So we engaged in a conversation about why people use insults. And after discussing the reasons – it's to hurt people's feelings, and to make

others feel bad, and to make yourself feel bigger than them, in whatever respect that may be – told the children that in order for us to have the knowledge of what everybody knew, we were going to say, all of us, the worst word we knew to insult another person. And I started, to kill that anxiety of 'This is my teacher I don't ...' And so one of the children said 'homo' again. And immediately another child said, 'What is that?' And another child answered, 'It's when a man loves another man instead of a woman'. And something sparked that before I knew it they were talking about how a baby is made and how the sperm needs to reach the egg. So at that moment I realised I needed to do something, because the first thing in my mind was, 'District! Parents!' and so the most important thing in my mind was, 'How do I stop this conversation without stripping them of that power of that incredible spontaneity of this interest? [...] Before stopping the conversation I said, 'You know what guys, I want you to know, I want you to understand, how comfortable you just made me feel, because you have proven to me that we are friends. But I want you to realise that what we are talking about right now is something that society at large, parents, that parents are not comfortable with, and in order for us to do this we need to have permission from your parents. And so I asked them, 'Do you really want to do this?' and they said, 'Yes.' (A. Rivera, personal communication, February, 1995)

This multi-aged class thus decided to learn about the human reproductive system. Given the age of the children and topic (a topic not part of the official primary school curriculum), the teacher and the children designed a sophisticated, yet age appropriate unit that involved 100% parental and district approval and participation. Conflict in this community became the catalyst for expanding learning in the Third Space.

This new activity was neither part of the normative practice of the school nor of the home. As Figure 2 shows, this became a hybrid activity that bridged the official and unofficial spaces of

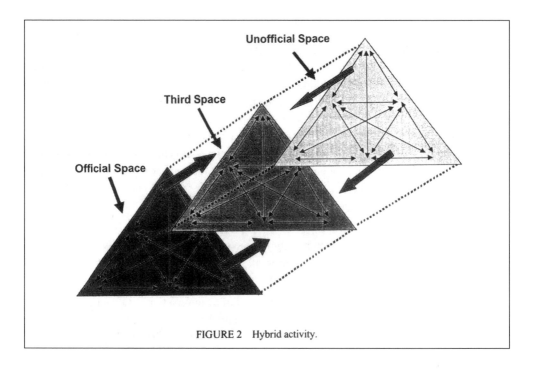

FIGURE 2 Hybrid activity.

both home and school. Further, this new activity system invoked novel forms of participation that also required new resources for making sense of the classroom participants' new collective activity.

As this case demonstrates, this hybrid culture is constituted at multiple levels. The new unit on human reproduction broke new terrain both at home and school – after all, these were second- and third-graders for whom human reproduction was not generally a topic of study. Moreover, the topic itself, and then the formal adoption of the topic into an official unit, merged official and unofficial classroom spaces.

Across this six-week learning event, the children and teacher participated in a variety of learning activities. For example, one Monday morning, students wiggled through cardboard fallopian tubes – simulating sperm travelling through a vagina to fertilise an egg. In another activity, students curled up in a papier-mâché womb to recreate the experience of a foetus. On yet another day the teacher found herself sitting in the principal's office, having to explain that she was not using a banana to teach the students how to wear condoms, as rumour had it. These were moments in Ms. Rivera's classroom during an instructional unit resulting from sustained inter-action in the third space. Although this unit resembled other instructional thematic units in many respects, its origin and content were different in other significant ways, especially in its ability to mediate home and school knowledge and language practices.

Hybrid language practices

In this learning context, no single language or register is privileged, and the larger linguistic repertoires of participants become tools for participating and making meaning in this new collaborative activity (Gutiérrez et al., 1999). In fact, these hybrid language practices became the central mediating tool. From a Bakhtinian (1981) perspective, hybridity increased the possibility of dialogue – and thus interpretation. Such practices built local interpretive communities and interpretive practices that included the use of humour, local knowledge, personal experience, and narrative. These creative strategies both challenged the normative scripts, practices and partici-pation frameworks of the official curriculum and became viable tools for meaning-making.

In the following transcripts of interaction[2] in this new human reproduction unit, we discuss how hybrid language practices mediate students' learning. The following interaction captures the unfolding of a new activity. The teacher has just returned papers to the students in which they had generated a list of questions they wanted to discuss.

Reorganising the Activity
1. ¿Podemos compartir? {{Can we share?}}

T: Entonces, quiero que leyendo su papel= {{So, reading your papers I want=}}

S1: =¿Podemos, podemos? {{=Can we? Can we?=}}

T: Vamos a agregar preguntas a lo que queremos saber. {{=We are going to add questions to what we want to know.}}

S1: ¿Podemos *share the–* las?– {{Can we share the–the?–}}

T: ¿Eso es lo que vamos a hacer no? {{That is what we are going to do, isn't it?}}

S2: Compartir– {{Share–}}

T: ¿O quieren compartirlo primero?= {{Or do you want to first share it?=}}

As the talk and interaction reveal, students in this community can negotiate the goals of tasks. For example, in this brief interaction, the teacher, speaking within the official curriculum, directs students to a predefined task, but the students interject with an alternative task to share their questions with their classmates first: '¿Podemos compartir?' The teacher readily takes up one student's suggestion and reorganises the task. In this classroom, learning is organised so that ruptures are points of negotiation rather than disruption. This negotiation opens up the possibilities for alternative voices to become part of the official curriculum.

Incorporating local knowledge

Within the same lesson, a student-generated question, '¿Qué es esperma?' (What is sperm?), motivates Jorge, one of the students, to contribute his own verbal and nonverbal interpretation of the term *sperm*. The following discourse excerpt vividly exemplifies the possibility of drawing on alternative codes (English/Spanish, verbal/nonverbal) and registers (formal and informal) to convey meaning.

2. Es como un tadpole {{It's like a tadpole}}

Official Space	Third Space	Unofficial Space
S: ¿Qué es esperma? {{What is sperm?}}		Ss: ((*Student rumblings and side discussions sprouting* J:Es) como un *tadpole*. {{It's like a tadpole.}} ((*Makes swimming tadpole motions with his hands*))
T: Como vamos–esa es una buena pregunta. ¿Qué es esperma? Ahorita la apunto.		
¿Cómo: cre:ce:n lo:s esperma? {{Since we are–that is a good question. What is sperm? I'll write it down right now. How: do the sperm gr:o:w?}}		
T: ((*Still writing on board, laughs silently at Jorge's description*))		
T: ((*Chuckles at Jorge's description.*))		
	T: Jorge, parece como renacuajos ((Turns and faces Jorge, smiling)), pero no <u>son</u> renacuajos.	
T: ¿Qué son (.) lo:s espe:rma? {{What are sperms?}} ((*Writing or' the board*)) <u>Muy</u> buena pregunta. {{Very good question.}}	{{Jorge, they look like tadpoles but they are not tadpoles.}}	
	Anabel: ((Laughs out loud)) J: ((Grins widely))	

Jorge likens his image of sperm to tadpoles, while making a fishtail motion with his hand and arm. Jorge's contribution represents alternative ways to display knowledge through the use of different codes: English/Spanish and gestures. Here, Jorge draws from a larger linguistic repertoire, and he is validated by the teacher. The teacher allows code switching, 'Es como un *tadpole*,' as a viable practice for meaning-making. The teacher's reformulation, 'Parece un renacuajo' (It looks like a tadpole), helps to both ensure the children's understanding of the concept of 'esperma' and expand vocabulary in both languages. At this moment, the teacher and the student are in a new hybrid space, indeed in the third space, where student knowledge, including the use of alternative representations of meaning, become new tools for learning. Showing expertise in this learning event requires students to draw from their wider linguistic and sociocultural toolkit. Moreover, Jorge's creative and rather amusing contribution is received by the teacher and students with approving chuckles and laughter. In this classroom, affective stances can not only be displayed, they are also welcomed additions to classroom ethos and official knowledge.

When Counterscript is not Counterscript

As the lesson progressed, students' questions were displayed on large sheets of paper posted on the chalkboard. We observed that the children were eager, although uncomfortable, about the content of the questions they were asking; nervousness and giggles accompanied both public and private exchanges among the students. Ms. Rivera's knowledge of the language and social practices of the local community allowed her to anticipate the children's anxiety and the responses to taboo topics. In the excerpt below, Ms. Rivera invited student participation in the discussion of human reproduction and noticed that several students were grinning and giggling. These behaviours would be considered counterscript in most classrooms. The teacher, instead, publicly reframed the students' feelings as legitimate: the topic is not something that is talked about in most homes and classrooms. She further reassured them that their anxiety was understandable, that the topic had been addressed in class previously, and that the anxiety was transitory.

3. Ya hablamos sobre este tema ((We already talked about this topic}}

Official Space	Third Space	Unofficial Space
T: ¿O quieren compartirlo primero?= {{Or do you want to first share it?=}}		((*Students have been smiling and giggling quietly about the nature of the questions about human reproduction*))
T: Antes de= {{Before=}}	T: ((*To Marta*)) Marta. ¿Porque no?– {{Why don't?–}} ¿Tu crees si lo escribes, es algo que vamos a aprender? No? {{You think if we write it, it'll be something we are going to learn? Right?}} Ya hablamos sobre este tema, es algo que a noso–a algunas personas–como a Jorge–lo hacen reir. Okay. Mientras	Marta: ((*Whining a little*)) No::

> aprendamos sobre esto se nos
> va a quitar esa ansiedad
> porque no es que nos de <u>risa</u>,
> es que estamos nerviosos
> porque es algo que no
> placticamos. {{We already
> talked about this topic, it is
> something that makes
> us–some persons–like
> Jorge–they make him laugh.
> Okay. While we learn about
> this we'll lose that anxiety,
> because it's not that we just
> laugh, it's that we are
> nervous because it's not
> something we talk about.}}
> ((*Feigns nervousness and
> fear, playfully*))

> Ss: ((*Laughter all around*))

This tension between the local knowledge and the official curriculum reframed this interaction into a developmental space – one in which personal experience is negotiated into the institutional context. Ms. Rivera facilitated this negotiation through appropriation of the students' anxiety and even simulated their nervousness. Their nervous giggles became playful laughter as they shared humour about their feelings of legitimate anxiety.

In the next example, the teacher again anticipated counterscript related to the topic of breasts, even though it was generated by the student question, '¿Por qué las mujeres tienen busto y el hombre no?' (Why do women have breasts and not men?) Here the teacher's linguistic and cultural knowledge of the Spanish vernacular for breasts, 'chi-chis,' and her understanding that this term sometimes has sexual connotations prompted her to infuse the taboo language with positive affect ('Se le dice de cariño'/it's said with love). In doing so, she diffuses the need for counterscript:

4. Cuál es el nombre que usamos de cariño? {{What is another name we use affectionately?}}

Official Space	Third Space	Unofficial Space
T: Okay, Andrea?		
A: ¿Por qué las mujeres tienen busto y el hombre no? {{Why do women have breasts and men don't?}}		

T: ¿Por qué: las mujeres {{Why do women}} ((Writing on board)) tienen bu:sto y el hombres – {{have bre:asts and men don't –}}

T: ¿Cuál es otro nombre que usamos de cariño para busto? {{What is another name we use affectionately for chest?}}

S: U:M pecho? {{U:m chest?}}

S: Pecho. {{Chest.}}

S: No. Es esto. {{No. It is this.}}

T: ¿Pecho? {{Chest?}}

T: Pero el pecho tenemos los – las mujeres y también – ¿Tu tienes pecho? {{But women have a chest and also – Do you have a chest?}} ((*Pointing to her chest as she looks at Jorge*))

J: ((*Nods*))

T: También los hombres. {{Also men.}}

T: En algunas familias el busto se le dice de cariño se le dice 'chi-chis.' {{In some families the chest is affectionately called boobs.}}

Ss: ((Chuckles))

T: Okay, Piwi.

Ss: Uh huh. Si.

Ss: ((Testing it out)) Chi-chis.

The teacher not only builds on the children's local knowledge and vocabulary, she also uses formal ('busto' and 'pecho') and colloquial ('chi-chis') language to make explicit the range of registers that can be used to make meaning. As this example depicts, the use of hybrid language is not a random act; instead, it is the conscious use of both registers and forms of knowledge as mediating tools for language and content development.

Counterscript as Meaning-Making: An Active Underlife

Within the range of interpretive strategies-that the children used throughout this learning event, counterscript can also become an occasion for meaning-making. Recall that here counterscript was redefined as effective sense-making practice. Indeed, this community of learners was generally characterised by its high tolerance for alternative sense-making practices that drew on personal experience; however, such practices were particularly salient in the Third Space.

The subsequent discourse segment illustrates how literacy learning can be imbued with meaning when one's personal life experiences are referenced. Of significance here is that this hybrid learning context expands the participation framework to include side talk as a means of interpretation and understanding. The side talk, a form of counterscript, is a response to a question about how many children a woman can have. Once again, the task was for students to share their questions, but they were not expected to answer them yet. Several students, however, redefined the task by first answering the question, and then making it personally relevant through the telling of a personal narrative. The students' collective answer forms a narrative constitutive of individual narratives that build on each other incrementally.

5. Mi abuelita tuvo diez {{My grandmother had ten}}

Official Space	Third Space	Unofficial Space
T: Natalia		Ss: ((*Inaudible student discussions beginning to develop*))
N: ¿Cuántos bebes pueden tener una mujer? {{How many babies can a woman have?}}		S: Mi abuelita tuvo diez. {{My grandmother had ten.}}
T: O:h, muy buena pregunta. {{Oh, very good question.}}		S: ((*Impressed whistle*))
		A: Mi abuelita tuvo doce. {{My grandmother had twelve.}}
		J: Mi abuelita tuvo- – {{My grandmother had –}}
		A: ¿Cinco? {{Five?}}
		J: Trece. {{Thirteen.}}

This counterscript has coherence – it is linked through a series of mini-narratives of each child's grandmother's birthing experiences. The distinct parallel structure of the narrative: 'My abuelita tuvo ('diez, doce, y trece')' illustrates the playful competition among the participants. We have previously documented that this tension between play and learning is characteristic of productive hybrid learning communities (Gutiérrez *et al.*, 1999). These playful narratives contribute to the changing nature of meaning-making and collaboration in this learning activity. This interpretive strategy, then, was not simply a social occasion; it was linked to the official topic and activity at hand.

Counterscript as a Cognitive Building Activity

As the previous examples have illustrated, in this classroom students are allowed to take alternative paths to understanding. In the following example, the teacher has begun to read to the children from a book on the development of a foetus, more specifically about the development of foetus' spine. Simultaneously, Jorge, who is also known for his prankishness, has constructed an alternative narrative about the spine, his spine. Jorge makes a cognitive connection to the subject of development by constructing a narrative about the origin of his nickname, 'Huesudo' (Bony). His recognition of his own boniness and this link to the nickname his uncles have bestowed on him, 'huesudo/bony,' helps him relate to the official text of the class, the book on the development of the foetus.

6a. Huesudo {{Bony}}

T: ((*Reading from book describing the early development of a foetus, bending over to touch her own vertebrae*)) Ella ya tiene una espina vertebral. {{She already has a spine.}} ((*Puts book down and touches her vertebrae with both hands*)) Tóquense su espina vertebral. {{Touch your spine.}}

Ss: ((*Touch their spines as the teacher does*))

J: ((*Touching his spine, talking to himself*)) Con razón me llaman 'huesudo.' {{No wonder they call me 'bony.'}}

T: Con punto. Aqui. {{With a period. Here.}} Hasta {{Up to}} ((*Touches the bottom and top of her spine*)) Ella ya tiene una espina vertebral. {{She already has a spine.}}

J: ((*Looks around, smiles*))

J: ((*raises his hand for a full 70 seconds*))

The permeability of this hybrid community allowed Jorge to share his text and to move from the periphery to the centre by making his private ruminations available to the larger community (Rogoff, 1990). The teacher continued her lesson while conscious of Jorge's raised hand and talk. Eventually, she called on him to share his private musings, and even asked him to elaborate on them. 'Por qué?' Jorge's story becomes part of the classroom text, even though the teacher's intent to ask a question is not diverted:

6b. Huesudo ({{Bony}})

T: Jorge.

J: Con razón me llaman 'huesudo.' {{No wonder they call me 'bony'}}

T: ¿Por qué? {{Why?}}

J: Mis tíos. {{My uncles.}}

T: ¿Por qué? ¿Qué es lo más impor – {{Why? What is the most impor –}}

T: ¿Por qué? {{Why?}} ¿Qué es lo más impor – {{What is the most impor –}}

J: Y mis tíos, que tuvo muchos huesos. {{And my uncles, that I have a lot of bones.}}

T: ¿O:::::h? {{¿O:::::h?}}

J: Me siento como – que tuvo muchos huesos. {{I feel like if I had a lot of bones.}} Mi – y mis tíos. My – and my uncles.}}

T: ¿Pero qué es lo más importante de su cuerpo?{{But what is the most important part of your body?

Jorge's full participation in the community, however brief, has important consequences (Gutiérrez and Stone, 1997). Rather than being marginalised or silenced, Jorge, as shown in the following example, not only becomes a central part of the community but also reemerges as expert in the official space as he answers the question that the teacher had been so intent on asking. Story-telling becomes his ticket to the main event.

6c. Tu corazón {{Your heart}}

J: Tu corazón! {{Your heart!}}

T: ¿Por qué, Jorge? {{Why, Jorge?}}

J: Porque tu corazón te da vida. {{Because your heart gives you life.}}

T: ¿Por qué? {{Why?}

J: Porque es el que hace la sangre – la sangre circular – tu cuerpo. {{Because it's the one that makes the blood – the blood circulate – your body.}}

T: Ex – AC – taMEN – te, Jorge. {{Exactly, Jorge.}}

Jorge's shift from peripheral to a more primary role in the activity had cognitive consequences. Jorge was now positioned to contribute to the central topic of the class discussion. His answer and the teacher's enthusiastic assessment of his response co-constructs Jorge's identity as a knowing contributor. He is not simply the comical contributor; he is also a resource in the classroom. Jorge's interpretive journey from home to school was facilitated by his range of participation and talk.

Conclusion

The interpretive strategies used across and within the social spaces of the classroom help illustrate the range of linguistic and cultural resources available in this learning context. However, in this classroom, learning was organised so that the cultural and linguistic resources of the diverse participants were strategically combined to promote learning (Cole, 1998). Such varied experiences and knowledge provided the context for children's development. Table 1 summarises the recurring patterns of language use across the different social spaces of activity during one classroom's cycle of learning and transformation.

Of particular interest is the narrower range of resources and language practices employed in either the official and unofficial spaces of the classroom. The potential power of hybrid language practices in the third space lies in the broader range of linguistic and sociocultural resources and experiences available to both individuals and the larger interpretive community. The use of these hybrid language practices had important social and cognitive consequences. First, they mediated the ways the students and teacher communicated and interacted with one another, and they helped mediate the participants' intellectual development (Cole, 1996; Scribner, 1990a, 1990b; Wertsch and Ramírez, 1994). Thus, instead of focusing on the children's language designation or

TABLE 1: Hybrid Language Practices in the Third Space

Official Space	*Third Space*	*Unofficial Space*
Calling on students by name to provide questions.	Conflict leads to shared and negotiated understandings of human reproduction.	Name calling and/or colloquialisms (e.g., 'homo'): Giggling about sensitive topics.
Introducing formal or academic lexicon and information (e.g., 'busto' and 'esperma').	Drawing parallels between home and academic lexicon (e.g., 'busto' and 'chi-chis').	Using home lexicon and local knowledge (e.g., 'chi-chis' and abuelitas' stories).
Formal Spanish register (e.g., 'renacuajo').	Hybrid language practices (using ethnic and standard language varieties, e.g., 'renacuajos' and 'tadpoles' as metaphors for sperm).	Range of Spanish and English dialects (e.g., 'tadpoles,' 'chi-chis,' 'homo').
Teacher/adult speech genres, including humour.	Hybrid genres including cultural humour.	Student/children speech genres including joking, and playing.
Re-keying of student script as official knowledge.	Re-keying of either script as a resource for learning.	Re-keying of the teacher's script as unofficial knowledge.

fluency in either Spanish or English, the practices of this community facilitated movement across languages and registers toward particular learning goals.

We believe our long-term observation of classroom life has allowed us to see the evolution of activity and to observe movement through the developmental zone of the third space. The theoretical tool of hybridity has allowed us to document the potentiality of learning contexts where diversity is prominent. Of importance here is not simply the recognition of hybridity and diversity in the activity and in the language practices, but rather how hybridity and diversity can be used to promote learning. Finally, we believe the use of hybrid language practices can help educators negotiate or traverse the diverse and often conflictual urban classroom landscape.

Notes

1   The recent California initiative to eliminate bilingual education (Proposition 227) is one particularly salient example.

2   The following are the transcript notations used to denote naturally occurring talk. In some of the data samples, we have represented talk according to the conceptual spaces that we have outlined and discussed throughout the article. Double brackets indicate English translations. Equal signs indicate talk that is latched, that is, talk that immediately follows an utterance without pausing. Commas indicate rising intonation. Dashes indicate cutoffs, often interruptions and self-corrections. Italics marks emphasis. Double parentheses indicate gestures. T = teacher; S1, S2 = individual or unidentified students; Ss= numerous students; J = Jorge. Colons indicate elongated sound, underlining indicates emphasis, and periods inside parentheses indicate pauses.

References

Anzaldúa, G. (1987) *Borderlands/La Frontera: The new mestiza.* San Francisco: Aunt Lute Books.

Arteaga, A. (1994) *An other tongue: Nation and ethnicity in the linguistic borderlands.* Durham, NC: Duke University Press.

Bakhtin, M. (1981) *The dialogic imagination* (M. Holquist and C. Emerson, Trans.) Austin: University of Texas Press.

Baquedano-López, P., Alvarez, H., and Gutiérrez, K. (1998, December) Negotiating fairness at an after-school club. Paper presented at the 98th annual meeting of the American Anthropological Association, Philadelphia, PA.

Becquer, M., and Gatti, J. (1991) Elements in vogue. *Third Text* 16/17. 65-81.

Bhabha, H. (1994) *The location of culture.* London: Routledge.

Cole, M. (1996) *Cultural psychology: A once and future discipline*. Cambridge, MA: Harvard University Press.

Cole, M. (1998, April) *Cultural psychology: Can it help us think about diversity?* Paper presented at the annual meeting of the American Educational Research Association, San Diego, CA.

Engeström. Y. (1987) *Learning by expanding*. Helsinki, Finland: Orienta-Konsultit Oy.

Engeström, Y. (1990) *Learning. working and imagining: Twelve studies in activity theory*. Helsinki, Finland: Orienta-Konsultit Oy.

Engeström, Y. (1993) Developmental studies on work as a testbench of activity theory. In S. Chaiklin and J. Lave (Eds.), *Understanding practice: Perspectives on activity' and context* (64-l03) New York: Cambridge University Press.

Engeström. Y. (1999) Activity theory and individual and social transformation. In Y. Engeströin, R. Miettinen, and R. Punamaki (Eds.), *Perspectives on activity theory* (19-38) Cambridge, England: Cambridge University Press.

Gómez-Peña, G. (1996) *The new world order: Prophecies, poems and locuras for the end of the century.* San Francisco: City Lights Books.

Griffin, P., and Cole, M. (1984) Current activity for the future: The zo-ped. In B. Roggoffand J. Wertsch (Eds.), *New directions for child development* (45-63) San Francisco: Jossey-Bass.

Gutiérrez, K. (1992) A comparison of instructional contexts in writing process classrooms with Latino children. *Education and Urban Society*, 24.224-262.

Gutiérrez, K. (1993) How talk, context, and script shape contexts for learning: A cross case comparison of journal sharing. *Linguistics and Education*, 5,335-365.

Gutiérrez, K. (1995) Unpackaging academic discourse. *Discourse Processes,* 19.21-37.

Gutiérrez, K., Baquedano-López, P., Alvarez, H., and Chiu, M. (1999) A cultural-historical approach to collaboration: Building a culture of collaboration through hybrid language practices. *Theory into Practice*, 83(2) 87-93.

Gutiérrez, K., Baquedano-López, P., and Alvarez, H. (in press) Using hybridity to build literacy in urban classrooms. In M. Reyes and J. Halcon (Eds.) *The best for our children: Latina/Latino voices on literacy.* New York: Teachers College Press.

Gutiérrez, K., Baquedano-López, P., and Turner, M. G. (1997) Putting language back into language arts: when the radical middle meets the third space. *Language Arts,* 74,368-378.

Gutiérrez, K., and Larson, J. (1994) Language borders: Recitation as hegemonic discourse. *International Journal of Educational Reform*, 3(l), 22-36.

Gutiérrez, K., and Meyer, B. (1995) Creating communities of effective practice: Building literacy for language minority children. In J. Oakes and K. Quartz (Eds.), *94th NSSE Yearbook: Creating new educational communities*. Chicago: University of Chicago Press.

Gutiérrez, K., Rymes, B., and Larson, J. (1995) Script, counterscript, and underlife in the classroom: James Brown versus Brown v. Board of Education. *Harvard Educational Review*, 65, 445-47 1.

Gutiérrez, K., and Stone, L. (2000) Synchronic and diachronic dimensions of social practice: An emerging methodology for cultural-historical perspectives on literacy learning. In C. Lee and P. Smagorinsky (Eds.), *Vygotskian perspectives on literacy research: Constructing meaning through collaborative inquiry* (150-164) New York: Cambridge University Press.

Gutiérrez, K., and Stone, L. (1997) A cultural-historical view of learning and learning disabilities: Participating in a community of learners. *Learning Disabilities: Research and Practice*, 12. 123-131.

Lipsitz, G. (1994) The bands of tomorrow are here today: The proud, progressive, and postmodern sounds of Las Tres and Goddess 13. In S. Loza (Ed.), *Musical aesthetics and multiculturalism in Los Angeles* (139-147), Vol.10 of Selected Reports in Ethnomusicology. Los Angeles: Department of Ethnomusicology and Systematic Musicology, University of California.

Lipsitz, G. (I 998) *The possessive investment in whiteness: How white people profit from identity politics*. Philadelphia: Temple University Press.

Moll, L. (1998, February) *Funds of knowledge for teaching. A new approach to culture in education*. Keynote address delivered to the Illinois State Board of Education, 21st Annual Statewide Conference for Teachers of Linguistically and Culturally Diverse Students, Chicago, Illinois.

Moll, L., and Greenberg, J. (1990) Creating zones of possibilities: Combining social contexts for instruction. In L. C. Moll (Ed.), *Vygotsky and education* (319-348) Cambridge, England: Cambridge University Press.

Newman, D., Griffin, P., and Cole, C. (1989) *The construction zone. Working for cognitive change in school*. New York: Cambridge University Press.

Rogoff, B. (1994) Developing understanding of the idea of communities of learners. *Mind, Culture, and Activity: An International Journal*. 1. 202-229.

Rogoff, B. (1990) *Apprenticeship in thinking: Cognitive development in social context.* New York: Oxford University Press.

Scribner, S. (l 990a) Reflection on a model. *The Quarterly Newsletter of the Laboratory of Comparative Human Cognition*, 12 (3), 90-94.

Scribner, S. (1990b) A sociocultural approach to the study of mind. In C. Greenberg and E. Tobach (Eds.), *Theories of the evolution of knowing.* Hillsdale, NJ: Lawrence Erlbaum Associates, Inc.

Shohat, E., and Stam, R. (1994) *Unthinking eurocentrism: Multiculturalism and the media.* New York and London: Routledge.

Valle, V., and Torres, R. (1995) The idea of mestizaje and the 'race' problematic: Racialized media discourse in a post-Fordist landscape. In A. Darder (Ed.), *Culture and difference: Critical perspectives on the bicultural experience in the United States* (139-153) Westport, CT: Bergin and Garvey.

Vasquez, 0. (1994) The magic of La Clase Mágica: Enhancing the learning potential of bilingual children. *Australian Journal of Language and Literacy*, 17. 120-128.

Vygotsky, L. S. (1978) *Mind in society': The development of higher psychological processes.* Cambridge, MA: Harvard University Press.

Wertsch, J. V., and Ramírez, J. D. (1994) Literacy and other forms of mediated action. In P. del Rio, A. Alvarez, and J. V. wertsch (Eds.), *Explorations in socia-cultural studies* (Vol.2) Madrid: Fundación Infancia Y Aprendizaje.

CHAPTER 13

Developing critical literacy in a changing context: the challenges of 'critique' in South Africa
Carolyn McKinney

Introduction

I begin this chapter with a discussion of definitions of critical literacy and briefly explore its diverse influences. I then look at some illustrations of critical literacy in classroom practice across different educational sites in Australia, the UK and South Africa. In the second part of the chapter I address tensions raised by critical literacy pedagogy, both at the theoretical level and in classroom practice. Using examples of work from South Africa, I explore the ways in which critical literacy pedagogy is linked to the particular socio-historical context in which it takes place and why it may be resisted by particular groups of students.

What is critical literacy?

Perhaps unsurprisingly, critical literacy is not one thing. It has diverse intellectual roots, a complex relationship with pedagogy and can take many different forms in practice. A number of researchers have been involved in theorising critical literacy in Australia. Luke and Walton (1994), for example, make a useful distinction between more conventional or conservative approaches to critical literacy defined 'in terms of personal response to literature, and in terms of the comprehension of disciplinary, non-fiction texts, and a 'critical social literacy' which 'entails the analysis and evaluation of textual ideologies and cultural messages, and an understanding of the linguistic and discursive techniques with which texts represent social reality, relations, and identity'. Lankshear (1997) has taken up this notion of critical social literacy and argues that it should aim to develop 'powerfully literate' readers and writers who can approach texts and social life critically as well as master the range of genres and techniques in writing, needed for effective participation in society and in a participatory democracy. It is with the latter definition of a critical social literacy, i.e. literacy that is concerned with the workings of ideologies in texts and in the social world, and with the relationship between language and power, that I am concerned here. Understanding the socially constructed nature of texts, knowledge and of one's own reading response is crucial to the project of critical literacy as defined here.

Intellectual roots of critical literacy

Critical literacy has different origins. Firstly, there is the overwhelming influence of the Brazilian literacy theorist and educator Paulo Freire. Freire's ideas, (first expressed in *Pedagogy of the Oppressed,* 1972) have had an enormous influence on North American critical pedagogy and critical literacy through the work of people like Giroux (1989), Aronowitz and Giroux (1986) and Lankshear and McLaren (1993). Freire's statement that we need to learn to 'read the world' through 'reading the word' is now famous (Freire and Macedo, 1987). Secondly there is the influence of British Critical Discourse Analysis following Fairclough and others, which was translated into Critical Language Awareness in the late 1980s. Critical Language Awareness (CLA) aims to raise consciousness of the language/power and language/society relationship, showing how sociolinguistic practices are 'socially created' and 'socially changeable' (Clark *et al*, 1990:250) and to develop 'practices of critical and oppositional reading, listening and viewing,' (Clark *et al* 1991:46-47). Thirdly, there is the influence of poststructuralism with its emphasis on multiple possible readings of texts, the discursive construction of the social and the consequent mutually constitutive relationship between language and subjectivity (Weedon, 1987).

Early writing on critical literacy emphasised rather grand aims, describing it as an emancipatory and empowering approach to literacy education. Freire was writing about the adult literacy process in a developing world context when he argued that any literacy learning worth the effort should be critical and emancipatory. For Freire, literacy was a tool for conscientisation, which he describes as

> The process in which [people], not as recipients but as knowing subjects, achieve a deepening awareness both of the sociocultural reality that shapes their lives and of their capacity to transform that reality (Freire, 1985:93).

Thus, it was expected that through reflecting on the forces shaping their lives and developing a deep awareness of social inequality, people would become engaged in transforming the sources of their oppression. Building on Freire's ideas, Giroux, who writes more generally about critical pedagogy in the North American context, outlines a notion of critical literacy as a way of infusing education with radical democracy, and a particular kind of citizenship education, across the school curriculum (i.e. into different subjects and disciplines). Giroux argues that critical literacy offers 'the opportunity for students to interrogate how knowledge is constituted as both a historical and social construction' and should provide them with the 'knowledge and skills necessary for them to understand and analyse their own historically constructed voices and experiences as part of a project of self and social empowerment' (Giroux, 1989:33-34). The role of power in the regulation of knowledge is an important focus. The aim is for students to examine how knowledge and power come together to legitimate different discourses. Giroux's notion of critical literacy is thus not dissimilar to that of the UK based researcher, Fairclough, who in an early discussion of Critical Language Awareness (CLA), stated his aim as 'to help increase consciousness of how language contributes to the domination of some people by others, because consciousness is the first step towards emancipation' (1989:232). While there is less emphasis on emancipation and empowerment in more recent writing on critical literacy (see Morgan, 1997; Christie and Misson, 1998 and Wallace, 1999), a broader vision of social justice and social equity is still embraced and can be traced throughout the discussion of definitions and origins of critical literacy above.

Critical literacy as a form of pedagogy

The relationship between critical literacy and pedagogy differs across different contexts. This means that people both claim and do quite different things with critical literacy across countries and educational sites. Writing on critical literacy in North America tends to be more theoretical than practical. The terms literacy and reading are used very broadly and critical literacy can refer to 'reading' the social world critically without necessarily working with specific texts. This is illustrated in the discussion of Giroux's ideas above and, as Cazden (2000:263) points out, specific examples of text-focused critical literacy practice in the United States are extremely hard to find. However critical literacy pedagogy has flourished in Australia, to a lesser extent in South Africa, and there are some examples of practice in the UK even though it is not a mainstream approach there. In this section of the chapter I shall begin by outlining two examples of practice in Australia, one from a primary classroom (O'Brien, 1994; Comber, 1993) and another from an English Second Language programme with adult immigrant women (Bee, 1993). I shall then move on to look at an example of a critical reading course with English Foreign Language higher education students in the UK (Wallace, 1992, 1999). Finally I will present an example of critical literacy materials developed for upper-secondary schools in South Africa (Janks, 1993, 2001).

Critical literacy in the early years

Working with primary school children in Australia, O'Brien has developed a number of strategies for introducing critical literacy in the early years classroom (O'Brien, 1994 and reported in Comber, 1993). In particular, she has developed activities around fiction and non-fiction texts which highlight the way in which gender stereotypes are presented in texts. For example, after reading Roald Dahl's *The Fantastic Mr Fox* to her 6 year olds, O'Brien engages the children in an activity which allows them to critique the story and to present an alternative version with the following instructions:

> In this story Roald Dahl shows Mrs Fox to be weak and scared. Draw a different Mrs Fox helping to save her family. Use speech bubbles to show what she could say and do to save her family. (1994:38).

O'Brien reports how the children responded enthusiastically to this task by drawing pictures of a strong and adventurous Mrs Fox making plans and digging to save her family. Another example (reported in Comber, 1993) is of work with 5-7 year olds around the junk mail and catalogues that circulate in their area around the time of Mother's Day. O'Brien gets the children to examine the examples of junk mail and catalogues critically through tasks such as the following:

(1) Draw and label six presents for mothers you expect to see in mother's day catalogues.

(2) Draw and label some presents you wouldn't expect to find in mother's day catalogues.

(3) What groups of people get the most out of mother's day?

(4) Look through the catalogue. Draw and label six kinds of presents you can find.

(5) Make two lists: how the mothers in the catalogues are like real mothers; how the mothers in the catalogues aren't like real mothers.

Through such activities the children begin to realise how they are positioned by the texts; that the purpose of the texts is to sell products and that it is the shop owners who make the most out of this occasion. O'Brien also raises a number of general critical reading questions with the children over the period of the school year:

(1) What do writers say about girls, boys, mothers and fathers in the books you read?

(2) What do adults think that children like to read about?

(3) If you knew about families only from reading this book what would you know about what mothers do?

(4) What would you know about what fathers do? (in Comber, 1993:76).

O'Brien's activities described above represent an attempt to involve even small children success-fully in using literacy to read their social world with a critical eye and in resisting the powerful ideologies which are often represented in texts, both of which are seen to be crucial elements in Luke and Walton's definition of critical literacy outlined above.

Critical literacy in adult education

In a very different context, Barbara Bee describes an English Second Language (ESL) course she taught with adult immigrant women in inner-city Sydney, Australia. After an unsuccessful start to the course using conventional formal language schemes, Bee decided to focus on the parti-cipants' life experiences and their oppressive circumstances as women in order to gain their interest and enthusiasm. Bee describes a series of successful classes, all of which centred around themes relevant to the women's lives, in which the women began for the first time to interact meaningfully in the class with each other and herself. In the first of these, Bee explains how she came to class 'armed only with three words: *wife, mother, woman*' (1993:111). These words were used as a stimulus for talking about these different roles and about the individual women's ex-periences of these roles. With Bee's help, each woman generated her own sentence in relation to the words. The sentences were then written up on the board for the students to read back. She describes the women's difficulty in coming up with positive sentences around the word 'woman' which were separate from the role of mother and wife:

> When asked what had made it difficult to say something positive about themselves, the women thought it was because they were rarely called upon to think or act in a capacity other than as caretaker of their husbands' or children's needs. 'I don't get any time to think about myself,' replied one. (p.113).

Bee's practice represents an explicit attempt to apply the Freirean conscientisation process dis-cussed above. She describes how developing literacy in English became a process for them women of learning to read their worlds critically and where possible working to change these. However, Bee also points to the difficulties such an approach can raise. In this case the women sometimes felt more depressed about their life circumstances when they felt unable to make the radical life changes required to escape them.

Critical literacy in the EFL context

Working in the area of Critical Language Awareness, which is synonymous in the UK with critical literacy, Catherine Wallace (1992, 1999) has described a number of critical reading courses which she ran with first year undergraduate English as a Foreign Language (EFL) students in London. In these courses she aimed to help students develop not only the ability to respond critically to texts, but also 'a critical awareness in a broader sense, of what reading itself is' (1992:61) including the way that reading is embedded in a social context. In line with this aim, Wallace began her critical reading courses with a focus on literacy practices, before engaging students in the analysis of specific texts. She outlines some of the tasks in which students were involved during this initial period of the course as: observation of reading and writing practices in everyday contexts; observation of the presence and physical location of texts in homes and public places; classification of community texts into genres in order to identify culturally significant text types and to locate cross-cultural difference in genres and their defining features; and a preliminary discussion of the cultural significance of both the practices and genres observed (1999:105).

In the second part of the courses, students turned their attention to particular texts. Wallace used the following questions posed by Kress (1989:7 in Wallace, 1992:71) in order to 'raise awareness of the ideology of texts':

1. Why is this topic written about?
2. How is the topic being written about?
3. What other ways of writing about the topic are there?

And added a further two questions:

4. Who is writing to whom?
5. What is the topic?

In a later course (Wallace, 1999) she shows how she used a simplified version of Hallidayan systemic functional grammar to closely examine a series of texts from the UK women's magazine *Marie Claire*, in which women from around the world were frequently exoticised and 'othered'. The students examined pronoun use, modality, thematisation and cohesion, among other features, in identifying the working of ideologies in the texts. Wallace's approach is thus strongly text-focused and engages students in linguistic analyses of textual ideologies in line with Luke and Walton's definition of critical social literacy above.

Critical literacy in secondary school

In South Africa, Hilary Janks co-ordinated the development and piloting of a series of Critical Language Awareness workbooks, focusing on the relationship between language and power, for use with secondary school students[1]. As editor of the series, Janks begins each workbook with an explanation of the critical literacy process and includes the following statement in her rubric:

> Critical Language Awareness emphasises the fact that texts are constructed. Anything that has been constructed can be de-constructed. This unmaking or unpicking of the text increases our awareness of the [constrained] choices that the writer or speaker has made. Every choice foregrounds what was selected and hides, silences or backgrounds what was not selected. Awareness of this prepares the reader to ask critical questions: why did the writer or speaker make these choices? Whose interests do they serve? Who is empowered or disempowered by the language used? (Janks, 1993, p. iii)

Janks had a particular goal in her critical literacy work which began during the late apartheid years. This was to highlight the ways in which language was manipulated by the apartheid state, including through their control of the media, and to develop an 'emancipatory discourse' (Janks, 2000, Janks and Ivanič, 1992). In one of the activities from her workbook, *Language and Position*, Janks gets students to examine how the writing of history has been manipulated in South Africa (see Figure 1).

It is worth noting that these CLA materials had a mixed reception from students. In interviews with some of the student recipients, Janks found resistance around the issue of gender roles, which was tied up in complex ways with race (see Janks, 2001). She links the difficulties students had with some of the materials to their own sense of threatened identity. I return to this issue in the discussion of my own classroom data below.

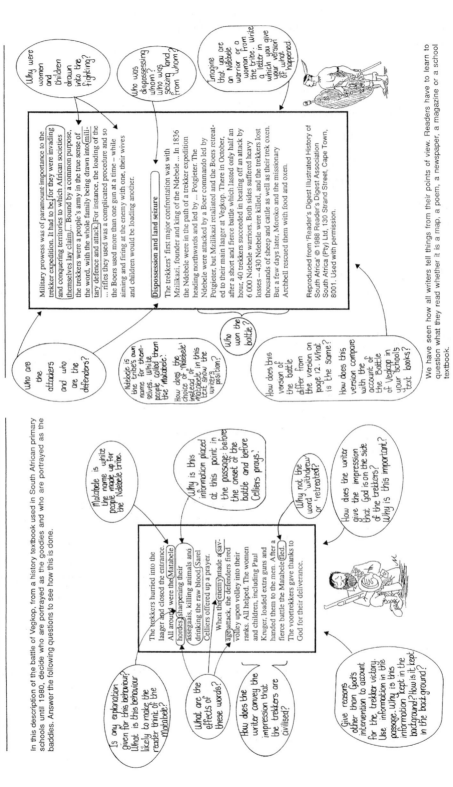

Figure 1

Challenges to critique/being critical: insights from the South African context

Central to critical literacy, and thus to the examples of pedagogy outlined above is, as the term indicates, the notion of being critical. However, as the examples above show, exactly what being critical means is powerfully dependent on the local social and political contexts in which teaching and learning take place. In this section I want to focus on the particular context of apartheid and post-apartheid South Africa to examine what critical in this context means to teachers and students, and to explore the limitations of working within a critical framing. I look at how the role of critique may differ in the post-apartheid context from that during apartheid, and highlight the need to consider student identities in critical literacy pedagogy.

In the example of Janks's materials above, I pointed out that her aim was tied to the socio-political and historical moment in apartheid South Africa. Apartheid was euphemistically glossed by the white minority government at the time as a policy of 'separate development'. In reality this meant the development and privileging of white people through the exploitation and dehumanisation of black people, the effects of which are still clearly evident today in the continuing widespread poverty of many black South Africans. Under apartheid, race and racial differentiation controlled every aspect of people's lives, and this was always designed to advantage white people: where you lived, worked, went to school, who you interacted with socially, and what amenities you had access to were all racially and legally governed. Resistance to the apartheid system, which gathered momentum in the 1980s, was met with violent and bloody repression from the totalitarian apartheid regime.

Under such circumstances, Janks felt that there was a particularly urgent need for the development of critical literacy skills in South African schools 'to enable readings that took up different positions from those offered by the state' (1995:5). In a more recent discussion of her work she explains:

> I cut my critical literacy teeth in the struggle against apartheid. I saw my own work as both a moral and a political project which valued education as an important factor in achieving a just society. In the days of apartheid it was easy to understand power as a negative force which constructed and maintained relations of domination by protecting the interests of the small white minority....my work set out to deconstruct the language of the oppressor, and to search for an 'emancipatory discourse'. (Janks, 2000:175)

Janks argues that after two democratic elections (the historic first in 1994 and the second in 1999) the critical literacy project in South Africa has changed and requires a re-imagining of how critical literacy can contribute to reconstruction and development, and 'to our reinventing our nation and ourselves' (Janks, 2000:175). As Janks makes clear, the critical literacy project during apartheid South Africa was unquestionably oppositional. Although this was tied to the socio-political moment, there does seem to be an assumption in critical pedagogy, and in many forms of critical literacy, that we should be working against, critiquing, the insufficiently democratic state (especially in Giroux and Freire's writing). Such social critique made sense in South Africa when the target was the apartheid government. Critique in the current South African context is however more complex and varied, and may involve criticism of particular policies and activities (e.g. health policy on HIV/AIDS) rather than of the entire government system. Indeed, new government educational policy advocates taking up issues of social inequality and injustice (especially racism and sexism) in the curriculum, both at school level and in higher education. I would therefore argue that the goals and practices of critical literacy pedagogy will inevitably change according to the historical and socio-political context in which they take place.

Kress argues that the notion of critique itself is a 'response to particular circumstances in a particular period' and thus is an 'historical phenomenon' (2000:160). He elaborates:

> In periods of relative social stability critique has the function of introducing a dynamic into the system. In a situation of intense social change, the rules of constitution both of texts and of social arrangements are in crisis: they're not settled, but in process of change. (2000:160)

Applying Kress's argument to South Africa, one could see apartheid South Africa as the relatively 'stable period' in which critique was crucial in 'introducing a dynamic into the system'. The present highly dynamic, transitional environment could then be defined as more in need of a forward looking approach and a focus on solutions and productive activity. Kress argues that the focus during times of intense social change should shift from critique to that of 'design'.

> While critique looks at the present through the means of past production, Design shapes the future through deliberate deployment of representational resources in the designer's interest. Design is the essential textual principle and pedagogic/political goal for periods characterised by intense and far-reaching change. (2000:160)

Kress explains that critique is one of the processes on which Design rests, and thus he is not arguing for its abandonment. Indeed, deploying resources in the 'designer's interests' could be dangerous without an examination of what these interests might be. But, while critique is often focused on the deconstruction of texts (for example much critical literacy practice focuses on critical reading rather than on writing, or creating texts), design is focused more on the production of new texts.

A second major criticism of critical pedagogy, and thus of critical literacy, are their conception of criticism as an essentially rational activity. While it is true that critical pedagogy and critical literacy aim at wider social change, being critical is also about self-examination and self-critique. This means that examining the relationship between the self and the social by answering questions such as 'How am I implicated in the social world?', 'How am I implicated in social inequality?' is also an important part of the critical literacy process. The extent to which students participate in or resist critical pedagogy is bound up with their sense of identity, and thus with how they are positioned or identified through the texts under study. The importance of identity in critical pedagogy has been emphasised by feminist and post-structuralist researchers who argue that critical pedagogy, as an enlightenment project, mistakenly treats people as fully rational and unified subjects (e.g. Britzman *et al*, 1993; Ellsworth, 1989; Lather, 1991; Janks, 2001). Researchers have pointed out that underlying most critical literacy approaches is the false assumption that revealing social inequalities to people will necessarily bring about change, whether personal, or collective. As Elizabeth Ellsworth indicates, in one of the best known critiques of critical pedagogy, this assumption ignores the way in which people have investments in particular social positions and discourses, and that these kinds of investments are not lightly given up:

> As long as the literature on critical pedagogy fails to come to grips with issues of trust, risk, and the operations of fear and desire around such issues of identity and politics in the classroom, their rationalistic tools will continue to fail to loose deep-seated, self-interested investments in unjust relations of, for example, gender, ethnicity and sexual orientation. (Ellsworth, 1989:313)

Stranded in critique? A case study of resistance to critical literacy in South Africa

My own research was conducted within a first year undergraduate English studies programme at a relatively privileged and predominantly white, Afrikaans university[2] in South Africa from February to June in 2001. The English studies programme is described in the university hand-book as, among other things, developing students' ability to read texts critically, whether these are literary texts (novels, poems, plays) or other texts (films, news reports, advertisements) as well as developing students' awareness of language (what it is and how it influences us). As part of this programme I taught seminar courses on South African literature to one group of 17 students, 14 of whom were Afrikaans first language (including two so-called coloured students) and three of whom were white English first language. The students were 18-19 years old. I hoped to use a critical reading of the prescribed texts to focus on issues of social inequality in South Africa and to document my work with the students as a case study of critical literacy pedagogy. I used ethnographic methods to collect data, including video-recordings of the classes I taught and recorded interviews with a sample of students. My data also included the journals kept by students, which I hoped would enable me to engage in dialogue with them around issues raised through the course and their assignments.

Since the seminar course was to deal with representations of South Africa in South African litera-ture (short stories and poetry), I decided to begin my teaching with two more general critical reading classes in which students explored the ways in which South Africa has been represented by outsiders, in foreign travel guides[3]. The introductions to the travel guides and the entries on the students' university town addressed South Africa's apartheid past to varying degrees. Partly in response to these outsider representations and also as a preparation for looking at the South Africanness of the short stories to follow, I asked my students to respond to the following ques-tions in their journal writing: 'How would you describe being South African?' and 'Do you think there is a collective South African identity'? Most of the students responded optimistically about present-day South Africa, but they frequently expressed the desire for South Africa to be free from racial tensions and divisions, acknowledging the continuing deep-seated racial divisions which characterise our society. J-M writes

> ...It's exciting being South African. Who knows what's going to happen in the future. There are so much potential, because we have such a lot of cultures and people who never had the chance to do something is now getting it ....Although there's more interaction between racial/cultural groups than ever before we're still divided into groups and that makes it dif-ficult to have a collective identity. (white female, Journal entry, Tutorial 3)

And KvW writes:

> ...I believe that all true South Africans share a positive attitude towards their motherland.
>
> South Africans are those people who have turned their backs on the past and decided to start afresh. Racial prejudice is still prevalent among people and until they turn over a new leaf, they will never truly be South African. (white male, Journal entry, Tutorial 3)

Other students were more overwhelmingly positive, for example LO:

> Being South African means you're living in one of the most beautiful and diverse countries in the world... South Africa is a passionate and sociable nation and there is a bigger sense of

respect and together[ness] between South Africans than the world might think. (white, male, Journal entry, Tutorial 3)

One student was overwhelmingly negative, yet still with a desire for optimism:

Being South African nowadays is all about being negative and I would like it dearly for that negative to change to a positive. (white male, Journal entry, Tutorial 3)

In the same journal writing on South African identity outlined above, one student in particular expresses the genuine fear that if we continue to focus on the past (and related issues of inequality and racism), we will never be able to move beyond it:

...I know that apartheid is far not over. But I believe we can have the identity of a liberal land...We can have the identity which I picture in South Africa in a few years, but South Africans has got to want that and work for that and stop focusing on previous issues and problems. ...Only being born in the eighties and growing up in a quite liberal town, I don't think I know the first thing about apartheid. In my mind things had always been complicated, but not nearly as much as I found it was later. For me being South African is therefore not about racial issues. It's never been about black, white and brown. *I don't believe that that is all a land can be about.* For me, being South African, is about *something more... it's about something more positive.* (MW, white female, journal entry, my emphasis. Tutorial 3)

This expression that 'there must be more' than the apartheid past, echoed above – and which MW repeats in writing later in the course – to me expresses a wish, desire, that apartheid were not the grand narrative of our past and the dominant narrative of our current times. I would argue that MW is resisting the representation of South Africa's past in the travel guide entries, two of which were explicitly political in focus.

With the expression of such optimism in some students' journals, and/or a strong desire for others to share this view, as well as to be part of a non-racist and unified society and to resist racial categories, it is perhaps not surprising that some students would resist going where the critical literacy course was taking them – into examinations of the recent apartheid past and its continuing effects in South African society.

After the travel guide classes we moved on to the short story section of the course. This progressed smoothly until the third class where, during a group-work session, a heated discussion broke out in one group about why students had to study South African literature. It is significant that students were working on the story 'The Toilet' by Gcina Mhlope. The story is partly autobiographical, dealing with Mhlope's development as a writer under oppressive circumstances in apartheid South Africa. In particular, it caricatures the Maid/Madam (domestic worker/ employer) relationship common at the time and portrays the white madam particularly scathingly. The story also represents the stark contrast between the luxurious living conditions of the white employer and the vastly inadequate living conditions of the domestic worker. In response to the group's complaints, I asked for the views of other students in the class on studying South African literature:

CB (white male): Yes, I think everything we have read is racially connected

CM (tutor and author): Racially connected, OK

CB And, and no just like saying, listen here how bad you know the white people treated the black people and because it's in the past, we just don't, we don't feel like dealing with that, because it's in the past. It's not our problem. We are a whole new generation and we live in harmony with each other and we don't feel like dealing with other people's problems

CM Uhhmm [disapproval]

CB and it gets thrown in our faces all the time

[MT – white male – points to MW to speak]

MW I can see the argument that we should know about it and it is part of our lives also. But that's why we should do one or two of these, but OK, we've been doing these (laughs) I don't know if it's just our school

CB romanticises the present situation in South Africa, 'we [new generation] live in harmony with each other', glossing over the continuing racial divisions which most students showed awareness of in their journal entries following the travel guide work. He also expresses frustration: 'we don't feel like dealing with that... It's not our problem', but this is coupled with a need to be absolved from any responsibility in dealing with the past in the present or from any connection whatsoever with the past. MW's response, which follows directly on CB's, is more moderate. Later in the discussion after a lengthy contribution from CB where he attempts to play down apartheid atrocities, MW again distances herself from his view while at the same time maintaining her own feelings of frustration over dealing with apartheid:

MW I just want to say about the issues. I don't think we shouldn't address them, I just wonder if we can get over it at some stage?

Although MW doesn't explicitly attack CB's argument at this point, by saying 'I don't think we shouldn't address them' she is in effect countering his position, while also returning to her expression of the fear, 'can we ever get over [apartheid]?'

Such resistance became a silent presence in the classroom and towards the end of the course I devoted a class to discussing the problems in South Africa with dealing with our past. At this point I could connect the discussion to a debate in the media about teaching history in South African schools and thus the problem was presented as a wider issue. In a journal entry following this class discussion, MW wrote, 'We are smothered with this issue, coming from all sides.' The violent metaphor of suffocation shows the extent to which MW feels trapped in a past that is not of her making. This deep frustration is accompanied by a strong desire to move beyond current social divisions and inequalities in South African society. Yet there is a danger in reading resistance in this way since it masks the fact that these fears and desires frequently arise from the continued feelings of guilt which white students may feel. Despite being only seven years old upon Mandela's release from prison and thus having no involvement in the apartheid regime, young white people such as MW continue to benefit from privileges granted under apartheid. Consequently, no longer discussing the past means no longer having the uncomfortable reminder of how one has benefited from it. That MW does feel guilt about her connections with the past, and also anger that she is positioned as guilty, is clear from another extract of this journal entry:

I think [South African history] should be teached in such a way that pupils understand that it is over and not really their [emphasis in original] issue, but history, that just explain why we are where we are now. I don't think it is fair to guilt people who is really innocent and the way this can be done is by not overteaching it! (Journal entry, Tutorial 22)

Within MW's resistance, expressed through her journal entries and in the class discussion, there is a tension between the desire to escape the past, and attendant feelings of guilt, and a real desire for a new, non-racist and egalitarian South Africa. Her position contrasts with that of one or two other students, such as CB, who seemed to be more concerned with escaping the past and avoiding any acknowledgement of their continuing position of privilege in South Africa, than with building a more equitable future. In my research example, students' identities as 'New' (post-apartheid) South Africans, and their desire to be part of a unified non-racial South Africa, are under threat when reminders of the past evoke feelings of guilt over past atrocities committed by whites which are responsible for their continuing privilege. Thus white students can feel uncomfortably positioned by the undesirable identity of oppressor which is represented in some of the South African literature from the apartheid era. In this case, critical literacy is working to disempower these students, rather than engaging them in a process of 'self-empowerment' outlined as one of the goals of critical literacy by Giroux (see Giroux, 1989, quoted above). For MW in particular, this connects with her feeling of being stranded in the moment of critique – if we continue to focus on critiques of the past, how can we move on in the present?

Conclusion

In this paper I have attempted to give a sense of the diversity of the critical literacy field. I have also indicated the differing relationships between critical literacy and pedagogy that exist in different contexts. In South Africa today it is clear that the role of critique is different from what it was under apartheid. I have argued through my case study that we need to ensure that we don't get stranded in the critique mode but need also to find ways of developing productive alternative approaches. Kress's notion of 'design' may be useful here. Perhaps my students could engage more successfully with South Africa's apartheid past if they were also given the opportunity to design and produce their own alternative fictional texts which represent South Africa now, as well as their visions for this, in addition to more traditional analytical writing. My case study also problematises notions of empowerment and difference in critical literacy. While more recent writing on critical literacy has moved away from simplistic notions of self-empowerment, it has not adequately addressed questions such as who is being critical of whom and what might happen when critical literacy pedagogy works to disempower certain students. Issues of desire and identity are crucial here. When critical literacy positions students in undesirable ways (as was the case with MW when certain texts positioned her such that she was unable to take up the identity of 'new South African' which she desired), it is not surprising that it will be resisted. While in some situations difference can be a rich resource for learning, it can also confront students with problematic evaluations of their own and their families positioning which are painful and difficult to deal with. This could also happen in other contexts, for example with young children recognising the inequalities in gender roles played by their parents at home. This calls for more complex approaches to critical literacy pedagogy which are always sensitive to the micro-politics of the classroom and the identity positions students either choose or feel compelled to take up, as well as to their wider social, cultural, political and historical contexts.

Acknowledgement

I would like to thank Ermien van Pletzen, Theresa Lillis and Janet Maybin for their invaluable comments on earlier drafts of this chapter.

Notes

1   Janks has links with Lancaster University group where CLA originated and thus works within this frame, though she uses the descriptors critical literacy and CLA interchangeably in referring to her work.

2   This is unusual in South Africa, where universities at present generally have a minimum of 50% 'black' students. While I do not want to support the myth of race as a biological category, the use of race terms is unavoidable here because of the continuing role which race plays in organising social life in South Africa.

3   Four different guidebooks were used: the *Rough Guide, Lonely Planet, Footprint* Guide and Dorling Kindersley *Eyewitness* guides respectively.

References

Aronowitz, S. and Giroux, H (1986) *Education under Siege: the conservative, liberal and radical debate over schooling.* London: Routledge and Kegan Paul

Bee, B. (1993) Critical literacy and the politics of gender in C. Lankshear and P.L. McLaren (eds) *Critical Literacy: Politics, Praxis and the Postmodern.* Albany: State University of New York Press, 105-131

Britzman, D., Santiago-Valles, K.A, Jiménez-Muñoz, G.M and Lamash, L.M. (1993) Slips that show and tell: fashioning multiculture as a problem of representation. In C. McCarthy and W. Crichlow (eds) *Race, Identity and Representation in Education.* New York and London: Routledge

Cazden, C. (2000) Taking Cultural Differences into Account in B. Cope and M. Kalantzis (eds) *Multiliteracies: Literacy learning and the design of social futures.* South Yarra: Macmillan Publishers Australia

Christie, F. and Misson, R. (1998) Framing the issues in literacy education in F. Christie and R. Misson *Literacy and Schooling.* London and New York: Routledge

Clark, R., Fairclough, N., Ivanič, R., and Martin-Jones, M. (1990) Critical Language Awareness Part 1: A critical review of three current approaches to language awareness, *Language and Education.* Vol 4, no 4

Clark *et al* (1991) Critical Language Awareness Part 2: Towards critical alternatives, *Language and Education.* Vol 5, no 1

Comber, B. (1993) Classroom exploration in literacy, *Australian Journal of Language and Literacy.* Vol 16, no 1, 73-84

Ellsworth, E (1989) Why doesn't this feel empowering? Working through the repressive myths of critical pedagogy, *Harvard Educational Review.* 59(3), 297-324

Fairclough, N. (1989) *Language and Power,* London: Longman

Freire, P. (1972) *Pedagogy of the Oppressed,* London: Penguin

Freire, P. (1985) *The Politics of Education: Culture, Power and Liberation.* Westport, Connecticut: Bergin and Garvey

Freire, P. and Macedo, D. (1987) *Literacy: Reading the Word and the World.* London: Routledge and Kegan Paul

Giroux, H. (1989) *Schooling for Democracy.* London: Routledge

Janks, H. (Ed.) (1993) *Critical Language Awareness Series.* Johannesburg: Hodder and Stoughton and Wits University Press

Janks, H. (2000) Domination, Access, Diversity and Design: a synthesis for critical literacy education. *Educational Review,* vol 52, no 2, 175-186

Janks, H. (2001) Identity and conflict in the critical literacy classroom, in B. Comber and A. Simpson (eds) *Negotiating Critical Literacies in Classrooms.* New Jersey and London: Lawrence Erlbaum Associates

Janks, H. and Ivanič, R. (1992) Critical language awareness and emancipatory discourse in N. Fairclough (ed) *Critical Language Awareness.* London: Longman

Kress, G. (1996) Representational resources and the production of subjectivity: Questions for the theoretical development of Critical Discourse Analysis in a multicultural society in Carmen Rosa Caldas-Coulthard and Malcolm Coulthard (eds) *Texts and Practices readings in Critical Discourse Analysis.* London: Routledge

Kress, G. (2000) Design and transformation: new theories of meaning in B. Cope and M. Kalantzis (eds) *Multiliteracies: Literacy Learning and the Design of Social Futures.* South Yarra: Macmillan Publishers Australia

Lankshear, C. (1997) (with J.P. Gee, M. Knobel and C. Searle) *Changing Literacies.* Buckingham: Open University Press

Lankshear, C. and McLaren, P. (1993) (eds) *Critical Literacy: politics, praxis and the postmodern. Albany: State* University of New York Press

Lather, P. (1991) *Getting Smart: Feminist research and pedagogy with/in the postmodern.* New York and London: Routledge

Luke, A. and Walton, C. (1994) Critical reading: teaching and assessing in T. Husen and T.N. Postlethwaite *International Encyclopaedia of Education*, 2nd edition. Oxford: Pergamon

Morgan, W. (1997) *Critical Literacy in the Classroom: the art of the possible*. London and New York: Routledge

O'Brien, J. (1994) Critical literacy in an early childhood classroom, *Australian Journal of Language and Literacy*, 17(1), 36-44

Tutu, D. M. (1986/1996) Foreword to Magubane, P. *June 16, 1976 Never, Never Again*. Johannesburg: Skotaville Publishers (1996, 20th anniversary edition)

Wallace, C. (1992) Critical literacy awareness in the EFL classroom in N. Fairclough (ed) *Critical Language Awareness*. Longman: London

Wallace, C. (1999) Critical language Awareness: Key principles for a course in critical reading, *Language Awareness*. Vol 8 no 2 , 98-110 [Special edition on Critical Language Awareness edited by Romy Clark and Roz Ivanič]

Weedon, C. (1987/1997) *Feminist Practice and Poststructuralist Theory* 2nd edition. Oxford: Blackwells (1st edition, 1987)

CHAPTER 14

'English is here to stay': a critical look at institutional and educational practices in India

Vai Ramanathan

Studies of World Englishes in the 1980s and 1990s have called attention to the growing number of Englishes used internationally (Kachru, 1985; Quirk, 1985) by documenting features of the varieties of English (Pakir, 1991) and raising issues about the socio-ideological underpinnings of their use (Canagarajah, 1993). A key assumption has been that the inner circle of countries, Britain, the U.S., Canada and Australia, with native speakers of the language, sets English language standards for countries in the outer circle – e.g., India and parts of Africa, where English is used non-natively but extensively and has been given official-language status. The different varieties of English used in outer-circle countries make inner-circle standards difficult or impossible for them to meet. Research has largely concentrated on describing English language varieties or discussing the unequal power relations between inner and outer circles of countries resulting from the privileged standard-setting position of inner-circle countries (Pennycook, 1998; Phillipson, 1992), but little attention has been paid to examining how power relations operate within the outer circle itself.

Extending the study of hegemonic practices associated with English language use to the outer-circle country of India, this chapter examines how English and the privileges associated with it remain inaccessible to those who are disadvantaged because of their economic situation, their caste, or both. Thus, even within an outer-circle country, an English-related inner-outer power dichotomy appears to exist. The Indian middle class assumes a position of relative power through its access to English in Circle 1, with Dalit, or lower caste, students and students from so-called Other Backward Classes (OBCs)[1] in Circle 2 (see Figure 1). By focusing on three specific educational and institutional practices influencing their access to Indian English, I show how some students remain within the relatively less powerful Circle 2. The three practices I address are (a) tracking students into college-level streams that bar some students from English-medium instruction; (b) teaching English literature rather than the English language throughout India, which limits English to the elite and middle class; and (c) using grammar-translation methods, which inhibit the communicative competence of some students, thus keeping them in their disadvantaged position.

The discussion and conclusions offered in this study are based on an ongoing ethnographic case study of an English-medium college (Ramanathan and Atkinson, 1998) that explores how students in India who have used the vernacular in Grades K-12 adjust to the use of English at the tertiary level. Rooted in the same context and data, this article focuses on how the people most

---

* First published in *TESOL Quarterly*, 1999, 33, 2:211-233.

Figure 1: Inner and outer circles of power in India

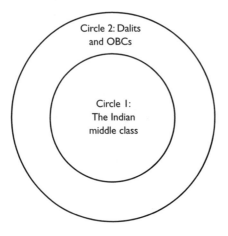

disadvantaged in Indian society – namely, Dalits and OBCs, who are also typically the most economically and educationally handicapped – negotiate with English but are unable to acquire proficiency in it. I draw on a range of data types, including interviews with students, faculty members and administrators; class observations; and textbooks and other written documents.

The primary motivation for this study stemmed from the fact that, when I was a student at the college myself 14 years before, several friends who had been educated in Gujarati-medium schools experienced serious difficulty with English at the college level. Some were constantly on the verge of dropping out because they found English classes too difficult; many felt enormous pressure to perform in exams and would even go to great lengths to get 'leaked' exam questions beforehand in order to prepare responses to them. Only much later in my graduate education and teaching career and during the research for this project did I realise how integrally their problems were tied to the above-mentioned institutional and educational practices. Although I had received a bachelor's degree from the institution and was thus very familiar with the general workings of the system when I began the research, some aspects of the college, including its general focus and the arrangement of classes, had changed. Thus, as a researcher, I returned to the site as both an outsider (having lived outside the culture for the past 11 years) and a relative former insider (having spent the first 23 years of my life in India and having attended the institution now to be researched).

To provide some cultural orientation for the research, I begin with a brief exploration of societal practices in India. I then describe the institution, the students, and the data collected and report on the institutional and educational practices that keep Dalit and OBC students out of Circle 1. Finally, I locate the findings within the larger issue of the role of English in India and offer suggestions for improving the language situation at the institution.

Hegemony, caste, and discrimination: some general connections

Hegemonic practices, as Gramsci (1988) maintains, are repressive practices in any given social structure, that ensure that the means and ownership of production remain in the hands of a few. These practices are perpetuated at every stratum of society by a variety of invisible factors – including institutions, religions, and legal practices – that justify unequal distribution of goods (Gee, 1990) and disallow minority groups access to and ownership of means of production. The construct of caste and its entailing social practices in India exemplify hegemonic practices that are historically and currently associated with keeping Dalit and OBCs in a disadvantaged position (Sarkar, 1984). According to Quigley (1993, p. 1), the Hindu world is made up of a number of castes, which are closed social groups: one may marry only within one's caste, and the children of the marriage belong to the caste of the parents. In this way the system is perpetuated ad infinitum.[2] Castes are hierarchically ranked on a purity-pollution scale according to their traditional occupations.[3] *Brahmins*, the caste traditionally associated with people who became priests, are considered in some ways the most pure. *Kshtriyas*, or the traditional warriors, are second on the scale; *Vaishyas*, who were originally business oriented, are third; and the *Shudras*, the scheduled caste people or labourers, are fourth.[4]

Method

As mentioned, this study draws on data gathered over two years as part of a larger ethnographic project (Ramanathan and Atkinson, 1998) that seeks to understand how students who have been socialised in Gujarati throughout Grades K-12 adjust to English in a largely English-medium college. In keeping with the ethnographic tradition (Ramanathan and Atkinson, 1999), our research questions evolved only after we had spent some time immersed in the field (Holliday, 1994; Prior, 1995), and our larger, somewhat inexplicit goals narrowed over time.

Data

The Students and the Institution

All the students under investigation in this study were attending a well-established college in Ahmedabad, Gujarat, India. After observing a range of students and classes for some weeks, we chose to focus on Dalit and OBC students for two reasons. First, the institution had in recent years committed itself to empowering them in a variety of ways.[5] Apart from adopting an open-door policy regarding admission for all Dalit and OBC students,[6] the institution, run by the Jesuit community based in the city, also offered them extracurricular support during their first year in the form of tutorials in English language, one area in which these students needed a great deal of help. We felt an investigation of how the institution handled its commitment to Dalit and OBC students would be potentially revealing. Second, because these students were taught in separate English classes during their first year at the college, we were able to conveniently narrow our focus and observe them intensely in a classroom context.

The choice of the institution was deliberate as well. Not only did the college have the reputation of being one of the premier English-medium colleges in the state, it was also the only college in the city that catered extensively to Dalit and OBC students. Furthermore, several departments in the college, including biochemistry, English, Sanskrit, and economics, were recognised as strong departments that were active in research and that graduated students with top marks on university final exams. In recent years, however, the institution's academic standards were thought to have gone down because it was willing to admit Dalit and OBC students who had not done as well as the other students in their 12th-grade exams.[7] Despite this college's deliberate pro-Dalit and OBC stance, its institutional and educational practices were representative of all English-medium colleges in the state.

According to the vice-principal of the college, an average of 1,500 students were enrolled at any given time. Of these, 500-600 students were enrolled in the arts, and the remaining were in the sciences. Approximately 375 of the arts students came from Gujarati-medium schools, and more than half of this number (56%) were Dalit or OBC students. The proportion of Dalit and OBC students in the science section was lower (30-40%). The number of Dalit and OBC students admitted each year to both the arts and the sciences had increased steadily because of the Jesuit community's commitment to 'serve the poor and the oppressed' (F4, p.2).[8]

The Exam System

All students were expected to take external exams set by the university with which the college was affiliated. Performance on these exams determined admission to the next year in the college as well as to master's programmes. Much instruction in the college was therefore geared toward getting students ready to take the exams. Instructors typically began the first day of English Compulsory (EC) classes by putting up the university exam format on the board (see Table 1), and every new topic in the class was introduced in terms of its relative importance (i.e., the point value assigned to it) in the exam. Such stress on the exam at every crucial stage of the teaching and learning process partially accounts for students' resorting to extensive memorisation of material (especially material they did not fully understand) only to get through the exams. Memorising seemed to be a way to succeed at all levels of college, but it was particularly prevalent among the group of students relevant to this article; it became a way for the Dalit and OBC students to manage despite their English language handicap.

Procedures

Data were gathered from multiple sources: 75 hours of classroom observation; interviews with 27 students, with all five faculty members of the English department, and with two chief administrators (the principal and vice principal of the college); and copies of required class texts, diagnostic exams, exam questions, and students' writing. Total time in the field was 12 weeks: six weeks in 1997 and six weeks in 1998; I conducted follow-up interviews with four of the students during the latter period.

TABLE 1: Structure of the Second-Year English Compulsory Exam

Test section	Task	Marks assigned
Short notes	write a paragraph on a specific term, concept, or character	10
Short-answer question	write a paragraph in response to a question	10
Advertisements	Answer questions based on advertisements (e.g., for jobs available, products for sale)	5
Short news items	Interpret excerpts from newspapers or other general news sources	5
Reading passage	Note the main points	5
Letter writing	Write a job application letter or a letter to a friend	7
Pronunciation	Identify which syllable in a list of words is stressed	10
Word building	In Scrabble-like games, create a certain number of words from an assortment of letters	10
One-word substitutes	Choose one of four phrases that best represents the meaning of a word	7

Interviews with teachers and administrators took place entirely in English and typically lasted 1-$1^1/_2$ hours. Interviews with Gujarati-medium students took place primarily in Gujarati or Hindi and were translated into English during transcription.

Contact with first-year (FY) students was made when we began to observe their EC classes; contact with second-year (SY) and third-year (TY) Gujarati-medium students was made when we went into their classes and asked for volunteers to participate in our project. Student interviews were conducted at times when students did not have class and in relatively quiet areas on campus, such as an empty classroom or the basketball court. Typically lasting for about an hour, these interviews sometimes involved groups of two or three students (generally friends) and at other times just one student.

For the purposes of this article, I draw primarily on 16 of the 27 student interviews with Dalit and OBC students as well as on the rest of the data collected over the two six-week periods. Of these students, three were FY students who had just gained admission to the college, six were SY students who had opted to major in English literature, and seven were TY students.

The students were interviewed about a range of issues: their general background in English, aspects of learning English that they liked or didn't like, the advantages that fluency in English would bring them, possible resistance to learning the language, the quality of English language instruction they had received in school, the adequacy of the instruction they were receiving in college, the relative importance they gave to spoken English, and any feelings of cultural conflict they experienced when reading literary texts based in US or British culture. The interviews were largely open-ended and unstructured, with the students' views and responses informing the flow of talk (see Appendix for a general schema of interview questions). Most of the students felt shy about speaking in English; many of them worried about how 'wrong' their English would sound ('Maaru English khotuu chhe, sharam aaveh chhe' [My English is wrong, I am shy]; S6, p.2). In the sections that follow, I draw on themes that emerged in at least 12 of the 16 interviews.

Findings
Within the setting described above, I found the following institutional and educational practices that appear to keep Dalit and OBC students out of the more powerful Circle 1.

Practice 1: Tracking
Instruction in the college is broken down into two divisions: the A division, in which Gujarati is the medium of instruction for all courses, and the B division, in which English is the medium of instruction. Students are placed in these divisions depending on whether their primary medium of instruction in Grades K-12 was Gujarati or English.

Unlike students in the B division, students in the A division are tracked into either the *a* or the *b* stream[9] depending on the years of English language instruction they have had in school (see Table 2). Students in the a stream typically had English as a subject in Grades 5-12 and are assumed to have a moderate grasp of the language. According to the *Teacher's Handbook* issued by the central university of which the college is an affiliate, this group is at the intermediate level. Students in this stream are generally from middle-class homes, and their literacy levels in Gujarati are relatively high. Three of the six SY students interviewed for this study came from this background.

Students in the *b* stream, on the other hand, are those who opted to drop English as a subject in Grades 10-12, thus having had instruction in it only from the fifth to the ninth grade. Students in this stream are primarily Dalit and OBC students with rural backgrounds. Many come from farming communities outside Ahmedabad, and most have attended municipal schools. Mainstream Gujarati is, in some instances, an L2 or second dialect, with English constituting the third (or sometimes fourth) language. The three FY, the remaining three SY and the seven TY students whose views inform this article shared this background. Although the *b*-stream students are of most concern in this article, when relevant I call attention to *a*-stream and English-medium students to highlight the general condition of *b* streamers and their position relative to Circle 1.

TABLE 2: Placement of students in English compulsory classes

Student's K-12 medium	Division	Prior English language instruction	Stream (EC placement)
Gujarati	A	Grades 5-12	a
		Grades 5-9	b
English	B	n.a.	None

Several themes related to this tracking emerged from the student interviews. None of the students articulated any resentment at being tracked into *a* and *b* streams in the college because this tracking was seen as a consequence of an individual choice to continue or to stop taking English in Grades 10-12. However, all the students believed that the quality of English language instruction they were currently receiving in their EC classes was not markedly different from what they had received in school; they felt that instruction in neither place prepared them to use English in the real world. Many explained their struggle in EC classes as a result of the poor English language instruction they had received in school. Twelve of the 16 students said that they had felt pressure to drop English after the ninth grade because they could not cope with it. According to the students, their teachers were themselves poor speakers of English, and it was thus not surprising that the students found English difficult ('Teacher ne English nathi aavadthu ne, tho amne kevi phaave?' [The teacher does not know English, so how do we cope?]; S3, p. 1). Tracking into *a* and *b* streams, then, although justified by the institution on the basis of these students' need for special attention, built on their already disadvantaged position with regard to English.

Practice 2: Extensive use of grammar-translation
The special attention given to students tracked into the *b* stream resulted in EC classes with methods that may have inhibited the communicative competence of these students and limited the choices students could make at the institution.

FY SY and TY EC classes for both *a*- and *b*-stream students were observed to get a comprehensive sense of the general focus of the classes. These classes emphasised language tasks, with grammar being the primary focus in the FY classes and more text- and comprehension-based tasks being incorporated at the SY and TY levels. However, grammar was not entirely discarded at the SY and TY levels because at least two of five sections of the final exams for these years were devoted to grammar.

Eventually, we observed only the FY *a*- and *b*-stream EC classes intensively because all FY Dalit and OBC students are placed into the *b* stream. These classes were typically held four days a week for 50 minutes each. Detailed notes were taken on any aspect of the class that had a bearing on how English was being taught and learned there. We noted that the young women sat toward one side of the class, that the young men sat toward the other, and that the two groups seldom had anything to say to each other. By contrast, in English-medium classes interaction between the sexes was more common. The instructor began the class sometimes with a joke and sometimes by referring to homework assigned in the previous class. Typically, the teacher asked questions; the students almost never did. Female students were especially shy about reading aloud in class. All the students were generally very careful to note down the homework expected of them for the next class.

Two pedagogical practices in particular seemed to be significant.

Use of Gujarati and Hindi

First, the teachers of both *a*- and *b*-stream classes frequently resorted to Gujarati and Hindi while teaching the class. A TY instructor who tended to use more English in class was generally seen as more difficult to understand and was not seen as a good teacher. ('Gujarati ane Hindi nathi vaparthi, ane amne mushkil laage chhe' [She doesn't use either Gujarati or Hindi and we find that difficult]; S19, p.3). On the whole, faculty members believed that they had to use native languages (Flowerdew, Li, and Miller, 1998) because it was the only way they could 'get through to the students' (F5, p.4). Students, likewise, had come to expect this way of teaching because they had been used to it in their English language classrooms in schools.

Almost all language in the *b*-stream class – directives, vocabulary items, entire paragraphs from short stories – was translated. Teachers frequently called on students to read a passage aloud from their textbooks and then had them translate it into either Gujarati or Hindi as a way to check comprehension. This reliance on translation extended to directions in grammar workbooks as well. When asked if using Gujarati and Hindi in the classroom hindered their English language learning, all the students maintained that it helped; translating everything into the vernacular helped them understand ('samjan padeh'; S8, p.1). None of them seemed to see how it could take away from their gaining fluency in English.

The almost exclusive focus on grammar (discussed below), combined with little or no attention to developing speaking skills (because developing fluency in speaking English was not part of the university-mandated curriculum) left students shy about using English outside the classroom ('sharam aave che' [I am shy about using it]; S14, p.6). Indeed, when asked to read passages or their responses to grammar drills aloud, many students seemed self-conscious.

Emphasis on Grammar

The second significant pedagogical practice was that all of the FY *b*-stream classes were devoted exclusively to the teaching of grammar. The class instructor felt that such intensive attention was warranted because 'the students' hold on grammar and the basics was so poor' (F4, p.6) that he could proceed with the readings in the textbook only after he had addressed all the necessary grammar points. Thus, the EC instructor taught various grammatical features in class, with tenses taught in one class, nouns in the next, and verbs in the class after. Although the instructor occasionally established connections between different grammatical units – how nouns and verbs are related to each other in sentences, for instance – he did not do so in a communicative context (as is common in language classrooms in the West; Holliday, 1994).

Equally strong emphasis on discrete units of language was evident in the FY *a*-stream classes, although the focus in these classes seemed less on sentence-level units than on paragraph-level features (e.g., students reordered jumbled sentences into the correct order).

When asked, all of the students said that this almost exclusive attention to grammar helped them speak correctly but did not really prepare them to use English in contexts like job interviews ('Amne tho ahinya grammaraj sikhwade chhe; English ma vaat karvani practice nathi malthu ... tho job interviews maa mushkil hoye amne' [We only get taught grammar here; we don't get to practice speaking English ... so we find job interviews difficult]; S9, p.2). Despite the students' feeling that they might not have been learning exactly what they needed to learn, their recognition that English was a passport to social successes in their culture prompted them to take the grammar instruction in EC classes seriously. ('Thoda kuch tho seekh lenge' [At least I'll learn something]; S6, p.1). All students in the a and the b stream alike voiced the need to be able to speak English fluently, because, as one student put it, this would give them an 'impressive personality' (in English; 86, p.2).

Regarding their study methods, 13 of the 16 students said that they dealt with the material in the EC classes by memorising grammar rules, entire chunks of lessons, texts, and ready-made responses from study guides or notes of students who had taken the class previously ('ghokhi kaadwaa nu' [we parrot it all]; 86, p.4). They reported being unable to comprehend what they read and saw teachers as generally ineffectual at helping them understand what they were reading or learning about (features noted as well by Bhattacharya, 1992). Although all the students conceded that extensive memorising did little to enhance their fluency – a concern that was echoed over and over in the interviews – many thought they had little choice.

Practice 3: The teaching of English literature

The teaching of English literature in English departments in India is best interpreted within a historical context. Thomas Babington Macaulay, who in 1834 was put in charge of reforming the educational system in India (MacCabe, 1985; Suleri, 1992), defended the teaching of English literature in India in a proclamation – often referred to as the Macaulay Minute – that announced the general superiority of English literature:

> I have no knowledge of either Sanskrit or Arabic-But I have done what I could to form a correct estimate of their value... I am quite ready to take the Oriental learning at the valuation of the Orientalists themselves. I have never found one of them who could deny that a single shelf of a good European library was worth the whole native literature of India and Arabia. (cited in MacCabe, 1985, pp.38-39)

Macaulay further maintained that 'all historical information which had been collected from all the books written in the Sanskrit language is less valuable than what may be found in the most paltry abridgements used at preparatory schools in England' (Moorhouse, 1984, pp.77-78). Views such as these, coupled with the sense that the British needed Indians who were English in every sense but colour, set in motion the intensive study of British literature in India's schools and colleges in the 1800s (Rajan, l992; Vishwanathan, 1989).

Today, majoring in English literature – including British, US, and Indian writings in English – seems to be one of the only ways Gujarati-medium students in the college feel they can master the English language. Four relevant themes emerged from the data regarding the effect of literature teaching on students' access to English. These factors, related to bureaucratic procedures, cultural practices regarding learning, and areas of cultural conflict, apply to all *a*- and *b*-stream students, although the implications for *b*-stream students are the most extreme. Cumulatively these issues shed light on the complexity and conflict surrounding literature teaching in a postcolonial context and the fact that practices associated with literature teaching keep English within the reach of a few and out of the grasp of millions.

Gatekeeping

One important theme related to literature involves the gatekeeping procedures that affected the Gujarati-medium students. Majoring in English literature appeared to be an option largely available only to English-medium students. As one faculty member put it, 'With English-medium students you can at least assume a degree of language proficiency that does not make the task of teaching Chaucer and Shakespeare seem insurmountable' (Fl, p.11). Among Gujarati-medium students, only a handful of exceptionally good *a*-stream students were allowed to major in English, but only after they had successfully passed a test administered by the English faculty. Because their English language proficiency was generally deemed poorer than that of their English-medium counterparts, Gujarati-medium *a*-stream students majoring in English were required to take intensive grammar, reading, and writing instruction in a remedial English class or tutorial. As for Dalit and OBC *b*-stream students, who had stopped studying English after Grade 9, majoring in English literature was not even a possibility. The institutionalised practice of tracking, therefore, affects who can major in literature, which in turn has consequences regarding the general accessibility of English for both *a*- and *b*-stream students.

English teachers' views of their role

A second important theme that emerged through the faculty interviews was that English department faculty saw themselves as literature not language teachers. All five faculty members mentioned that the language problems of the Gujarati-medium students were not really their responsibility. None of the faculty had had any formal training in applied linguistics or language teaching methods, and all felt at a loss at having to address grammar-related problems when teaching Chaucer and Shakespeare. All but one teacher also expressed discomfort at teaching EC classes, where language-related concerns were addressed. Many of the faculty also believed that the college's recently adopted stance on promoting the English language skills of Dalit and OBC students worked at odds with the faculty's literature background. Many seemed to resent the management's not fully understanding that 'literature and language teaching are two separate endeavors' (F3, p. 4). Thus the value historically placed on teaching British literature manifests itself today in an English faculty composed solely of literature teachers who lack the expertise to help Gujarati-medium students to access English.

Heavy use of study guides

A third significant practice that emerged was the students' extensive use of study guides. Several of the Gujarati-medium students who were majoring in English literature admitted to relying heavily on such guides to get them through exams (Ramanathan and Atkinson, 1998). Many students felt that their English language proficiency was inadequate for understanding and explaining concepts in literary theory and poetry. Study guides, several maintained, explained difficult literary concepts in Gujarati. As for poetry, all the students believed unequivocally that poetic language and metaphors (especially in contemporary poetry as opposed, e.g., to the nature poetry of the romantics) were generally difficult to grasp. Resorting to memorising summaries and explanations of such poetry from their study guides afforded the students a way of comprehending these poems

Cultural dissonance

A final finding related to literature teaching was the students' feeling of cultural dissonance between themselves and the topics portrayed in the literature. Students in literature classes also voiced feelings of alienation from texts with overly Western themes. When asked what sense they made of romantic love – a theme predominant in much Western literature – several students admitted to sometimes being at a loss ('mushkil laage chhe' [I find it difficult]; S3, p.2). This is understandable, as in India's culture love between the sexes typically operates in the framework of an arranged marriage. Some students said they had come to terms with such Western themes by experiencing them vicariously; others would try to translate them into local terms. Students contending with race relations in the abridged version of *Uncle Tom's Cabin* (the required text for the TYEC class), for example, made sense of the text by understanding race-related issues in terms of unequal power relations between castes in India ('Vaat jevi chhe?' [Is it like caste?]; 'Tho bahu power inequality chhe?' [So is there a lot of power inequality involved?]; S6, p.2). Several students also believed that they often had to forego comprehending certain experiences and themes that were too far removed from their everyday realities or that could not be culturally transposed into local terms. Lukmani (1992), drawing on an in-depth survey of Marathi-speaking literature students, surmises that 'Indian students... tend to remain aloof from involvement in the representation of life in English texts. Their interest is in the medium rather than the message, the language rather than the culture, and the benefit they hope to attain is proficiency in English rather than integration in a western, cultural ethos' (p.170), a generalisation that seems applicable to the study of English literature at this institution.

Athough students may have been interested in literature for its potential to improve their English, the institutional practice of keeping *b*-stream students from majoring in literature precluded any potential benefit from this interest. This practice, like the teaching of grammar and the streaming of students, may seem on the surface to have made good sense for all involved. In fact, however, these practices worked together to deny *b*-stream students access to English proficiency.

Discussion implications and conclusions

The data from this institution illuminate the institutional and educational practices that keep standard Indian English within the reach of the middle class and inaccessible to those students that it is attempting to help. In this section I locate the discussion of this institution within a larger framework of the general role of English in India and offer some suggestions for ways that English language inequality at the institute can be rectified.

English versus regional languages in India

Dua (1994) maintains that English in India no longer coexists with other languages in a complementary relationship but seems to have acquired such a privileged status that literacy in local, indigenous languages is threatened[10] (Pennycook, 1994, 1998; Phillipson, 1992; Skutnabb-Kangas and Phillipson, 1995). Indeed, many of the students we interviewed wished that their parents had kept them in English-medium schools because good jobs and social successes are directly tied to how fluent one is in English (Kumar, 1993). This preference for English medium schools is echoed in other studies as well. Jayaram (1992) cites Reddy's (1979) study, wherein he examined 'students' reactions towards English and regional languages as media of instruction' (p.103) and found that students overwhelmingly favoured English. On the basis of this study and others, Jayaram concludes that a 'fear of being treated as an inferior category among the educated unless the courses are taken in the English medium' is an important factor in 'their aversion to the regional language medium' (p.103).

The Indian government has tried to balance English language teaching with the teaching of other languages by promoting the teaching of regional languages, including the students' L1 and Hindi as an official language (see Jayaram, 1992, for an in-depth discussion of the *three-language formula* adopted by the Indian educational system). It has not been easy. According to several scholars (e.g., Chitnis, 1993; Jayaram, 1992), not much has been done to build infrastructure that would support regional languages, such as developing reading materials or ensuring administrative autonomy. Although anti-English advocates frequently voice the need to do away with English in the curriculum altogether because it represents colonial and neocolonial vestiges, academics such as Chitnis (1993) maintain that India can give up English only at the grave peril of the educational system. Certainly the students at the institution under study echoed this sentiment. Although the quality of language teaching – of regional languages and English, but of English in particular – needs to be addressed seriously; the fact remains, as one student put it, that 'English is here to stay; we have to deal with it' (S4, p.5). Thus, it looks as if English language teaching will continue in India whether or not the teaching of regional languages develops.

Widening access to the inner circle

Although the motivation to learn English is very strong in India (Altbach, 1993; Chitnis, 1993; Lukmani, 1992), practices such as those at the institution under investigation keep the poorest and the most disadvantaged students from learning it. The cumulative effect of institutional and university wide mandates is to keep *b*-stream students in India's own outer circle. The specific factors creating this effect were found to be the institutional practices of teaching, teaching practices in the EC classrooms, the faculty's lack of training in language teaching despite the administration's resolve to provide English instruction to Dalit and OBC students, and the students' own prior learning practices and views about effective language teaching and learning.

Multi-pronged as this problem is, some measures may ameliorate the general situation:

1. The administration as well as the university should be aware that English language teaching is a completely separate enterprise from the teaching of literature. The English department faculty recognised this distinction clearly and acutely because they had to contend with the vagaries involved on an everyday, local level, but the management seemed to be less conscious of the pedagogical problems involved in having literature faculty teach language. Certainly, raising the consciousness of the administration to classroom problems is necessary.

2. Especially at the university level, the EC class is an area that begs for change. Because fluency in spoken English is so important but currently neglected in the lives of all the *a*- and *b*-stream students, the EC class must include a speaking component that actually helps the students communicate in the real world. The current, almost exclusive emphasis on grammar and the general use of native languages in these classes (Flowerdew *et al.*, 1998), although aiding comprehension and accuracy, does not provide an opportunity for the development of communicative fluency. Balancing these methods with those intended to develop the communicative skills of students while being mindful of local constraints (Holliday, 1994; Li, 1998) is a possible first step.

As a relative outsider to the scene now, I realise that these changes are easier to recommend than to carry out, especially because both faculty and management feel they can do little to alter the situation. The syllabi, the curricula, and the final, external exams, they say, are out of their hands. Their role, as one teacher cynically put it, 'lies in merely dispensing what is in a prescribed set of texts into the heads of the students' (F3, p.6). This lack of autonomy on the part of both the management and the teachers may partially explain why teaching is oriented toward exams, why teachers opt for particular teaching methods over others, why the students resort to memorising and using study guides to get through the exams, and why English language speaking skills are not emphasised.

The Dalit and OBC students seem to struggle more than others. Not only do they enter the college on the fringes of Circle 2 with poor English language skills, having been educated entirely in Gujarati, but they are also unable to develop their English in the college because they are tracked into streams. These are the students most in need of English, yet English seems farthest from them. Their economically disadvantaged status does not permit them to enroll in language classes in the city, nor does it afford them access to other realia available to learners in Circle 1: the Internet, newspapers, TV shows in English, and English movies. They realise more and more that they need to be computer literate for the simplest of jobs, but to gain access to knowledge about computers they have to first become fluent in English – that is, they have to develop the language that allows them to enter and become part of Circle 1. For most, however, their worst fears become reality: they never really gain fluency in English or entry into that circle and thus never become qualified for the jobs they desire.

This in-depth look at one English language teaching situation in a postcolonial context raises several questions. Will current English language teaching methods remain? How can the communicative fluency of the most disadvantaged students be facilitated? Would Western communicative language teaching practices work well in the Indian context? What local constraints will influence attempts to implement change? Much more research needs to be done to reveal additional insights, but this article represents a beginning toward understanding some of these issues in a postcolonial reality; in the meantime 'education [in India] drifts along' (Jayaram, 1992, p.111), and English stays.

Notes

1   Patronising as this term is, I use it because it is the current political term used in India for members of tribal groups who are not Hindu (and therefore do not fall into the caste system). Like Dalits, OBCs have been and still are discriminated against.

2   Marrying within one's caste is definitely a criterion for arranged marriages. Marriages of choice, on the other hand, are not particularly stringent about matters of caste, although marriages between an upper- and lower-caste person are not common.

3   Caste and occupation, as Quigley (1993) points out, do not necessarily go hand-in-hand. Although the relationship between the two is one way of explaining the social stratification in the caste system, it is extremely outdated. Today, a person born into the tailor caste may not be locked into the tailoring profession but may simply have once had an ancestor who was a tailor.

4   These four divisions are the broadest in the caste scale. Each contains several subcastes, with rules regulating social practices and behaviour – including language use – within and across caste groups.

5   These included awakening them to their rights by organising regular group meetings wherein Dalits and OBCs talked about discrimination and practiced and performed street plays depicting problems in their current general condition. One such meeting, called United Ahmedabad, became so well known that many non-Dalits and non-OBCs began to join.

6   Most institutions in the state do not have such a policy in place. Although all state- and government-funded institutions must reserve seats for students from this group, the college under investigation had chosen in recent years to open more than the required quota of seats as a way of generally uplifting this historically disadvantaged group.

7   In fact, Dalit and OBC students need only passing marks to gain admission into the college whereas all other students have to secure a minimum percentage of marks on their 12th-grade exams (in 1997, 62% for the arts section and 65% for the sciences).

8   Each interview excerpt is identified by the participant (S = student, F = faculty member), a number assigned to the participant, and the transcription page on which the quotation is found. All interviews took place between June 15 and August 3, 1997. Excerpts from field notes are designated FN; the date the notes were taken is indicated.

9   This division into *a* and *b* streams occurs only in the first and second years; in) the third year all *a*- and *b*-stream students are amalgamated into one EC class, as *b*-stream students are assumed to have picked up enough English to compete with the *a*-stream students.

10   Gujarat, the state in which the institution under investigation is located, is one of the few states in India that offers tertiary-level education in the regional language as well as in English. Most other states impart college education exclusively in English.

References

Altbach, P. (1993). The dilemma of change in Indian higher education. In S. Chitnis and P. Altbach (Eds.), *Higher education reform in India* (13-37). New Delhi, India: Sage.

Bhattacharya, R. (1992) Siting the teacher. In R. S. Rajan (Ed.), *The lie of the land.* Delhi, India: Oxford University Press.

Canagarajah, S. (1993) Critical ethnography of a Sri Lankan classroom: Ambiguities in student opposition to reproduction through TESOL. *TESOL Quarterly,* 27, 601-626.

Chitnis, S. (1993) Gearing a colonial system of education to take independent India toward development. In S. Chitnis and P. Altbach (Eds.), *Higher education reform in India* (400-427) New Delhi, India: Sage.

Dua, H. (1994) *The hegemony of English.* Mysore, India: Yashoda.

Flowerdew, J., Li, D., and Miller, L. (1998) Attitudes toward English and Cantonese among Hong Kong Chinese university lecturers. *TESOL Quarterly,* 32, 201-231.

Gee, J. (1990) *Social linguistics and literacies: Ideologies in discourses.* Philadelphia: Falmer Press.

Gramsci, A. (1988) *A Gramsci reader: Selected writings* (D. Forgacs, Ed.) London: Lawrence and Wishart.

Holliday, A. (1994) *Appropriate methodology and social context.* Cambridge: Cambridge University Press.

Jayaram, N. (1992) The language question in higher education. In S. Chitnis and P. Altbach (Eds.), *Higher education reform in India* (84-114) New Delhi, India: Sage.

Kachru, B. (1985) *Standards, codifications, and sociolinguistic realism: The English language in the outer circle.* Cambridge: Cambridge University Press.

Kamble, N. D. (1983) *Deprived castes and their struggle for equality.* New Delhi, India: Ashish.

Kumar, K (1993) Literacy and primary education in India. In P. Freebody and A. Welch (Eds.), *Knowledge, culture and power: International perspectives on literacy as policy and practice* (102-113) Pittsburgh, PA: University of Pittsburgh Press.

Li, D. (1998) 'It's always more difficult than you plan and imagine': Teachers' perceived difficulties in introducing the communicative approach in South Korea. *TESOL Quarterly,* 32, 677-702.

Lukmani, Y. (1992) Attitudinal orientation toward studying English literature in India. In R. S. Rajan (Ed.), *The lie of the land* (156-186) Delhi, India: Oxford University Press.

MacCabe, C. (1985) English literature in a global context. In R. Quirk and H. G. Widdowson (Eds.), *English in the world: Teaching and learning the language and literature* (37-46) Cambridge: Cambridge University Press.

Moorhouse, G. (1984) *India Britannica*. London: Paladin.

Pakir, A. (1991) The range and depth of English-knowing bilinguals in Singapore. *World Englishes*, 10, 167-180.

Pennycook, A. (1994) *The cultural politics of English as an international language*. Mahwah, NJ: Erlbaum.

Pennycook, A. (1998) *English and the discourses of colonialism*. London: Routledge.

Phillipson, R. (1992) *Linguistic imperialism*. Oxford: Oxford University Press.

Prior, P. (1995) Redefining the task: An ethnographic examination of writing and response in graduate seminars. In D. Belcher and G. Braine (Eds.), *Second language writing* (47-82) Norwood, NJ: Ablex.

Quigley, D. (1993) *The interpretation of caste*. New York: Clarendon Press.

Quirk, R. (1985) *The English language in a global context*. Cambridge: Cambridge University Press.

Rajan, S. R. (1986) After 'Orientalism': Colonialism and English literary studies in India. *Social Scientist*, 158, 23-35.

Rajan, S. R. (1992) *The lie of the land*. Delhi, India: Oxford University Press.

Ramanathan, V., and Atkinson D. (1998) English on the ground: The search for English and educational equality in Gujarat, India. Unpublished manuscript.

Ramanathan, V., and Atkinson, D. (1999) Ethnographic approaches and methods in L2 writing research: A critical guide and review. *Applied Linguistics*, 21, 44-70.

Sarkar, J. (1984) *Caste, occupation and change*. Delhi, India: B. R. Publishing.

Skutnabb-Kangas, T., and Phillipson, R. (1995) (Eds.) *Linguistic human rights*. Berlin: Mouton de Gruyter.

Suleri, S (1992) *The rhetoric of English India*. Chicago: University of Chicago Press.

Vishwanathan, G. (1989) *Masks of conquest: Literary study and British rule in India*, New York: Columbia University Press.

APPENDIX
Schema of interviews with students
General information
Name
Place of origin
Parents' occupation
Name of high school
Major in college
Plans after graduation
Stream in the college (a or b)

English language learning and teaching

1. How do you view English? How long have you had exposure to it?

2. Do you use English outside the classroom? (with whom? access to TV, newspapers, radio?) What are some ways you seek exposure to English?

3. What were your English language classes in middle and high school like?

4. How would you rate your high school preparation in English? Was it adequate for dealing with English in the college?

5. What is the general importance you give English in your life? What advantages is fluency in it likely to give you?

6. Can you tell me about specific instances illustrating your struggles with English?

7. Are English Compulsory classes a help? What would you like to see changed about these classes?

8. Should the college provide you with more English language instruction?

9. Do you have difficulty dealing with American and British literary texts? What are some of the difficulties? How do you overcome them?

PART FOUR
Multimodal Communication

Introduction

The fourth and final section of this book considers an increasingly important area in the study of language, literacy and communication. Multimodal communication (often called multimodality) involves the study of the different semiotic modes which come into play whenever we speak, gesture, write or draw in order to communicate a message. All communication is, of course, multimodal – we gesture while we speak; we use a variety of typefaces in our writing to signal different levels of importance or a change of meaning – but it is only fairly recently that these additional resources for meaning-making have started to be studied as closely as language itself and their importance in education explored.

Multimodality as an academic area of study is undertaken by researchers from a wide range of disciplines, including linguistics, visual communication, media studies, anthropology and information technology. The chapters in this section cover a number of approaches and focus on different types of multimodal communication.

The first chapter looks at the meaning-making practices of an indigenous Brazilian community, where words and pictures are traditionally combined. Lynn Mario T. Menezes de Souza studied the multimodal practices of the Kashinawá people during a national literacy campaign. He documents how traditional drawings (used in ceremonial tattoos and woven into textiles) have recently been introduced into writing. The relationship of words and pictures in the Kashinawá texts is highly codified – individual elements are placed in specific ways in specific relationships to each other in the complete texts, and meanings are derived from this interplay. Crucially, the role of the images is a meaning-making one, not an illustrative one as has been the case in most traditional 'western' texts: for the Kashinawá, a text is not a text unless it is multimodal. De Souza uses his study of these texts to underline the fact that social processes, including cultural practices, shape the ways we use language and create meaning.

In chapter 16, Ruth Swanwick describes a different domain, that of Deaf education, where multimodality has traditionally been the norm. Her study of Deaf schoolchildren learning to write in English highlights a number of issues relevant to both deaf and hearing children. Swanwick points out that deaf children have simultaneously to shift between, and make sense of, three modes of communication: visual sign language, spoken English and written English; whereas hearing children only have to cope with two. The degree of hearing of the children in her study varies, as does the hearing and signing ability of their family members. Some of these children may have a visual-gestural code as their 'inner speech', which makes it harder for them to translate into written English than their hearing or partially deaf counterparts, whose inner speech is spoken English. Swanwick notes that differences between the two languages, such as the importance of facial gesture and word order, make the literacy development of deaf children different from the biliteracy development of hearing children. Some meanings in sign language, moreover, are not amenable to direct translation.

Chapter 17 by Ron Carter and Svenja Adolphs explores the use of creativity in spoken language, using a corpus based approach. Creative uses of language, such as metaphor and figures of speech, are usually associated with written modes of communication – literary language – but the authors' use of computer software for collecting data both quantitatively and qualitatively enables them not only to say that creativity is a common feature of spoken language but to explore in detail where and how it happens.

In the next chapter, Ilana Snyder takes up the theme of technology, language and literacy, mapping out some broad conclusions about literacy in an electronic world, based on a study which investigated literacy, technology and student learning. Snyder states that literacy now entails not only the encoding and decoding of meanings but also the capability to actively create, shape and transform meanings. In our definitions of literacy, we need to include the ways modes of meaning – audiovisual, oral and written – combine in multimodal texts. Images have moved significantly from being illustrative to being communicative, and technology brings audiovisual modalities to the classroom which challenge traditional print based understandings of literacy. The computer is seen as a site for the social construction of knowledge.

In chapter 19 Carey Jewitt and Gunther Kress look at the range of modes of communication employed in the science classroom. They analyse the meanings made by the teacher as he speaks to the class while he gestures and writes on the whiteboard, points to a model of the human body, and directs the students to look at an image in a book. The starting point is the visual image drawn on the whiteboard, which is central to how the lesson develops. Jewitt and Kress's analysis of the science lesson exemplifies the fact that all communication is intrinsically multimodal: the authors consider each mode, note how each is alternately foregrounded or backgrounded and then analyse how meaning is constructed as modes combine ('orchestration'). They conclude that each mode represents different ways of shaping and conveying meaning, and point to the inadequacy of conceptualising classroom teaching and learning as being primarily based on linguistic resources.

In the final chapter, Anita Wilson uses the concept of a Third Space in the context of her research into literacy practices in prisons, to describe a non-institutional space constructed by the prisoners to keep some sense of self while they are imprisoned. As well as reporting the prisoners' communication with their families and others outside the prison, Wilson describes how prisoners communicate with each other from their cells via electric cables, customise their clothing, transform common objects such as pillows into sites for literacy, and utilise a host of language and literacy practices to remain 'uninstitutionalised' while in prison. The visual, material and sensory aspects of many such texts are of vital significance to the prisoners she studied.

CHAPTER 15

Literacy and Dreamspace: multimodal texts in a Brazilian indigenous community

Lynn Mario T. Menezes de Souza

Introduction

The Kashinawá indigenous community of South America belongs to the Pano linguistic family. Inhabiting the western Amazon region of Brazil and Peru, it is a community of little more than 4000 members, of which 1,200 occupy the Brazilian side of the border (Monte, 1996, Aquino and Iglesias, 1994). In the past two decades the community has been the focus of literacy campaigns both in Portuguese and in the Kashinawá language and this has led to a recent boom in writing.

This research is part of a project which initially set out to study the teaching and learning of Portuguese in the bilingual contexts of indigenous schools in Brazil (where Portuguese largely co-exists in varying degrees with local indigenous languages) from the perspective of applied linguistics, ultimately aiming at developing a body of knowledge and methodologies for the teaching of Portuguese as the national language in bilingual indigenous schools. This wider project focused on communities where literacy had recently been introduced, in both the indigenous languages and Portuguese. The written material produced in both languages by the Kashinawá, especially adult male teachers in a training course for Kashinawá teachers of Portuguese demonstrated a high degree of multimodality. Initially this posed a problem: the visual components of these multimodal texts had been considered by local anthropologists, literacy campaigners and teacher trainers as no more than decorative elements, having no connection to the alphabetic content of the texts themselves. However, given the degree and recurrence of multimodality involved, a new perspective was clearly called for, especially as there were clear indications that writing, besides modifying the cultural practices of the Kashinawá, was itself being modified by the Kashinawá. This new perspective on Kashinawá multimodality has since begun with the ethnographic collection of written material, interviews with the writers and the consultation of ethnological studies of the culture of the Kashinawá.

Multimodality is the term used (Kress and van Leeuwen, 1996) to refer to texts in which the alphabetic/verbal and visual elements interact with each other and jointly contribute to construct the meaning of the texts; more specifically, Kashinawá multimodal texts consist of a profusion of highly coloured hand-drawn visual texts which accompany the alphabetic writing. These visual texts consist of two basic types of drawing, *kene* and *dami*.

Kene drawing refers to a set of highly codified geometric patterns which can be multi-coloured or monochromatic. The *kene* patterns are codified, in the sense that they rigorously follow pre-established rules which define the shapes, combinations and patterns they may have. Before the introduction of literacy, the *kene* geometric graphic patterns traditionally only appeared woven

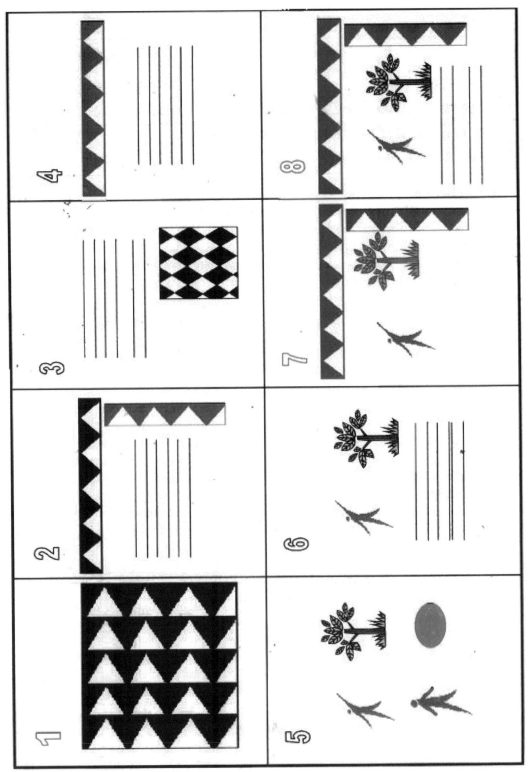

Figure 1

into textiles and basketry and in ceremonial body tattoos. It was – and still is – the prerogative of women to produce *kene* graphics on surfaces other than paper; with the advent of literacy however, this has changed and men now produce these graphics on paper, closely interrelating them with alphabetic writing and thus creating profusely multimodal texts. Permitting men to produce *kene* graphic patterns on paper has modified local cultural practices. A *kene* pattern on paper may appear on its own, for example on the cover page of an exercise book; it may also appear in miniature form in a corner of a page (see Fig. 1 no. 3), as a right-angled frame on one, two and sometimes three sides of a page (see Fig. 1 nos. 2 and 4), or as part of a multimodal set containing alphabetic text and figurative drawings called *dami* (see Fig. 1 nos. 6-8). And *kene* drawings may also cover – in the form of tattoos – *dami* figures.

The second type of drawing, called *dami* is a soft figurative line drawing, not necessarily in colour, depicting plants, animals or humans. Unlike *kene*, it is not codified or rule-governed, so there are no fixed forms or shapes and there is no preoccupation with using excessive detail or perspective. In the western tradition, perspective is rule-governed and presupposes that reality is three-dimensional. In the west perspective is employed to make a drawing or painting appear as three-dimensional reality, almost like a photograph. It is what gives apparent depth to a visual representation, allowing the perceiver to distinguish between visual elements in a 'foreground' – which must be presented as being larger – nearer to the viewer, and visual elements in a 'background' – which must appear as being smaller, more distant from the viewer. This use of perspective to give the viewer a sense of the 'real' in visual representation, far from being natural or universal, is thus a western cultural convention whose rules must be learned. (Note that in drawings by very young children perspective does not appear until it is learned much later.) This means that visual representation depends not only on *what* a particular culture considers to be real, but also on *how* it chooses to visually represent this reality. *Dami* drawing for the Kashinawá does not follow the western rules of perspective and therefore does not distinguish between foreground and background. The figures are generally organised in a scene or narrative form representing an action or sequence of actions, rather like a part of a comic strip. *Dami* drawing may appear alone or together with alphabetic text or with both alphabetic text and *kene* drawing (see Fig. 1 nos. 5-8).

In order to understand the meaning of these drawings and therefore the literacy practices of this community, these practices have to be seen as a part of the local indigenous knowledge and hence deeply interconnected with other practices of Kashinawá culture such as their belief systems, their rituals and their identity.

Kashinawá systems of meaning

In the Kashinawá belief system, in certain significant situations such as venturing away from home and deep into the jungle, or facing other threatening situations such as modernisation or environmental change, the observer and the observed, the subject and the object (and by implication, the reader and the text) are not separate from each other but instead *constitute each other* (Keifenheim, 1999). In a situation of this kind the meaning of what one sees/reads depends on who the observer/reader is; that is, their understanding of the object being seen/read will depend on what they already know about the object. So for the Kashinawá in these situations, meaning is not fixed or stable, nor is it located singularly and unquestionably within a text. The observer/reader not only transforms or modifies the text or image being seen/read, but they are also transformed by the very text or image.

The geometric *kene* drawings illustrate this belief. If one looks long enough at the wavy intricately interconnected line patterns of the *kene* drawings, one becomes almost hypnotically drawn into the patterns, figuratively losing one's ground and falling victim to the patterns, as if being drawn by them into another dimension or dreamspace (see below for an explanation on the ritual of dreaming). When the viewer stops concentrating visually on the pattern, he or she seems to emerge from this apparently hypnotic state, this other dimension of 'dreamspace' and the pattern seems to go back to being once again a harmless drawing. For the Kashinawá, this visual experience of being drawn into and emerging from 'dreamspace' is understood as having already transformed the observer . What does this mean? To understand the concept of 'dreamspace', the *kene* patterns and this process of mutual transformation between the observer and the observed, the reader and the text, it is first of all important to know that for the Kashinawá, the wavy intricate geometric lines of *kene* figuratively represent the designs on the skin of the anaconda snake who is for them the goddess spirit of wisdom and culture, and hence the source of all knowledge.

Like other Amazonian shamanic indigenous cultures, Kashinawá culture is ritualistically a culture of visions or 'dreaming' (Lagrou, 1996, 1998). Traditionally, when they need to seek knowledge on a particular topic or issue, the Kashinawá, with the help of the shaman or medicine man and a special drink, ritually lie down and (consciously) 'dream' or have a vision in which they enter into dreamspace where they meet and receive knowledge from the anaconda spirit. For the Kashinawá, dreamspace is another dimension and part of reality. Hence visions or dreams are texts – a significant source of knowledge in much the same manner that written texts function in a literate culture.

In a typical Kashinawá visionary 'text', the dreamer first sees the geometric patterns on the skin of the anaconda spirit; he/she is then hypnotically drawn into the pattern (this is understood as being received into the world of the anaconda spirit) and then, in a second phase of the vision, receives the knowledge sought after. This second phase of the vision occurs in figurative and narrative form, as a kind of film sequence of actions with human, animal or mythical characters organised into a sequential plot structure, bringing with it the knowledge sought after by the dreamer. Just like staring at the geometric *kene* patterns as described above, any entrance into dreamspace transforms the Kashinawá perceiver/dreamer, who always emerges transformed by the knowledge acquired in the visionary dream process. This ritual of dreaming, entering into dreamspace, having visions or consulting visionary 'texts' is one important knowledge-acquisition cultural practice of the Kashinawá. Another is the contact with difference. Again, like most Amazonian indigenous cultures, Kashinawá culture emphasises the need to maintain periodical contact with other cultures and communities in order to survive and seeks to obtain from them information, values and objects.

Both these knowledge-acquisition practices of the Kashinawá – the ritual dreaming and the contact with difference – illustrate that knowledge-acquisition is for them a *process*; that is, knowledge or new information is not seen as a *product* or object that one can simply acquire wholesale. One is *transformed* by knowledge or new information, and in turn one has to *transform* or process this knowledge or new information. In a western literate culture this would be equivalent to assuming that the reader of a text is not only transformed by a text read but also transforms the significance or import of the text itself. The importance given to transformation in knowledge-acquisition, and hence in cultural survival, in Kashinawá culture is symbolised by the important figure of the anaconda spirit itself as the source of knowledge; like all snakes, the anaconda periodically sheds its skin and transforms itself in order to survive.

Adapting practices, adapting texts

Given that literacy is not merely a technical or linguistic skill but a cultural practice, when a particular culture takes on literacy, this new practice of writing interacts with pre-existing practices within the culture and may either generate new practices or transform existing ones. In the case of the Kashinawá, the pre-existing practice of knowledge-acquisition was transformed by literacy. Before writing and literacy, a major source of knowledge for this indigenous culture was the visionary 'text'; with the advent of literacy the written text has become a significant source of knowledge. However, though the *practice* of knowledge-acquisition may have been modified or westernised – from the vision to paper, from dreaming to writing and reading – the *process* has been maintained. This means that *transformation* is still an essential element for the Kashinawá even in their more recent literacy practices. This is clearly illustrated by their multimodal writing.

Rather than merely learning to read and write an alphabet, this indigenous community, in keeping with its traditional value of transforming and being transformed by new knowledge, allowed itself to be transformed by becoming literate, but in turn transformed the concept of alphabetic writing into multimodal writing so as to accommodate its own pre-literate practices such as the visionary text (Kress, 1997). The visionary text acquired a new format on paper and now appears as a multimodal text where the alphabetic and the visual interact.

How then can one read the multimodal Kashinawá texts containing *kene*, *dami* and/or alphabetic writing? As we have seen, in a visionary text, *kene* patterns do not contain any message but are seen to signify the presence of the anaconda spirit, the bearer of knowledge; the same is true when *kene* appears on paper in a multimodal text. In such a text, the presence of a *kene* pattern may be seen as an indication or marker of the importance of the information of the text. *Dami* figures on the other hand represent the actual information or message sought after. So whereas *kene* may be said to stand for the presence of the messenger and the process of knowledge acquisition, *dami* indicates the message received and the product of knowledge-acquisition. Without *kene*, *dami* drawing is merely illustrative i.e. it simply repeats the information given in the alphabetic text; the absence of *kene* indicates that the information in the alphabetic text, with or without *dami*, is not considered by the writer to be of great importance. That is, the transformative capacity of the information in the text is considered to be low (see Figure 2).

Figure 2

kene	dami
Geometric	Figurative
Messenger	Message
Process	Product
Marker of importance of information	Does not mark importance of information
Reinforces the value of the alphabetic text	Repeats/illustrates something in the alphabetic text or something already known

In view of this, six possible multimodal combinations of Kashinawá writing on paper may be read:

1. **kene** geometric pattern on its own: the text *following* (i.e. on another page) the geometric pattern is considered to contain important information (see Fig. 1 no.1).

2. **kene** + alphabetic text: the alphabetic text accompanying the geometric pattern (on the same page) is considered to contain important information (see Fig. 1 nos. 2,3,4).

3. **dami** drawing on its own on a page: such a text is considered to carry information of little or no importance.; it may be a simply decorative drawing as art for art's sake (see Fig. 1 no.5).

4. **dami** + alphabetic text: the figurative drawing on the page repeats, paraphrases or illustrates the alphabetic text which it accompanies; such a multimodal text is considered to contain information of no great importance (see Fig. 1 no.6).

5. **kene** + **dami**: such a multimodal text, with these two visual elements, is considered to contain important information even without an alphabetic text to complement it (see Fig. 1 no.7).

6. **kene** + **dami** + alphabetic script: such a multimodal text, with the two types of visual element plus the alphabetic verbal text, is considered to contain highly important information (see Fig. 1 no.8).

Figure 3

Consider the example of the multimodal text in Figure 3. This text was composed by a Kashinawá male teacher attending a course in written Portuguese (functional literacy skills) for indigenous teachers in the Amazonian state of Acre given by a volunteer female teacher from the distant, affluent and westernised urban industrialised southeast of the country. The text represents a kind of homage or vote of thanks to the volunteer teacher.

There are three different types of coloured *kene* patterns framing the text at the top and on the right-hand edges. Monochromatic *kene* patterns in the form of tattoos cover the body of the *dami* male character on the left of the text. Within the space framed by the *kene*, two *dami* figures compose the figurative-narrative *dami* message of the text: there is a masculine figure on the left and a feminine figure on the right. The feminine figure is delivering a fruit to the masculine figure who, arms outstretched, is ready to receive it. Note the curious lack of fixed perspective in the *dami* drawings: whereas the legs of each character appear in pairs, the same does not apply to their eyes and outstretched arms.

Note the alphabetic text which accompanies the *kene* and *dami* elements and which appears on two different planes: a vertical plane on the left of the page containing the official and complete Christian name, status and tribal origin of the author, and two blocs of handwritten alphabetic text grouped on a vaguely horizontal plane in the centre and to the right of the page. The right-hand block consists of a narrative text in Portuguese, in the past tense, telling of the arrival in the Brazilian Amazonian region of Acre of a female teacher from the distant – urban and industrialised – Southeast of the country, bringing a seed (knowledge, i.e. new literacy practices) for indigenous teachers to take to their students in the indigenous schools. Below this bloc of text, there is a referential caption indicating the female character as the teacher from the Southeast. Above this bloc is a date, either of the encounter or when the text was originally composed. The left-hand block of alphabetic text is in the present tense and describes the fact that the indigenous teacher is receiving the fruit, which is to be passed on to his students. Below this bloc of text, the indigenous name of the author appears again, this time in caption form indicating referentially that the male character is a representation of the author of the text himself. Apart from the specific details such as names, dates and origins, the information contained in the alphabetic text is largely redundant and repeats what is already apparent in the figurative *dami* composition.

The presence of the *kene* patterns framing the page indicates the transformative high value information-acquisition import of the text as a whole. The *kene* tattoos on the male character indicate that he is undergoing a process of transformative knowledge-acquisition; this information is also repeated figuratively by the *dami* drawings showing the same character receiving a transformative fruit from the female character. As we have seen, the two blocs of alphabetic text repeat in alphabetic form the same process of transformation of the male character through the acquisition of information from outside.

Because the male character is also the author of the text, undergoing a course in literacy skills, this multimodal text as a whole closely follows the Kashinawá indigenous notion of the interconnectedness between the subject and object of new knowledge; that is, the person who is undergoing transformation by acquiring new literacy skills from outside is himself transforming the knowledge he has acquired. In other words, he is interconnecting alphabetic writing in Portuguese, acquired as a new literacy practice from the course via the outsider teacher, with pre-existing Kashinawá *kene* and *dami* elements, thus transforming the very alphabetic literacy practice which has also, through the acquisition of new knowledge, transformed him. Thus, as well as being a text illustrating the transformative power of literacy, the multimodality of this text simultaneously makes an illustration of how the Kashinawá have transformed the notion and practice of alphabetic literacy.

The predominant western view of writing is that it represents speech or the sound system of a language, and is consequently a system of secondary representation (Derrida, 1976) because the primary phenomenon that writing represents, i.e. speech, is considered to be elsewhere – in the mind or the voice of the writer, himself absent from the written text. Taking this western concept of writing as representation to its logical conclusion, writing would seem to function as a form of visual illustration of something – in this case speech – which it merely complements, as a form of appendage. In this sense, the western notion of writing would seem to approximate the Kashinawá concept of *dami*. Significantly, however, in the Kashinawá language, the word for writing is *kene*; by equating writing with *kene* – the marker of information of high transformative value – the Kashinawá demonstrate how much they value writing, seeing it not as mere secondary representation of the speech of an absent or dislocated speaker but, like *kene*, a path towards transformation.

One may thus conclude that for the Kashinawá, a text with only alphabetic writing but neither of the two types of drawing cannot be considered a text *per se* as 'text' is seen to be a container of high value information/knowledge/meaning. This is because alphabetic writing that appears on its own on paper would acquire the value of *kene* – the word in Kashinawá that means 'writing'. The purely alphabetic text would indicate only a process, or the presence of a messenger but no message or content. This explains why the Kashinawá need to add figures or sets of figures to an alphabetic text, consequently producing multimodal texts.

Literacy practices and identity

What do these multimodal texts tell us about Kashinawá identity? Firstly, one has to consider the fact that identity is not something fixed and stable which one is born with and retains all one's life; identity is discursive in the sense that it is constructed socially and culturally, with and through language. We are born into our culture and we learn to see ourselves and the world around us by and large as permitted by our culture and our language (Foucault, 1980, 1982). However, cultures are not homogeneous units and nor are languages, so our identities are constructed by the various discourses and language practices in which we participate and through which we pass in the course of our lives.

Considering literacy as a set of social and cultural practices, it becomes clear that, like the other language and discourse practices of our culture, our identities are constructed also by our specific literacy practices (Gee, 1990; McKay, 1994).

Whereas some cultures are closed to difference and tend to see change as derogatory, giving more value to conservation and preservation, indigenous Amazonian cultures such as that of the Kashinawá are open to difference, and highly prize transformation (Levi-Strauss, 1995). Whereas in most western cultures one remains the same by resisting change, for the Kashinawá one remains the same by undergoing constant change. The glimpse of Kashinawá multimodal texts offered here tells us much about Kashinawá identity and its valorisation of transformation.

What can westerners learn from this look at Kashinawá multimodality? Though we may be aware of the fact that different indigenous cultures have different identities, it is often not so clear how these identities are interconnected with language, culture and, hence, literacy practices. As a result, one's own language and literacy practices may be used as a yardstick to judge the practices of indigenous cultures negatively. This situation is worsened if one sees literacy as no more than a neutral, value-free technology of alphabetic writing unrelated to the people's other cultural practices. In this sense one may wreak havoc on an indigenous culture if one seeks to teach that culture to read and write as one does in the West, without taking into account the pre-existing cultural practices with which literacy, once introduced, will interact.

From a Western perspective, the visual element in alphabetic texts is sometimes used as mere decoration; most often, however, the visual element has a high degree of redundancy in that it is generally secondary in relation to the alphabetic text and normally illustrates or repeats, for purposes of clarity, a particular, generally small portion of the content of a text. Greater importance is attributed to the alphabetic component of the text. Moreover, in the West, solely alphabetic texts in general possess greater truth value and are considered more serious than multimodal texts. Kashinawá multimodal texts could erroneously be seen as texts with excessive illustrations or doodles with little textual, i.e. alphabetical, content, and hence containing information of little importance. If the nature of **kene** and **dami** is not understood it could mistakenly be thought that the texts were childish, reinforcing cultural stereotypes of indigenous cultures as 'primitive'.

Another common and related misconception of literacy in the West, this time on the part of those who often claim to protect and preserve indigenous cultures, is that the introduction of literacy may jeopardise indigenous cultures by putting an end to preexisting cultural practices in the community. This standpoint is based on the view that literacy transforms and modifies. With the Kashinawá, it is apparent that this is not as simple as it may seem; the pre-existing practices of visionary texts as an important source of knowledge-acquisition have not ceased to exist but on the contrary have given rise to a new form of writing – multimodal writing. Here the alphabetic element far from predominating, interacts with **kene** and **dami** as only one of three possible elements. It becomes clear then that literacy not only transforms and modifies but it may be itself re-contextualised, re-signified, transformed and modified.

Implications for literacy education

We have seen that literacy is not simply an innocuous means of representing spoken language. It interacts directly with the cultural practices of a community. As the Kashinawá demonstrate, literacy not only modified their existing cultural practices but was itself modified by these practices. Besides visions and dreamspace, written texts are now also a source of important information; likewise, with multimodality, a written alphabetic text acquires qualities of visions and dreamspace which defy the boundaries of the written page. What are the implications for literacy education? The most pressing seems to be that, like literacy, no knowledge is value-free, nor is it acquired wholesale; it inevitably interacts with, and thus may modify and itself be modified by, pre-existing knowledge in a particular culture. This highlights the need to respect the fact that several knowledges are in contact in the teaching-learning situation, and as a teacher one should ideally at least attempt to familiarise oneself with and be aware of these local knowledges. One needs to recognise that one's own knowledge – even as an experienced teacher – is always local.

References

Aquino, T. and Iglesias, M. (1994) 'Kaxinawá do Rio Jordão' *História, Território, Economia e Desenvolvimento Sustentado*. Rio Branco: CPI do Acre

Derrida, J. (1976) *Of Grammatology*. Baltimore: Johns Hopkins University Press

Dreyfus, H. and Rabinow, P. (1982) (eds) *Beyond Structuralism and Hermeneutics*. Brighton: Harvester

Foucault, M. (1980) *Power/Knowledge*. Brighton: Harvester

Foucault, M. (1982) 'The Subject and Power' in Dreyfus and Rabinow (eds)

Gee, J. (1990) *Social Linguistics and Literacies: ideology in discourse*. London: Falmer Press

Keifenheim, B. (1999) 'Concepts of Perception, Visual Practice and Pattern Art among the Cashinahua Indians (Peruvian Amazon Area)' *Visual Anthropology* vol. 12, 27-48

Kress, G. (1997) *Before Writing: rethinking the paths to literacy*. London: Routledge

Kress, G. and van Leeuwen, T. (1996) *Reading Images: the grammar of visual design*. Nova York: Routledge

Lagrou, E.M. (1996) *Xamanismo e Representação entre os Kaxinawá*, in Langdon, 1996

Lagrou, E.M. (1998) Caminhos, Duplos e Corpos: uma abordagem perspectivista da identidade e alteridade entre os kaxinawá. Unpublished PhD thesis, University of São Paulo, São Paulo

Langdon, E.J.M. (1996) (ed) *Xamanismo no Brasil: Novas Perspectivas*. Florianópolis: Editora da UFSC

Levi-Strauss, C. (1995) *The Story of Lynx*. Chicago: University of Chicago Press

McKay, S.L. (1994) 'Literacy and literacies' in McKay and Hornberger (eds) 1994

McKay, S.L. and Hornberger, N. (1994) (eds) *Sociolinguistics and Language Teaching*. Cambridge: Cambridge University Press

Monte, N. (no date) Quem são os Kaxinawá?, in *Shenipabu Miyui: história dos antigos*. Rio Branco: Comissão Pró Índio do Acre

Monte, N.L. (1996) *Escolas da Floresta: entre o passado oral e o presente letrado*. Rio de Janeiro: Multiletra

CHAPTER 16
Sign bilingual deaf children's approaches to writing: individual strategies for bridging the gap between BSL and written English
Ruth Swanwick

Introduction
Deaf children's performance in literacy is very well documented but the majority of reports reference deaf children's achievements to hearing models of literacy development and pedagogy. This body of research provides a useful framework for considering literacy development but it is not comprehensive, as many deaf children use sign language and are learning English as a second or additional language. Whilst many of the findings regarding deaf children's difficulties may be relevant to all deaf children (Paul, 1998), investigations into literacy from this cultural and linguistic perspective are more likely to reveal the different learning styles and strategies of sign bilingual deaf children.

What is different for these children is that they have to make a shift from the visual (live) mode to the written (static) mode. This requires an appreciation of the different conventions and characteristics of each modality, particularly regarding the way in which different meanings are specified in both languages. Sign bilingual children have to incorporate a third modality into their linguistic repertoire, many of the features of which have no equivalent in spoken or written languages. While we might accept that deaf children make similar errors in their written English to other learners of English as a second language, we need to consider whether or not the writing processes that they go through are similar. This paper focuses specifically on sign bilingual children and their experiences of writing in English. The term 'sign bilingual' is used throughout to describe deaf children and adults who are bilingual in a spoken and a signed language such as English and BSL (Pickersgill and Gregory, 1998).

Theoretical framework
Proponents of sign bilingual education propose that deaf children's developing skills in sign language (e.g., American Sign Language (ASL), or BSL) will provide a foundation for their subsequent English language development, including literacy skills (Mahshie, 1995; Rodda and Eleweke, 2000; Singleton *et al.*, 1998). Sign bilingual deaf children should therefore approach the learning of literacy with sign language skills through which English language learning can be mediated. While sign bilingual policy and practice has already gone a long way to improving the quality of education for many deaf children, there are theoretical and practical issues relating to this premise which remain to be resolved.

* First published in *Deafness and Education International*, 2002, 4.2:65:83

Theoretically, professionals working with sign bilingual deaf children have adopted a 'best fit' model of literacy instruction based on research into the bilingual language development of hearing children. This model draws on the developmental interdependence theory (Cummins, 1991, 1994) and proposes that the most appropriate route to bilingualism for deaf children involves using the learner's well-developed skills in sign language as a basis for developing literacy skills in the second language. It is suggested that in this way literacy skills in the second language can be achieved without exposure to the spoken form. Adopting this theory wholesale is problematic because it rests on two key assumptions that cannot be applied to sign bilingualism.

The first assumption is that learners bring age-appropriate receptive and expressive first language skills to the learning context and that literacy instruction will therefore be based on their established skills as communicators and language users. While we know that sign language can be acquired as a first language for deaf children who grow up in a sign language environment with one or more deaf parents, most deaf children are born into hearing families who do not know a natural sign language. We cannot make assumptions, therefore, about the level of deaf children's sign language skills when they enter school, and certainly not all sign bilingual deaf children will have age-appropriate sign language skills when they first begin to learn English as a second language.

Secondly, it is assumed in the theory proposed by Cummins that aspects of literate proficiency will be transferred from the first language to the second language. In their critique of this theory, Mayer and Wells (1996) point out that bilingual deaf children have not had the opportunity to acquire literacy skills in their primary language because sign language has no orthography. There are some parallels with other learners whose first language (L1) does not have a written form, but these learners are still able to benefit from the support of the spoken form of the second language (L2) when learning the use of the written form of the L2.

Mayer and Wells examine this problem of applying the theory of transfer between L1 and L2 in some depth by exploring the role of 'inner speech' in the writing process and how this relates to deaf children. The work of Vygotsky (1978) suggests that the spoken and the written forms of language are interdependent and linked by what he describes as inner speech. This is not to say that text is simply speech written down but rather that inner speech is a means to rehearse, self-direct and mediate between the spoken and the written form. Although inner speech is usually associated with spoken language there is evidence to suggest that deaf children may not have inner speech based on the spoken word but that some may have inner language based on the visual-gestural properties of sign. For these children there is evidence to suggest that their inner language might be a visual-gestural code (Klima and Bellugi, 1979) but we cannot assume that meaning which has been constructed in internal visual-gestural language can be transferred to linear written language. Mayer and Wells suggest that areas where deaf children might experience particular difficulties in moving from a mental representation in sign language to the written form would include:

- encoding in written English bound morphemes in sign language which are not represented by individual signs but through the manner or style of presentation of the lexical sign

- representing the signed utterance in the correct English word order as sign language has specific rules about sign order which differ from word order rules in English (in BSL the topic is usually established first)

- capturing the non-manual signals, which convey critical semantic and syntactic information, in printed form

- providing the context of the meaning, such as the attitude and intention of the characters, which can be conveyed in sign language through the use of facial markers.

As this critique by Mayer and Wells demonstrates, we cannot simply lift a second language learning model from research into hearing bilingualism and apply the same principles to sign bilingualism. The model we must work from needs to be tailored to match the second language learning situation of bilingual deaf children. With regard to literacy development, a model for sign bilingual deaf children needs specifically to address how sign language might serve as the mediating function between inner language and written language.

In practical terms we still need to know more about how to use both languages in the teaching context, and how to bridge the gap between the two languages (Albertini, 2000; Musselman, 2000). Most descriptions of sign bilingual programmes incorporate a strong metalinguistic component; that is, the ability to reflect upon and discuss the properties of both languages is emphasised (e.g., Mahshie, 1995; Neuroth-Gimbrone and Logiodice, 1992; Strong, 1988). Central to these teaching programmes are translation and comparison work between languages with an emphasis on the development of fluent skills in sign language as L1 and on the written form of the second language. These programmes successfully exploit the strengths of sign bilingualism by using the children's well-developed sign language skills as the medium of instruction. However, they do not fully address the early challenges of learning to read and write such as the decoding process, the development of phonological awareness and the role of inner language.

In search of a more holistic approach to sign bilingual literacy development, which takes into account the role of inner language, some researchers in the United States have explored the role of manually coded English in the writing process for sign bilingual children (Mayer, 1999; Mayer and Akamatsu, 2000). These studies suggest that deaf pupils' development of writing competence benefits where English-based signing is used as an intermediary between ASL and written English. It is suggested that English-based signing should have a specific role with regard to preparing for writing rather than become the single mode of face-to-face communication. To complement this, introductory and preparatory work in ASL is suggested, thus supporting the pupils' comprehension and conceptual understanding. These studies suggest that, even for deaf pupils with significant sign language abilities, writing in English involves thinking in English and this should be supported in the learning environment.

Other research into sign bilingual deaf children's writing questions whether this would be an appropriate learning route for all and points instead to the role of the pupils' established sign language skills in the writing process. Some studies have explored the use of written glosses for ASL or BSL to support deaf children's English literacy development. It is argued that the writing of a English gloss in response to an ASL or BSL source reflects the pupils' sign language knowledge and hence provides evidence of an attempt to create their own structures using a language they already know (Gregory, 1997; Mozzer-Mather, 1990; Neuroth-Gimbrone and Logiodice, 1992; Singleton *et al.*, 1998). Gregory, for example, considers the strategies that bilingual deaf children use for writing and the extent to which their knowledge of BSL influences their writing, in both positive – facilitative – and negative – interference – terms. From analysis of the types of errors which appeared in children's writing she concludes that deaf children use their knowledge of BSL in their English writing. Gregory argues, echoing the other related studies, that this should be considered as a positive transitional stage, which could open up the possibilities of the use of BSL for the discussion of English and how it expresses grammatical information in comparison to sign language.

This study furthers this debate by exploring the bridging processes used by individual bilingual deaf children between BSL and written English. The methodology for the study draws on the approaches to the teaching of literacy described in sign bilingual programmes where metalinguistic skills and the role of translation and comparative analysis work are considered to be central. The study investigates how individual deaf children move between BSL and written English in response to a translation task and what the implications of these findings are for the continued development of strategies for teaching literacy skills to sign bilingual deaf pupils.

Research context

The research took place within an inclusive education service for deaf pupils which has a sign bilingual policy. The service concerned promotes the role of deaf adults and BSL in the education of deaf children. The development and use of BSL is encouraged through the employment of deaf native-users and hearing staff proficient in sign language. The service staff and the children's parents were fully consulted prior to and throughout this research project. The researcher was able to meet regularly with staff and parents at service development meetings and family support groups respectively. These provided forums for informal discussion about the research as well as the opportunity to report on progress and preliminary findings. The parents' permission to involve the children in the research, including reporting and presentations, was sought in writing but the informal meetings ensured that the parents fully understood the procedures and the implications for the children.

The subjects

Six primary-aged children, in two different inclusive primary schools, were selected as subjects for the study. All those selected used both BSL and English for learning and for socialising at home and at school, and so could be considered to be bilingual to varying degrees. These children were also all in a bilingual educational programme where deaf and hearing adults worked together and where both BSL and English (spoken and written) were used in the teaching situation. The children had varying degrees of hearing and although this is considered in the analysis, the main criterion for the choice of the subjects was the functional use of both languages in the learning context.

For the purposes of this article just three of the six children are discussed in depth, although examples of use of language have been selected which illustrate characteristics and patterns across the whole group. Short descriptions of the three children are given below. Real names are not used.

Hannah is 8 years old. She has a pre-lingual, severe, bilateral, sensorineural hearing loss. She has a partially deaf mother, deaf father and a deaf sibling. She is currently undergoing transition from accessing the full curriculum through BSL to accessing most of the mainstream curriculum through English with sign support (SSE). Her spoken English consists of the intelligible use of voice and appropriate lip patterns with increasing grammatical accuracy. The adults report that she is able to use BSL and SSE equally well but her use of SSE is dominant. This balance was also reflected in Hannah's own stated language preference when asked by the researcher, which was 'all ... sign and voice'.

Jake is 8 years old. He has a pre-lingual, profound, bilateral, sensorineural hearing loss. He has hearing parents and a hearing sibling. Jake accesses the school curriculum entirely through BSL. He has strong receptive and expressive BSL skills but very limited receptive and expressive English skills. His spoken English consists of lip patterns and some vocalisation using only simple sentence structures. The adults report that BSL is his most fluent language and proficient means of accessing and conveying information and that he experiences frequent frustration with spoken and written English. Jake's own stated language preference when asked by the researcher was 'sign best'.

Lucy is 8 years old. She has a pre-lingual, profound, bilateral, sensorineural hearing loss. She has a partially deaf mother and a hearing father and sibling. She accesses the school curriculum through BSL, although the influence of English is present in her expressive BSL skills. Her spoken English consists of intelligible speech with appropriate intonation and pitch. She demonstrates some knowledge of English sentence and grammatical structures. The adults report that she is able to receive and express complex information more efficiently in BSL but is always willing to attempt English and that she frequently mixes SSE with BSL. Lucy's own statement when asked about her preferred language use was 'signing and talking a little bit', which reflects this mixed repertoire of skills.

Three of the six children, including Hannah, were able to use some spoken language as part of their bilingual repertoire. The other three children, including Jake and Lucy, had only limited spoken language abilities and so the dominance of BSL was easier to recognise. What is important is a recognition that this mixed profile of subjects and the inconclusive descriptions of their preferred language is likely to be representative of other cohorts of deaf pupils and it is this diversity that needs further exploration.

Research approach rationale

A set of six individual exploratory case studies with clearly defined techniques for data collection were used in the investigation. It was recognised that studying six rather than one case study would still not lead to opportunities to generalise about all sign bilingual children. However, as Yin (1989) states, the different results achieved may facilitate the generation of a theory about sign bilingual children's language learning strategies.

Although the researcher worked with the individual children on the data collection activities, the teachers of the children played a significant role in planning and reviewing these. The teachers were interested in learning more about the children's linguistic potential so that they might adapt and develop their teaching strategies. The collaborative nature of this study points to an action research approach in that the project aimed to address some of the practical concerns of teachers regarding the teaching of English (Rapoport 1970; Stenhouse, 1985).

Elicitation task

The study involved the use of a translation writing task. The language demands of this activity reflected the typical language demands placed on the children in their school settings, although the activity necessarily concentrated this experience for the purposes of the research. This structured task was intended to elicit richer and more concentrated data about the processes of language learning than unstructured observation would yield.

For this task the children were asked to view a BSL story on video being told by a familiar native sign language user. Although the BSL story was presented as a personal account by the deaf adult, the length, structure and style of the story reflected that of the picture sequence stories with which the children were familiar. The children were asked to watch the BSL story on video and to write their English version. The tape was reviewed as often as they requested. Any help they requested was given and noted. This work had been piloted previously with the children by their teachers and this informed decisions about the appropriate length and content of the BSL source story.

Focus of analysis

The analysis concentrated on the process that children went through to complete the translation task as well as the final written products. Analysis of the process focused on how each child prepared for the written task. This was undertaken because it became evident during pilot work that the children had various mediation strategies for writing. Strategies included repetition of the BSL as used in the source story; prior rehearsal in the child's own choice of BSL (paraphrase); or prior rehearsal in spoken English. The nature of the help that each child requested was also considered to be significant in terms of the conclusions drawn about individual children's sign bilingualism.

The other area of analysis focused on the strategies each child used to translate BSL structures where information was specified in such a way that it could not be directly re-coded in written English. It was intended that information would be gained about each child regarding:

- their ability to interpret the meaning of the BSL source
- their awareness of the shortcomings of writing down an English gloss of the BSL
- their understanding of the separate nature of the two languages
- their ability to work creatively with their repertoire of English skills.

Three specific BSL phrases and the children's attempts at a written translation of these phrases were selected for the purposes of analysis. These three items were selected because each phrase incorporates particular features of BSL which cannot be reliably translated into English using direct sign/word equivalents. Some interpretation of the BSL phrases is therefore needed for an English meaning equivalent to be constructed. Each phrase is discussed separately and the individual children's written translation attempts described and analysed in turn. The children's full written translations of the BSL story are included in Appendix 3.

Transcripts of the story

In order to provide a context for the analysis of each child's translation work, a gloss of the BSL story is provided in Appendix 1. English punctuation has been added to the gloss to preserve the meaning of the story. A full written English translation of the story has also been provided (Appendix 2). The conventions used to describe the children's writing (process and outcomes) are outlined below in Table 1.

Written translation problem 1

In the BSL story the deaf adult used a BSL sequence which appeared to be made up of two English words but which was a BSL structure in its own right, meaning in this context 'he wants to come with us'. The BSL sequence that was presented can be glossed as WANT WITH. The

---

Table 1: Transcription conventions

- A word in capital letters (e.g. LOOK) denotes an English gloss for a BSL sign. (A gloss represents the meaning of the basic form of the sign taken out of context.)

- Words in upper-case connected by a hyphen (e.g. LOOK-AT-ME) are used when a single sign requires more than one English word to give a gloss of the meaning.

- Words in upper-case italics separated by a hyphen (e.g. *J-O-S-H*) denote a finger-spelled word.

- A single capital in italics (e.g. *J*) denotes initialisation (finger-spelling of initial letter of a word, e.g. for people's names).

- Lower-case text in italics denotes written English.

---

reason this is interesting for analysis is that, because the lip patterns given relate to familiar English words, the children had a cue for some English that they could write, although if they simply wrote the BSL down this would not be correct English. It was interesting to see to what extent each individual tried to provide a translation and not a transliteration (gloss) of the BSL phrase.

Lucy wrote *My little son billy new. dog want come with in shoP*. Lucy rehearsed what she was going to write in BSL first and then picked out the key words she wanted to write down. She rehearsed DOG WANTS *T-O* COME WITH and then asked for the spelling of *want* and then of *come with* but wrote *in shop* independently.

It is not entirely clear whether Lucy intended *dog* to be the end of the first sentence of her written story or the beginning of the second phrase. If it was intended to be a part of the second phrase then she correctly inserted the subject of the English sentence. She also added *come* and in *shop*, both of which are English features not specified in the original BSL of WANT WITH. It seems that although Lucy did not always use spoken English to rehearse her writing, she had a model of English which she used to build on the key words extracted from the BSL and she had some idea of what an English sentence should look or sound like. The gloss was Lucy's starting point; this was a strategy deployed by three out of the six in the group.

Jake wrote *Not Dog with got shop*. Jake rehearsed DOG WANTS WITH and then added NO STAY and then began to try to write down what he had rehearsed. This was a long and arduous task during which Jake lost the thread of his writing several times. Jake rehearsed WITH DADDY AND JOSH, DOG WANTS WITH NO STAY. He then wrote *dog*. Jake then rehearsed NOT WITH JOSH and wrote *not*. He rehearsed WITH and then wrote *with*. Having got this far, Jake rubbed out all his work to start again.

To move Jake forward the researcher prompted him about the story in BSL. Jake's reply was DOG and then he wrote *dog*. He then rehearsed GO WITH and wrote *with*. Then he rehearsed GO WITH SHOPPING and wrote *got*. Then he wrote *sohop* but corrected it using text written earlier to *shop*.

Jake tried to write down the English gloss of the BSL and struggled with retaining any meaning of what he was writing as well as with the actual mechanics of writing. He clearly comprehended the BSL as he rehearsed several different possible phrases in an attempt to plan something to write. The discrepancy between Jake's BSL and English skills was very marked here and he seemed to be frustrated by his lack of independence with the written form. Jake relied heavily here on the use of an intermediary gloss to tackle the writing task.

Hannah wrote *BiLLy was HaPPy to buy the Cake*. Hannah did not discuss or rehearse this phrase but watched the BSL tape and wrote her version independently.

Hannah demonstrated here a very useful strategy as a language learner. She tried to actually translate the BSL phrase into an appropriate English phrase and so moved away from the BSL structure and, instead of relying on cues from the BSL, she used the English she was confident with to write a 'close-enough' translation. What was interesting about her written phrase is that it was very much in her own words and that she did not try to go beyond her own English resources. Her writing did not seem to be influenced by the BSL. She had a picture of what had happened and was able to paraphrase this to get the main idea across. This possibly points to her ability to think in English.

Written translation problem 2

In the BSL story the deaf adult used the BSL feature of repetition to indicate that an action was repeated over time or prolonged. In this instance, she used the sign for WAIT three times to convey the idea that Josh waited for a while for his daddy to come home. She then used the sign for FINISH, which is a perfective marker, to indicate that the waiting was over. The English gloss of the BSL phrase would be WAIT WAIT WAIT DADDY HOME, FINISH DADDY HOME. A full translation could be *Josh waited and waited for daddy to come home and then at last daddy came home*. Alternatively, instead of repeating waited in English a different written translation could be *Josh waited for a long time for daddy to come home and then at last daddy came home*.

The use of the written English phrase *at last* is an attempt by the researcher to provide an appropriate translation for FINISHED in this context and an appropriate connective between the two clauses. The reason this is interesting for analysis is that because of the match between the sign WAIT and the familiar English word *wait* the children had a cue for writing, although it would obviously have been inappropriate English to write *wait* three times. How then did they convey the sense of waiting over some period of time which is conveyed by this BSL phrase? In addition to this problem, the children had to decide how to address the translation of the sign FINISH in this context. There were no cues from this BSL sign for the written English and an appropriate translation relied heavily on an understanding of the context of the whole phrase as well as sufficient competence in English to construct an appropriate translation.

Lucy wrote *wait for DaDDy at last home*. Lucy rehearsed WAIT WAIT WAIT as it was expressed in the BSL version of the story. She then asked for the spelling of *wait*. She then rehearsed for using voice before she wrote it independently and then rehearsed FINISH as produced in the BSL version and used exactly the same sign to ask the researcher for the written version. The researcher gave the written translation *at last,* as she assumed that the child already knew the spelling of the English word *finish* and was asking for help with the correct translation of the sign. The researcher drew on her knowledge of the child to make this response and could therefore have over-interpreted the request. However, for the purposes of analysis it is sufficient to note that Lucy did not attempt to translate FINISH herself.

Lucy was able to use her English skills to correctly translate WAIT WAIT WAIT and use the English verb appropriately with *for.* She found herself out of depth, however, with FINISH and made no attempt to find an English equivalent for this. Lucy seemed again to begin with a gloss but to add to this using her English knowledge.

Jake wrote *wait Daddy*. Jake rehearsed his ideas in BSL before writing. In this instance he rehearsed WAIT DADDY but he did not repeat WAIT as signed in the BSL version. He also added DADDY, indicating what Josh was waiting for. Jake then wrote *W* to start off his English text and then asked for the spelling of *wait* and then wrote *Daddy* independently.

The fact that Jake rehearsed the phrase not repeating WAIT in the BSL leads us to speculate that he was perhaps aware of the difference between the two languages and of some of the rules governing written English. What is certain is his confidence and ability to interpret the BSL, as he was able to take the central meaning out of this and either paraphrase it in his rehearsal or attempt to prepare an English version. Jake re-worked the BSL before tackling the writing task.

Hannah wrote *Josh was waiting for DaDDy back DaDDy was back.* Hannah rehearsed out loud in spoken English 'Josh was waiting for daddy to come back' before she wrote. She then asked for help with the spellings of *waiting*, *back* and *was*.

Hannah was able to put together a complete translation of the BSL into written English using the spoken form to plan and rehearse her text. She went beyond a literal translation or gloss of the BSL signs and added both the subject and the object as well as tense and function words. Her writing was clearly supported by her spoken language skills as she was able to write down most of what she had planned out loud.

Written translation problem 3

In the BSL story the deaf adult used a BSL phrase which visually describes that the dog has chocolate cake all round his mouth and indeed all over his face. To illustrate this the deaf adult represented the dog in her story-telling and dragged her fingers down her cheeks and round the corners of her mouth whilst also wearing a glazed but contented facial expression. This type of characterisation is a common device in BSL, although this description could be described as non-linguistic, which presents the children with a complex translation problem. The meaning of the BSL phrase in this context was unmistakable as the description was so vivid, but because the whole meaning is expressed through one sign, the children had to use their own English resources to create a written English equivalent. Because no separate signs are used, writing a gloss of this BSL phrase was not a straightforward task. The children in this instance were therefore left in no doubt as to the meaning of the BSL but with the task of creating their own English equivalent of this colourful scene.

Lucy wrote *dog chocolate all over his mouth*. Lucy rehearsed what she wanted to say by repeating the BSL phrase from the story. She then asked for help in written English using the exact signs from the BSL.

There are two main factors likely to be influencing Lucy's choice to ask for help with the whole translation. Firstly, it is very difficult to take the BSL apart as so much information is given in one sign. The second factor is that the researcher was there and help was available all the way through the tasks and so to flounder and possibly fail was unnecessary. Help was given throughout these tasks because the data collection took place in a natural setting. Without this support the individuals may not have been able to engage in the tasks to the extent that they did. We can speculate however that this was Lucy's limit. The nature of this part of the task was difficult enough for her not to even attempt the English herself. This suggests that without the gloss as a starting point Lucy could not use her own English resources as a starting point.

This is interesting because, based on the writing collected from Lucy, it seems probable that she had the English vocabulary and grammar knowledge needed to construct an English translation. She also demonstrated that she was able to paraphrase BSL information and put it into her own writing. It may be that the unpacking of this BSL phrase was more daunting than finding the actual English words needed. Without the starting point of the gloss Lucy, and others in the group, had difficulty in attempting this problem.

Jake wrote *cholate all over his face*. Jake rehearsed this by repeating the BSL exactly as viewed on the video and then he asked for the English for CHOCOLATE. Having copied this down he then asked for ALL-OVER-FACE by repeating the BSL version and he copied the English given.

It is arguable that Jake made some attempt to re-construct the meaning in English because he started his written version off with *chocolate*, whereas in the BSL chocolate was not specified. Alternatively we could interpret Jake's beginning differently. It may be that he was thinking through the meaning of the BSL and interpreting the BSL phrase, and so to clarify the BSL meaning for himself he added CHOCOLATE. The latter suggestion seems more likely given his lack of confidence with English.

Hannah wrote *BiLLy got a chocolate round Billy mouh*. Hannah talked through the English translation out loud before tackling the writing. She said 'daddy saw Billy's mouth was all over chocolate'. She then wrote *got* and then *a chocolate*. Next she rehearsed 'round Billy's mouth' and wrote this down, asking for help with the spelling of *mouth*.

Interestingly, Hannah did not write down exactly what she rehearsed aloud but put together a modified or paraphrased version for the English text. She interpreted the BSL and then constructed the English but was not restricted by her initial verbal translation of the BSL.

Discussion

The first translation problem allows us to see the difference between the children who relied on a written gloss as part of the writing process and those who were able to think in English. In the case of Lucy and Jake, the English gloss of WANT WITH was used as a cue to help them make a start on the written English even though they then added their own English features. This BSL phrase does lend itself to being transliterated as a starting point and this is certainly the strategy which the children without strong spoken language skills favoured. In contrast, Hannah, who used spoken English as a strategy to prepare her writing, seemed to do the actual translating part of the task before she began on the written English. Her spoken preparation was already structurally very different from the BSL phrase.

The complexity of the translation task increased with the BSL sequence WAIT WAIT WAIT DADDY HOME, FINISH DADDY HOME because of the repetition used in the BSL and because of the use of the sign FINISH in this context. Some children did however take up the cue of WAIT and, as with the first task, they then added certain English features such as *dad* and *for*. Jake actually modified the BSL in his preparation before attempting the writing, in that he took out the repetition. This seemed to be a very useful strategy but because of his lack of written English skills he was not able to capitalise on this. Several of the children also asked for help with the complete translation of FINISH, but notably not the children with stronger spoken

English skills. These children did not overtly search for a translation of this but conveyed it nevertheless in the way they structured their English text. These children's confidence with the spoken form seemed to enable them to move away from the BSL structure and allow them to prepare their English translation with the actual meaning and not the BSL structure in their minds.

The BSL phrase CHOCOLATE-ALL-OVER-MOUTH presented an even more complex task because the potential sign/word equivalents are reduced to an absolute minimum. Mouth is really the only English gloss you might pick out if you were trying to write a word for sign transliteration of this. The children with weaker spoken English skills all asked for help with a direct translation. Out of the other three children, two of them wrote a translation very much in their own words which conveyed the meaning and the tone of the BSL phrase.

From this analysis we can learn a certain amount about the children's awareness of the two languages and their inner representation of English, as well as their strategies for moving from BSL to written English. It is interesting that all the children seemed to be aware of the limitations of writing down an English gloss of the BSL, although Lucy and Jake used this strategy as a starting point. Even though this seemed to provide the link between the BSL and English writing for them, we can argue that their awareness of the differences between the two languages was still evident. This is suggested by their attempts to add other English features to their text such as the subject or object in a sentence.

It seems that this translation task was a different activity for each individual depending on the starting point. For the deaf children without strong spoken language skills the actual writing was more like the first stage of the translation process. These children seemed to accept that certain content words are transferable from BSL to written English, but that English requires additional details and linguistic features such as the naming of people and places and the addition of function words. The writing of the gloss of the BSL provided a link from the BSL to the written English, thus allowing them to commence the writing and then incorporate their own English knowledge as appropriate. This supports findings from other studies which stress the value of using a written gloss as an intermediary between ASL or BSL and written English (Mozzer-Mather, 1990; Neuroth-Gimbrone and Logiodice 1992; Singleton *et al.*, 1998).

For the children with more spoken English skills, the writing down of the English was more like the end of the translation process. It seems that translation for these children took place internally, enabling them to then verbalise their English version before writing. It is likely that the children with more developed spoken language skills have a model of written English which is more similar that of hearing children, which allows them to think in English.

These pupils were clearly thinking in English and as a result their written texts successfully conveyed the sense of the BSL story but were not hide-bound by the structure of the BSL narrative. Their internal model of English does allow them to be more proficient writers, confirming other similar reports (Mayer, 1999; Mayer and Akamatsu, 2000).

The analysis of the different strategies the individual children used provides some useful pointers for how to use both languages in the teaching context and how to bridge the gap between the two languages. Ideally we would all like to see deaf pupils with sufficiently well-developed internal models of English which allow them to think in English. However, it is evident from this small sample that for some deaf pupils this may never be a route. Certainly, meaningful exposure to good models of spoken and written English should be a goal in all sign bilingual programmes.

This exposure may include the use of some English-based signing but where this is used its role should be explicitly and clearly defined for pupils and adults. Teachers should be mindful of their own language use and be explicit where possible about their separate or mixed use of BSL and English (Swanwick, 2001).

It is equally important that the languages are clearly separated and that good models of spoken and/or written English are provided alongside instruction through BSL. The children need to be made aware of the differences between the mixed and separate use of their two languages as well as the characteristics of their own mixed language use and the contexts in which this usually occurs. How the two languages (BSL and English) and the three modalities (sign, speech and text) are used in a sign bilingual classroom is a crucial part of the children's bilingual development. The combined and separate use of sign language and English needs to respond to the bilingual profiles of the individuals.

In English teaching, the children's BSL skills need to become a more holistic and integral part of the process rather than a means to an end. For example, in translation work, more talk in BSL about writing might support the children's concept development and steer them away from writing down the English gloss of the BSL and accepting this as a meaningful translation. Within-language translation work would be particularly helpful as it would broaden the children's language repertoire and enable them to focus on the actual meaning to be translated rather than the structure.

The findings from this analysis reveal a range of strategies for moving between the two languages that the children use intuitively, without prior training. In addition to this the children's emerging language awareness and some of their perceptions of the two languages are exposed. We should be aiming to further develop the children's tacit language awareness that is a result of their bilingual experience. Both of these factors support the development of the use of translation work as a language teaching tool as well as a research technique. This study also demonstrates the potential of the translation task for providing an insight into the interaction between the two languages and the language learning process.

Although this study touches on individual experiences of moving across languages, we certainly need further understanding of what it is to be sign bilingual and how individual deaf children move between their two languages and three modalities.

References

Albertini, J. (2000) Advances in Literacy Research and Practice. *Journal of Deaf Studies and Deaf Education*; 5:123.

Cummins, J. (1991) Interdependence of First- and Second-Language Proficiency in Bilingual Children. In E. Bialystok (ed), *Language Processing in Bilingual Children*. Cambridge: Cambridge University Press.

Cummins, J. (1994) Knowledge, Power and Identity in Teaching English as a Second Language. In Genesee F (ed), *Educating Second Language Children*. Cambridge: Cambridge University Press.

Gregory, S. (1997) Deaf Children's Writing: The Influence of British Sign Language on Written English. Paper presented to the International Symposium on Bilingualism, University of Newcastle-Upon-Tyne, April.

Klima, E. and Bellugi, U. (1979) *The Signs of Language*. Cambridge, MA: Harvard University Press.

Mahshie, S.N. (1995) *Educating Deaf Children Bilingually*. Washington, DC: Gallaudet University Press.

Mayer, C. (1999) Shaping at the Point of Utterance: An Investigation of the Composing Processes of the Deaf Student Writer. *Journal of Deaf Studies and Deaf Education*; 4: 37-49.

Mayer, C. and Akamatsu, C.T. (2000) Deaf Children Creating Written Texts: Contributions of American Sign Language and Signed Forms of English. *American Annals of the Deaf*; 145: 394-403.

Mayer, C. and Wells, G. (1996) Can the Linguistic Interdependence Theory Support a Bilingual-Bicultural Model of Literacy Education for Deaf Students? *Journal of Deaf Studies and Deaf Education*; 1: 93-107.

Mozzer-Mather. S. (1990) *A Strategy to Improve Deaf Students' Writing Through the use of Glosses of Signed Narratives.* Gallaudet Research Institute Working paper 90-4, Washington, DC: Gallaudet University.

Musselman, C. (2000) How do Children who Can't Hear Learn to Read an Alphabetic Script? A review of the literature on reading and deafness. *Journal of Deaf Studies and Deaf Education*; 5: 9-31.

Neuroth-Gimbrone, C. and Logiodice, C.M. (1992) A Co-operative Bilingual Language Programme for Deaf Adolescents. *Sign Language Studies*; 74:79-91.

Paul, P.V. (1998) *Literacy and Deafness: The Development of Reading, Writing and Literate Thought*. London: Allyn and Bacon.

Pickersgill, M. and Gregory, S. (1998) *Sign Bilingualism. A Model*. A LASER Publication.

Rapoport, R.N. (1970) Three Dilemmas in Action Research. *Human Relations*; 23: 499-513.

Rodda, M. and Eleweke, J. (2000) *Theories of Literacy Development in Deaf People with Limited English Proficiency*. DEI 2:101-113.

Singleton, J.L., Supalla, S., Litchfield, S. and Schley, S. (1998) From Sign to Word: Considering Modality Constraints in ASL/English Bilingual Education. *Topics in Language Disorders*; 18: 16-29.

Stenhouse, L. (1985) Action research and the teacher's responsibility for the educational process. In J Rudduck, D Hopkins (eds), *Research as a Basis for Teaching*. London: Heinemann.

Strong, M.A. (1988) Bilingual Approach to the Education of Young Deaf Children: ASL and English. In M Strong (ed), *Language Learning and Deafness*. Cambridge: Cambridge University Press.

Swanwick, R. (2001) *The Demands of a Sign Context for Bilingual Teachers and Learners: An Observation of Language use and Learning Experiences*. DEI; 3: 62-79.

Vygotsky, L. (1978) *Mind in Society: The Development of Higher Psychological Processes*. Cambridge, MA: Harvard University Press.

Yin, R.K. (1989) *Case Study Research: Design and Methods* (2nd edn). London: Sage.

APPENDIX 1: GLOSS OF THE BSL STORY

Below is the English gloss of the BSL story. Sections in bold indicate the sections of the story selected for analysis.

HI! I WANT TELL-STORY SHORT. I HAVE BOY NAME *J-O-S-H*. HE HAVE NEW DOG WHAT NAME *B-I-L-L-Y*.

BEFORE BEEN HIS DADDY'S BIRTHDAY I THOUGHT...TAP...*S-A-T* BIRTHDAY WHO?...DADDY'S!

J-O-S-H EXCITED WHAT DO? THOUGHT WHAT...WHY-NOT MAKE CAKE. JOSH YEAH!

BOTH WENT SHOP. HIS DOG SIT-UP **WANT WITH**... HMM... BETTER STAY. BOTH WENT SHOP LOOK-AROUND BUY WHAT? THINK WHAT BUY... CHOCOLATE.. YES... MAKE CHOCOLATE CAKE RIGHT. BUY THINGS HOME MAKE CAKE.

LOVELY CAKE SMELL GOOD. **WAIT WAIT WAIT DADDY HOME. FINISH DADDY HOME.** COME SHOW... GONE CAKE.

DADDY THINK WHERE DOG. JOSH LOOK SAW OH AWFUL! DOG-WALKING – HAPPY **CHOCOLATE-ALL-OVER-FACE**.

APPENDIX 2: WRITTEN TRANSLATION OF THE BSL STORY

A full written English translation of the story is also provided. The sections in bold are those which relate to the sections of the BSL story selected for analysis in the children's written translations.

Hi, I want to tell you a short story.

I have a little boy; his name is Josh. He has a new dog. His name is Billy.

A little while ago, it was his daddy's birthday. I thought about it and said to Josh 'On Saturday, you know whose birthday it is?'

'It's daddy's!'

Josh was really excited 'Oh, what shall we do?'

I suggested 'Why not make a cake?'

'Oh yeah!' said Josh.

We were setting off for the shop. The dog wagged his tail hopefully. **He wanted to come with us.** We thought that he had better stay at home. We got all of the things to make a chocolate cake and then went home and made the cake. It was a lovely cake and smelt wonderful.

Josh waited for daddy to come home. At last, daddy came home and we called him to show him the cake. Oh, it had disappeared!

Dad was puzzled. 'Where's the dog?' he asked. Josh looked at the dog. Oh no! The dog came tottering happily along with **chocolate cake all over his face!**

APPENDIX 3: THE CHILDREN'S TEXTS WRITTEN FROM THE BSL STORY

The texts are reproduced as written by the children including the use of capital, line breaks, punctuation and spelling. Sections of the texts in italics indicate where the children asked for and were given an English translation for a particular part of the BSL story.

Hannah

'Josh and BiLLy'
Josh got a new dog its NaMe BiLLy.
Josh got a idea for DADDY BirtHday Cake.
BiLLy was HaPPy to buy the Cake.
Josh was waiting for DADDy back
DADDy was back Josh said COME here
there you are it *disappear* DADDy saw BiLLy
got a chocolate round Billy mouh.

Jake

I Josh DaDD saiD
Birthday Josh excited
Saturday thought
cak shop with Daddy
Not Dog with got
shop Daddy Josh
make caks make Josh caks
wait Daddy cak
dissapeared thought
Dog chocolate eat
Dog Josh saw Dog
cholate *all over his face*

Lucy

Hi My little son billy new.
dog want come with in shoP.
better leave house went to shoP look
around idea make chocolate cake.
Chocolate cake leave smell nice
wait for DaDDy *at last* home
cake gone where dog chocolate
all over his mouth.

CHAPTER 17
Creativity and a corpus of spoken English
Ronald Carter and Svenja Adolphs

Introduction

In this paper our aim is to explore the relationship between language, especially spoken language, and creativity. We examine data from a five-million-word computerised language corpus – the CANCODE spoken English corpus [CANCODE stands for 'Cambridge and Nottingham Corpus of Discourse in English']. The corpus was developed at the University of Nottingham, UK between 1994 and 2001, and was funded by Cambridge University Press©, with whom sole copyright resides. The spoken data were recorded in a wide variety of mostly informal settings across the islands of Britain and Ireland and then transcribed and stored in computer-readable form.

What is a computerised language corpus?

A computerised language corpus is a collection of texts electronically stored in computers, in which information about the language is made accessible through software designed to analyse patterns of language. For example, computerised language corpora can give information about the frequency of words in the corpus, the most common partnerships formed by the words with other words, the different uses of such patterns in speech and writing and the different grammatical structures found in different varieties in the corpus such as newspaper or legal language.

Most language corpora in the world are assembled with the aim of making statements about language which can be statistically supported. Examples in English are the 400m word Bank of English, held at the University of Birmingham, UK and the 100m word British National Corpus (BNC). These and other corpora have proved invaluable in the construction of authentic reference materials such as dictionaries for learners of English. Both these corpora contain spoken samples but they contain mainly written data and there is still a tendency for written language to predominate in computerised corpora because such data are so much easier to collect.

In spite of trends to ever larger, multi-million-word corpora and associated quantitative analysis, in the case of CANCODE the main aim has been to construct a corpus which can allow both quantitative and qualitative investigation. The data have been carefully collected and sociolinguistically-profiled with reference to a range of different speech genres and with an emphasis on everyday communication. The corpus has been designed with a particular aim of relating grammatical and lexical choice to variation in social context and is also used in connection with a range of teaching projects, being especially concerned with differences between spoken and written language (Carter and McCarthy, 1995a,b; 1997). What all these corpora have in common is a concern with language as it is really used. They reinforce a tradition of examining how language is authentically and actually used, rather than armchair conceptions of language use in which a linguist tests hypotheses based on made-up or invented examples.

Why spoken creativity?

However, in addition to this more pedagogic work, researchers have been unable to ignore the pervasive instances of word play and creative language use in many parts of the corpus and have begun to investigate these phenomena further (Carter, 1998a). The research reported here takes a different direction to most previous accounts of creativity which normally pursue the topic in relation to written and, in particular, canonical written and canonical literary text, often drawing on traditions of creativity and composition theory (Nash, 1998; Nash and Stacey, 1997). The research reported here allows us to question the significance of terms such as figures of speech – which are, ironically, rarely illustrated with speech examples – and to begin to question whether words such as *literary* can be reserved only for contexts of writing. Explorations of creativity in language were not the main purpose of the CANCODE project and we stress that the investigations described here are no more than preliminary steps.

Types of speech in the corpus

The data collected for the CANCODE project were classified along two main axes according to *context type* and **interaction type**. The axes were selected with the aim of providing frameworks which are neither too broad nor too narrow. The classification scheme emerged both pre- and post-hoc in that the researchers had presuppositions concerning the contexts in which they wanted to have evidence of language use and yet had to respond and develop the categories in response to the developing data bank. There were no prior conceptions concerning instances of creative language use, since that was not a primary concern of the project in its earliest stages.

CONTEXT TYPE

This axis of categorisation reflects the interpersonal relationships that hold between speakers. Four broad types were identified: *intimate, socialising, professional* and *transactional*. A fifth, somewhat narrower category embracing *pedagogic* contexts to support the teaching and learning underpinning of CANCODE is not considered here. The categories embrace both dyadic and multi-party conversations. In multi-party conversations in particular it was initially thought to be problematic that relationships, especially changing relationships or relationships affected by new members joining the group, might be difficult to monitor, but a strong tendency has existed for speakers to converge towards one interaction type in their linguistic behaviour. For example, two intimates sharing a common place of work will adopt a professional attitude in the company of colleagues. To safeguard against possible misinterpretation by the analyst, information on speaker relationships is provided in the majority of cases by the person contributing the data to the corpus. An assessment of speakers' own goals thus remains central to the analysis.

An *intimate* relationship is a private relationship which typically, but not exclusively, centres round cohabitation and where speakers can be assumed to be linguistically most off-guard. All participants in a conversation must belong to the intimate sphere for the text to be categorised thus. So, for example, a conversation between two or more intimates and the family doctor on a home visit will be not intimate but transactional.

The *professional* category refers to the relationship that holds between people who are interacting as part of their regular daily work. The speakers in a professional encounter need not be peers but they do need to share either a profession or a regular place of work. So-called casual talk at work is also included in this category, based on the assumption that colleagues retain the same professional interpersonal relationships whether they are discussing work matters or not.

Colleagues can also be friends, in which case their conversations could be classed as 'socialising'.

An important characteristic of the *transactional* category is that often there is no previous relationship established between speakers. If the intimate relationship is the most private, the transactional is the most public – which is one of the reasons why transactional data is relatively easy to acquire. The transactional category includes job interviews, asking a passer-by for information, goods and service encounters and so on.

Typical contexts for *socialising* are recreational settings such as sports clubs and pubs, as well as political, environmental, religious and other group meetings. Note, however, that it is the relationship between speakers, that is, their wish to communicate at this level, which qualifies data for inclusion in the category, and not the particular environment in which the recording is made. So, for example, a married couple engaged in private conversation in a pub will remain *intimate.* Two couples in a similar setting, however, are more likely to conform to a socialising text.

Although there are points of overlap between categories, the relationship categories do represent, albeit roughly, a cline of private to public speech, with the intimate and transactional categories respectively at each end of the cline. The professional category is more public than the socialising category, which in turn is more public than intimate.

Along the axis of ***interaction type*** distinctions were made between data that are predominantly collaborative and those that are non-collaborative and, further, for the collaborative type, those which are task-oriented and those which are not.

Non-collaborative texts are those in which one speaker dominates significantly, supported by back-channelling from the other speaker(s). Typically, the dominant speaker in these texts is relating an event, telling a joke, giving instructions or explanations or professional presentations. On one level these exchanges are also collaborative, but there is a level at which they resemble narration or the unilinear, asymmetrical transfer of information, rather than dialogue. The blanket term adopted to account for such an interaction type is **information provision**.

The two other interaction types classified represent more collaborative, interactive and symmetrical speech encounters. **Collaborative idea** involves the interactive sharing of thoughts, opinions and attitudes, while the category of **collaborative task**, as the term implies, is reserved for task-oriented communication.

Overall, ***interaction type*** texts have proved more difficult to categorise because of the embedding of one context-type within another. Category membership is thus allocated according to the activity that is dominant in each conversation. A significantly more detailed account of the CANCODE corpus and its design may be found in McCarthy (1998), where the dangers inherent in reifying the categories are also fully acknowledged.

Combining the two axes of categorisation provides a matrix of twelve text types as shown in Figure 1, which also suggests some situations in which the text types might be found.

Figure 1: CANCODE text types and typical situations in which they might be found

	Context-type	Interaction – type	
	Information-provision	Collaborative idea	Collaborative task
Transactional	commentary by museum guide	chatting with local shopkeeper	choosing and buying a CD
Professional	oral report at group meeting	planning meeting at place of work	colleagues window-dressing
Socialising	telling friends about a recent holiday	reminiscing with friends	flatmates cooking together
Intimate	partner relating the plot of a novel	siblings discussing their childhood	couple planting a small tree in their garden

The creativity continuum: credit controllers, student couple and flatmates

Our working definition of creativity is broadly based. It embraces uses of language which both depart from and reinforce expectations. Figures of speech such as metaphor, puns, hyperbole, idioms and repetition in various forms are deployed creatively when they produce either divergence or convergence in participants' responses to the information content of a message. Creative language acts as a trigger for such responses in speakers and writers – here speakers – by generating a different way of seeing or a new way of seeing the same thing. The main purpose of this section is to investigate the notion further focusing mainly on degrees of creativity in different kinds of everyday situation.

Credit security controllers

The following two extracts, both from spoken exchanges, involve contrasting social and inter-personal occasions. In this first extract participants are concluding a meeting concerned with credit control. In the second example two flatmates are talking about a neighbour. It is not pos-sible to cite the full version of the first extract used because it runs to several minutes of record-ing but analysis of the transcript reveals no examples of creative choices in over ten minutes of exchanges which mainly involve a generic reproduction of: professional and transactional/infor-mation provision. The extract here occurs when the meeting is coming to a close.

[Contextual information: The primary purpose of the meeting is an examination of the legal particulars of documents relating to Credit Security. The extract here is taken from the end of the meeting: <S 01> manager: male (55); <S 02> company representative: male (40s); <S 03> company representative: male (40s). Speakers <S 02> and <S 03> report to the manager, speaker <S 01>.]

1   <S 03> But the release now of savings is going to be an issue all right isn't it.

2   <S 02> Yeah.

3   <S 01> Yes.

4   <S 02> How is it approved. And can the board delegate that authority to somebody. To to release erm can, yeah that's right. Can the board delegate it?

5   <S 03> Well I [unintelligible] Well my reading of that would say that that is quite specific.

6   <S 02> Yeah.

7   <S 03> You don't know whether there's provision for the appointment of loans officers and credit officers and all this kind of.

8   <S 02> Mm.

9   <S 03> I wouldn't..There doesn't seem to be anything there except to say that the board must approve this.

10   <S 02> But but in accordance with the registered rules.

11   <S 03> [unintelligible]

12   <S 02> That's the only pos=, so it's, the question is thirty two three B. What's the inter=, can that, can the board delegate its authority under that section Geoff.

13   <S 01> Yeah.

14   <S 02> Thirty two three B.

15   <S 03> Or I wonder is that a limit according to the registered rules. Monitoring of it.

16   <S 01> [unintelligible]

17   <S 03> [whistles]

18   <S 02> I know.

19   <S 01> I used to [unintelligible].

20   <S 03> [unintelligible]

21   [laughter]

22   <S 01> I used to think I was a pair of curtains but then I pulled myself together.

23   [laughter]

24   <S 01> I used to think I was being ignored but nobody still talks to me.

25   <S 02> [laughs]

26   <S 01> Cowardly [unintelligible] this morning. What was in the tea? It's that s=, it's that bloody foreign coffee [laughs] that's what is it.

27   <S 03> Foreign coffee?

28   <S 01> That's that foreign coffee [unintelligible].

After such a long time in which documents are pored over and during which the main purpose of the exchanges has been to transmit or obtain information, the meeting finally erupts in a kind of carnivalesque spirit, in which the speakers take a holiday from information transfer and joke and banter their way through to the end of the formal proceedings of the meeting (ll.20-28). The business done, it seems, they are free to play with words and the labels for what is in their immediate environment. The context and interaction type have restricted opportunities for such uses of language. In this particular instance an increase in creativity even seems to coincide for all the speakers with points of release from their institutional roles.

The social and interactive context of the following exchange is less hierarchical and much less obviously concerned with the transfer and retrieval of information. The speakers are partners who are clearly very familiar with each other and who partake in a more symmetrical relationship. The speech genre is closest to that of: intimate collaborative idea.

Student couple

[Contextual information: The couple in this extract reminisce about the time when they first met. The conversation starts off with a narrative by speaker <S 01> who talks about his drinking habits and later develops into gossip about an acquaintance. <S 01> student: male (26) <S 02>student: female (22)]

1   <S 01> I'd wake up like in the middle of the night er er anything disturbed me and I wake up feeling shit. I wouldn't be ill or anything I'd just feel Oh God.

2   <S 02> Yeah.

3   <S 01> I'd fall back to sleep and then+

4   <S 02> [laughs]

5   <S 01> +maybe er I'll have shivers for about an hour.

6   <S 02> Oh God.

7   <S 01> Go back to sleep.

8   <S 02> You're a right alcoholic.

9   <S 01> And wake up fine. I know. [unintelligible]

10   <S 02> Just think that's what that's what you could be now.

11   <S 01> I know. I could be eighteen stone.

12   <S 02> Could have been Adam Potter with a massive pot pregnant belly.

13   <S 01> I know. [tuts]

14   <S 02> With heart disease and all

15   <S 01> I know.

16   <S 02> sorts of horrible liver conditions.

17   <S 01> So easy to fall into though. I mean you like [unintelligible] at dinner time and Kevin gets tanked up.

18   <S 02> I know.

19   <S 01> Then goes to work. But he don't get drunk you know he just gets tanked up.

20   <S 02> But he drives as well.

21   <S 01> I know. I thought he did.

22   <S 02> Aye. You know and they're

23   <S 01> I've not seen them for about a year now.

24   <S 02> They're both still at home living with their mum aren't they.

25   <S 01> I know. Bit weird family though aren't they.

26   <S 02> Very. Very strange.

27 <S 01> Strange old world.

28 <S 02> I know. It's like I see his mum and dad up the street and I'm sure they must recognise me I've been there often enough and they

29 <S 01> Oh yeah.

30 <S 02> never speak.

31 <S 01> I know. Mm. Odd. A strange family.

32 <S 02> You know I'm like somebody to say hello to anybody who I vaguely know you know.

33 <S 01> E=even if you do.

34 <S 02> I even say hello to people I don't know. [laughs]

35 <S 01> Even if you just say hello to them though they're like weird with it aren't they.

36 <S 02> Yeah.

37 <S 01> He's completely off his trolley.

38 <S 02> Yeah. He's a bit barking isn't he.

39 <S 01> And she she's friendly enough. But she's

40 <S 02> But I don't know when I to their house I always feel like she doesn't want you there. That she's fed up of visitors and Can't you bog off or something.

41 <S 01> Well they do have like twenty visitors a day don't they.

42 <S 02> Oh. Yeah I think I'd been annoyed. And Dave just sits up there waiting for people to call doesn't he.

43 <S 01> Yeah.

44 <S 02> Don't think he moves from that room. Oh well.

45 <S 01> [unintelligible]

46 <S 02> He's off our Christmas card list anyway.

In this extract the two speakers adopt a range of creative strategies. They engage in playful insults which are direct but clearly to be interpreted indirectly as banter; they deploy hyperbolic expressions (*with a massive pot pregnant belly; don't think he moves from that room; they do have like twenty visitors a day*); there is a liberal use of metaphoric and fixed expressions, some creatively extended (*he's completely off his trolley*), some deliberately ellipted (*he's a bit barking* (mad)); and there is a creative play with cultural allusions (*he's off our Christmas card list anyway*). Also noticeable is a particular strategy, with creative outcomes, of quoting other speakers' words for humorous effect (e.g. *that she's fed up of visitors and can't you bog off or something.*) Such a strategy involves grammatical and discourse patterns more than it does specifically lexical or figure of speech patterns. It serves, however, to contribute to the marked density of creative formulation in the extract.

Flatmates

In spoken discourse puns are more directly connected with humour and with the kind of humorous wordplay which reinforces group solidarity. In more intimate encounters the humour is also often scatological, as in the following example where the common coincidence of puns with parts of the body and with the sexual act is very much in evidence. The genre classification is that of 'socialising/collaborative task'.

[Contextual information: four friends meeting at <S 02>'s house. Following on from a prolonged stretch of casual conversation, <S 02> diverts the attention to some DIY task. Two of the friends are attempting to drill a hole in a wall in order to put up shelves: <S 01> secretary: female (31); <S 02> scientist: female(31); <S 03> unemployed: female (28); <S 04> production chemist (29); <S 03> and <S 04> are partners]

1   <S 03> Have you finished screwing it in then?

2   <S 02> [laughs] Well no. [unintelligible]

3   <S 03> [unintelligible] again.

4   <S 02> We've all had a go.

5   <S 04> Yeah. Go on you have a go.

6   <S 03> It's quite hard.

7   <S 02> It's it's getting there. You can do alternate turns but then your wrist starts to hurt.

8   <S 03> Mm.

9   [laughter]

10 [unintelligible]

11 <S 01> It's cos you can't get a foot in. If you could get a decent er lean on it.

12 <S 03> It doesn't happen fast enough for me.

13 [unintelligible]

14 <S 03> Ah. I can't move that at all. Am I exceptionally weak and crap?

15 <S 01> Yeah. It was just an exceptionally large screw for a small hole I think.

16 <S 02> Oh dear. I wouldn't wanna to do that.

17 [laughter]

18 <S 02> I'll heave it.

19 <S 01> It's not moving at all Margaret.

20 [unintelligible]

21 <S 03> We'll put this [unintelligible] away now and never touch it again.

22 [laughter]

The above example also illustrates how punning and wordplay are not unconnected with a lack of control or order. One sexual pun leads to another and a semantic flow is created by the participants in which language as it were takes over and becomes itself a main point of communicative reference. Such a process inverts rationalist assumptions that language use is wholly for ideational reference and for purposeful communication. The participants here are creating an alternative reality in which, albeit momentarily, representation takes over from reference. The event does not lead to increased knowledge on the part of the participants and the point of the exchange is not necessarily to prompt action or to transfer information. The laughter and obvious pleasure derived by the group as a result of the wordplay is sufficient justification for the event (see Chiaro, 1992; Cook, 1996,2000; Crystal, 1998). Similar claims have been made for the functions of gossip (Dunbar, 1996; Eggins and Slade, 1997: ch 7).

Creativity and formulaicness: the example of idioms

Several of the features noted in the data so far could be considered to be formulaic rather than creative. Formulaic language poses a particular problem for analysis because it appears to counter Chomskyan claims concerning the creative-generative human capacity for language production (Chomsky, 1964: 7-9). For Chomsky, the ability to create language forms that could not previously have been heard is part of a natural and universal endowment of the mind for creating language. The position we hold is that some language choices are more openly creative than others but that the potential exists in all uses, even the most formulaic, for making new formations, that the seemingly least open choices can also, as we hope to have shown, contribute to creative functioning, and that creativity, whether a universal component of the mind or not, operates for social and interactive purposes and not simply as an innate mentalistic reflex.

One particular aspect of creativity with idiomatic expressions in spoken discourse has been noted by McGlone, Glucksberg and Cacciari (1994) and more specifically by McCarthy (1998:117):

> Another noteworthy feature of idioms in everyday talk is the way speakers use them creatively by a process of 'unpacking' them into their literal elements and exploiting these, ... even in opaque idioms, literal meanings of component words are in some sense activated, or are at least potentially available.

A good example of this feature in CANCODE data involves part of a conversation between two schoolteachers who are reminiscing about former pupils and colleagues.

[Contextual information: two retired schoolteachers meeting at <S 02>'s house reminiscing about the times that they spent as teaching colleagues in the late 1960s. The speakers have known each other for over 25 years: <S 01> male (50s); <S 02> male (50s)]

> <S 01> The second year I had, I started off with 37 in the class I know that, of what you call dead wood the real dregs had been taken off the bottom and the cream the sour cream in our case up there had been creamed off the top and I just had this dead wood. I mean it really was and he was so impressed with the job that I did with them and the way that I got on with them and he immediately said right how do you feel about taking a special class next year and I took one from then on.
>
> <S 02> Rather you than me.

The first speaker begins with the metaphor of bottled liquid in which bad elements (*dregs*) fall to the bottom. The liquid metaphor is then extended to *cream* (which means the best and which floats to the top of the milk) which is then idiomatised into the phrase *sour cream* (meaning something unpleasant) and then further extended into the phrase *creamed off* (meaning to select the most worthwhile. The metaphor of liquids is then mixed with the idiom of *dead wood*, something which is of little value. The comments of the first teacher are then responded to by the second teacher with a more routinised fixed phrase *rather you than me* which evaluates what has just been said. There are naturally difficulties of overlap and unclear borderlines between fixed and unfixed and between metaphor and idiom in this extract. For example, to what extent is *dead wood* or for that matter *sour cream* or the reference to *dregs* metaphoric or idiomatic? But this instance does underline the extent to which in fixed expressions some component parts remain alive and open to pattern-reforming and innovative extension (for further examples see Carter, 1998a; McCarthy, 1998: ch 7; and for the affective functions of formulaic language in context, Cameron, 1999; Moon, 1998).

What has not yet been established in current research is how and why particular items are selected for metaphoric extension or for further play with ambiguity or how and why idioms vary in the way in which literal meanings are blocked. Giora (1999 and 1997:185) has suggested that there is a semantic core to some idioms which invokes a different comprehension process:

> If a word has meanings that can be retrieved directly from the lexicon, the meaning more popular, or prototypical or more frequently used in a certain community is more salient.

Such a suggestion may well lead us back to the notion of core vocabulary (see Carter, 1998b: ch 2; Stubbs, 1998) and to the fact that certain lexical items have a greater salience than others. Core vocabulary is vocabulary which plays a central communicative role, by means of its frequency, its perceptual and protypical functions or even because of its simplicity of structure. Initial corpus analysis in this area does suggest, for example, that words for parts of the body and basic perceptual processes are active in this kind of way. Corpus searches for words such as *back, head, arm, shoulder, head, eye, teeth, foot, heart,* together with *see, hear, talk, breathe* show how regularly such prototypical items enter into idiomatic form. For example:

> *catch someone's eye; keep an eye on; turn a blind eye to; eye up; eye to eye; to turn one's back on; back to back; to back out; to back up; to stab you in the back*

are all items which seem to invoke metonymic and metaphoric readings and can thus activate both literal and metaphoric interpretation and be open to creative pattern reformation (see also Goddard, 1996; Gibbs, 1994: ch 5; Tannen, 1989; Turner and Fauconnier, 1999).

Interlingual creativity and *crossings*

So far an impression has probably been created that that there is a kind of linguistic purity to these practices, that creativity and language play reside within a single language or that creativity is only triggered in monolingual contexts. However, bilingual and multilingual communities have been especially rich in the production of creative artefacts and there is some evidence to suggest that conditions of multilingualism may favour creative production.

Recent research by Rampton (1995) describes a phenomenon which he terms *crossings*, a feature of cross-lingual play and of creativity with language codes which is distinctively oral rather than written in mode. The specific focus of language crossing in Rampton's studies is centred on multi-racial urban adolescents in the South Midlands of Britain and concerns 'the use of Creole by adolescents of Asian and Anglo descent, the use of Panjabi by Anglos and Afro-Caribbeans and the use of stylised Indian English by all three' (Rampton, 1995). Rampton's study is in a tradition of sociolinguistics which explores the relationship between language and social roles, with particular reference to race and ethnicity. However, the data also goes a long way to illustrate the degree to which members of the groups studied engaged in crossing from one language to another as part of day-to-day exchanges. Other typical samples of data include contexts in which a fifteen-year-old Afro-Caribbean boy teases a classmate, a fifteen year old Asian girl, about her having an older boyfriend, by using stylised Asian English with marked Panjabi intonation in order to tease and encourage her to engage in playful banter.

Most instances found by Rampton involve the use of Creole and of Creole crossing. In Rampton's data Creole is much more extensively integrated by all speakers, indicating the extent to which it is symbolic of all that is valued in the culture shared by the adolescents in the study. In the following example, two boys, one Anglo (Alan) and one Asian (Asif), both aged fifteen are being held in detention at school. The extract shows them speaking with an Anglo female teacher, (Ms J) aged in her mid-twenties. She says why she is a little late for the supervision of the detention, explaining that she had to contact the headteacher and then why she now needs to go to fetch her lunch before the detention proper begins. The boys attempt to undermine and criticise her position by locking her into a sequence of question and answer. When she departs and the boys are left on their own, they mock her statements using a markedly Creole intonation, most markedly on the word 'lunch'.

Creative Crossings

Ms J:	I had to go and see the headmaster
Asif:	why
Ms J:	none of your business
Alan:	a-about us
Ms J:	no, I'll be back
Asif:	hey how can you see the headmaster when he was in dinner
Ms J:	that's precisely why I didn't see him
Asif:	what
Ms J:	I'll be back in a second with my lunch
Asif:	NO, dat's sad man I'll be... I had to miss my play right I've gotta go
Alan:	with mine
Asif:	**LL**unch.. You don't need no...
Alan:	**Ll**unch....
Asif:	have you eat your lunch Alan

These creative mixes indicate an underlying artistry in the appropriate handling of two voices. However, the resulting hybrid discourse is not creative simply for its own sake. In many of Rampton's examples this double-voicing is put to social use either for the purpose of criticism, for banter and verbal duelling which reinforces group values and affiliations or simply to express identities and values which are separate from the dominant discourses and which could not be altogether articulated within the domain of single voice (see also Bauman and Briggs, 1990). In many cases the choices are creative choices and the speakers learn to make the choices; but the choices are not merely aesthetic – they are socially and culturally motivated.

The significance of the relationship between creative communication, language crossing and more intimate speech genres is further evidenced in a sub-corpus of emails and IRC [Internet Relay Chat] data collected in Nottingham as a supplement to the CANCODE corpus. Several thousand emails and several hours of IRC data (Fung, 2003; Gillen and Goddard, 2000) on a variety of topics are being collected in order to examine the continua between planned and un-planned discourse, the interpenetration of spoken discourse features into written text (Baron, 2000; Cherny, 1999) as well as the creativity manifest in these more informal, mixed-mode forms of communication (Crystal, 2001). The data collected by Fung also illustrate the extent to which different languages can be creatively combined. The resulting hybrid is written rather than spoken but, as in the manner of much email discourse, is sufficiently informal, pervasive and everyday to count as demotic. In the following IRC example transliterated Cantonese, text-messaging shorthand and English are used to mark out an interpersonal territory in which emotion and affect are expressed in a private discourse in which form and the meaning of form are overtly played with. The two writer/speakers (W/S0) are girls and are both undergraduate students at the University of Nottingham, England <W/S01> is 21 years old; <W/S02> is 22 years old.

Viki:	it=s snowing quite strong outside....be careful
Sue:	I will, thx
Viki:	wei wei...lei dim ar?
Sue:	ok, la, juz got bk from Amsterdam loh, how r u?
Viki:	ok la.. I have 9 tmrw
Sue:	haha, I have 2-4 ....soooooooooooo happy
Viki:	che...anyway...have your rash gone?
Sue:	yes, but I have scar oh...ho ugly ar!
Viki:	icic...ng gan yiu la...still a pretty girl, haha!!

[Cantonese translations: *wei wei...lei dim ar* – hi, how are you?; *ng gan yiu la* – it doesn't matter; *ar* and *la* are discourse markers in Cantonese]

Some may argue that such a discourse underlines the irreversible decline of standard English into a series of mutually unintelligible sub-languages; another way of seeing such exchanges is, however, to observe the richness and invention of which everyday users of English are capable and to praise the creative invention which results from the mixing. An even stronger interpretation would be to recognise the clear need the two girls have to appropriate a language which is not just English but their own English and, for them, to develop a repertoire of mixed codes which enable them to give expression to their feelings of friendship, intimacy and involvement with each others' feelings and attitudes – a discourse which would not be available to them to the same degree through the medium of standard English. Here there is no overt expression of social critique as in the crossings into Creole made by many of the adolescent speakers captured by Rampton. But there is nonetheless an implicit recognition that standard English has no clear value for them for the purposes of daily intimate email exchange and accordingly new modes of speaking/writing are invented and developed.

As we continue to investigate all the above data, we acknowledge that we are interpreting the data as outsiders, ascribing to participants particular intentions, assigning to stretches of language particular functions and framing accounts of effects and of emotional contours which may not accord with the value systems of participants. But we also acknowledge the provisional nature of all interpretations of language use; even participants' own accounts of intentions and responses fall foul of a circular dialectic of relativity and intentionality. We also accept that categories of description are provisional and that at this stage the analysis is necessarily largely qualitative rather than quantitative. We also accept that we have not yet fully investigated relationships between the gender of the speaker and their interaction with creative utterances.[1]

Conclusion

Corpus-based research into spoken discourse underlines the extent and significance of creativity in a range of encounters and for a range of functions; the research so far reinforces the relative narrowness of investigations based solely on written text. Evidence from a naturally-occurring five-million word corpus of spoken English reveals an interplay of complex patterns and choices, a clustering of features and a density of creative language forms relative to particular speech genres and particular social contexts. Indeed, preliminary research so far has suggested that creativity is more likely to occur in certain social contexts rather than others; notice for example that in the above examples creativity is more pervasive in informal 'socialising' and 'intimate' contexts such as 'collaborative idea' or 'collaborative task' where there is a more distinctly symmetrical and equal relationship between speakers. Such hypotheses will be tested further on a wider range of data. Evidence also suggests that theories of creativity within cognitive psychology which are rooted in studies of specially gifted individuals or theories based on timeless or autonomous aesthetic values are limited (see Gardner, 1993).

We are already beginning to conclude that creativity is more of an everyday phenomenon than is normally assumed and that it is not simply a capacity of special people but also a special capacity of all people. Creative language in spoken discourse does not exist wholly as written, aesthetic presentation but it exists for social and critical-social purposes in speech too; it is often co-produced and regularly emergent from particular interpersonal and affective platforms. Our provisional findings are beginning to force us to re-consider the instances and contexts to which we conventionally ascribe words such as literary creativity.

Notes on transcription:

Transcription convention for:	Symbol	Explanation
Speaker codes	<S 01>, <S 02>, etc.	Each speaker is numbered <S 01>, <S 02>, etc.
Extralinguistic information	[ ]	This includes things like laughter, coughing and inaudible speech on the tape.
Interrupted sentence	+	These instances are marked by a + at the point of where one speaker's utterance is interrupted and are followed by another + when the speaker resumes his or her utterance:
		<S 01> I think I would like+
		<S 02> Right.
		<S 03> + to teach.
		These interruptions may overlap with the previous speaker's utterance or occupy an individual turn after which the interrupted speaker resumes his or her turn. Or: These interruptions occupy turns by themselves and do not overlap with the utterance that has been interrupted.
Back-channel	( )	Back-channel items tend to overlap with the turn of the current speaker and are therefore inserted into his or her utterance, e.g.:
		<S 01> I think I would like (<S 02> Right) to teach.

Transcription convention for:	Symbol	Explanation
Unfinished words	=	Speakers not only change their course in mid-sentence but also in the middle of individual words which has been marked as follows:
		<S 01> I wouldn't ha=, I wouldn't have thought so.
Punctuation	. ? ,	A full stop or question mark is used to mark the end of a sentence (depending on intonation). 'Sentences' are anything felt to be a complete utterance, such as:
		<S 01> What did you think of the film?
		<S 02> Lovely.
		'Lovely' is considered as a sentence here.
		Unfinished sentences are not followed by a full stop.
		A comma indicates that the speaker has re-cast what he/she was saying, e.g.:
		<S 01> I bet, is that supposed to be straight?
		These include false starts.

Notes

1   We are grateful to Janet Maybin for the observations that female speakers in our data sometimes use creatively marked language as a means to break into male-dominated talk. We are also currently exploring how non-literal hyperbolic speech acts such 'Why don't you just cut my throat?' are used for humorous effect and how these speech acts are distributed according to different social and gender roles.

References

Baron, N. (2000) *Alphabet to Email: How written English evolved and where it's heading*. London: Routledge

Bauman, R. and Briggs, C.L. (1990) 'Poetics and performance as critical perspectives on language and social life' *Annual Review of Anthropology*, 19: 59-88

Cameron, L. (1999) 'Identifying and describing metaphor in spoken discourse data', in L. Cameron and G. Low (eds) *Researching and Applying Metaphor*. Cambridge: CUP, 105-133

Carter, R. (1998a) 'Common Language: corpus, creativity and cognition', *Language and Literature*, 8, 3: 195-216

Carter, R. (1998b) *Vocabulary: Applied Linguistic Perspectives* (2nd ed). Routledge: London

Carter, R. and McCarthy, M. (1995a) 'Grammar and the spoken language', *Applied Linguistics*, 16, 2: 141-158

Carter, R. and McCarthy, M. (1995b) 'Discourse and creativity: Bridging the gap between language and literature', in G. Cook and B. Seidlhofer (eds) *Principle and Practice in Applied Linguistics*. Oxford: Oxford University Press, 303-323

Carter, R. and McCarthy, M. (1997) *Exploring Spoken English*. Cambridge: Cambridge University Press

Cherny, L . (1999) *Conversation and Community: Chat in a Virtual World*. Stanford, CSLI Publications

Chiaro, D. (1992) *The Language of Jokes: Analysing Verbal Play*. Routledge, London

Chomsky, N. (1964) *Current Issues in Linguistic Theory*. The Hague: Mouton

Cook, G. (1996) 'Language Play in English', in J. Maybin and N. Mercer (eds) *Using English: From Conversation to Canon*. London: Routledge, 198-234

Cook, G. (2000) *Language Play, Language Learning*. Oxford: Oxford University Press

Crystal, D. (1998) *Language Play*. Harmondsworth: Penguin

Crystal, D. (2001) *Language and the Internet*. Cambridge University Press, Cambridge

Dunbar, R. (1996) *Grooming, Gossip and the Evolution of Language*. London and Boston: Faber

Eggins, S. and Slade, D. (1997) *Analysing Casual Conversation*. London: Cassell

Fung, L. (2003) From Discourse Markers to Hong Kong English. Unpublished PhD dissertation, School of English Studies, University of Nottingham

Gardner, H. (1993) *Creating Minds: an anatomy of creativity as seen through the lives of Freud, Einstein, Picasso, Stravinsky, Eliot, Graham and Gandhi*. London: Harper Collins

Gibbs, R.W. (1994) *The Poetics of Mind: Figurative thought, language and understanding*. Cambridge: Cambridge University Press

Gillen, J and Goddard, A. (2000) 'Is there anybody out there?': creative language play and 'literariness' in internet relay chat (IRC)' mimeo, Centre for language and Communication, Manchester: Manchester Metropolitan University

Giora, R.(1999) 'On the priority of salient meanings: Studies of literal and figurative language.' *Journal of Pragmatics*, 31: 919-29

Goddard, A. (1996) 'Tall stories: The metaphorical nature of everyday talk.' *English in Education* 30, 2: 4-12

McCarthy, M. (1998) *Spoken Language and Applied Linguistics*. Cambridge: Cambridge University Press

McGlone, M.S., Glucksberg, S. and Cacciari, C. (1994) 'Semantic productivity and idiom comprehension.' *Discourse Processes,* 17, 169-190

Moon, R. (1998) *Fixed Expressions and Idioms*. Oxford: Clarendon Press

Nash, W. and Stacey, D. (1997) *Creating Texts*. Harlow: Longman

Nash, W. (1998) *Language and Creative Illusion*. Harlow: Longman

Rampton, B. (1995) *Crossing: Language and Ethnicity among Adolescents* Harlow: Longman.

Stubbs, M . (1998) 'A note on phraseological tendencies in the core vocabulary of English' *Studia Anglica Posnaniensia,* vol. 23: 399-410

Tannen, D. (1989) *Talking Voices: Repetition, dialogue and imagery in conversational discourse*. Cambridge: Cambridge University Press

Turner, M. and Fauconnier, G. (1999) 'A mechanism of creativity.' *Poetics Today* 20, 3: 397-418

CHAPTER 18
A new communication order: researching literacy practices in the network society
Ilana Snyder

Introduction

In the Prologue to *The Rise of the Network Society*, Manuel Castells argues that:

> a new communication system, increasingly speaking a universal, digital language is both integrating globally the production and distribution of words, sounds and images of our culture, and customising them to the tastes and identities and moods of individuals. Interactive computer networks are growing exponentially, creating new forms and channels of communication, shaping life and being shaped by life at the same time. (Castells, 1996: 2)

This new communication system, centred around information technologies, is part of the technological revolution that is reshaping the material bases of society.

Much has been said and written about the technological revolution and its implications for education. Discussions, however, are often clouded by hype. Enthusiasts openly embrace the technologies, claiming they offer a panacea for educational problems, enhance communication, empower users and democratise classrooms. By contrast, demonisers express cynicism about the technologies' apparent powers, either dismissing them as new instructional and communication tools or rejecting them as yet a further form of social control or enforced consumption, which promotes the interests of the state and the corporate sectors. Clearly, extreme responses and entrenched positions are of limited use in education, and the need to move beyond them increasingly urgent. But there is one response that is indisputable: the new technologies have altered everyday modes of communication and are becoming so fundamental to society that most areas of life have been affected.

The upshot is that in a world increasingly mediated by information and communication technologies, literacy researchers cannot afford to ignore the implications of their use for literacy practices. Labbo and Reinking (1999:486) go so far as to suggest that literacy 'researchers who fail to acknowledge issues of technology in their work may have to face the reality that their findings... may seem outdated, incomplete or irrelevant'. In the diverse field of language and literacy education, the challenge for research is to extend and enhance understanding of the ways in which the use of new technologies influences, shapes, even transforms, literacy practices. Researchers need to investigate the nature of the changes and to find illuminating ways to theorise them that are useful for teachers.

* First published in *Language and Education*, 2001, 15,2/3, 117-131.

At the risk of sounding glib, teachers also need to understand the changes so that they can learn how to use the new technologies efficiently, ethically and responsibly with a view to tapping their educational potential. But this is not to ignore the enormous pressure many teachers are now under – and not just to technologise learning. Unfortunately, the incursion of new technologies into schools coincides with many other things. These include an intensification of teachers' work, concerted attacks on teachers' conditions, and the openness with which interested groups conspire to undermine confidence in public schools by manufacturing successive 'crises' in school performance. Moreover, there is also a broad-based assault on schools which is designed to lay the ground for corporatising education and opening it up as a new frontier for business activity and entrepreneurship (Robertson, 1998). It seems that the push to technologise education is intimately tied up with interests most eager to undermine the tradition of public education. More than ever, teachers need 'to ensure that education remains the main game and that technologies, new or old, remain faithfully in the service of that main game' (Lankshear and Snyder, 2000: xvi).

Features of the New Communication Order

Increasingly, attention in the New Literacy Studies (NLS) – independent yet linked work produced over the past 20 or so years across a number of disciplines including anthropology, history, psychology and sociolinguistics (Graff, 1979; Scribner and Cole, 1981; Heath, 1983; Street, 1984) – has been directed towards the understanding that there is a need to move beyond narrowly defined accounts of literacy to ones that capture the complexity of real literacy practices in contemporary society. Literacy needs to be conceived within a broader social order, what Street and others have called a 'new communicative order' (Kress and van Leeuwen, 1996; Lankshear, 1997; Street, 1998). The emergence of this new order is directly associated with the development of an electronic communication system characterised by 'its global reach, its integration of all communication media, and its potential interactivity' (Castells, 1996: 329).

In particular, this new communication order takes account of the literacy practices associated with screen-based technologies – widely known as computer-mediated communication. It recognises that reading and writing practices, conceived traditionally as print-based and logocentric, are only part of what people have to learn to be literate. Now, for the first time in history, the written, oral and audiovisual modalities of communication are integrated into the same electronic system – multimodal hypertext systems made accessible via the Internet and the World Wide Web. Being literate in the context of these technologies is to do with understanding how the different modalities are combined in complex ways to create meaning.

The Internet is a complex network of networked computers that can convey all kinds of messages, including sound, images and data. And within the global communication networks provided by the Internet, the World Wide Web provides a flexible network of networks 'where institutions, businesses, associations and individuals create their own 'sites' on the basis of which everybody with access can produce their own 'home page' made of a variable collage of text and images' (Castells, 1996: 355). Significantly, the question of access to the new communication system should not be passed over lightly. Unlike television, computer-mediated communication is not a general medium and will not be for a long time. It is the medium of communication for the most educated and affluent countries and within those countries, primarily for the most educated and affluent groups. So although computer-mediated communication is radically altering communication practices, the changes are developing in what Castells calls 'concentric waves, starting from the higher levels of education and wealth, and probably unable to reach large segments of the uneducated masses and poor countries' (p.360).

The use of the Internet and the Web has significant implications for communication practices noticeable in a number of domains (Snyder, 1997). Social relations are considerably affected, as in e-mail, online discussion groups and chatrooms. Virtual communities – electronic networks of communication organised around shared interests – are formed, providing new fora for communication (Rheingold, 1993). More specifically, class, race and gender relations are affected. For example, it seems that women and members of non-white male middle-class groups are more likely to express themselves openly through the protection of the electronic medium. Some argue that computer-mediated communication could offer a chance to reverse traditional power relationships in communication practices. By contrast, others argue that there is enough accumulated knowledge about the social uses of technology to know that people tend to adapt the new technology to meet their needs. Rather than creating radically new patterns, computer-mediated communication is more likely to reinforce existing patterns of social practice (McConaghy and Snyder, 2000). It seems that further exploration of these complex issues is required.

In the new structures of communication, the social practices related to work, education, home and entertainment are becoming increasingly blurred. Nicholas Negroponte (1996: 221), one of the creators of multimedia and a well-known enthusiast for new technologies, predicts that 'tomorrow people of all ages will find a more harmonious continuum in their lives, because, increasingly, the tools to work with and the toys to play with will be the same. There will be a more common palette for love and duty, for self-expression and group work'. Predictably, Negroponte puts a positive spin on the convergence of social practices that he anticipates. By contrast, Chuck Darrah, a cultural anthropologist, who has made a study of the people working and living in Silicon Valley, describes a more sinister world. It is a world of frenetic lifestyles, of constant connectedness: via beepers, cell phones and wireless modems; a world in which corporate rhetoric is seeping into the home-life vernacular: a child is asked by his father to assess the 'value-added' of going fishing (Schonfeld, 2000).

Although, at this point in time, the overwhelming proportion of computer-mediated communication takes place at work or in work-related situations, it seems that progressively, the computer will connect work, education, home and entertainment, which were once more or less discrete domains of social practice, into the same system of communication. This convergence of experience in the same medium may serve to blur the institutional separation of these particular domains of activity. A further consequence may be that codes of social behaviour will become more hybridised or perhaps more confused (Castells, 1996). Whether the impact is positive or negative – in Negroponte's view 'more harmonious', in Castell's 'more confused' – it is clear that under the new communication regime, the main social institutions are beginning to articulate with each other in very complex ways. This poses dilemmas for language and literacy educators and for students in current school settings for which there are not yet clear resolutions. To what extent will work, home, school and entertainment all be connected into the same system of symbol processing? To what extent does the particular context determine the perceptions and uses of the medium? Of course, these dilemmas need to be understood if language and literacy education is to serve the young people of today and tomorrow.

'The turn to the visual' also represents a significant change associated with computer-mediated communication as to how meanings are made. Certain developments in technology – electronic text and data processing and reproduction, image and colour reproduction, and layout practices – are all making the shift from the verbal to the visual possible. A direct consequence is that the visual is becoming more prominent in many domains of public communication. But the shift from verbal to visual language cannot be attributed only to the increased use of the new technologies – it has profound social and political causes such as changes to the global economy and the growth of multiculturalism (Kress, 1995). Indeed, 'the globalisation of mass media makes the visual a seemingly more accessible medium, certainly more accessible than any particular language' (Kress, 1995:48). Visual language can move across cultural and linguistic distinctions with greater ease than verbal language. This is not to argue that images are devoid of cultural specificity. The point is that in many situations, visual communication is more likely than verbal to be effective.

However, probably the most significant feature of the new communication order is that many kinds of messages are communicated within the same hypertext or multimedia system such as the Web: 'they capture within their domain most cultural expressions, in all their diversity' (Castells, 1996: 372). There is no longer a clear separation between audiovisual media and printed media, popular culture and high culture, entertainment and education, information and knowledge. Everything – 'from the worst to the best, from the most elitist to the most popular' (Castells, 1996: 372) – comes together in this electronic world. What is created is a new symbolic environment: a 'multifaceted semantic context made of a random mixture of various meanings' (Castells, 1996: 371).

As computing power increases, the potential of the Internet and, in particular, the Web is accelerating. Without doubt there are possible benefits for education and there are many advocates for the wiring of schools. The reality, however, is a communication system that is predominantly dedicated to the construction of access to commercial sites where tele-gambling and pornography predominate. Business interests have controlled the first stages of the development of the Web, despite the dreams of visionaries such as Ted Nelson who, in the mid-1960s, imagined a time when all the 'texts' in the world would be available electronically to all people in all places via a universal supertext (Nelson, 1992; Snyder, 1996). It may be that these early uses of the technologies for commercial purposes shape the social possibilities of the new communication media for the future, thereby limiting their educational usefulness.

But even if commercial interests continue to dominate the Web, the multimodal formations in which the verbal and the visual are combined in new ways represent different kinds of texts and invite different kinds of literacy practices. On the whole, the multimodality made possible by the new communication system has been culturally overlooked. The new texts are often approached through ways of seeing conceived in an older mode of communication. People of a certain age who are products of a print generation have been shaped by print-based understandings of literacy. Unlike the younger generation, they do not feel altogether at ease in virtual environments. For them, images are more often than not thought of as illustrations – even when they fill the entire page or screen and constitute the major mode of communication (Kress, 1997; Snyder, 2001). By contrast, young people who regularly use the Web have a different understanding of images. Their homepages, for example, suggest that images are treated not simply as illustrations; rather, they are integral to the ways in which meanings are made.

Theoretical work that begins to examine facets of multimodality provides useful frameworks within which language and literacy educators might consider the cultural significance of the new media. In the book, *Remediation: Understanding New Media*, Bolter and Grusin (1999) present their theory of 'remediation' which offers an explanation of the complex ways in which old and new media interact. They contend that the new media achieve their cultural significance by paying homage to, rivalling and refashioning earlier media such as perspective painting, photography, film and television. They call this process of refashioning 'remediation' and note that earlier media have also refashioned one another: photography remediated painting, film remediated stage production and photography, and television remediated film, vaudeville and radio. Accessing audiovisual, news, education and entertainment shows on the same medium even from different sources blurs the distinctions between the contexts in which each originated. Castells makes a similar point when he explains how different media borrow codes from each other so that 'interactive educational programs look like video games; newscasts are constructed as audiovisual shows; trial cases are broadcast as soap operas; pop music is composed for MTV' (Castells, 1996: 371).

Other theoretical approaches are also useful for teachers in their encounters with multimodality. Kress and van Leeuwen's (1996) book, *Reading Images: The Grammar of Visual Design*, provides a systematic account of the ways in which images communicate meaning. The authors examine how visual depictions of people, places and things are combined into a meaningful whole. It seems that the time is ripe for a book that concentrates on the grammar of multimodal texts: a theoretical examination of the grammar of verbal-visual-audio language: how words, images and sounds combine to create multimodal statements of greater and lesser complexity and extension. Kress and van Leeuwen's *Multimodal Discourse* (2001) may fill this gap.

Discussion of the connections between verbal, visual and aural modes of representation provoke some important questions about the changes to literacy practices and formations associated with multimodal texts. Are graphics and video as informative as, or even more informative than, verbal text? Is it possible to determine whether the image, the sound or the word is the principal carrier of meaning in the text? How do the words, pictures and sound interact to make meaning? How are the ambiguities created by that interaction recognised and interpreted? The integration of video, film and still photography into the computer means that it is necessary to understand the aesthetic differences between these media and, in particular, how those differences might affect the ways in which meanings are made.

In the new communication order, where words, images and sound all play an important role, people are now required to link communication practices from one domain such as print-based literacy with those of another such as visual images. The implications for language education is that teachers should be attending to the whole spectrum of communication practices and communicative competence no longer ignoring the skills involved in relating them to each other.

Altered social practices, the blurring of the boundaries between significant social institutions, the growing importance of the visual in communication, and the increasing significance of multimodal communication systems: these then are some of the salient features of the new communication order. The material and cultural conditions of the new communication order provide a context for the overview of research in the field of literacy and technology studies which follows.

Literacy and Technology Studies: emerging understandings of literacy as social practice

Integral to the New Literacy Studies (NLS) are 'approaches to language and literacy that treat them as social practices and resources rather than as a set of rules formally and narrowly defined' (Street, 1998: 1). These social practices and resources are 'embedded in specific contexts, discourses and positions' (Street, 1996:1). The NLS reject the dominant view of literacy as a 'neutral' technical skill, conceptualising it instead as 'an ideological practice, implicated in power relations and embedded in specific cultural meanings and practices' (Street, 1995: 1). The fine-grained accounts of the social uses of literacy in a range of contexts in post-apartheid South Africa reported in Prinsloo and Breir's (1996) *The Social Uses of Literacy* and the rich description of how people use literacy in their day-to-day lives in a particular community in Britain presented in Barton and Hamilton's (1998) *Local Literacies* are remarkable examples of this approach. In the field of literacy and technology studies, similarly textured reports also did not appear till the mid to late 1990s. However, by the mid-1980s researchers, examining the educational impact of the use of new technologies and associated changes to literacy practices, began to pay attention to social context.

Following a decade of research dominated by a plethora of quasi-experimental studies that set out to determine whether the use of computers 'enhanced' writing and in the main drew upon accounts of literacy somewhat narrowly conceived, by the mid-1980s understandings of literacy as social practice became more widely accepted. Some researchers shifted the focus from the isolated writer to the writer in context; some began to explore the possibilities of the computer as a site for the social construction of knowledge. With this increased sensitivity to the social setting in which the computers were used, studies became more distinctively qualitative (Dickinson, 1986; Herrmann, 1987). More recent studies have adopted multiple perspectives which draw on methods from both quantitative and qualitative traditions, while others examine computer-mediated literacies through a particular ideological lens such as feminism. It would be a mistake, however, to represent the three decades of research in literacy and technology studies as a process of evolution. Each of the earlier waves is still operating in the present as a set of practices that researchers follow or argue against.

The social approach to computers and their use made gender issues central to discussions of technology (Kramarae, 1988). Early research on computers and gender focused on women's exclusion from the computer revolution (Gerrard, 1999). Women and girls of the 1980s and 1990s were found to be anxious about computers (Collis, 1985; Gerrard, 1999); unchallenged by the unstimulating assignments and lack of hands-on experience they received in school (Levin and Gordon, 1989); discouraged from pursuing a career in technology (Abtan, 1993); and stereotyped in advertising as phobics (Hawkins, 1985).

By contrast with the studies which exposed women's problems of access to computers and computer culture, research has also examined gender from a broader perspective. Studies have suggested ways to inform the computer-based classroom with feminist pedagogy (Selfe, 1990); considered the computer conference as a medium that promotes or shuts out women's voices (Flores, 1990; Romano, 1993); and investigated girls' use of the Internet (Kaplan and Farrell, 1994). The most contemporary studies take account of the factors that have alienated women from computer technology, but focus more on 'how gender influences what men and women are doing with computers and what this technology is doing for them' (Gerrard, 1999:1).

More generally, there was a growing recognition that computers in classrooms appear 'unlikely to negate the powerful influence of the differential socialisation of students by social class and its effects on their success or failure in school' (Herrmann, 1987: 86). In fact, the contrary may be the case. It may be that computers in classrooms make the impact of students' differential socialisation and enculturation experiences more severe. For example, a Scandinavian study shows that adolescent girls are rejecting computers in disproportionate numbers, presumably because of their lack of sympathy for the control ideology that drives the construction and invention of computers, and because of the obstacle to quality interaction between people that they may erect (Staberg, 1994).

Increasingly, researchers examined computer-mediated communication (CMC). Researchers observed that the electronic spaces in which writers and readers can create, exchange, and comment on texts have the potential for supporting student-centred learning and discursive practices that can be different in form, and, some claim, more engaging and democratic than those in traditional classrooms (Batson, 1988).

More recently, the Internet has become a site for research. Informed by the understanding of literacy as a set of social practices, located in the interactions between people, new literacy practices (Burbules, 1997; Sorapure *et al.,* 1998; Burbules and Callister, 2000); issues of identity (Turkle, 1995; Alexander, 1997); class and access (Castner, 1997; Richardson, 1997; Grabill, 1998); and the maleness of the Web (Takayoshi *et al.*, 1999) have been the focus of investigations. Research has emphasised the need to teach students how to assess the reliability or value of the information they find on the Web by understanding not only its textual but also its non-textual features such as images, links and interactivity (Burbules and Callister, 2000).

The Digital Rhetorics Project

Digital Rhetorics exemplifies the shift towards research in the area of literacy and technology studies informed by the understanding of literacy as social practice. The two-year Australian study investigated the relationship between literacy and technology in teaching and learning (Lankshear *et al.*, 1997; Lankshear and Snyder, 2000). It focused on four main elements:

- the development of a theoretical position to inform the approach to the study as a whole

- a study of selected key policy documents concerned with teaching and learning in relation to literacy, technology and learning

- an investigation of technology and literacy practices in a range of learning contexts, mainly primary and secondary classrooms

- the articulation of a set of recommendations resulting from the investigations.

The project was conducted by a research consortium, with members from New South Wales, Queensland, Victoria and Western Australia, under the joint leadership of Colin Lankshear and Chris Bigum. It was funded by the Department of Education, Employment, Training and Youth Affairs through the Children's Literacy National Projects Program. As it is impossible to do justice to all four aspects of the study here, attention is given to the two components relevant to the focus of this article: the 'three-dimensional' theoretical approach to literacy and technology that informed the project and the findings of the empirical investigation. A complete report of the study is presented in *Teachers and Technoliteracy: Managing Literacy, Technology and Learning* (Lankshear and Snyder, 2000).

In the Digital Rhetorics project, being literate is seen as more than the capacity to encode and decode – to grasp meanings inscribed on a page or a screen or within an established social practice (Street, 1984). Being literate also involves the capacity and disposition to scrutinise the practices and universes of meanings within which texts are embedded. Being literate entails the capability to enter actively into creating, shaping and transforming social practices and universes of meanings (Lankshear and Snyder, 2000).

The study argues that in the context of increasing and changing demands for literacy and technology learning worldwide, education must enable students to become proficient in the 'operational', 'cultural' and 'critical' dimensions of literacy and technology – a formulation originally developed by Green (1988). The 'operational' dimension of literacy education, as it involves new technologies, focuses on how to operate the language system as well as on how to operate the technology system. With respect to the language system, this involves learning how to make it work for individuals' own meaning-making purposes. With respect to the technology system, it involves learning how to make a computer operational, how to 'turn it on' and make it 'work'.

Understanding and being able to draw upon the 'cultural' dimension of literacy involves realising that the ability to operate language and technology systems is always in the service of participating in 'authentic' forms of social practice and meaning. People always use texts and technologies to do things in the world, and to achieve their own and others' purposes, whether in the context of school, work or everyday life. This means putting the emphasis on authentic contexts, forms and purposes, and of learning along the axes of literacy and technology and text and information.

The 'critical' dimension means that teachers and students need to be able to assess and evaluate software and other technology resources (Lankshear and Snyder, 2000). That is, they need the ability not only to use such resources and to participate effectively and creatively in their associated cultures, but also to critique them, to read and use them against the grain, to appropriate and even re-design them, as well as to be able to actively envisage and contribute to transforming social practices as they judge appropriate.

Most importantly, understanding the 'operational', 'cultural' and 'critical' dimensions suggested to the Digital Rhetorics team how to frame research questions for the empirical component of the study about the changes to literacy practices associated with the use of new technologies. In opposition to reductionist and mechanistic views of literacy and learning, the study focused not simply on 'how-to' knowledge, understood as technical competence and 'functional literacy'. Instead, it sought research knowledge that is contextualised in ways that pays due attention to matters of culture, history and power, and which recognises that it is counter-productive to start with issues of 'skill' or 'technique' outside of an 'authentic' context of situated social practice (Lankshear and Snyder, 2000).

The Site Studies
The aim in the site studies was to research, describe and analyse practices in a range of exemplars. Exemplars did not necessarily represent best practice in the sense of ideals to be emulated, although some of the sites did approximate to this meaning. Instead, the exemplars represented informative and illuminating examples of what was going on in learning on an everyday basis, across a range of circumstances, policy and resourcing arrangements and professional knowledge bases.

The classroom portraits the study produced describe diverse models and circumstances that colour instances of current practice. The portraits drew on brief, but intensive and highly focused, investigations of eleven research sites – 20 teachers, who agreed to participate in the project, and their classrooms – in three Australian states. Selection of sites drew on advice from personnel in state education departments, and on the local knowledge and professional development connections of the investigators. A range of geographical locations were represented: inner city suburbs, outer city suburbs, satellite cites, regional towns and small settlements in rural areas. Classrooms from lower primary to upper secondary were covered. Key Learning Areas were English, Technology, Studies of Society and the Environment, Science, Maths and the Arts.

The aim was to witness, capture and describe a range of illuminating instances of practice using new technologies in literacy education. In most cases, data were collected over just three or four days. These data included contextual or background information; artefacts (for example, policy documents and statements, lists of technology resources, descriptions of student work); audio-tapes and transcripts of interviews; and observation notes. The emphasis was on finding and describing illustrative instances of practice – particular events or episodes that were likely to be similar to other events and episodes, both at that site and at others. The focus of the analysis and interpretation of the data was on what the descriptions suggested about how to achieve what were judged to be effective practices and outcomes.

Consequently, the investigations were not exhaustive of all that went on in the sites. Neither do the portraits claim to be representative of practice as a whole in these sites, still less of schools at large. Practices were described to illustrate significant points about literacy, technology and learning. The aim was to use portraits of classroom activities for illustrative purposes. The ideas emerging from classroom portraits were then linked to larger patterns and principles which were intended to enhance future practice on a more extensive scale.

A template was developed for writing the sites studies. The components were: the study at a glance; the site; the policy context; the practice; distinctive features; and issues and implications. Detailed accounts of each site were produced. Data from different collection sources – policy documents and other artefacts, interview material, observations – were 'triangulated' both across different episodes within single sites and between different sites. Consistencies across these variables increased confidence in the data collected.

Five broad patterns – 'complexity', 'fragility', 'discontinuity', 'conservation' and 'limited authenticity' – were identified. In addition, the data were analysed in terms of five principles: 'teachers first', 'complementarity', 'workability', 'equity' and 'focus on trajectories'. These patterns and principles were useful for making sense of the site studies; making decisions and judgments about various aspects of what was seen; and helping to formulate concrete recommendations for future actions.

Relatively little critical emphasis was evident in the sessions observed across the entire project. This may indicate the extent to which classroom practices involving new technologies are being exhausted on merely getting to grips with the operational dimensions. If this is what is happening, it is perfectly understandable, given the relatively limited prior experience many teachers have with information and communication technologies. But it reinforces the importance of attending to all the patterns and principles identified in the study within future policy directions, teacher education programmes and professional development initiatives.

Future Directions

The research agenda is rich with possibilities. In this section, a number of suggestions for further research that will extend understanding of the new communication order are presented, acknowledging that the ideas are by no means exhaustive. The challenge is to devise research initiatives that will inform effective practice, mediated by new information and communication technologies, at all levels of education.

Digital Rhetorics was essentially a qualitative study with the researchers visiting sites, often for just three or four days, and describing, then interpreting what they observed. Schools, classrooms and teachers grappling with literacy, technology and learning, however, also provide a site for practical intervention. A study in which teachers and researchers collaborate to implement the recommendations that emerged from the project, evaluate what happens, then refine the recommendations for further implementation could result in enhanced administrative and pedagogical practices.

It would be salutary to concentrate on students who have grown up with the technologies. A longitudinal approach to the study of young people immersed in computer culture will yield new understandings of computer-mediated literacy practices. As students represent a different generation, one with a different relationship to computers and to print text, researchers must observe them, ask them questions and listen to their responses.

Attention needs to be directed towards the intersection between multiple languages and the multiple modalities of the new technologies. There are many schools in which the presence of multiple languages is inescapable both inside and outside classrooms. At the same time, there are also tensions around attempts to legislate English as the dominant or sole language of instruction and commerce. Research could investigate the place of multilingualism and multiculturalism in the new communication order.

Issues of access and equity can no longer be ignored by researchers. Moran (1999) points out that those working in schools and universities know that there are the 'haves' and 'have nots' and that the situation seems to be getting worse. It is also widely understood that the overriding factor in determining who gets access and who does not is wealth: the *per capita* funding of a given school, college or university and the income level of the student's family/caregivers determine the likelihood that a given student will have access, at school and/or at home to the new technologies. Much of Comber's (1997) research in Australia has focused on literacy, disadvantage and school education. Also in Australia, Snyder and Angus (2000) have initiated a study of home and school technology-mediated communication practices in low socioeconomic communities. Although the study is not placing greater value on schooled literacies, it recognises the power issues associated with access to standard linguistic and literacy conventions (Gee, 1996). The study aims to produce a textured, micro-account of the computer-mediated communication practices in which children engage that can explain the link between social factors and school success. The need for further research investigating the complex relationships between literacy, new technologies and disadvantage is manifest.

An important aspect of the new communication order requiring further investigation is the increasing dominance of images. Research projects aimed at investigating the relationships between the verbal and the visual in communication and representation would also provide opportunities to examine at close hand new literacy practices in real contexts: to observe teachers and students, to discuss the emerging computer-mediated communication practices with them, and to apply to those practices understandings which draw on the work of theorists such as Bolter (1998), Kress (1997), Kress and van Leeuwen (1996), Lemke (1997), Reinking (1998) and Bolter and Grusin (1999).

Conclusion

This article has argued that the use of new information and communication technologies has significant implications for literacy practices (Snyder, 1997, 2001), so much so that a new communication order is emerging. With the changes associated with the use of the new technologies, language and literacy educators are beginning to take account of the increasingly blurred boundaries between different areas of knowledge and different theoretical perspectives. To regard 'literacy and technology studies' and 'media studies' as separate enterprises is becoming increasingly untenable. Theorists in both fields now have a common concern: making sense of the construction of meaning within a new communication order.

Education is at a crossroad. Language and literacy educators have within their power the opportunity to shift their own and their students' beliefs and understandings about the new technologies – about their place in education as well as their wider cultural importance. And this process is now happening. As the new information and communication technologies are used more and more widely, language and literacy educators are beginning to think critically about their use and to provide their students with the skills to do likewise. They realise that if they dismiss information and communication technologies simply as new tools, using them to do what earlier technologies did, only faster and more efficiently, then they perpetuate acceptance of a limited notion of their cultural significance: they overlook the technologies' material bases and the expanding global economic dependence on them. Increasingly, they are acknowledging that when they present the technologies as both an important part of the cultural and communication landscape, and as a potentially valuable resource, they engender a realistic conception of the technologies' significance and of their own and their students' place in an information and knowledge-based society.

References

Abtan, P. (1993) The gender gap. *Computing Canada* 19, 9.

Alexander, J. (1997) Out of the closet and into the network: Sexual orientation and the computerised classroom. *Computers and Composition: An International Journal for Teachers of Writing* 14 (2), 207-16.

Barton, D. and Hamilton, M. (1998) *Local Literacies: Reading and Writing in One Community.* London: Routledge.

Batson, T. (1988) The ENFI project: A networked classroom approach to writing instruction. *Academic Computing* 2, 32-33, 55-56.

Bolter, J.D. (1998) Hypertext and the question of visual literacy. In D. Reinking, M.C. McKenna, L.D. Labbo and R.D. Kieffer (eds) *Handbook of Literacy and Technology: Transformations in a Post-typographic World* (3-13). Mahwah, NJ: Lawrence Erlbaum.

Bolter, J.D. and Grusin, R. (1999) *Remediation: Understanding New Media.* Cambridge, MA: MIT Press.

Burbules, N.C. (1997) Rhetorics of the Web: Hyperreading and critical literacy. In I. Snyder (ed.) *Page to Screen: Taking Literacy into the Electronic Era* (102-22). Sydney: Allen and Unwin.

Burbules, N.C. and Callister, T.A., Jr (2000) *Watch IT: The Risky Promises and Promising Risks of New Information Technologies in Education.* Boulder, CO: Westview Press.

Castells, M. (1996) *The Rise of the Network Society, Volume 1, The Information Age: Economy, Society and Culture.* London: Blackwell.

Castner, J. (1997) The clash of social categories: Egalitarianism in networked writing class-rooms. *Computers and Composition: An International Journal for Teachers of Writing* 14 (2), 257-68.

Collis, B. (1985) Reflections on inequities in computer education: Do the rich get richer? *Education and Computing* 1, 179-86.

Comber, B. 1997) Literacy, poverty and schooling: working against deficit equations. *English in Australia* 119-20, 22-34.

Dickinson, D.K. (1986) Cooperation, collaboration and computers: Integrating a computer into a second grade writing program. *Research in the Teaching of English* 20(4), 357-78.

Flores, M.J. (1990) Computer conferencing: Composing a feminist community of writers. In C. Handa (ed.) *Computers and Community: Teaching Composition in the Twenty first Century* (pp.106-17). Portsmouth, NH: Boynton Cook.

Gee, J.P. (1996) *Social Linguistics and Literacies* (2nd edn). London: Falmer Press.

Gerrard, L. (1999) Letter from the guest editor. *Computers and Composition: An International Journal for Teachers of Writing, Special Issue: Computers, Composition and Gender* 16(1), 1-5.

Grabill, J.T. (1998) Utopic visions, the technopoor, and public access: Writing technologies in a community literacy program. *Computers and Composition: An International Journal for Teachers of Writing* 15 (3), 297-315.

Graff, H. (1979) *The Literacy Myth: Literacy and Social Structure in the Nineteenth-century City.* London: Academic Press.

Green, B. (1988) Subject-specific literacy and school learning: A focus on writing. *Australian Journal of Education* 32 (2), 156-79.

Hawkins, J. (1985) Computers and girls: Rethinking the issues. *Sex Roles* 13, 165-80.

Heath, S.B. (1983) *Ways with Words.* Cambridge: Cambridge University Press.

Herrmann, A. (1987) Ethnographic study of a high school writing class using computers: Marginal, technically proficient and productive learners. In L. Gerrard (ed.) *Writing at Century's End: Essays on Computer-Assisted Instruction* (pp. 79-91). New York: Random.

Kaplan, N. and Farrell, E. (1994) Weavers of webs: A portrait of young women on the Net. *Arachnet Electronic Journal on Virtual Culture* 2, 3.

Kramarae, C. (1988) *Technology and Women's Voices: Keeping in Touch.* New York: Routledge and Kegan Paul.

Kress, G. (1995) *Writing the Future: English and the Making of a Culture of Innovation.* Sheffield: National Association for the Teaching of English.

Kress, G. (1997) Visual and verbal modes of representation in electronically mediated communication: The potentials of new forms of text. In I. Snyder (ed.) *Page to Screen: Taking Literacy into the Electronic Era* (53-79). St Leonards, Sydney: Allen and Unwin.

Kress, G. and van Leeuwen, T. (1996) *Reading Images: The Grammar of Visual Design.* London: Routledge.

Kress, G. and van Leeuwen, T. (2001) *Multimodal Discourse.* London: Arnold.

Labbo, L.D. and Reinking, D. (1999) Negotiating the multiple realities of technology in literacy research and instruction. *Theory and Research into Practice* 34 (4), 478-92.

Lankshear, C. (1997) *Changing Literacies.* Buckingham: Open University Press.

Lankshear, C., Bigum, C., Durrant, C., Green, B., Ronan, E., Morgan, W., Murray, J., Snyder, I. and Wild, M. (1997) *Digital Rhetorics: Literacies and Technologies in Education – Current Practices and Future Directions.* Canberra: Department of Employment, Education, Training and Youth Affairs.

Lankshear, C. and Snyder, I. with Green, B. (2000) *Teachers and Technoliteracy: Managing Literacy, Technology and Learning in Schools.* St Leonards, Sydney: Allen and Unwin.

Lemke, J. (1997) Metamedia literacy: Transforming meanings and media. In D. Reinking, L. Labbo, M. McKenna and R. Kieffer (eds) *Literacy for the 21st Century: Technological Transformation in a Post-Typographic World* (283-301). Mahwah, NJ: Lawrence Erlbaum.

Levin, T. and Gordon, C. (1989) Effect of gender and computer experience on attitudes towards computers. *Journal of Educational Computing Research* 5, 69-88.

McConaghy, C. and Snyder, 1(2000) Working the Web in postcolonial Australia. In G.E. Hawisher and C.L. Selfe (eds) *Global Literacies and the World Wide Web* (74-92). London and New York: Routledge.

Moran, C. (1999) Access: The A-word in technology studies. In G.L. Hawisher and C.L. Selfe (eds) *Passions, Pedagogies and 21st Century Technologies* (205-20). Logan, UT and NCTE, Urbana, IL: Utah University Press.

Negroponte, N. (1996) *Being Digital. Rydalmere*, NSW: Hodder and Stoughton.

Nelson, T. H. (1992) Opening hypertext: A memoir. In M. Tuman (ed.) *Literacy Online* (43-57). Pittsburgh, PA: University of Pittsburgh Press.

Prinsloo, M. and Breier, M. (eds) (1996) *The Social Uses of Literacy: Theory and Practice in Contemporary South Africa.* Cape Town: Sached Books, and Amsterdam: John Benjamins.

Reinking, D. (1998) Introduction: Synthesising technological transformations of literacy in a post-typographic world. In D. Reinking, M.C. McKenna, L.D. Labbo and R.D. Kieffer (eds) *Handbook of Literacy and Technology: Transformations in a Post-Typographic World* (xi-xxx). Mahwah, NJ: Lawrence Erlbaum.

Rheingold, H. (1993) *The Virtual Community.* Reading, MA: Addison Wesley.

Richardson, E.B. (1997) African women instructors: In a net. *Computers and Composition: An International Journal for Teachers of Writing* 14 (2), 279-87.

Robertson, H-J. (1998) *No More Teachers, No More Books: The Commercialisation of Canada's Schools.* Toronto: McClelland and Stewart.

Romano, S. (1993) The egalitarianism narrative: Whose story? Whose yardstick? *Computers and Composition: An International Journal for Teachers of Writing* 10 (3), 5-28.

Schonfeld, E. (2000) http: / /www.Ecompany.com/articles/web /0,1653,6821,00.htm (accessed December 2000).

Scribner, S. and Cole, M. (1981) *The Psychology of Literacy.* Cambridge MA: Harvard University Press.

Selfe, C.L. (1990) Technology in the English classroom: Computers through the lens of feminist theory. In C. Handa (ed.) *Computers and Community: Teaching Composition in the Twenty-First Century* (118-39). Portsmouth, NH: Boynton Cook.

Snyder, I. (1996) *Hypertext: The Electronic Labyrinth.* Melbourne: Melbourne University Press.

Snyder, I. (ed.) (1997) *Page to Screen: Taking Literacy into the Electronic Era.* St Leonards, Sydney: Allen and Unwin.

Snyder, I. (2001) 'Hybrid vigour': Reconciling the verbal and the visual in electronic communication. In A. Loveless and V. Ellis (eds) *ICT, Pedagogy and the Curriculum: Subject to Change* (41-59). London: Routledge.

Snyder, I. and Angus, L. (2000) Home and school computer-mediated communication practices. Paper presented at the Australian Association for Research in Education (AARE) Annual Conference, Sydney 4-7 December, http://www.aare.edu.au/ index.htm.

Sorapure, M., Inglesby, P. and Yatchisin, G. (1998) Web literacy: Challenges and opportunities for research in a new medium. *Computers and Composition: An International Journal for Teachers of Writing* 15 (3), 409-24.

Staberg, E.M. (1994) Gender and science in the Swedish compulsory school. *Gender and Education* 6 (1), 35-45.

Street, B. (1984) Literacy in Theory and Practice. Cambridge: Cambridge University Press. Street, B. (1995) *Social Literacies: Critical Approaches to Literacy in Development*, Ethnography and Education. London: Longman.

Street, B. (1996) Preface. In M. Prinsloo and M. Breier (eds) *The Social Uses of Literacy: Theory and Practice in Contemporary South Africa* (1-9) Cape Town: Sached Books, and Amsterdam: John Benjamins.

Street, B. (1998) New literacies in theory and practice: What are the implications for language in education? *Linguistics and Education* 10 (1), 1-24.

Talayoshi, P., Huot, E. and Huot, M. (1999) No boys allowed: The World Wide Web as a clubhouse for girls. *Computers and Composition: An International Journal for Teachers of Writing* 16 (1), 89-106.

Turkle, S. (1995) *Life on the Screen: Identity in the Age of the Internet.* New York: Simon and Schuster.

CHAPTER 19
A multimodal approach to research in education
Carey Jewitt and Gunther Kress

Introduction

Language is widely taken to be the dominant mode of communication, particularly so in contexts of learning and teaching (Edwards and Westgate, 1994; Mercer, 1995; Christie, 2000). Image, gesture and action tend to be considered illustrative supports to speech or writing. Our observation of teaching and learning, in both Science and English classrooms, casts doubt on this assumption. In the teaching and learning of Science it is entirely common practice for teachers to use demonstrations and gestures, images and models, to explain phenomena, and to set tasks which require a response using visual, written, actional means for the production of concept maps, diagrams, 3-D models, as well as written texts, and mixtures of these. The English teacher uses a range of modes of representation, in the joint construction of school English. Students are asked to use a variety of modes, although the modes and their uses and combinations differ from those of Science: visual and actional resources for instance tend to be used less often and differently.

The older approach has served to maintain the dominant view of learning as occurring primarily through language in the mainstream of research; and indeed it has been strengthened, if anything by the renewed emphasis on the importance of literacy in all classrooms (Unsworth, 2000; Wagner, Venezky, and Street, 1999). Yet increasingly, texts-as-communicational-entities use more than one mode for meaning-making – speech and gesture has of course always been significant. Now texts using writing and image, for instance, are becoming commonplace, in part through the potentials of the new media of information and communication. The facts of multimodal communication raise a crucial question: is a theoretical stance, and its attendant analytical procedures, which see communication as a linguistic event, capable of providing plausible accounts of the functions of multimodal texts and practices? Once this question is asked, several others arise. Do semiotic modes other than language show regularities such as those of speech or writing? How do modes interact with one another to make meaning? What effects do the representational uses of these modes have on the very forms of language itself, and hence on the theorisation of what language is and can do? Such questions arise from multimodal analysis.

We proceed on the assumption that representation and communication always draw on a multiplicity of modes, all of which contribute to meaning. We focus on means for analysing and describing the full repertoire of meaning-making resources which students and teachers bring to the classroom (actional, visual, spoken, gestural, written, three-dimensional, and others, depending on the domain of representation), and on developing means that show how these are organised to make meaning. That is, we focus on a multimodal approach to classroom interaction (Kress *et al*, 1998; Kress and van Leeuwen, 2001; Kress *et al*, 2001).

Three theoretical points inform our account of multimodal communication in the classroom. First, material media are socially shaped to become, over time, meaning making resources which articulate the (social, individual/affective) meanings demanded by the requirements of different communities. These we call *modes*. All modes have potential for making meanings, differently. Modes are socially and culturally specific. Second, the meanings in any mode are always interwoven with the meanings made with those of all other modes co-present and co-operating in the communicative event. This interaction produces meaning. Third, what is considered a mode is always contingent: resources of meaning are not static or stable; they are fluid. Modes are constantly transformed by their users in response to the communicative needs of society; new modes are created, existing modes are transformed.

Halliday's social semiotic theory of communication (Halliday, 1978) provides the starting point for such a theory. The exploration of multimodal representation, as in our recent work on teaching and learning in the science classroom, is founded on developments of that theory (Kress and Hodge, 1988; Kress and Van Leeuwen, 1996; Kress *et al*, 2001). Halliday argues that as members of a culture we have at our disposal networks of options (sets of semiotic alternatives) which constitute the meaning potential of a culture; these are realised as sets of options of resources through which meanings can be realised in (material) form. These realizational resources are the *modes* of a multimodal approach: speech, for instance is the materiality of sound organised by a culture as a resource through which meanings can be realised in a regular fashion. Image is inscription on a surface through the materiality of light, again organised, in quite different ways, by a culture into a resource for realising meanings in a regular fashion. For Halliday, whose approach focuses on language alone, the semantic system is shaped by the social functions of the utterance as representation, as interaction, and as message; which are realised by the grammar and by the words/lexis – the lexico-grammar – of a language. The principal assumption is that language is as it is because of the social functions it has evolved to serve: it is organised to serve the interests of those who use it in their social lives. In other words, language can be understood to be the result of constant social/cultural working on and shaping of a *material medium* – sound in the case of language-as-speech – into a resource for representation, which displays regularities as mode, the – material yet socially/culturally shaped – resource – as signifier-material – for meaning in the constant new making of signs.

We start from the position that all modes have, like speech or writing, been shaped in their social use into fully or partially articulated semiotic resources: modes. Extending Halliday's theory, we assume that all modes have been developed as networks of interrelated options for making signs. The choices made within these networks of meaning-potential by a sign-maker are then traces of a sign-maker's decisions about the expression of the meaning that she or he wishes to make in a given context. They are the expression of the sign maker's interest (Halliday, 1985; Kress, 1994; 1997).

From this perspective, teaching – and, differently, learning – is the material expression, the evidence, of the motivated – social and affective – choices of teachers and students from the meaning-making resources available in a particular situation at a given moment in our discussion (the science classroom).

In Hallidayan linguistics meaning is the effect of the interplay of choices made from the ideational, interpersonal and textual functions of language, realised in texts. A multimodal perspective involves attending to this interplay between these three functions in each of the modes in use. This multiplies the complexity of meaning. Each mode interacts with all others, contributes to all others. At times the meanings realised in two modes may be equivalent, often they are complementary, sometimes one repeats information presented in the other, at yet other times each may refer to quite different aspects of meaning; or the two may be contradictory (Kress, 1994, 1989; Lemke, 1998). In the instances of multimodal communication that we have studied, the different modes are often used for specialised tasks, along lines of their inherent *affordances* and their historical shaping, as specialised meaning resources, in *functional specialisation.*

Here we demonstrate the application of multimodal analysis to an example of teaching and learning in the science classroom.

A MULTIMODAL APPROACH TO COMMUNICATION

The account is a description of the first of five lessons on the circulation of blood with year nine students (age 13-14) in a London Community and Technical College. The school is a large, all ability mixed comprehensive.

Data collection

A multimodal approach to classroom interaction requires methods of data collection which facilitate a focus on all modes in the classroom; can accurately record multimodal classroom interactions, given their speed and complexity; and will provide a record from which all modes can be transcribed. These requirements, and our conception of teaching and learning as a *rhetorical process* in which the teacher shapes meaning in response to the students' responses, in which the students are involved in the process of re-making signs, shaped our decision to use video-recording as the central data collection method in the project. Two video cameras were used, one focused on the teacher, the other on the students. The use of the two cameras in the recording of teacher and students at the same time, enabled the analysis to explore the dialogic nature of teacher-student interaction. (For discussion of video recording as a way of collecting data, see Lomax and Casey, 1998.) The video-data was supported by observation notes, which recorded interactions that the video could not, for example certain shifting spatial arrangements of objects, furniture, and people in the classroom.

Sampling the data

Due to the intensive nature of multimodal analysis, criteria are needed for selecting a representative range of examples for analysis. Successive viewing of the video data played a large role in the generation of analytical themes. The process of logging and organising the video data yielded insights through intensive engagement with the material. This generated insights and questions, drawing attention to important aspects of communication.

The video recordings were classified into discrete analytical/descriptive units by applying the concept of 'rhetorical frame'. These are units of form and content, defined by a configuration of factors, such as: a clear framing of beginning and end; positioning of the teacher in the classroom; positioning of the students in relation to knowledge, e.g.: 'draw on your own experiences'; choice of content; dominant mode; the means, props, or objects used in the lesson; teacher and student agency and activities; teacher and students' posture and movement in the classroom; the genre of interchange, e.g. monologue or question and answer sequences; and lexical style (Scheflen, 1973; Bateson, 1987).

The video data was catalogued in chunks, using the concept of *rhetorical frame* ranging from one to 15 minutes in length. This classification enabled us to produce a descriptive account of each video-taped lessons in terms of rhetorical frame. These segments were then classified by mode, to produce a modal-catalogue of the units of the lesson. We then selected a representative range of these units, and produced modal transcripts of each, to see how each mode contributed to the realisation of rhetorical intentions across a range of topics.

Multimodal transcription

Our theoretical perspective of teaching and learning as multimodal processes demands a transcription process which takes account of how all modal resources work together to make meanings. To achieve a multimodal transcript we used a theoretically integrated set of descriptive dimensions highlighted as important in a review of the literature and in our engagement with the data. These included eye-movement; gaze and direction of gaze; facial expression; hand and arm movement/configurations; the use of the whole body to make gestures; body posture; the position of people in the room and their use of space; the location and context of the action – e.g. the semiotics of architecture; the semiotic objects of action – for instance 3D models; and speech (Bateson, 1987; Bitti and Poggi, 1991; Merleu-Ponty, 1969; Crowder, 1996). Each of these modes was recorded, using time as an anchor. That is, we decided that we did not wish to privilege speech, say, by recording it in the left-hand column of a transcription, and scoring or calibrating other modes – say gesture, or action on a model, or the use of an image – against speech as the metric. We attempted to provide a 'thick descriptive' multimodal account of the video data.

Multimodal analysis

The units in sequence were analysed as detailed trails, or traces of the teaching and learning practices in which students and teachers engage. The analysis sought to identify the communicational and representational potentials available to teachers and students in the science classroom, and the use made of them. The concepts provided us with a range of tools to prise open the multimodal environment of the science classroom. They included a focus both on realizational resources – the modes – and units such as medium, mode, materiality, rhetorical frame; concepts related to these, such as the rhetorical orchestration of meaning; theoretical resources such as functional specialisation, functional load, grammar and meaning making functions; interest, within an over-arching hypothesis of learning as a dynamic process of sign making.

Stage One: Mode and Meaning

The first stage of our analysis involved exploring our data through intensive viewing by attending to each of the modes operating in the lesson separately, using the concepts above, and classification of the data by meaning functions. This allowed us to see how modes realise different meanings.

Here we focus on a five minute episode, half way through the first in a series of five lessons on blood circulation. The teacher starts with a spoken account of the circulation of blood, which he transposes through gesture onto an image (figure 1) on the whiteboard behind him.

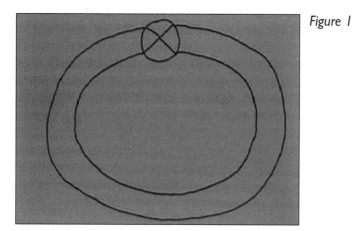

Figure 1

Speech	Action
We can think about it as a circle of	points at heart, traces finger around circle
blood like this, going round, and at	returns hand to heart, draws on arrows
various points say, the lungs are	places opened hand at left of diagram
here, the small intestine here, and	places opened hand at bottom left of diagram
the cells are here, the kidneys	places opened hand bottom right of diagram
up here, okay so it's going all the	places opened hand at top right of diagram
way around and what it needs	draws arrows on circle, points at heart
is something to start pumping it	bends elbows, arms at side, 'bellows' action
again to give it a bit more motion	makes 'bellows' action three times
to go around okay	puts pen lid on

He then gave a more complex spoken description of the cycle of blood as a 'double loop', blood going to the lungs, and to the rest of the body. He added this second loop to the drawing, transforming it (figure 2).

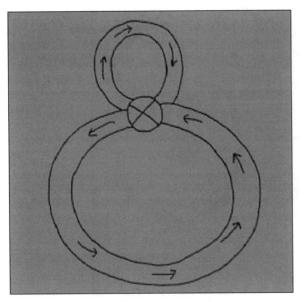

Figure 2

Having described the route of the blood, the teacher placed a model of the upper part of the human body on the bench in front of him (figure 3).

Figure 3

He handled the model heart while talking about the blood's movement through the heart, and the contracting of the heart's muscles. Cyclicity was represented through the teacher's animation of the model, and by his use of the verbs 'goes', 'comes'.

Speech	Action
Now if we look at that on our	Places model on front desk
model you can actually see here	stands behind model, arms in front
the heart has four main blood	picks up heart, points at heart
vessels okay now...	puts heart back in model
and if we take the front off, you can	takes front panel off heart
see what's going on inside,	lifts heart out of model to in front of him
basically blood is coming round	sticks out index finger, traces loop from
from the rest of the body into this	his head to heart, puts finger in chamber
first chamber here...okay it goes	moves finger about in chamber
from this chamber into this	moves finger to next chamber
bottom chamber on this	
side that's where the first	slowly contracts hand into a fist, twice
pump happens	

Figure 4

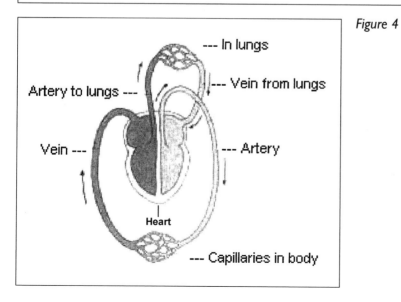

The teacher then directed the students to look at an image in their textbook (figure 4). He used his finger to indicate the circulation of the blood on the image, providing a multimodal – visual, verbal, and gestural – summary of the lesson.

The teacher then instructed the students to complete a series of activities from their textbook, focusing on the functions of the different organs, in particular the heart, in the process of blood-circulation.

Over the course of the lesson the scientific entity blood circulation was constructed from the interweaving of meanings created by the teacher's shifting between modes. The function of each of the modes in this episode is discussed in the following sections.

Speech: Creating difference: At the beginning of this segment, the teacher contrasted the initial schematic verbal description of the blood's circuit, developed in the first half of the lesson, with a second more detailed version of 'what actually happens'. He said: 'It would be very simple if that is what it was like... But it's not quite that simple...'. The contrast was achieved by a juxta-position of the teacher's more detailed verbal description with the image of the abstract cycle drawn on the white board. The contrast between what the teacher said, the abstract diagram of one circuit, and what he went on to say 'actually happens', set up the need for an explanation.

The Image on the white-board: a visual backdrop: The image provided the starting point for the lesson and formed the ground on which the other modes were developed. It presented a view (figure 1) of the circulatory system as a highly abstract entity. It provided an adaptable visual backdrop – an abstract map onto which the spoken account was overlaid. The teacher mentioned the 'places' on the route of the blood – the lungs, the small intestines, the cells, the kidneys. He did not draw these onto this map; rather, his speech and gesture served to form an imagined trans-parent overlay onto this abstract image.

The materiality of the white board and the mode of gesture together afforded a flexibility which enabled the organs to be there as a momentary presence overlaid on the stable image, a presence which evaporated once it had served its purpose. The teacher's engagement with the abstract image avoided having to change the position of the lungs when he later extended the image to reflect a more complex view of the circuit of the blood. Similarly, it obviated both the problem of representing the organ cells, and the placing of it in one location on the diagram. In this com-bination of modes such questions couldn't really arise. The adapted image (see figure 2) provided a visual analogy of a figure eight, which translated the teacher's verbal explanation of 'what actually happens' to an abstracted image rooted in the everyday, serving as a tool for memory.

The two-dimensionality of the visual mode reorganised the representation of the heart and lungs, so that in front became up, and behind became down. The framework developed by Kress and van Leeuwen (1996) to look at composition as meaningful was applied to this image: that is, the compositional values in a two-dimensional rectangular space where bottom = real, top = ideal, left = given, and right = new. The resulting analysis suggests that the composition of the image provided information about the process and the direction of the blood's circulation around the body. The left section was used for the blood needing oxygen, going to the lungs to get it. So left, the area of the given – the issue which causes the problem that the body needs oxygen, in the first place, the lungs are the supplier of the oxygen, and the causal problem is the absence of oxygen – was used to represent 'before': left had the meanings of old, used up, waiting and com-ing. The right section of the image, the new, was used to represent after: the blood now has oxygen. The top and bottom of the images corresponded to the opposition source *vs.* sink, supply *vs.* things supplied. The heart and lungs at the top were source, the organs below were use. So the space of the top, the ideal, was used to represent source, and the space of the bottom, the actual, was used to represent use.

Manipulating the Model: locating the discussion in a physical setting

The images used by the teacher provided schematic knowledge of 'how to think about this'. The model (figure 3) provided a sense of the scientific process of exploration: going deeper into the subject. Inside is brought out onto the surface, literally. The model is used to take a surface view inside, to say: 'when this schematic process works, here is where it works'. What is explored is how the actual contains the ideal.

The model made visible the usually unseen insides of the human body, and in the process transformed the everyday human body into the scientific entity human body. Colour was used modally, as a visual representation of the transformative process of blood circulation: grey/blue for used blood and red for oxygenated blood. The model presented the spatial relation between the parts, the organs, and the whole, the human body, in a realistic dimensional relationship, representing depth and layered relationships between the organs. The static, solid materiality of the model limited its role in the explanation of a dynamic and organic process, by representing the organs as hard, lifeless things that do not move. However the limitation of this mode enabled the heart to be physically handled in ways that living hearts cannot be.

Action: Making Dynamic: The teacher's gestures introduced the dynamic nature of the circulation of blood and the pumping of the heart, and this compensated for the limitations of image and model. He used gesture as mode throughout the lesson to represent the movement of the different imagined entities. He gestured the movement of the entities the students were required to imagine: the body; the heart; the heart's valves; and the blood. For example, at the start of the segment he used his own body as a model to provide a physical location for circulation of blood. Later, in a passage not recorded here, he held his hand flat open in a gesture of being winded and shocked, representing the material effect of the content of his speech: 'it's got no oxygen in it, okay, where does it need to go to get oxygen?'

The teacher's use of his body had a textual function: it was the location for the verbally and visually given information. It connected the empirically real – a human body – with the theoretically schematic – the model which is made in accordance with the classifications of the theory. In doing so he re-oriented the students to think about their bodies not as they usually experience them but to imagine their internal structure. His body provided a real for the theoretical; it, and his gesture, made the entity body dynamic and real, while the model classified it. His body showed 'how it actually looks', how it is for us; the model showed body analysed into the parts of the scientific classification scheme. The modes jointly realised three levels of analysis of the body: movement, parts, and functions.

The teacher repeatedly made three gestures: a circular motion, specifically, with his hand and arm around his upper torso; a contracting gesture made with his hands, holding his palm wide open and closing it in a grabbing motion to form a fist; and a gesture of arms pressed against his body. These are lexis in the gestural mode – they gave specific meaning to central words of his speech, for instance 'pump' and 'squeeze'. Here gesture, and other modes, function ideationally: whether it is when he used his arm and hand to trace the circles of the image on the white-board, or used his arms to encircle the model, or to show the circular route of the imagined blood from the heart. This contrasts with the textual use of gesture when he traces the circular route of the blood on the image in the textbook – a kind of textual deixis and modal linking. At one point he made this circular gesture a total of 16 times in five minutes, realising the movement of the blood as a cycle. Here we would say that the function is ideational too: signalling intensity, a gestural very. During the same five minute segment he made the contracting gesture a total of 23 times. This contraction-gesture, as well as the arm-compression-gesture, represented the 'pump', the squeezing of the heart and the compression of the lung-cavity, all ideational functions of gesture, lexically. In this way the gestures realised two key themes of the lesson, and elements in the ideational function: cyclical movement and contraction. At the same time these provided both a rhythmic back-drop for the lesson, and coherence across modes: both functioning textually.

The Image in the Textbook: a stable summary: The image in the text book (figure 4) serves the function of providing a stable summary – the knowledge at issue in canonical form – of the two and three-dimensional images and actions presented by the teacher. It offers a topographical representation of heart and blood-circulation, drawing on the visual analogy of a figure eight, on the knowledge introduced by the teacher's actions with the model.

Stage Two: The orchestration of modes

In the second stage of our analysis the focus was on an exploration of how each mode was used to make meaning with all others. This entailed further viewing and comparisons across the meaning functions in each mode, examining how one can read the meaning of one mode with co-occurring modes. To do this we focused on aspects of meaning in three main ways.

First we looked at the role of different semiotic objects in the classroom: what things were manipulated, pointed at, and how did teachers' and students' interaction with them either bring them into existence, or momentarily transform them. Second, modes in relation to each other: through examining the co-occurring modes, and viewing modes across the lesson, we identified repetitions, reiterations and transformations of modes and elements. Through this comparison we were able to identify what Scheflen (1973) calls 'customary acts': acts that happen in a particular context at a particular time and have an established function. Third, the representational and communicational tension between modes, for example, what was spoken and what was performed through action. Why might action have been introduced at a particular point in a lesson? What did it enable the teacher or student to do? Through this process of comparison and contrast we attempted to unpick the role of each mode in the communicative event seen holistically. Here, as elsewhere, modes interact in different ways. Specific modes are foregrounded at particular points. At times the teacher's speech was independently coherent, at others its meaning was entirely intertwined with his action, to the extent that neither speech nor actions were coherent independently.

The model was made salient through the teacher's manipulation, to display the parts named in his speech. It was then backgrounded as he focused on his body as a canvas for explanation. These shifts can be seen as one effect of the material potentials and limitations of the mode 3D model to convey the meaning. As the focus of the teacher's communication shifted from organic movement to explaining blood circulation as a process which unfolds over time, he shifted from action to speech. Each of the modes came to realise specific meanings in line with their functional specialisation in this science classroom.

The teacher's speech was foregrounded in the first part of the episode – it carried the central part of his message. Verbally and visually he set up the issue for discussion by building the notion of blood flow as a cycle. He presented and then refuted his initial explanation of how the heart works, creating the need for an explanation, which he then provided. Image and action alongside speech realised the continuous cyclical movement of blood and the contraction of the heart. His speech combined with his actions and use of image to build a schematised version of circulation. The figure-of-eight image offered a basic map with which to read what was to follow in the lesson.

Standing in front of the image on the white board, he introduced the model of the insides of the human body, using his own body as a model for the outside: it mediated the transition between the image on the board and the model on the bench, in a layering effect: his body overlaid the image; the model overlaid his body. Speech, gesture and model were fully integrated. Speech provided an explanation; gesture indicated the players, acting out and dynamiting the verbal account; the model provided an analytical representation of the body as the physical location, and the relationship between the parts and the whole. The textbook image offered a detailed visual summary of all that had happened.

The different semiotic modes worked together to form a coherent text through a range of textual features. They produced similarity and contrast: schematic *vs.* actual; inside *vs.* outside; idea *vs.* object. They all worked together to create coherence through repetition. In the second half of the lesson, the verbal description was repeated seven times, the visual depiction three times, and the actional cycles 16 times. Coherence was also achieved through the linking of spoken account with all modes, each mode contributing a different part to the whole communicative event. At one point, the actor/entity blood was carried in the teacher's speech, the physical location of the action was provided in the model, and the teacher's manipulation of the model was the representation of the process (movement of the blood). At other times, the teacher's synchronisation of different semiotic modes produced meaning: the teacher's speech, his action of tracing the arrows on the textbook image of the blood's movement around the heart, and the textbook image itself, worked in combination to produce an abstract directional map of the process-entity blood circulation.

Multimodal Repositioning

During the lesson the teacher's use of different modes repositioned the students in relation to the human body. The teacher's talk and his use of the image he had drawn required the students to imagine themselves inside the body. His gesture and use of his body as a model asked them to imagine themselves as observers outside of the body. Through his gesture of the pumping action of the heart, he took the students a layer deeper – they were *in* the heart 'seeing the movement of the valves'. With the model, the teacher pointed out and handled the organs, a dissection reminiscent of an autopsy. This required the students to imagine the model as once moving and placed them in the role of medical students looking in at the dead body – observers of the transformation from the process of experiencing the body as an external entity to experiencing it as an internal entity. The textbook image required the students to imagine the context the rest of the body. Finally, the homework which the teacher set, to write 'as a blood cell' of their journey around the body, required them to move into the cell itself – to become a blood cell, so to say. In this way all of the modes worked to achieve the rhetorical repositioning of students and the construction of the entity the human body.

In summary, throughout the second half of the lesson the students were required to shift their view of the body between that of an internal and an external entity.

Internal:	Talk and image – Body as process
External:	Gesture – Body as location
Internal – deeper:	Gestures – Body as movement, heart as pump
External – distant:	Manipulation of the model – Body as parts
Internal – deeper still:	Writing in Homework – Blood as entity – cell

Each shift involved metaphorically re-entering the body at a deeper level and exiting at a more distant level. The direction of these moves echoed the process of science as immersion and observation.

The students were required to do different imaginative work in order to make sense of different aspects of the circulatory system. The image required them to imagine the movement of blood around a circuit; to envisage the size and position of organs and the relationships between them, in a highly abstract fashion; to think of the organs in a circuit, and of the cells as collected up into one place as an organ; to transform the spatial relationship between the heart and lungs from a three-dimensional relationship into a two-dimensional relationship: front became up, behind became down. The teacher's use of gesture and his body required the students to imagine what goes on beneath the skin. The model required the students to think about elements of the cycle, for instance, the size and position of the organs, differently to that suggested by speech and image. The teacher's actions with the model realised movement and direction of actions which were named in his speech, and required envisaging the agent of this action – the blood. Each mode both repositioned the students in relation to the human body and demanded different cognitive work of them. The complex meaning of this part of the science curriculum was realised through this interweaving of modes.

The analysis demonstrates that the work of teachers and students was not accomplished through language alone.

Conclusion
Implications for policy and practice
Taking a multimodal approach to communication in the classroom has wide implications for learning, teaching and assessment.

Learning
Theorising the classroom as a multimodal environment has profound implications for thinking about learning. Central among these is the relationship between mode, thinking and the shape of knowledge. If the affordances of different modes enable different representational work to be done, shaping and conveying information and meaning in distinct ways, then it follows that each mode entails different cognitive work, and has different conceptual, cognitive and affective consequences.

A multimodal approach to classroom interaction demands serious reading of signs made by students, to see their 'interest' through their representational choices in terms of mode, elements and arrangements (Jewitt *et al,* 2001). Previous educational research has tended to focus on linguistic resources (talk, reading and writing), a view of learning as primarily a linguistic accomplishment. We explore the full repertoire of meaning-making resources which students and teachers bring to the classroom, and show how these are organised to make meaning (Kress *et al*, 1998; Franks and Jewitt, 2001). The material, multimodal characteristics of students' texts – for instance the use of colour in drawing, of layout in writing, the disposition of image and texts on a page – have rarely been attended to in educational research. Where attention has been given to such characteristics, it has provided a link between the study of texts and the study of practices, giving insight into children's literacy practices (Ormerod and Ivanič, 1999). The multimodal resources students draw on to make meaning are instances of their cultural working with a material medium as a semiotic mode. In this way, such representations reflect the material, cultural-historical, and functional specialisation of all modes of communication. Students are engaged in complex decisions when selecting how to represent materially. For them, as for all sign makers, form and meaning are interconnected and motivated: form is meaning. Any easy dismissal of any text-as-the-realisation-of-meaning produced by a student – in whatever mode or multimode – becomes impossible; the text which ostensibly shows a refusal by the student to engage with available resources can, with this method, reveal the principles of the lack of engagement – in itself a valuable pedagogic resource for the teacher.

Extending our range of what is encompassed as communication, and of meaning-making highlights the need to consider how all modes express social meanings. This opens the way to seeing differences between students' texts in whatever modes, not so much as markers of individual aesthetic, affective or social position, but as an expression of distinct interests: always a transformation of the teacher's signs into new signs. Importantly, it opens a way to connect the modal practices of school with the modal practices outside school, a task of absolute urgency, and not only around notions of literacy.

Teaching and assessment

A multimodal approach highlights the complexity of classroom interaction, and of the tasks of pedagogy (Jewitt *et al*, 2000a). Multimodal descriptions will, we hope, contribute to a full understanding of the meaning-making resources in the classroom and the development of a language of description for these resources. Making them explicit would, as work on linguistic resources has done, provide teachers with an extended range of tools for reflective design and practice.

Is all this special to science? Our answer is no. All communication is multimodal. Science education makes some aspects more salient than do other school subjects, especially the combination of abstraction and analysis; the use of images as contentful and not just as illustration; the emphasis on action through experiment and demonstration; and the over-riding importance of things as against words.

The major implications for teacher education of a multimodal approach to learning and teaching are: first, the need to attend consciously to the range of modal resources available to and selected by teachers and available to pupils, but particularly, in the evaluation and assessment of learning. Second is the need to develop an awareness of how these modes are used in the classroom, asking: 'What modes are used?'; 'When are specific modes used?' 'Are modes used to attend to different aspects of concepts, phenomena, explanations?'. Third, the exploration of what mode may best suit a task, and the different cognitive, affective and representational demands modes may place on pupils. Fourth is the consideration of relations between modes and the shaping of knowledge. There is a need for the work of all modes to become explicitly articulated in teacher education and practice, so that all are available for reflection, refinement and improvement as teaching and learning resources.

Critical review of methodology and of the ways it shaped the research

The enterprise of multimodality in this form is new. Yet there are already some criticisms of this project; in part these are issues which concern us also.

Multimodality is frequently criticised as 'just another form of linguistics'. Its focus on the materiality of representation, and the interest in form, seem to give rise to this. We share with Hallidayan linguistics the assumption that any full semiotic resource needs to meet the social-semiotic functions of representation and communication: to represent what is happening in the world – the ideational function; focus on the modes used in representation – the textual function; and what social relations are at issue in communication – the interpersonal function. But for us these are semiotic principles which apply to all modes, to gesture and image no less and no more than to speech and writing. Our attempt, as here, is to use descriptive/analytical terms which stem from the materiality of the mode and of its cultural working. We do not import linguistic terms. We do not ask of the visual mode 'what are the nouns, where are the clauses, where is the subject of the sentence?' In our examples we have stressed the textual function, for after all, this chapter is precisely about mode; though we have drawn attention, for instance, to the ideational function of gesture, and the ideational affordance of 3D models, and to a lesser extent to matters of affect, something we would put – somewhat uncomfortably into the interpersonal function – in the use of gesture. Being interested in the rhetorical reasons for the use of mode, the orientation of the chapter is interpersonal in any case.

A second criticism is: 'But how do you know?' How do you know that this gesture means this, or that that image means that? This problem exists, however, in exactly the same way in speech or in writing. The principles for establishing the 'security' of a meaning or a category are the same for multimodality as for linguistics – or Philosophy, Fine Art, etc. A related criticism is 'why do semioticians assume that they can read/see things that ordinary readers cannot?' Our answer is: on the one hand we assume that developing explicit means for description/analysis is the route to reflective engagement with the objects at issue; on the other hand we assume that within a specific community readings are relatively secure, but that outside that community they are less so. We do not presume to produce secure readings, rather we attempt to establish principled means for arriving at secure readings. Beyond that, it is the case that the readings of the everyday are made in different ways and for different purposes than the readings of the theorist. But the latter should inform the former.

Because multimodality attends to everything as meaningful, it is regarded as imperialistic. Multimodality is a new enterprise, and as such it needs to test, precisely, where the boundaries of its effective work are located. In Social Semiotics, of which it is a part, it is recognised that there are such limits, beyond which other approaches work much more effectively. In part this is a question of the size of the data, and of the need to configure the data appropriately to the demands of the analysis. Semiotic analysis works best with small elements, or with larger level elements treated as small, namely as 'signs'. When the aims of enquiry shift to larger-level relations in process it may be necessary to shift theoretical paradigms. This is not to say that semiotics, and multimodal analysis, does not deal with events in time: such sequences of signs in time, as in series of transformations in teaching and learning.

Implications of findings/interpretations for methodological and theoretical issues

A multimodal approach opens paths to a newly intense focus on work on meaning, learning, language and semiosis. In a multimodal approach it is clear – in a way that in the term 'extra-linguistic' it is not – that language, whether as speech or as writing, is only ever a partial means for representing. But if it is partial, then the question arises as to how that partiality works, in and across cultures.

We see multimodality as crucial to linguists or applied linguistics, so as to know, for instance, which meanings speech or writing carry and which they don't. This is especially so in all contexts of language learning: it cannot be taken for granted that the meanings carried by language in one culture will be carried by language in another. The distribution of meanings between modes is now an issue; it is not likely that all cultures follow the same principles for such distribution: that which is named in one culture may be gestured in another.

Multimodality places new questions against all modes, and their roles in representation and in communication. All are partial; and the need is to understand that partiality. The emphasis on the materiality of modes issues a deep challenge to abstract notions of semiosis, which have proved problematic in linguistic theorising.

References

Bateson, G. (1987) 'A theory of play and fantasy'. In *Steps to an ecology of mind*. USA: Aronson

Bitti, P. and Poggi, I. (1991) 'Symbolic nonverbal behaviour: talking through gestures'. In Feldman, R. and Rime, B. (eds) *Fundamentals of nonverbal behaviour*. USA: Cambridge University Press

Christie, F. (2000) 'The language of classroom interaction and learning' in Unsworth, L. (ed.) *Researching language in schools and communities*. London: Cassell, 184-203

Crowder, E.M. (1996) 'Gestures at work in Sense-Making Science Talk'. In *The Journal of Learning Sciences*, 5 (3), 173-208

Edwards, A. and Westgate, D. (1994) *Investigating classroom talk*. London: Falmer Press

Franks, A. and Jewitt, C. (2001) 'The meaning of action in learning and teaching'. *British Education Research Journal*, 27(2)

Halliday, M.A.K. (1978) *Language as a social semiotic*. London: Edward Arnold

Halliday, M.A.K (1985) *An introduction to functional grammar*. London: Edward Arnold

Jewitt, C., Kress, G., Ogborn, J. and Tsatsarelis, C. (2000a) 'Teaching and learning: Beyond language'. *Teaching Education*. December 11(3)

Jewitt, C., Kress, G., Ogborn, J. and Tsatsarelis, C. (2000b) 'Learning as sign making: Materiality as an aspect of learning in the science classroom'. *ZFE* (2)

Jewitt, C., Kress, G., Ogborn, J. and Tsatsarelis, C. (2001) 'Exploring learning through visual, actional, and linguistic communication: the multimodal environment of the classroom'. *Educational Review* 53(1)

Kress, G. (1989) *Linguistic processes in socio-cultural practice*. London: Oxford University Press

Kress, G. (1994) *Learning to write* (2nd edition). London: Routledge

Kress, G. (1997) *Before Writing: Rethinking the paths to literacy*. London: Routledge

Kress, G., Jewitt, C., Ogborn, J. and Tsatsarelis, C. (2001) *Multimodal teaching and learning: Rhetorics of the science classroom*. London: Continuum

Kress, G., Ogborn, J., and Martins, I. (1998): A satellite view of language. *Language Awareness*, Vol. 2 & 3., 69-89

Kress, G. and van Leeuwen, T. (1996) *Reading images: the grammar of visual design*. London: Routledge

Kress, G., and van Leeuwen, T. (2001) *Multimodal discourse: the modes and media of contemporary communication*. London: Edward Arnold

Lemke, J. (1998) 'Multiplying meaning: visual and verbal semiotics in scientific text.' In J. Martin and R. Veel (eds). *Reading Science*. London: Routledge

Lomax, H. and Casey, N. (1998) 'Recording social life: Reflexivity and video methodology'. *Sociological Research Online*, Vol 3, No 2

Mercer, N. (1995) *The guided construction of knowledge: talk amongst teachers and learners.* Clevedon: Multilingual Matters

Merleau-Ponty, A. (1969) *The essential writings of Merleau-Ponty.* A. Fisher (ed) New York: Harcourt, Brace and World

Ormerod, F. and Ivanič, R. (1999) 'Texts in practices: interpreting the physical characteristics of texts'. In Barton, D., Hamilton, M., and Ivanič, R. (ed) *Situated literacies.* London: Routledge

Scheflen, A. (1973) *How behaviour means.* London: Gordon and Breach

Unsworth, L. (2000) 'Investigating subject-specific literacies in school learning'. In Unsworth, L. (ed.) *Researching language in schools and communities.* London: Cassell, 245-276

Wagner, D., Venezky, R. and Street, B. (1999) *Literacy an international handbook.* Oxford, UK: Westview Press

CHAPTER 20
Researching in the Third Space:
locating, claiming and valuing the research domain
Anita Wilson

All those who spend time in prisons remain aware both of the outside worlds they have left behind and the perceived threat of Prisonisation with which they are faced. Rather than forget the former or be drawn into the latter, I maintain – and prisoners validate – that acquired knowledge of both 'Prison' and 'Outside' allows them to create a culturally-specific environment – a 'third space' – in which to live out their everyday lives. (Wilson, 1999: 20)

Introduction

In this chapter I want to discuss various aspects of space – how we locate the space where our research is conducted, who can claim a place within it, and how we can value what that space has to offer, particularly in its inter-relation with language and literacy-oriented activities and practices. I want to talk about space in both the physical and metaphorical sense, and in general and specific terms. I also want to talk about language and literacy in equally broad terms, expanding our understanding of text beyond its conventional interpretation as marks on the page. My focus will be to change the way we look at language and literacy by recognising where they are situated in our changing world. As a way of grounding the discussion in experience I will draw heavily from my own work researching in prison – a paradoxical world that can be both static and changing at almost the same time – where the identification of a third space can offer new ways of looking at the people we are researching with and the language and literacy-related activities and practices that they employ.

To guide you through the process of locating, claiming and valuing the spaces where we locate our data and our participants, I am going to structure the discussion in the following way. I begin by reflecting on how space – particularly a third space – became a central issue in my work. Then I go on to focus in depth on three main issues – firstly, the importance of locating this space in a way that is meaningful and appropriate, secondly, the importance of recognising who operates within it, and finally the importance of valuing the inter-relationship between the space and the unique, site-specific materials and experiences generated within it. I discuss each topic in turn, moving the readers towards considering the spaces in which they conduct their inquiry by using the experiences from my own locations and methods. I do not deny that any one site may incorporate a variety of different spaces, or that any number of research sites can have common patterns of language-oriented activities, practices and materials. What I stress here is that diligent and sustained ethnographic research can tease out the links between space/s and communicative practices that are unique and special to every project, highlighting the importance of being receptive to the dynamics of the research environment and of the need to observe culturally-regulated rather than research-driven practices.

Rationale and framework for the third space

> Dear Anita Wilson, Thank you for calling by the byway here. I'm glad you enjoyed yourself, so did I, and would be pleased to see you anytime you are able to call by...All that is required is that you ring the front door bell and ask to see me at the visitors reception desk there at the main gate area of the prison. (personal correspondence 6/8/91)

Over a period of ten of years ethnographic research in prison I have worked with adult prisoners and young offenders, male and female, long and short term, remanded and convicted. With some, our projects have lasted little more than a year, with others our ten-year association is still ongoing. Over time I have frequently found myself invited into what can only be termed 'non-prison' spaces. Non-prison in the sense that they are not those associated with an environment traditionally described as a total institution (Goffman, 1961; Cressey, 1961) where inmates are presented as 'docile bodies' (Foucault, 1977), anonymised, dehumanised, and institutionalised by an autonomous system of control, completely cut off from the outside world. On being invited to revisit a particularly high security prison, noted in the quotation above, my instructions did not focus on the very necessary and complex negotiation of close surveillance and tight security. Instead – from that prisoner's perspective – I was invited to enter an informal space where the requirement was to 'ring the front door bell and ask to see me'. On reflection, that invitation gave a clear indication that prisoners already constructed some prison space as un-institutional. It would take me many visits, conversations and observations to recognise it myself.

I subsequently began to find myself invited into prisoners' cells which I discovered were decorated with artefacts and materials associated with their outside worlds. Alan succinctly explained this need for personalisation in our correspondence:

> I see it like this, at home you do your bedroom how you like it and to me it's the same. (personal correspondence, Alan 27/11/96).

Prisoners and I engaged in personal conversations that had little to do with prison and more to do with their social worlds, including anything from the finer points of whippet racing to the responsibilities of imminent fatherhood and naming the baby.

Through further observation and correspondence, I noted young prisoners behaving socially, singing or dancing to the radio alone in their cells, for example, as noted by Mick:

> Sorry about the gap [in the letter] but I've just been dancing to the track that starts by someone saying 'Subterranean Homesick Blues, take two', the song is great. (Mick in personal correspondence)

Long-term prisoners were also telling me they kept plants and pets in their cells and men in prison showed me their fine embroidery work.

In addition to being invited into non-institutional spaces, I was also discovering decidedly non-prison language usage and literacy-oriented activities and practices. Prisoners told me about secret languages that they used to communicate with each other. They shared copious amounts of personal poetry. They told me of the importance of corresponding with their family and friends and activities and practices such as choosing a birthday card, purchasing stationery and 'posting letters'. Things that were undertaken in the prison context but connected to their outside worlds. Rather than allowing themselves to become totally institutionalised, it seemed they managed their everyday lives through a combination of prison and non-prison activities, as described by Mark in a prison literacy diary that he kept at my request.

Thursday 26th

Wrote a V.O. [visiting order] application out.

Just started reading a book 'Lust at Large, Noel Amos'

it's about a woman who goes round robbing bank's topless. It has a funny story to it.

Wrote another letter to my girlfriend.

Wrote a Valentine's card out.

Read the news paper about Eric Cantona punching a supporter in the face.

(Mark's diary)

I also discovered that prisoners developed highly sophisticated networks, subverting institutional spaces in order to maintain personal communication. I observed first-hand a variety of ingenious ways of passing subversive notes or verbal messages, as illustrated by one such incident written into my research journal.

[Two prisoners send a message to the guy next door] by calling through the wall via the electric cable which drills straight through [to the next door cell] – the answer comes back via the toilet bowl and it is answered from this side through the air vent ... which is reached by climbing onto the toilet seat

It was becoming more and more apparent to me that even though they were confined within a space that the institution named prison, prisoners' activities and attitudes were more strongly linked to those associated with their various outside worlds.

Language and literacy played a central role and situating my research in a 'prison space' seemed highly inappropriate. The greater my levels of observation and the more refined my avenues of inquiry, the more convinced I became that prisoners continually tried to remain non-institutionalised. It was finally, after five years of such observation that I began the search for an appropriate theoretical framework in which to situate the experiences and practices that I continued to discover.

After much deliberation I discovered that theories of community (Bell and Newby, 1971), rather than institution, best described the way that the prison population operated. Clemmer (1940) had already linked prison to community but while his ethnographic stance and attention to the detail of everyday prison life still make his work a seminal text, it was difficult to resituate his observations of US prisons in the 1940s in UK prisons in the 1990s. In the light of my observations and the views of prisoners, I needed to position the prison community as a flexible and organic unit, able to accommodate people other than prisoners, such as friends, families, ex-offenders and even myself. However, this community still needed to be bounded in some way and I needed to set its parameters. In order to both limit and delimit this diverse and transient population with its key and peripheral players, I set *the experience of prison* as the criterion for membership.

There was no denying, however, that aspects of prison and prisonisation continued to impact on the daily lives of prisoners that I was working with. I needed to find a way to describe this community in a way that would reflect prisoners' capacity to utilise activities and practices from both prison and outside worlds.

'Ringing the door bell' was, after all, linked to the visitors reception desk and the main gate area of the prison. Thus the concept of a 'third space', positioned between prison and the outside world began to take shape (see Wilson 2000a for overview).

Although not previously applied to the prison domain, concepts of a third space already existed. Most relevant to my work was that of Bhaba (1994) who applies it to migratory post-colonial cultures seeking to redefine themselves in culturally-appropriate ways. In highlighting the need for individuals to retain a sense of belonging and their desire to find appropriate commonality of identity and purpose, his work provided a strong framework for my own theory. Importantly, his views on the agency of the individual in (re)constructing a sense of personal and community identity resonates with my observations that prisoners were taking hold of at least some aspects of their daily lives in order to keep a sense of their own selfhood. 'Borderland' territory is also identified by Gee (1990) as the physical and metaphorical space between school and home where children negotiate culturally-appropriate ways of operating – Gee's related notion of Discourse I refer to later. Rampton (1995) also uses the equivalent concept of a liminal space in which to position the code-switching language practices of urban adolescents. Importantly, in each case, third spaces appear to be generated from necessity, at sites of struggle, or when existing spaces do not provide the necessary feeling of belonging.

Third spaces do not exist in a vacuum, occupying a neutral place between two worlds. They require a set of rules – in other words a form of discourse – which distinguishes them from other spaces with other sets of rules. I found Gee's (1990) concept of Discourse an appropriate frame for the rules that drive the third space of the prison community. For Gee, Discourse is not to be understood in its conventional usage as a term to describe some form of linguistic interaction but as

> a sort of 'identity kit' which comes with the appropriate costume and instructions on how to act, talk, and often write so as to take on a particular social role that others will recognise (1990:142)

The prison community draws up an appropriate set of rules that allows its members to engage with 'ringing the doorbell', cell dancing, talking about whippet racing or doing embroidery, for example. These activities are seen as entirely appropriate for the prison third space and form part of the identity kit which guarantees membership. As an aside, I found one 'rule' of particular interest. While some outside world practices were known to prisoners, they were not actively engaged with until that person came to jail. A male prisoner, for example, could gain prestige by the quality of his romantic poetry or his skill in embroidery, but it is only in a small number of very discrete communities in the outside world that such activities would be equally well received. Re-gendered activities where men take on social roles that might be considered in Western society as conventionally female, only appear to exist when they are confined to single sex, isolated communities such as prisoners of war, miners, religious orders, submariners or prisoners. It is a point that I return to later under the section on locating the space.

Central to the appropriate costume and instructions, central to my research interests and central to the model for the third space is communicative practices. From the day that I had 'rung the front door bell' (alongside using a variety of spoken protocols and writing my name in the visitors' book), I had become increasingly aware of the central role played by language and literacy-related activities and practices. It became more and more evident that engagement with language and literacy was a central means by which prisoners sustained the third space. This belief was not only my own but shared and articulated by prisoners I consulted as my ideas took shape.

To assist the reader in envisaging the concept, a model illustrating the various components that I have just discussed is reproduced below.

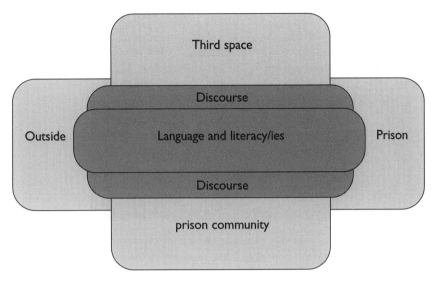

Having set out the rationale and framework for the third space for prison I now move on to discuss the three issues I identified in the introduction. I begin with discussion around the location of the space – where and how it manifests itself in the daily life of prisoners.

Locating the third space

> I was talking to my son, Brian on the phone, he's teaching himself to swim... it breaks my heart that he can splash a few wild strokes and thinks he can swim the ocean. I'm teaching him over the phone that rivers are different animals from swimming pools. (Thomas in personal correspondence)

The institution does not concern itself with providing a space in which to 'teach Brian to swim' and yet prisoners continue to re-locate prison space as personal space where they try to draw in and continue to engage with outside world activities. Visits to prisons in other parts of the world convince me that third spaces are not confined only to jails in the UK. In the United States, for example, the third space appears on a prisoner's body when prison issue t-shirts are taken by prisoners and re-defined as personal garments by the addition of personalised texts and images. In Hungary, I have seen the institutional spaces of prison dormitories drawn into a third space by the introduction of creeping vines and ivy plants. The image of an overcrowded cell occupied by 30 men and an abundance of foliage is a lasting one. Colleagues from South Africa tell me that on Robben Island, political prisoners brought ballroom dancing into their incarcerated lives. This last example reinforces my earlier claim that prisoners do not have to have actively engaged in certain outside world activities in order for them to be acceptable in the third space. Ballroom dancing – as a white colonialist activity – would not normally be considered appropriate behaviour for a black activist. Choosing an activity from which one would normally wish to be disassociated – such as ballroom dancing, embroidery or romantic poetry – highlights again that prisoners are prepared to go to extremes in order to reposition themselves as social rather than institutional beings. Existing belief systems around discrimination or masculinity are shifted to become accommodated by third space Discourse.

Figure 1

The pillow pictured above illustrates a third space which prisoners have constructed through their use of language. The photograph was taken in the punishment block and highlights how literacy as a social practice can colonise institutional spaces. The pillow itself is taken out of its institutional role and re-located as a site for graffiti, conventionally linked to outside world activity. The graffiti, usually understood as an act of defiance, desecration and disregard in the outside world (Conquergood, 1997) is brought into the prison space in order to disrupt the order of the institution. In one statement, 'John Lomax' has chosen to place himself as a person – and name both himself and the object of his affection – even though this act will identify him as damaging the property of the institution, an offence which carries with it a substantial punishment. The pillow is itself a reflection of the organic nature of prison communication, open to the additions of other authors, whose activities are sanctioned and supported by any number of future writers equally keen to risk punishment in order to identify themselves as sentient beings. The visuality of the pillow is something I return to further along in the discussion.

As the concept of a third space crystallised for me into a working model, language-based examples continued to support its existence. In prison, young men write their laundry lists in order to 'do their washing', young women take their personal shopping lists with them when they 'go shopping' at the prison canteen and adult males read and memorise their lines for the annual prison pantomime while worrying at the prospect of wearing ladies' tights. These are non-institutional activities undertaken in an institutional world, that reflect personal rather than organisational identities and supported by language and literacy activities and practices.

Who claims a place in a third space?

[today I discovered] a whole new supply of [prisoners'] letters [which are] are picked up by the censor, copies are taken and put into the files as Security risks – [it would seem] that if everyone was doing what they say they are there would be no-one in the jail who wasn't permanently stoned or buzzin' – apart from that they all say the same things – best wishes to family – telling their mates what they will do when they come out – to girlfriends the usual terms of endearment – while reading them I spoke to an Officer who tells me about his letter-writing habits as a Marine in Ulster – they used to write to people they didn't know ie firms, page 3 girls, Elton John etc etc and received many replies and goodies in return – he says that he doesn't write to anyone now not even his mates who he knows well. (personal research journal)

The 'experience of prison' which I set as the boundary of the prison community is sufficiently flexible to allow a variety of members to inhabit the third space. In this section I discuss four – the researcher, the prison staff, the families and friends of prisoners and of course, most importantly, prisoners themselves. I want to use the quote from my research journal above as a point of reference.

The researcher

Mace (1986) suggests that in our efforts to give fair and equitable voice to those with whom we research, we often deny that we ourselves occupy a space within the project.

My reflections led me to believe that not only could a concept of the third space be applied to the prison community – and include me as a member – but that the concept could be applied to other dimensions.

For example, as the researcher, I found that I inhabited a third space of my own. On the one hand I was academically part of the university and on the other ethnographically part of the prison. Subconsciously, constantly moving between two institutions and seeing the comparisons and contrasts between them may well have influenced the way my thoughts developed. From a methodological perspective, persuading young men that I was indeed a part of the academic community did nothing to reduce my credibility as someone who challenged the system. They frequently found my academic credentials very amusing and often voiced the opinion that 'they don't let people like you [me, the researcher] into university'.

In the academic milieu, it was equally interesting to disrupt the norm by putting forward a reasoned argument which drew on obscene graffiti or prisoners' less attractive modes of communication such as the toilet bowl scenario described earlier. Researcher reflexivity is an essential part of the research process and in which third space theory may well have a part to play.

Prison staff

Prison staff have frequently been the gate-keepers of my research. Without their co-operation I would have had little access to prisoners and without their support, my projects might have been terminated much sooner. As part of the orientation process, I had many conversations with staff who often went on to become key players in the research. Although formally positioned in institutional space, prison officers nevertheless often joined third space domains and Discourses. As the quote illustrates, willingly bringing personal experience into institutional time reflects third-space-approved activities and practices. I also found that it was not only prisoners who personalised institutional space through literacy. Prison staff displayed pictures of their families on office desks, communal work areas were decorated with cartoons – usually subverting official notices – and it was not uncommon to find staff rooms displaying mottos such as 'abandon hope all ye who enter here' or 'this is a prisoner-free zone'. Official documents such as journals and observation manuals often contained graffiti and non-institutional remarks.

Prisoners' families and friends

The importance of peripheral players is reflected in the influence on the third space of prisoners' families and friends. As noted in the quote above, many letters contained in the security files were sent between people inside and outside the prison. This constant exchange of information between inside and outside worlds not only places the activity within the third space but also helps to denounce the institutional model of prison, cut off from the outside world. As noted from the journal, confiscated correspondence between prisoners and family or friends drew on both prison and personal worlds. Mostly written on prison issue paper and sent using institutional protocols, it moved from official text to subversive text – often about getting hold of drugs, intimate text – sending affectionate messages to girlfriends, or threatening text – about what would happen if certain other things did or did not occur, or adolescent text – bragging about what the correspondent was alleged to have done or might do in his personal life-world. Little reference was ever made to prison business.

The physicality of prison correspondence is also important to the maintenance of a third space. Letters and photographs sent in to prisoners are used to personalise prison cells, validating personal as well as institutional identity. The visual importance of this correspondence is something that I return to in the next section.

Prisoners

Prisoners are undoubtedly the primary force in the creation and sustaining of a prison third space and locating them centrally to the research project and the space itself highlights a number of important issues. Firstly, little research features prisoners as social beings. Most criminological research focuses on general rates of offending or overall prison populations, reflecting an institutional approach linked to quantification and depersonalisation. Proposing a third space model for the prison community which rests on prisoners themselves shifts them away from quantification or the anthropological exotica of 'the other' and instead recognises the agency and creativity of a specific community. Ethically, I could not have found the third space without the engagement of prisoners in my project, nor would it have been articulated in an appropriate way had prisoners not felt themselves to be a fully recognised and valued force in the research. Methodologically, my invitation to 'ring the front door bell' sanctioned my entry into the third space of their prison world, a space in which prisoners were already situated and to which they went on to allow me access. Sharing information, donating materials and writing their responses to my emerging ideas has helped to concretise not only the third space but also the central place of language and literacy required for its support. As one prisoner noted:

> I have been coming in and out of prison since 1979 and learnt a great deal about reading and writing. It's all I do. I must have read a library and written a book. (Howard's comments from prison in personal correspondence)

In engaging with poetry, official documentation, judicial texts, and personal reading and writing prisoners themselves recognised the centrality of language and literacy to their prison lives. It is to their language related activities, practices and materials that I now turn, focusing on valuing what third space literacy – in the singular and the plural – have to offer.

Third space data – valuing what it offers

> someone has an excellent letter holder in yellow made from some kind of a box – he says that his mate made it for him – it is amazing and [he tells me] his letters are sorted in it according to size. (excerpt from my research journal)

So far we have established that prison can operate as a community, whose members use language and literacy to sustain a space in which they can hold on to a sense of personal identity. However, the literacy-related activities and practices of the third space are rarely to be found in education departments, nor can they be easily evaluated in terms of skills, or fit a pedagogical model of reading and writing. To find third space language and literacy, I took Street's (1984) autonomous/ ideological model as a framework. There is no doubt that prison contains traces of what Street describes as 'autonomous' literacy – a discrete set of skills and official texts that can be imposed, assessed and evaluated – and which prisoners recognise as institutional and choose to subvert. But the majority of literacy oriented activities and practices of the third space sit within Street's ideological model where language is situated in context and literacy is recognised as multiple and contextualised. The 'ideological' approach to literacy/ies has produced a wide range of studies such as Kapitske's (1995) work on Seventh Day Adventism, Caniesco-Dorinila's (1996) work with island people, and Barton and Hamilton's study (1998) of a language community in the north of England.

When language and literacy/ies are researched in this way, every site – third space or not – will offer up fresh and contextual data. In the prison third space, young men file their correspondence in 'an excellent letter holder in yellow' and even autonomous forms of literacy in official documentation throw up new readings. Cell cards pinned outside each cell, for example, are intended to contain only official records of the prisoner's surname and prison number, with minimal details limited to religion, length of sentence and/or status (remanded/convicted). Prisoners never participate in their production, which acts as an institutional gatekeeper to direct communication with a prisoner. Their message reinforces the autonomy of institutional spaces through regulation, compartmentalisation and dehumanisation of the prisoner. However, I have seen instances where prisoners challenge this institutional message by drawing the artefact back into the third space. Outside the cell of one young woman, for example, I noticed that someone had written 'and she's a really nice person' while another had added 'Kentucky fried chicken and a large fries please' at the bottom.

It is with prisoners' less official activities and practices, however, that the true extent of third space literacy/ies can be valued and acknowledged. I want to illustrate how multi-modality – the notion of making meaning through various modes – can be applied both within and beyond a single text. The three aspects touched on here are the reliance of messages on intra-literacy features, the importance of visuality to a text, and how the message can go beyond the text to where the text itself is the message carrier.

'Intra-literacy' features

I use the term 'intra-literacy features' to describe qualities within texts and attached to texts and the activities and practices associated with them that form an intrinsic part of prisoners' meaning making. They include sensory features such as smell, touch, taste or sound, so that the message is transmitted in ways that are embedded in or around the text. For example, a prisoner may tell me that he can 'smell' from my letters whether I have been using cleaning materials or am wear-

Soul Mate
Yes, sayeth I, forgot is that
Which hath gone before,
The past is passed
And therefore let it lie,
Let me love thee for loves sake
What thou art
Not what thou wert
Nor what I hoped thoud be,
...Equal...
Neither to the fore
Nor hidden by my stride,
Strengthen where my weakness lies
And light such place where shadow makes its lair,
Do-not speak what thou think'st I'd like to hear,
Rather the truth of thine own heart and mind
Lest all be lost of that whith one we make.

Figure 2

ing perfume while writing the letter. Conversely, within my considerable collection of prisoners' correspondence – over 400 letters – I can identify the 'smell' of different establishments from whence the letters have been sent. I have observed prison staff singing 'Happy Birthday' to prisoners as they 'post' cards through the hinge in the prison cell door and prisoners have told me that the 'taste' of envelopes or stamps can be modified to include 'tabs of acid'. (This practice has since been identified by the authorities and new protocols are in place to prevent it.) Prisoners tell me that the (lack of) quality and 'feel' of prison notepaper is considered inappropriate for personal correspondence and only used for emergencies or writing to one's solicitor. I am told that filing letters away (as in the quote above), re-ordering them and re-reading them provides a tactile reminder that helps the prisoner retain comforting and physical links to an outside world.

Looking more closely at these intra-literacy features shows that each activity or practice draws on the inter-relation of prison and outside world experiences. Scented letters are not part of an institutional world, nor is singing Happy Birthday, nor is the flavouring or feel of correspondence and yet each is central to the activities and practices around prison correspondence and thus integral to sustaining a third space.

Visuality also forms an intrinsic part of intra-literacy features, but it is given sufficient importance by prisoners to warrant its own discussion and it is to this that I now turn.

Visuality

It is possible to respond in many ways to a written text – reading for pleasure, reading as critique, reading as information-gathering, for example – and the third space supports a reading of messages which pays attention to the visuality of the artefact itself. As I noted in the quotation, one young man had 'a yellow letter holder', which sent the message through the vibrancy of the item that he and his correspondence should not be ignored. Other prisoners use visuality to keep a sense of cultural as well as personal identity. A prisoner from the Travelling community – known for its attention to colour and creative detail – spent considerable time choosing the colours of pens that he wanted to use for our collaborative letter-writing. A prisoner from the Turkish community – see the illustration (Figure 2 opposite) – drew culturally-appropriate decoration into the artistic embellishments of his prison poetry.

In an environment where drabness and conformity are the preferred norm, prisoners place great emphasis on redressing the balance by using bright colours, extreme language and bold statements. The 'excellent letter holder in yellow' was displayed with such prominence that neither it nor its colour could possibly be ignored. The visuality of graffiti text in punishment blocks is often written in the boldest lettering – sometimes even burned onto the walls or written in blood or excrement – and bald statements make the message as clear as possible that a human presence has made its mark on an institutional void.

The specific visuality of prisoners' correspondence I have noted elsewhere (Wilson, 2000b) and in the third space the rules dictate that the decoration of envelopes and letters should be a stylised replica of outside world images. Flowers and birds are exaggerated and colours are unrefined as though to counteract the bleakness of the environment in which they are executed. Images which might appear kitsch in the outside world are taken as the norm in the prison third space by men who would protest machismo and masculinity in every element of their every day life. Colour, form and visuality are brought together most strongly in the decoration of personal space where the text – be it book, photograph, correspondence, certificate, magazine, personal artefact or

Figure 3

poster – become transformed into a visual image intended to identify a prisoner as remaining un-institutionalised and part of a world wider than that of prison. It is at this point in the third space that a text is no longer thought of merely as a text.

Texts beyond the text

By texts beyond the text I mean instances where prisoners take texts not for the marks on the page but for the materiality of the artefact itself. Just as pillows are taken from their conventional use and re-positioned as organic message boards, so books and correspondence are given new roles as message carriers rather than message providers. They still remain, however, within the parameters of third space language and literacy activities and practices. Returning once again to the punishment block, the austerity of the environment requires considerable imagination and creativity to sustain any non-institutional space. Social interaction is restricted, books are scarce and take on a special significance.

As the illustration suggests, prisoners not only use reading as a way of passing the time but use the books themselves as organic message carriers, writing on the front and back cover or in the margins and circulating them from one reader to the next. In the punishment block, paper is scarce and prisoners often use books as a means by which they can send discrete messages to one another or to re-create texts for themselves. Books often show an absence of the blank sheets of paper which are conventionally found towards the back cover. In times of necessity, pages are

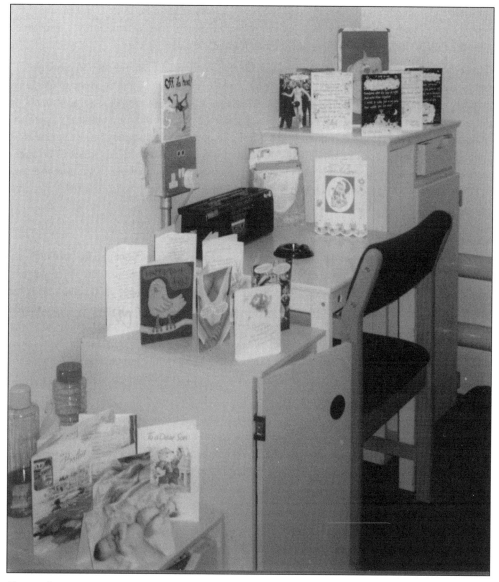

Figure 4

also torn out to make 'skins' for smoking tobacco. What is significant here is the message that young men risk punishable acts of vandalism in order to retain non-institutional identities.

Texts also go beyond their meaning as materials associated with reading and writing when they become transformed into artefacts for personal cell decoration, as noted earlier in the chapter by Alan, who stated that he thought of his cell as a room and decorated it accordingly. My observations suggest that the most common materials used are those that have a strong link to language and literacy. In addition to posters, photographs and correspondence, prisoners use books, certificates, magazine articles and personal items to make up a visual image of how they wish to be seen.

Invariably this has more to do with social status than prison identity. Letters and photographs denote contact with the outside world. Images reflect links with friends and family – sometimes even the family dog – or social interests such as football or cars.

Texts can sometimes take on an extra role of protector, sending out the message to other people not to disturb the owner's possessions. Prisoners place letters or books in front of personal property to prevent it from being disturbed. Messages transmitted from the arrangements of personal items operate on two levels. In a general sense they reflect the rules culturally approved as third space by the prison community as a whole. In a specific sense they reflect the rules as applied by the specific jail in which they are housed – each jail has different rules of arrangement. In each instance the text is seen less as a text and more as something to be used as a way of sustaining a third space in which non-institutional identity and culture is prioritised over that of the system.

Conclusion

Looking again at the spaces in which we research can give us fresh insights into the problems we seek to address and perhaps throw new light on situations and environments with which we may be already familiar. To be guided by the research setting and by those alongside whom we research gives us an opportunity to redress the imbalances which our investigations often run the risk of producing. The third space – as a negotiable and multi-layered concept – may be a way of re-positioning ourselves and our research and serve as a means by which we can write about those who provide our data. It offers a complete model, defining the parameters within which it can exist, a Discourse by which it can operate and a focus on language and literacy-related activities and practices which support and validate it.

In the third space of prison, looking at prisoners' literacy-related activities and practices clearly indicates that not only are they utilised to exert a sense of personal rather than institutional self, but that they can be seen across sites and shared by any number of prison community members. It also seems that the more extreme the environment – such as the punishment block – the more determined it makes prisoners to hold on to a sense of self. Importantly, researching in the third space can identify that language and literacy mean more to a prisoner than merely reading and writing.

Literacy-related activities and practices serve much more fundamental purposes and to this end prisoners stretch our meaning of literacy beyond conventional readings as marks on a page. They translate the text in truly imaginative ways, holding on to their existing experience, their knowledge of social worlds and using their creativity and imagination to change an institutional world into a place where language and literacy are meaningful and relevant. In addition to our recognising a changing world, we should remember the agency of others who have the ability to change their worlds and thus our understanding. The arenas in which we undertake our work should never be taken as neutral territories. Powerful ideologies may be at work within them. To take them as a benign givens would deny their capacity to influence the agency of those who operate within them and the language and materials they utilise in order to sustain them. Identifying and acknowledging where research is undertaken can produce richer, more grounded data and encourage reflective, more innovative processes of analysis.

References

Barton, D., Hamilton, M. (1998) *Local Literacies – Reading and Writing in One Community*. London: Routledge

Bell, C. and Newby, H. (1971) *Community Studies*. London: George Allen and Unwin

Bhaba, H.K. (1994) *The Location of Culture*. London: Routledge

Canieso-Dorinila, M.L. (1996) *Landscapes of Literacy – An Ethnographic Study of Functional Literacy in Marginal Philippine Communities*. Hamburg: UNESCO

Clemmer, D. (1940) *The Prison Community*. New York: Holt, Reinhardt and Winston

Conquergood, D. (1997) 'Street Literacy' in *Handbook of Research on Teaching Literacy through the Communicative and Visual Arts* by Flood, J., Heath, S.B. and Lapp, D. (eds). New York: Prentice Hall International

Cressey, D.R. (1961) *The Prison – Studies in Institutional Organisation and Change*. New York: Holt, Reinhardt and Winston

Foucault, M. (1977) *Discipline and Punish – the Birth of the Prison*. London: Penguin

Gee, J.P. (1990) *Social Linguistics and Literacies – Ideology in Discourse*. London: Falmer Press

Goffman, E. (1961) 'On the Characteristics of Total Institutions: The Inmate World' in *The Prison – Studies in Institutional Organisation and Change* by D. Cressey (ed). New York: Holt, Reinhardt and Winston

Kapitske, C. (1995) *Literacy and Religion – the Textual Politics of Seventh Day Adventism*. Amsterdam: John Benjamins

Mace, J. (1986) 'Double Dutch – Transcription and Interviewing' in *Doing Research* by M. Baynham and J. Mace. London: Goldsmiths College, University of London

Rampton, B. (1995) *Crossing – Language and Ethnicity among Adolescents*. London: Longman

Street, B.V. (1984) *Literacy in Theory and Practice*. Cambridge: Cambridge University Press

Wilson, A. (1999) *'Reading a Library – Writing a Book': The Significance of Literacies for the Prison Community*. Unpublished PhD Thesis, Lancaster University, Lancaster, England

Wilson, A. (2000a) 'There's no escape from Third-space Theory' in *Situated Literacies* by D. Barton, M. Hamilton, R. Ivanič (eds). London, Routledge

Wilson, A. (2000b) 'Absolute Truly Brill to See from You Again – Visuality in Prisoners' Correspondence' in *Letter Writing as a Social Practice* by D. Barton, N. Hall (eds). Chichester: John Benjamins

Index